NAMING NAMES

Who, What, Where in Irish Nomenclature

◆

BERNARD SHARE

Gill & Macmillan

Gill & Macmillan Ltd
Hume Avenue, Park West, Dublin 12
with associated companies throughout the world
www.gillmacmillan.ie
© Bernard Share 2001
0 7171 3125 4
Design and print origination by Carole Lynch
Printed by MPG Books Limited, Cornwall

This book is typeset in MBembo 11/14.5.

*The paper used in this book comes from the wood pulp
of managed forests. For every tree felled, at least one tree
is planted, thereby renewing natural resources.*

A CIP catalogue record for this book
is available from the British Library.

1 3 5 4 2

Seeing that *truth* consisteth in the right ordering of names
in our affirmations, a man that seeketh the precise *truth,*
had need to remember what every name he uses stands for;
and to place it accordingly or else he will find himself entangled in words,
as a bird in lime-twiggs ...'

Thomas Hobbes, *Leviathan* (1651)

Give it a name, citizen, says Joe.
Wine of the country, says he.

James Joyce, *Ulysses* (1922)

Sometimes I am in religious awe of the power of names.

Ciaran Carson, *The Star Factory* (1997)

Contents

Acknowledgements

The help of many people has been inadvertent – through a remark or comment overheard, a suggestion which has led to a fruitful follow-up, and clearly such assistance cannot be fully acknowledged individually. Others, on the other hand, responded with generosity to direct requests, and I would like to thank the following in this respect (and in no particular order): Dónall Mac Giolla Easpaig, Chief Placenames Officer of the Placenames Branch of the Department of Arts, Heritage, Gaeltacht and the Islands; Bord na gCon; the Jockey Club; the County Libraries North and South; the National Dairy Council; Dr Perry Share.

For reading the typescript and suggesting corrections and emendations I am indebted to Leslie Matson and Jonathan Williams, and I owe a particular debt to my editors at Gill & Macmillan. Elizabeth, while enduring with fortitude the customary authorial abstraction has contributed substantially both in fact and in spirit to what follows.

Some material in Chapter 4 has appeared in other forms in *History Ireland* and *Technology Ireland,* to the editors of which due acknowledgement is made.

NOTE. Newspapers, periodicals etc. referred to or quoted from are published in Dublin unless otherwise stated.

Abbreviations and Symbols

<	from	ed.	edited/editor
abbrev.	abbreviation; abbreviated	Eng.	England; English
		enter't	entertainment
adj.	adjective	*et al*	*et alii* ('and others')
advt.	advertisement; advertising	euphem.	euphemism
		fict.	fiction
agric.	agriculture	*fl.*	*floruit* ('flourished').
attrib.	attributed	Fr.	French
Aust.	Australia; Australian	GAA	Gaelic Athletic Association
biblio.	bibliography		
Brit.	British	Gael.	Gaelic
C	century	gen.	general(ly)
c.	circa	Gk.	Greek
Celt.	Celtic	Hib.-E.	Hiberno-English
cf.	compare	*idem*	'the same'
Co.	County	interj.	interjection
coll.	colloquial	Ir.	Irish
Dan.	Danish	Ire.	Ireland
derog.	derogatory	iron.	ironic
dial.	dialect	joc.	jocular
dimin.	diminutive	Lat.	Latin
Dinneen	P.S. Dinneen, *Irish-English Dictionary.*	lit.	literature
		medic.	medical; medicine
Du.	Dutch	milit.	military
Dub.	Dublin	myth.	mythology
econ.	economics	n.	noun

NI	Northern Ireland	pronun.	pronunciation
ODMS	*Oxford Dictionary of Modern Slang*	q.v.	*quod vide* ('which see')
		recte	'properly'
OE	Old English	RTÉ	Radio Telefís Éireann
OED	*Oxford English Dictionary*	Sc.	Scots; Scottish
		sl.	slang
OFr	Old French	soc.	society
ON	Old Norse	Sp.	Spanish
op.cit.	'work (previously) cited'	TD	Teachta Dála (M.P.]
personific.	personification	trad.	traditional (music)
phr.	phrase	trans.	translation
politic.	political; politics	typog.	typography
pop.	popular(ly)	US	United States of America
poss.	possibly		

Introduction

ACCORDING TO *LEBHAR GABHÁLA ÉRENN,* or *Book of Invasions,* one of the most informative of the ancient Irish annals, the goddess Ériu, together with her sisters Banba (Banbha) and Fótla (Fódhla), was on hand to welcome the Milesians, when they arrived in Ireland after travelling from an unspecified starting-point through Egypt, Crete, Sicily and Spain. Each of the sisters extracted from Amairgen, one of the Milesian leaders, the promise that her name should be enshrined as that of the island. Ériu, slain at the battle of Tailteann (now Teltown, County Meath) in 1698BC was the one who had her request fulfilled: her name, which came to be written *Éire*, was thereafter identified with the island and nation of Ireland, surviving the eclipse of Irish as the vernacular to be legally enshrined in the 1937 Constitution: 'The name of the State is Éire, or in the English language, *Ireland*'. And in the forms *Éireann, Erin, Erinn* and others it was, over the course of several millennia, to be utilised and exploited for a wide variety of purposes political, geographical, cultural, personal, institutional and commercial. Banbha and Fódhla, it might be added, did not entirely lose out on the deal with the Milesians, lending their own names not only to romantic evocations of their sister's terrain but, in the course of time, to an almost equally wide spectrum of undertakings and activities.

From these misted beginnings, Irish onomastics, or the theory and practice of name-giving, has developed in many directions, and it is the purpose of this book to attempt to document, discuss and characterise some of the more significant of these. Specific areas of this territory have already been the subject of detailed investigation, e.g. P.W. Joyce on placenames, Edward MacLysaght on family names. It is not proposed, therefore, to cover the same ground in detail, but rather to offer a conspectus, supported by individual examples, of a field which is altering rapidly under the pressure of wider social change but which nevertheless remains fundamental to the way we categorise and verbalise our culture and *mores.*

If evidence is demanded of the centrality of nomenclature to our society, one need look no further than the recent controversy over the renaming of the

RUC. Mr Les Rogers, addressing the annual conference of the Police Federation of Northern Ireland in June 2000 said that 'whatever happens to the name of the RUC in the Police Bill the name is carved on more than just the tombstones of our murdered colleagues throughout Northern Ireland. It is also imprinted in the hearts and minds among a wider community where qualities such as sacrifice, dedication and service are admired.' Similar, if more circumscribed, indignation, was engendered by the decision to rename, or, in the current jargon, to 'rebrand' Dublin's long-established **Shelbourne** hotel. 'For the Shelbourne to retain its physical existence but, like a fugitive criminal, adopt an alias instead of its real name is intolerable and insulting', *The Irish Times* thundered editorially (20 January 2001). These two examples, from very different positions in the geographical and cultural spectrum, are perhaps sufficient indication of the onomastic element in the linguistic fabric which, until a perceived misuse provokes controversy, is very widely taken for granted.

There is evidence, however, of a growing awareness of the role of names and naming in our everyday lives. With rampant urbanisation leaving its mark on hitherto demographically quiescent cities, towns and villages, the naming of new roads and estates, frequently by developers with no sense of history, ethnicity or, dare it be said, simple good taste, has led to protests by prospective buyers who have no wish to live in a tatty replica, linguistically speaking, of an English suburb. Residents of Johnstown, County Kildare, for example, voiced their anger at the proposal to name their new estate 'St John's Wood'. 'This is just the latest in a long line of inappropriate names proposed for estates in this part of the county,' said the secretary of the Residents' Association: 'We hope the council is not considering approving it.' The residents, according to the *Leinster Leader* (14 Dec. 2000), 'have called for consultation with bodies such as An Taisce, Naas Local History Group and Kildare Archaeological Society when names are being sought'.

Such protests have been replicated throughout the country and there is at last some evidence that they are not falling entirely on deaf ears. For better or worse, not only in this but in many other contexts, placenames and their associations remain a key element in our understanding of ourselves. If this can at times be carried to satirizable extremes ('Hitler's brother was married to an Athy woman' [*Leinster Leader*, 22 Feb. 2001]) it argues both an affinity with linguistic origins and in many cases a surviving transparency strong enough, one would hope, to survive the incursions of the Downs, the Meadows, the Groves and similar barbarities.

It is not too much to suggest, perhaps, that public nomenclature is currently at a crossroads. From the verbalisation of the national identity to the development of a whole new information technology nomenclature, new norms are being applied, new names coined in the pursuit of both identity and individuality; while in another sphere a glance at a telephone directory will confirm that the hitherto relatively straightforward matter of seeking the origin of Irish surnames in either Celtic or Anglo-Norman elements will in future have to take account of a much wider spectrum ranging from Lithuania to Malaysia and many cultures in between. A socio-historical assessment would therefore appear timely; and it is hoped that the present attempt will shed some light on the historical context of Irish onomastics in the light of contemporary change.

While the book as a whole is concerned with the origins and applications of proper names and related lexemes encountered in Hiberno-English usage and in references to Ireland and things Irish overseas, it takes into account the fact that in many instances names specific to the Irish language are employed and/or understood by the wider community and as such qualify for inclusion. This raises the wider question of the fortunes, in this context, of the Irish language; and here let it be said that the signs are not discouraging. Irish-language nomenclature, whether in the original or in unlovely phonetic transcription, is currently recommending itself in various fields and in a wide variety of applications. If, as may be safely posited, the motive is very largely commercial, it suggests nonetheless both a widening awareness of the language as a tool of identity and its growing acceptance, if on a limited scale and for a specific purpose. Cynics may object that this constitutes an exploitation for cosmetic purposes with no real commitment; but at the very least it represents a rural-urban shift which can only serve to put a wider community in touch with its linguistic heritage.

Since the Greek grammarian Julius Pollux produced what is thought to be the first study of the subject, *Onomasticon*, in the third century AD, there have been fashions in nomenclature as in every other branch of human expression, often manifesting themselves as political and/or moral imperatives. The change of name from **Long Kesh** to the Maze, one of the more recently obvious in our context, was preceded by Dublin's sanitizing of the streets of its brothel quarter in the 1920s, and the process of gentrification over the years offers many more examples, such as the renaming of the Dublin pub 'The Bleeding Horse' as 'The Falcon' (it has since happily reverted). In 1999 the American partners of a French company which had established themselves in the French town of Villeneuve-d'Ascq objected to the name of the street in which their premises were situated, rue Gay-Lussac: 'Gay', they felt, would send out the wrong signals. Their petition to the mayor was eventually successful and the street was renamed 'Newton'. This, however, prompted accusations of homophobia from several quarters and was restored to its original identity, but this time with the addition of the distinguished chemist's first names: Louis-Joseph Gay-Lussac. The absurdity of this particular example only serves to underline the fact that the naming and re-naming process constitutes a rich source of socio-linguistic study, and one which has only recently fallen within the scope of serious academic investigation.

∗ ∗ ∗

Naming Names comprises two parts. In Part One, four chapters provide an overview of the main themes, cross-referenced (in **bold**) to the Dictionary in Part Two. In the Dictionary each entry is supported, where possible, by one or more illustrative quotations intended to establish both usage and historico-linguistic context. Etymologies have been suggested only where these are of relevance. In the selection of entries preference has been given to names which possess a resonance effective beyond their primary definition – to those, for example, which cast a significant light upon the resources of the Irish/English diglottism. If the emphasis is upon the nomenclature of the late twentieth century, it is to be hoped that sufficient earlier material has been included to provide a useful historical perspective. It should be noted that names are listed in the form of common usage, e.g. SALLY O'BRIEN (protagonist in a television commercial series) appears thus rather than under O'BRIEN, SALLY – though a cross-reference will in most cases assist in locating the entry.

This study has been undertaken in the belief that names and nomenclature are as much a part of our linguistic and cultural heritage as the fecund corpus of Hiberno-English or colloquial discourse. In several areas, such as that of placenames, this could be said to be self-evident. Of others, beginning with the very names we use to connote nationality and status, there is a less general apprehension. It is to be hoped that an overview such as is offered here will serve to bring the whole conspectus into a clearer perspective and encourage, in the public area in particular, a more pro-active and imaginative approach to national, personal, institutional and topographical nomenclature. Names, after all, are an enduring part of what we are; or as the poet John Hewitt put it more memorably in a local context, 'I'll take my stand by the Ulster names, /Each clean, hard name like a weathered stone ...'.

xvi

Finally, a modest degree of ultra-national reference has been accessed as a palliative to Louis MacNeice's salutary castigation of the Irish 'assumption that everyone cares/Who is king of your castle'. I received such a corrective to unthinking insularity when, some time before direct telephone dialling became universally commonplace, I was attempting to phone home from a hotel in Chiang Rai in northern Thailand. Some hours after booking the call I had more or less given up on it when the phone in the room tinkled and a triumphant female voice hailed me: 'Mister Bernard! Your call to Iceland!'

PART ONE

THE OVERVIEW

1

What ish my nation?

HERE ARE FEW COUNTRIES in the modern world which are not engaged with the question of national identity. Some, particularly former colonies, have adopted a new name to formalise a break with the past or to reidentify themselves in their native language: thus Burma becomes Myanmar; the New Hebrides, Vanuatu; Haute-Volta, Burkina-Faso ('country of men of integrity'). Others, while retaining a long-established verbal identity, have attempted to relocate it within an altered political framework: Australia, in evolving from an Anglo–Celtic to a multicultural society, re-examined its colonial origins and moved to restore some aboriginal names such as Uluru for Ayer's Rock; while Ireland, in achieving partial political independence, confronted, with varying degrees of commitment and certainty, the onomastic legacy of what was defined in its 1937 Constitution as the first official language.

This concern with identity is, of course, by no means a contemporary phenomenon; and in the case of Ireland, Captain Macmorris's rhetorical question, 'What ish my nation?' had been posed in different guises for many centuries before Shakespeare codified it in *Henry V*. According to Charles O'Conor's *Dissertations on the Antient History of Ireland* (1753), 'The more general Names by which *Ireland* was known to the Learned, were HIBERNIA and SCOTIA; the one, as Ware justly observes, denoting the *Iberian,* and the other their *Scythian* original: We need go no farther ...' Or, as Sellar and Yeatman were to put it in their irreverent *1066 And All That* (1930): 'The

1

Scots (originally Irish, but by now Scotch) were at this time inhabiting Ireland, having driven the Irish (Picts) out of Scotland; while the Picts (originally Scots) were now Irish (living in brackets) and *vice versa.*' P.W. Joyce, in *The Origin and History of Irish Names of Places* (1869) explained it more formally: 'The name Scotia originally belonged to Ireland, and the Irish were called Scoti or Scots; Scotland, which was anciently called Alba, subsequently got the name of Scotia minor, as being peopled by Scots from Ireland, while the parent country was for distinction often called Scotia major. This continued down to about the eleventh century, when Ireland returned to the native name *Éire* ...'

If this confusion is now largely a matter of history, Ireland from the earliest times was identified by a number of names many of which still reverberate in a contemporary context. 'The natives called this island Erin,' wrote T. Comerford in *The History of Ireland* (4th ed. 1807): 'from which the names Ierna, Juverna, Iouernia, Overnia, and Hibernia are plainly derived. The Britons styled it Yverdon; the Romans, Hibernia; and the Saxons, Iren-landt, i.e. the country of Iren or Erin.' Comerford, as is the case with many of his contemporaries and antecedents, is not slow to embellish dubious history with equally questionable etymology: '... Bochartus derives Hibernis from Iberniae, a Phonoecian word, denoting the farthest habitation. Isidore and Bede style it Scotia, with respect to the inhabitants, who generally came from Scythia, and were therefore named Scots, and also Scotia Major, to distinguish it from North Britain, inhabited by the same nation. Plutarch calls it Ogygia, i.e. the most ancient isle; but others term it Britannia Parva, to distinguish it from great Britain, pretending that all the isles, in those parts, should be called the Britannic islands.'

By Any Other Name

Banba; Britannia Parva; Éire; Ériu; Emerald Isle; Erin; Fódhla; Free State; Hibernia; Ierland; Ierné; Inis Ealga; Irish Free State; Iren-Landt; Irish Republic; Irlanda; Irland; Irlande; Irlanthia; Irlanti; Irorszag; Irska; Irsko; Ivernia; Iwerddon; Juverna; Northern Ireland; Ogygia; Overnia; Paddyland; Republic of Éire; Republic of Ireland; Scotia; Six Counties; Twenty-Six Counties; Ulster; Yverdon.

Two millennia after Plutarch, that particular pretence remained a bone of contention: in 1999 Fintan O'Toole wrote of 'A place we don't even have a name for since "the British Isles" became unsayable ("these islands?", "Islands of the North Atlantic?", "the Anglo-Celtic Archipelago" ...' Though a variety of substitutes has been suggested, including the unlikely **Hibernian Archipelago**, the most frequent recourse is to the anodyne '**These Islands**', though this carries the unspoken implication of a common geographical/ cultural entity in some degree offensive to nationalist opinion.

More offensive, however, is the employment, both in Britain and in Northern Unionist circles, of the term '**mainland**' with reference to the neighbouring island. This is frequently a deliberate instance of political coat-trailing, more frequently, perhaps, particularly in Britain, a reminder of old assumptions dying hard. In response, an attempt has been made to apply the term to continental Europe, but this has met with little acceptance except when qualified by the adjective 'European'. 'This', in the view of Joe Lee, 'is merely to succumb to the type of arrested juvenilia which coined the term in the first place. The European continent is no more the "mainland" of Britain, or even England, than England is of Ireland ..." Mainland is another weapon in the war for people's minds".'

'For years', said Maurice Craig, 'we have had to endure the sloppy use of "Britain" to mean "Britain and Ireland".' A common instance is the persistence in UK media travel supplements, of the inclusion of Ireland under a 'UK' heading – a practice even observable, for example, in the Irish-owned *Independent on Sunday* (London). Craig, in *The Elephant and the Polish Question* (1990), perceives the root cause of this practice as British laziness or ignorance in failing to distinguish between the 'United Kingdom' (as at present consisting of Great Britain and Northern Ireland) and Britain (England, Scotland, Wales): 'so they use the term "Britain" when they mean the UK. In consequence they are left without a word to use when they actually mean Britain.' In fairness this confusion is evident also in Irish usage, the media in particular habitually failing to draw the distinction.

The Irish habit also persists, though to a lesser degree than formerly, of using 'England' when what is implied in the context is Britain as a whole. In the introduction to *Paddy and Mr Punch* (1993) R.F. Foster suggests that '... "England" carries a historical charge, an implication of attempted cultural dominance, an assertion of power, which is not conveyed to an Irish ear by Britain.' 'Brits' is an increasingly popular alternative, particularly among Northern nationalists, though the derogatory application of the term is counterpointed by that of many unionists, who accept it as an affirmation of their politico-cultural sensibilities. In 1993 a UK marketing campaign which used the slogan 'Beanz Buildz Britz' was modified for Northern Ireland consumption to 'Beanz Means Heinz', thereby incurring the wrath of the Democratic Unionist Party politician Sammy Wilson, who called for a boycott of the firm's products.

With the partial devolution of Scotland and Wales and its consequences it is likely that the whole question of nomenclature as affecting, in C.J. Haughey's term, 'the totality of relationships' between the two islands and their component geo-political elements will remain a subject of controversy. That generated by the naming of the British-Irish Council (BIC) is a case in point. The complexity of relationships between the two islands is exemplified by the consumer accounts issued by Telecom Éireann (subsequently **eircom**) which distinguish between calls to Britain and 'International' calls. If communications between two sovereign states are not international, one might ask, what are they?

But to return to the matter of the naming of Ireland itself independently of its neighbour. Charles O'Conor (*op.cit.*) quotes early authorities who derived *Hibernia* from '*Hiberoe* and *Nayon*, two Greek words, which, when compounded, signify the Western isle', or, alternatively, 'from the Phoenician IBERNAE, which, in that language, imports the remotest Habitation or Country; there being no Lands known to the Ancients beyond the Western Coasts of Ireland …' . (It derives, in fact, from a confusion with the Lat. *hibernus*, 'wintry'). With a certain amount of post-factum adjustment of history O'Connor also suggests that 'This island was also called IERNE by the Grecians, which, denoting the *Holy* or *Sacred* Island, was a Name imposed in Honour of its humane and pious Inhabitants …' To such a fanciful derivation might be added, by way of counterweight, that quoted by Brewer in his *Dictionary of Phrase and Fable*: '… the island is called *the land of Ire* because of the broils there, which have extended over four hundred years.'

It must be emphasised in the context of these and other early usages that the names were for the most part of external origin and application, the inhabitants themselves employing their own Irish-language nomenclature; though, as Joep Leersen suggests, 'even the very names that "nations" or tribes gave themselves are indicative of friction with, or opposition to, an "outside" – a suggestion borne out by the long history of the definition of Ireland and Irish in terms of non-Englishness'. The oldest native form of the name of Ireland was *Ériu* or *Heriu*, according to P.W. Joyce, 'but in the ancient Greek, Latin, Breton and Welsh forms of the name, the first syllable, *Er,* is represented by two syllables … From this it may be inferred, with every appearance of certainty, that the native name was originally *Ibheriu, Eberiu,*

Iveris, Hiberiu, Hivveriu, or some such form; but for this there is no native manuscript authority, even in the very oldest of our writings. Beyond this, all is uncertainty.'

Charles O'Conor, writing admittedly before the advances of nineteenth-century philology, ranged more widely. 'The vernacular Names of Ireland were many', he asserted (*op.cit.*); 'some descriptive, as *Crioch-fuinidh* (The Western Country), *Fiodh-Innis* (The Woody Isle), *Innis-Elga* (The Noble Isle); some poetical, as *Teach-Tuathail* (*Tuathal's* Habitation), *Cro-Cuinn, Iath-Ugaine* &c – Others general, as *Ere, Fodla* and *Banba*. The name of *Ere* ... I take to be of *Pheonician* Original: Those of *Fodla* and *Banba* are said to be owing to two *Danan* Queens, an Account which I take to be fabulous. *Innis Fail* was an honourary (*sic*) Name of *Ireland*, from the celebrated *Stone of Destiny*, over which the Monarchs of Ireland were formerly inaugurated ...' Fabulous or no, not a few of O'Conor's listing have passed into Hiberno–English usage.

Such names were fundamentally geographical in reference, the concept of the nation-state, as far as Ireland at least was concerned, being yet to be established. A nation, again according to Leersen, 'need have no clearer geographical outlines than, say, the demographical distribution of vegetarianism or of allegiance to the Jewish faith ... national definitions are protean and volatile, and, in fact, so ethereal and ephemeral that one is forced to wonder whether national denominations or identities have any real meaning at all.' 'The nation', wrote Peter Stalybrass, 'has to be invented or written; and written, what is more, in the crucial and troubling knowledge that it could be written otherwise.' Hence the core significance of the name in codifying the identity. National fervour, suggested H.L. Kopplemann, directs itself at the name, at the sound of the word, rather than at an apprehensible reality.

The name, however, is itself no simple label, a place on a map, but a variable element in terms of connotation and the evocation of emotive response. In this, 'Ireland', in its use and misuse over the centuries, has proved no exception; though until the modern period it remained coterminous with the geographical territory, signifying, in other words, the whole island. The establishment of the **Free State** in 1922 was to demonstrate, however, that nation and state are not one and the same thing. The name 'Ireland' was henceforth to exist in a realm of semantic anomaly, along with what had been proclaimed by the revolutionaries of 1798 as 'the common name of Irishman'. The naming of the new post–1922 entity 'The Irish Free State' on the model of the African Orange Free State significantly attempted to establish, at the same time, an Irish-language equivalent, **Saorstát** Éireann. That version found its way into some official and commercial titles and, of course, onto stamps and currency, but its popular usage remained limited while the English equivalent was quickly abbreviated to 'Free State' and to '**State**'. In the North, 'Free State' and 'State' had derogatory overtones and both versions long outlived the legal disappearance of Saorstát Éireann in 1937. At the same time, as a result of partition, the new entity of Northern Ireland was quickly and controversially equated, linguistically, with **Ulster**. With the enactment of the 1937 Constitution the onomastic situation was further confused, Article 4 of Bunreacht na hÉireann (Constitution of Ireland) stating that 'The name of the State is Éire, or in the English language, *Ireland*'.

The new name was adopted at all official levels and on stamps and coinage. Motorists travelling overseas were in due course issued with EIR stickers, the letters EI were applied to aircraft registrations and the new designation was accepted abroad, where Lithuania continues to derive its name for the country from the Irish rather than the English version, which is general. Britain in particular, which had been uneasy with the notion of another 'Free State' within its hegemony, was happier with Éire, though continuing to use the colonialist 'Southern Ireland', a usage that is still occasionally encountered. 'Éire' continued to recommend itself, political bias apart, for its brevity in advertising and similar contexts, though the British attitude to the naming of its former possession was the subject of an interesting comment by Martin Mansergh in his review (*Sunday Tribune*, 19 Nov. 2000) of a study of the Northern Ireland peace process. He wrote of 'the surreal efforts in the offices of a London law firm to persuade the Irish government to slash the preamble, to dilute Article One of the constitution, to get the state to call itself Éire in English, to downgrade the Irish language ...'

For much of the rest of the world, however, the country remained Ireland, where it was acknowledged or recognised at all. As *The Irish Times* sports columnist Tom Humphries put it: 'You grow up taking certain things for granted. The world revolves around Ireland. People are fascinated and charmed by us ... Not so. There are people in Arizona who have never heard of Ireland.'

More people, certainly, had never heard of Éire. And, predictably, the very fact that the British had adopted it in their dealings, both official and unofficial, was instrumental in fostering an adverse domestic reaction. The name was shunned in popular parlance, 'Ireland' concurrently shifting its reference from the island as a whole to what in 1949 became the Republic of Ireland. This variation, however, brought further problems in its wake. Its use was virtually confined to those areas where an unambiguous reference to the Twenty-six Counties was mandatory, as in the case of international soccer teams. The British refused to employ it at all, resorting to 'The Irish Republic', a term without legal sanction, on the grounds that the title Republic of Ireland implicitly claimed jurisdiction over Northern Ireland.

This objection was also implicit in the official attitude of Australia. It enacted legislation, as did other Commonwealth countries, preserving Ireland's favoured status in the wake of the 1949 declaration of the Republic. However, with the election of the conservative Menzies government in December of that year the matter of Ireland's title became a serious bone of contention. Australia refused to accept 'Ireland', the title under which diplomatic representatives were henceforth to be accredited, while the Dublin government objected to 'Éire' or 'Republic of Ireland'. The result was that there was no Australian representation in Dublin at ambassadorial level until 1964, when, as the historian Patrick O'Farrell put it, 'the matter, of diplomatic forms of address was resolved in a way commentators at the time regarded as "Irish" … In the exchange of ambassadors Ireland would use its legislative styles and titles, which implied its claim to government of all thirty-two counties of Ireland, including the North, and Australia would use its styles and titles, which recognised the Irish Republic and implied recognition of Britain's government of Northern Ireland.'

The practically universal recognition of the name of the 26–county state as 'Ireland', Australia notwithstanding, created its own anomalies and antagonisms. The antagonisms were most noticeable amongst those of the unionist persuasion, who, though in many instances describing themselves as 'Irish', employed the adjective geographically and could not accept association with an 'Ireland' which had in their view been hijacked by the southern entity. Hence the diplomatic recourse to 'the Island of Ireland' where the reference is to the 32 counties and the persistence in usage in loyalist circles of 'The Irish Republic' and even 'Éire'. The equally tautological 'All-Ireland' is common in sporting, and particularly GAA circles.

More recent political developments have furnished new anomalies. 'Even our sense of where Ireland *is*', wrote Fintan O'Toole (*The Irish Times,* 28 December 1999), 'has been radically unsettled. As the old, curiously comforting architecture of Ireland, Britain and the North falls away before the peace process and Tony Blair's constitutional reforms, people in the Republic find themselves having to use the very word "Ireland" differently, giving it a new inflection that half-includes the North, yet that contains all sorts of unspoken reservations and sensitivities.' In the North itself the reorientations consequent upon the establishment of the Assembly under the terms of the 1998 Good Friday Agreement created their own ambivalences. The new cross-border bodies, such as Waterways Ireland, refer to a 32-county entity; and as a correspondent signing him- or herself 'Fair Play' put it in a letter to the *Belfast Telegraph* (22 June 2000): 'I understand that some senior civil servants are already referring to Northern Ireland as the "North of Ireland" in papers which go to their Minister. This is hardly a good omen for the acceptance of the proposed new title for the RUC [**Royal Ulster Constabulary**]'; and a contemporaneous US usage, '**Regular Ireland**' indicated that the confusion was not confined to the native shores.

Meanwhile, although it has long passed from common currency as a national designation, Éire remains on stamps, the EI on aircraft (though EIR on car stickers has given way to IRL). It is also perpetuated in many trade and brand names employing 'Eire' or 'Eir-' as an element: Eirebus, **eircom**, Eircell, Eirpage. The country coding, 'IE', as established by the International Organisation for Standardisation, is derived from the first and third letters of 'Ireland', and not, as might appear, from the initial letters of 'Ireland' and 'Éire'.

The Internet, which employs this country designation, has had the effect of attaching significant value to unique or advantageous domain names, among them those of countries themselves. Ireland.com, owned by *The Irish Times*, was estimated to be worth up to £5 million in November 1999, the same month in which www.ireland.co.uk was put up for auction. On the other hand www.ireland.ie remains unavailable since the Irish domain registry authority does not permit the registration of generic terms. The .ie (<Ireland/Éire) suffix is now widely utilised – to designate, for example, Irish pounds (IE£) before their replacement by the euro. Meanwhile the academics, particularly the historical revisionists, have been busy. 'The titles of some recent critical works', wrote Willy Maley in his contribution to *Ireland in Proximity* (1999), 'suggest that there is a consensus forming around the idea that "Ireland" is a cultural construct. One thinks here of volumes like *Writing Ireland* (1988), *Representing Ireland* (1993), *Inventing Ireland* (1995) and *Translating Ireland* (1996). Indeed, Declan Kiberd's notorious observation that Ireland is a fiction created largely by England now seems to be taken for granted.' (One might ask by whom?)

As a sub-culture of the officially recognised national name there have persisted in various guises several associative and attributive designations employed in specialised areas such as transport names: (Hibernia/Ivernia and

8

more generally: Banba, Ierne, The **Four Green Fields**] and particularly **Erin**. Personifications, now rarely employed except in a semi-humorous or satirical context, include Dark Rosaleen, **Cathleen ní Houlihan**, the Hag of Beare, the **Shan Van Vocht**, the Sovrantry of Ireland and the **Washer of the Ford**; these most frequently epitomised the nadir of national fortunes. Ireland, in common with France (Marianne) and Britain (Britannia) is invariably personified in the feminine gender. Thus the attribution '**Mother Ireland**' – or, in Stephen Dedalus's somewhat less eschatological gloss, 'the sow that eats her farrow'.

Irish, Celts and Gaels

If the national identifier has known its semantic vicissitudes, the noun/adjective derivative, 'Irish', has enjoyed a colourful socio-linguistic existence, complicated by the English-language usage of 'Gael' carrying similar, but not always identical attributions. Both have carried their own semantic burdens down to the present day, reflecting the confusing distinctions made by the historian Geoffrey Keating, writing in Irish in the 1620s, between *Gaedhil, Sean-Gaedhil* and *Fíor-Ghaedhil, G*ael, Old Gael and True Gael, and his reference to both Gaels and Old English (those who had adopted the Irish language and habits), as *Éireannaigh*, or Irish in the context of the geographical location they jointly inhabit.

'Irish' began life under the Anglo-Norman conquest as close to a term of abuse: 'Irrois savages nos enemis' and 'Irroix rebelx' were included by England's Richard II in 1395 amongst the 'trois maners de gentz' in Ireland (the third were 'Engleis obbeisants', or loyal Englishmen). The neutral mediaeval usage 'mere Irish' (<Lat. *merus*, pure, unmixed) was to acquire the derogatory sense of its later definition ('that is barely or only what it is said to be', OED): 'Irish' and 'Irishman' meant, as they continue to mean, different things to those of differing social/political outlook. Philip O'Sullivan Beare, in his *Historia Catholicae Iberniae Compendium* (1622), categorised the population of the country as consisting of 'Iberni Ibernici' – the **Irish Irelanders**, otherwise the Gaels – and the 'Iberni Anglici', foreshadowing the Anglo-Irish of subsequent usage. A century later Jonathan Swift complained 'that all persons born in *Ireland* are called and treated as *Irishmen,* although their fathers and grandfathers were born in *England* ...' Sean Connolly, in *Irish Popular Culture 1650-1950* (1999) points to the role played by inherited prejudices 'in the difficulty that Irish Protestants experienced in finding a satisfactory vocabulary of national identity. In the seventeenth and early eighteenth

centuries they had used the term "Irish" as synonymous with Catholic, while referring to themselves as "English". From the 1720s onwards this latter usage was increasingly abandoned. Yet the term "Irish" continued to have strong negative associations.'

The pejorative attributions were to be exacerbated, particularly in England itself, in the nineteenth century and subsequently with the popularity of the 'Irish joke' and attributions such as 'Irish beauty – woman with black eyes'. At the same time, with the widening diaspora created by mass emigration, 'Irish' was coming into use, unqualified, for second and subsequent generations, especially in North America. 'Irish' in terms of qualification for soccer and other international sports teams was established as resting upon the possession of one native-born grandparent; while Conor Cruise O'Brien famously redefined 'Irishness' as 'not primarily a question of birth or blood or language; it is the condition of being involved in the Irish situation, and usually of being mauled by it'. One use of 'Irish' was, however, specifically challenged. Its employment by a number of British daily and Sunday papers to denote editions with a partially substitute or add-on Irish-interest content spawned the neologism '**Oirish**' in a mocking echo of stage-Irish speech.

With the rise of nationalism the term, with its equivocal socio-political connotations, was seen as requiring tautological reinforcement or replacement to create a new image devoid of pejorative overtones. Though it scarcely survived beyond the nineteenth century, the adjective '**Milesian**' was adopted to fulfil these requirements in perpetuating a fanciful national pedigree. More durable were 'Gael/Gaelic', effectively reinforcing the posited source of the Irish/Catholic tradition; while the virtually parallel 'Celt/Celtic' was promoted particularly by those of the Protestant tradition who interested themselves in archaeology and the 'Celtic Revival' as being somewhat less burdened with sectarian socio-political reference. The Celt, as Seamus Deane saw it in *Strange Country* (1997): 'was ecumenically useful, especially for Protestant writers, to indicate that there was an Ireland that, in its pre-Christian form, was remarkably identical to the Ireland of sectarian difference that at present existed … The Celt served both nationalist and liberal unionist purposes …' This Celtic/Gaelic reconstruction of national origins resulted, however, in the Irish pre-Celts being largely edited out of history. 'What was it like in Ireland before the Celtic yoke –' wrote Paul Durcan: 'Before war insinuated its slime into the forests of the folk?' There are few, indeed, who would honour the name of the Beaker People, while Firbolg (see **Bagmen**) has become a term of opprobrium.

'Gaelic', in the view of David Greene, gave a new word to the English language. In his Thomas Davis lecture in *The Shaping of Modern Ireland* series (1954), he suggested that 'Up to the nineteenth century the adjective corresponding to "Ireland", whether the people or the language, was "Irish". Both "Gaelic" and "**Erse**" came from the English of Scotland, and their use in this country was as much due to deliberate English avoidance of the uncompromising word "Irish" as to any other cause. But the nineteenth century nationalists fell easily for romantic words like "Gaelic" and "Celtic", and in any case, the new [athletic] association had a difficulty about its title; for the English-controlled body which it sought to replace was already calling itself the "Irish Amateur Athletic Association". So "Gaelic" it became – perhaps we are lucky it wasn't "Celtic"...' The name originally proposed at the founding meeting in Thurles in 1884 was 'The Gaelic Athletic Association for the Preservation and Cultivation of National Pastimes' – quickly reduced to acronym GAA. (The Irish title, Cumann Luthchleas Gael, appears to have been an afterthought and has never achieved significant popular currency.) 'Gaelic' thereafter became closely identified with the revitalised games, particularly football, with which the noun–usage became generally equated. Its wider application was to some extent inhibited by its employment as an alternative to 'Irish' when referring to the language, especially in instances where the latter word would lead to confusion. With the prefixing of the definite article it came to personify the resurgent national tradition in contradistinction to the Anglo-Irish, with the intensive 'True Gael' adopted as expressive of unsullied nationalism.

The Celtic Revival of the latter part of the eighteenth century, owing much to the Scot James Macpherson's *Ossian* and the work of both British and French racial theorists, was eagerly adopted by their Irish counterparts who in particular were anxious to rebut Scottish claims to the origins of Celtic civilisation and to establish, in Seamus Deane's words, 'the cultural annexation of a distant past'. By the end of the nineteenth century the Celt was being portrayed, particularly in the writings of W.B. Yeats and his associates, as a dreamer of dreams, remote from and unconcerned with the modern world and was most consistently characterised in the cultural-meteorological phenomenon of the **Celtic Twilight**.

This literary employment of Celt/Celtic was, however, only one aspect, if the most prominent, of a wider dissemination. It was taken up by commercial undertakings anxious to establish a national brand-image (see chapter 4) and 'Celtic' was applied to soccer teams – especially overseas teams with strong Irish connections. The juxtaposition of what were subsequently to be defined in the language of politico-cultural jargon as 'the two traditions' was codified by, for example, the Cavan newspaper title *The Anglo-Celt,* which, in common with the soccer usage, favours an initial sibilant rather than a hard 'C'.

Largely as a result of pressure from the Irish community, 'Anglo-Celt' began, in the latter part of the twentieth century, to replace the conventional 'Anglo-Saxon' in Australia, where the latter had long been in use as a label for those of both British and Irish origin. Continuing to inhabit less well-defined territory is the term 'Anglo-Irish', both in its substantive and adjectival usage. It is an expression, according to Willy Maley, 'that has been applied to Irish literature in English in the modern period, and also to the English colonial community in Ireland from the twelfth century. It is a disputed term, because some Irish critics point out that we do not call American literature "Anglo-American".' It is perhaps less controversially employed to denote writing in the second rather than the first official language.

Both 'Celt' and 'Gael' have carried forward into contemporary usage, perhaps most conspicuously in the apotheosis of the '**Celtic Tiger**'. This in turn has produced reaction from some for whom the concept of the Celt remains far removed from that invoked by the rapacious feline. In a letter to *The Irish Times* (25 May 2000) Claire Oakes, of the Celtic Christianity Group, complained that 'The word Celtic is much over-used these days. It is applied to all manner of things Irish, from the economy to chocolates, to perfume, to helicopters. What, if anything does the word Celtic have to do with our tiger economy? ... Celtic as a tradition speaks about hospitality, community, and affinity with nature ...' But it also, for better or worse, speaks about the often inhospitable world of Astérix and his friends and, increasingly, about calculated commercial exploitation. The 01 Area Telephone Directory (1999) listed 60 business names based on 'Celt' or 'Celtic' either singularly or in combination (Celtech, Celtward) as against 22 'Gael' derivatives, 11 of which were Irish-language Gaelscoil (Irish-speaking school) names. 'Gael/Gaelic', no doubt on account of the potential sporting/ language confusions, have in general proved less deployable than 'Celt/Celtic', even if contemporary punning usages have included Gael Force (see **Riverdance**) and a long-running stage show, Gaels of Laughter. These two 'new' noun/adjectives did not, however, substantially impinge upon the proscriptive territory occupied by 'Ireland/Irish'; which, with the birth of the new state and its independent, or quasi-independent institutions was extensively utilised, together with the similarly-functional adjectival prefix 'National' in an attempt to distance them from their British originals.

It would have been instructive to have been a bird in the elm tree in Dublin's **Phoenix Park** under which, in the spring or summer of 1842, three friends met to plan the publication of a new weekly newspaper. Sadly there is no record of the discussion which must have taken place between Thomas Davis, John Dillon and Charles Gavan Duffy before the name was decided upon. The choice, given the aims and objects of the projected publication, was limited. These were, in Duffy's words, to promote their country's affairs more vigorously, and it was thus apparent that the name must possess a strong national identity. In this context the English language is at a disadvantage in that it can find no words for the French *Patrie*, the German *Vaterland* ('Fatherland') or even 'Motherland'. These remain verbally alien concepts, while the bi-functional 'country' has to stand for what in Spanish is distinguished by *país* and *campo*, in French by *pays* and *campagne*. 'The State' is devoid of emotive resonance; 'The Republic', so shortly after the French Revolution, was freighted with extraneous associations. Thus **The Nation** it was, though it would have been fascinating to have been privy to any other suggestions offered: we do know that *The National* was proposed and wisely rejected.

'And Ireland long a province be/A Nation once again!' Davis was to write in his most popular poem, and 'The Nation' thereafter became at once a statement and an aspiration, bizarrely recalled by Winston Churchill in his secret telegram to Éamon de Valera on 8 December 1941 following the Japanese attack on Pearl Harbor: 'Now is your chance. Now or never. "A nation once again" …'. The offer was for the reunification of the country in exchange for the abandonment of neutrality, an offer which Churchill had not the power to make nor de Valera the naiveté to accept.

With nationhood partially achieved the adjective 'National' was by then in widespread usage, with reference to the 26-county state. There was an acceptance of this usage as reinforcing a sense of sovereignty, whereas the effect was frequently merely provincial if not patently exiguous – as in the tautological instance of the National Council for the Blind of Ireland: either 'National' or 'Ireland' surely, but not both. Nor was the term without its disabling ambiguities: the instance of the National Union of Journalists, where the adjective refers not to Ireland, but to Britain, being a case in point. With independence 'Irish' had equally come to be seen as a reinforcement of identity, latterly exemplified by the instance of the newspaper *The **Irish Examiner*** which has evolved from *The Cork Examiner* through *The Examiner* … though failing, through these successive reincarnations, to shed its colloquial appellation, both in its native city and beyond, of '**De Paper**'; the RTÉ Radio satirical programme 'Round Up the Usual Suspects' expressed the result of this process: 'Buy *De Irish De Paper*!'

Province and County

'Used her, mused her, licksed her and cuddled' – thus James Joyce, transmogrifying the four provinces in *Finnegans Wake*. The Irish *cúige* ('province'), one of five divisions, commemorates the fifth, Meath, long vanished, though not entirely erased from folk memory. On St Patrick's Day, 1936, one of the programmes broadcast to mark the occasion was listed in *Irish Radio News* as 'The Five Provinces Greet the Nation. Orchestra and Vocalists in Ballads of the Provinces. Alice Milligan for Ulster, Sean French for Munster, Frank Fahy for Connacht, James Montgomery for Leinster, and a message from Royal Meath.' And in January 2001, addressing the annual general seminar of the General Council of County Councils, the then Minister of State for the Arts, Éamon Ó Cuiv, proposed that the fifth province should be restored to the map to encompass the three counties created by the effective dismemberment (see below) of County Dublin.

Of the four existing provinces, the names **Ulster**, **Munster**, Leinster were formed from the original Irish with a Scandinavian suffix and as such the usage in English has remained fixed. However, Connacht and its colonial version, Connaught, still somewhat surprisingly co-exist in contemporary usage (*Connacht*, rugby team, *Connaught Telegraph*, newspaper, *et al*.), an attempt even having being made in official circles to dub what has become known as Knock Airport as Connaught Airport. Whereas any controversy over the current naming of Connacht is confined to this aspect and there is little to be said in the case of Leinster and Munster, no serious attempts having been made to restore the original Irish, the case of Ulster is very different.

Ulaidh originally defined the territory of the tribe of that name, and when they were defeated by the Anglo-Normans in 1177 John de Courcy assumed the title of *Princeps Ultoniae*, or Prince of Ulster. By the early seventeenth century the nine-county area now accorded recognition as the historical province was variously named Ulster, Ultonia and Provincia Ultoniae, though its early history of shifting and disputed boundaries was to be replicated with the 1922 partition. 'Ulster' then became coterminous, in unionist circles, with 'Northern Ireland' while nationalist usage favoured '**The Six Counties**'. The three sundered counties, **Monaghan**, Cavan and Donegal, continued meanwhile to assert their traditional Ulster identity, though for some administrative and electoral purposes being subsumed in a new concept, 'Connacht-Ulster'.

The individual counties themselves have undergone minimal boundary revision and little change in nomenclature since the original Anglo-Norman shiring, the exception being King's County and Queen's County, which at independence reverted to the names 'Laois' (for some time with the Anglicised spelling 'Leix', which remains in Abbeyleix as against Port Laoise) and 'Offaly', though the conversion was by no means instantaneous, southern unionists in particular continuing to employ the replaced names together with those of Kingstown (Dún Laoghaire) and Queenstown (Cóbh). There was no further change until, with the reorganisation of local government in Northern Ireland, new administrative areas (such as Newry & Mourne) were established, transcending the traditional county boundaries, though these later remained in popular use, thanks largely to the influence of the GAA.

The county divisions, with their colonial provenance, had in general received little popular recognition until, with the establishment of the GAA in 1884 and the organisation of teams on a county basis they became, and have remained, the focus of local identity – a recent proposal to amalgamate some of the weaker counties provoking a predictable protest. The extent to which the county name and identity have become the bedrock of GAA culture was exemplified in the account by Tom Humphries (*The Irish Times*, 22 May 2000) of a 'typical tail-sniffing encounter following strict rules. "What county man are ya?" A county name is offered up. The first party must then make a joke at the expense of the good name of this county. "Still locking referees in boots are ye/stonethrowers/ye pissed in the powder" etc, etc.'

County identities received an additional impetus with the development of the provincial press from the mid-nineteenth century onwards. While a few local newspapers claimed a province or even wider area (*Connacht Tribune; Leinster Leader; Munster Express; Ulster Herald; Western People; Midland Tribune*) many more were (and remain) content with a county identification: *Carlow Nationalist; Clare Champion; Derry Journal; Downshire Protestant; Fingal Independent; The Kerryman; Kilkenny People; Kings County Chronicle; Roscommon Herald; Sligo Champion; Tyrone Constitution; Westmeath Examiner; Wicklow People*. Ulster, however, generally favoured (and continues to favour) more localised titles such as *Ballymena Observer; Banbridge Chronicle; Coleraine Chronicle; Lurgan Mail; Newry Telegraph; Portadown News; Strabane Weekly News*.

Though the Irish forms of the county names are employed, if sparingly, in the GAA context and for official purposes such as postmarkings, the prevailing usage is English. This became a matter of controversy when in the 1980s a new system of car registration was introduced that, in the words of

Donnchadh Ó Corráin (*A Future for Irish Placenames*) 'was 100% anglicised in a country that constitutionally requires official bilingualism'. The original system, introduced under the British régime, assigned two-letter index marks (initially one, Z, in the case of Dublin) to each of the 32 counties and to county boroughs on the basis of the letter I or Z plus one other (later two). Thus CI Carlow; AI Meath; IL Fermanagh (see **MIL 2000**); IO, ZW Kildare.

The new system substituted a one- or two-letter code indicative of the county name in its English version. Ó Corráin claimed that 'By careful planning the abbreviations of 15 of the 26 counties could be bilingual (e.g. Donegal/Dún na nGall DL., Monaghan/Muineachán MN ....' And that the remainder could employ a three-letter Irish code and an alternative two-letter English code, as Kerry/Ciarraí KR/CRR. 'The fact is', he concluded, 'that nobody bothered to plan this operation in an intelligent bilingual way, even though the resources of modern technology made it perfectly feasible. The subsequent addition of the Irish county names in full on registration plates came not from officialdom but as a result of the continued protests of cultural groups.'

While the county, whether in Irish or English, remains the popular unit of local definition, particularly in the sporting context, throughout the country as a whole divisional identifications from an earlier tradition are sporadically encountered: Breffni; Decies; Desmond; Joyce's Country; Muskerry; The Kingdom (Kerry); Thomond; **Tyrconnell** amongst many. While such evocations are generally what might be termed romantic/historical, some, such as The Goldsmith Country, the Ely O'Carroll Country, the Yeats Country, the **Thoroughbred County** are neologisms or recent revivals exploited for tourism or other publicity purposes.

New Territories

On 30 July 1934, under the Tactical and Territorial Organisation of the Defence Forces, the newly-named Infantry Corps was restructured on the basis of ten new named regiments: The Regiment of Rifles; The Regiment of Oriel *(Counties Louth, Meath, Monaghan)*; The Regiment of Leinster *(Kildare, West Wicklow, Wexford, Carlow)*; The Regiment of Dublin *(Co & Borough of Dublin, East Wicklow)*; The Regiment of Ormond – renamed Ossory, 1935 *(Kilkenny, Waterford, Tipperary)*; The Regiment of Thomond *(Limerick, Clare)*; The Regiment of Connaught *(Galway, Mayo, Roscommon)*; The Regiment of Breffni *(Cavan, Longford, Leitrim, Sligo)*; The Regiment of Tírconnail *(Donegal)*; The Regiment of Uisneach *(Laois, Offaly, Westmeath)*.

Following the establishing of the County of Wicklow out of the lands of County Dublin in 1605 there were few changes to the 32-county pattern, apart from the abolishing of 'The County of the Town of Drogheda' and the renaming of King's and Queen's Counties until 1994 when protests, culminating in the uprooting of road signs, occurred following the division of County Dublin into three administrative divisions. One of them, Fingal, erected signs welcoming visitors to 'Co. Fingal', thus raising the ire of County Dublin loyalists. In this the Fingal authorities were technically within their rights, since there exists a body named 'Fingal County Council' which functions in exactly the same manner and with the same powers as that of County Meath or County Mayo – or as the other two new 'County Councils', Dún Laoghaire-Rathdown and South County Dublin. These latter, however, find themselves at an onomastic disadvantage, since neither name could be said to roll trippingly off the tongue: it is difficult, for example, to imagine a football crowd in Croke Park shouting 'Up Dún Laoghaire-Rathdown!'

Perhaps the choice of the new designations was made for this very reason; but in that case the selection of 'Fingal' has had the opposite result, creating a strong new name with a concomitant local identity. Evidence of the continuing confusion and ambivalence with regard to the new entities was provided by advertisements in November 2000 urging those living in the greater Dublin area to ensure their names were on the electoral register. These advertisements quaintly addressed themselves to 'Residents of Dublin City … South Dublin County Council … Fingal County Council … Dún Laoghaire/Rathdown County Council'. The housing crisis has created many anomalies, but living in a County Council must rank as one of the more bizarre. Such infelicities apart, the question remains, with the administrative eclipse of County Dublin, as to whether there are now 32 or 34 counties in the Republic. The matter is likely to remain in a legal limbo, however (the three new bodies are sometimes described as 'Electoral Counties'), until such time as Fingal fields its first 'county' GAA team. One should not underestimate, however, the residual power of the existing county names, by no means entirely residing in their sporting connotation. Similarly, the introduction of the new administrative entities in Northern Ireland (Newry & Mourne, Mid-Ulster *et al.*) has failed to undermine the strongly-felt identities of the six component counties.

The Place in the Song

The number of localities celebrated in song – many several times over – would fill a volume. The counties themselves are not lacking in lyrical tributes as the following highly selective listing suggests: *The Green Glens of Antrim; The Bard of Armagh; Follow Me Up to Carlow; My Cavan Girl; The Cork National Hunt; The Darlin' Girl from Clare; The Derry Hornpipe; The Hills of Donegal; The Star of the County Down; The Rocky Road to Dublin; Lovely Fermanagh; Bring Me a Shawl from Galway; The Kerry Dances; Norah the Pride of Kildare; The Boys of Kilkenny; Lovely Laois; Lovely Leitrim; The Limerick Rake; Longford On My Mind; The Wood of County Louth; Moonlight in Mayo; Beautiful Meath; The Little Hills of Monaghan; The Offaly Rover; If We Only had Roscommon Over Here; The Pride of Tipperary; Dear Old Tyrone; The Westmeath Bachelor; The Old Woman from Wexford; Among the Wicklow Hills.*

While many other jurisdictions have, in the process of local devolution, created new names for new administrative areas or given new life to old ones, the determination to retain centralised control in Dublin has inhibited any move in this direction as far as the Republic is concerned. The most consistent manifestation of attempted regional autonomy, that of the Shannon Region under the aegis of Shannon Development (formerly, the Shannon Free Airport Development Co. or SFADCO), has never enjoyed official recognition while the name itself suffers from confusion both with the airport, from which it was derived, and the river – as well as a prominent Limerick rugby football club. The frequently conflicting administrative and juridical divisions of the country over the years involving health boards, tourist regions and other similar authorities have produced nothing in the way of distinctive nomenclature. More recently the establishment, in response to EU requirements, of two new 'regions', has resulted in the utterly unimaginative titles of Border Midlands and Western Region (**BMW**) and Southern and Eastern Region. Given the traditional centralism of successive governments it is not unreasonable to see in this nomenclature a decided reluctance to apportion to these two new divisions any meaningful identity… in either of the two national languages.

2

O tell me about Anna Livia!

THOMAS MOORE, ACCORDING TO A. NORMAN JEFFARES in *Place, Space and Personality and the Irish Writer* (1977), was among those nineteenth-century poets who placed 'a fresh emphasis on place ... What he did was to invest Irish placenames with plangent sounds, often dwelling on them repetitively ...' Jeffares then listed examples from the first volume of Moore's *Irish Melodies:* ''Tis Innisfail'; 'Sweet Innisfallen fare thee well'; 'Silent, Oh Moyle'; 'Glendalough, thy gloomy wave'; 'Oh Arranmore, lov'd Arranmore'; 'Sweet vale of Avoca'; 'Tara's halls', amongst many others. While according to Jeffares the effects of the **Young Ireland** movement 'led to a rhetorical poetry, often using round tower, harp and cromlech as symbols, but generally associating placenames with battles ... Irish Victorian poets moved to a new kind of local poetry, enjoying the particularity given by naming places, and obviously expecting these names to be evocative in effect.' Such expectations were not to be disappointed. 'The place in the song' became, and remains, the common denominator of the popular ballad to a extent that probably exceeds that encountered in any other western culture.

The phenomenon is, of course, simply the current expression of a near-obsession with toponomy which has been evident at least since the twelfth-century *Dindshenchas* ('lake of high places'), a compilation of placenames, with etymological anecdotes, which probably drew on even earlier material.

And from the *Dindshenchas* to Paul Durcan the obsession has remained: as Fintan O'Toole wrote of the latter (*The Ex-Isle of Erin* [1996]): 'No living Irish poet and few dead ones can match the sheer range of Irish places reflected in the work ... Deeply embedded in his poetry is the idea that to name is to bless ... His insistent naming of places that would otherwise have remained unnamed in poetry and therefore have been denied a recognition of their preciousness is one of the most important aspects of Durcan's care for Irish reality.' In *Going Home to Mayo, Winter 1949* the poet recalls that

> Each town we passed through was another milestone
> And their names were magic passwords into eternity:
> Kilcock, Kinnegad, Strokestown, Elphin,
> Tarmonbarry, Tulsk, Ballaghaderreen, Ballavarry ...

This sense of preciousness is the theme of Brian Friel's play *Translations*, set in the period 1824-41 when the Ordnance Survey was occupied with establishing English equivalents for Irish toponomic identities. To Friel this represented a cultural assault of tragic significance, and he lends added weight to his argument by indicating that the characters in his drama, though ostensibly Anglophone, are in fact speaking in Irish. In the view of Joep Leerssen, however (*Remembrance and Imagination* [1996]), Friel has been guilty of serious distortion. The Survey, in his view, '... salvaged placenames by painstaking investigation of manuscripts, giving them English transliterations rather than translations' – a point which had been made in 1867 by P.W. Joyce: 'In anglicising Irish names, the leading general rule is, that the present forms are derived from the ancient Irish, as they were spoken, not as they were written. Those who first committed them to writing aimed at preserving the original pronunciation, by representing it as nearly as they were able in English letters.' Most prominent amongst these was the young fieldworker John O'Donovan, of whom Willie Smith, reviewing his *Ordnance Survey Letters Donegal* (*The Irish Times,* 16 Nov. 2000) wrote, 'he moved from parish to parish to become Ireland's greatest historical topographer and leave his stamp both on Irish placenames and the Irish psyche.'

Brien Friel's protest, however, was centred not upon how it was done but whether it should have been done at all; and in this he would have the support of many who cite, for example, the maintenance in a largely anglophone culture of Scottish Gaelic placenames in their original, or close to original form. With the coming of 26–county independence some moves were indeed made to restore the *status quo ante*, but these have proved to have been of sporadic efficacy. Kingstown and Queenstown, King's and Queen's Counties quickly shed their royal status; there was a trickle of displaced Parsons (Parsonstown > Birr); though whereas Newtownbarry reverted to Bunclody, Newtownmountkennedy retained its anglophone status and its position as the longest town or village name in that language (local and commercial pressures are now threatening to cut it back to 'Newtown'). **Navan** went full circle, becoming An Uaimh before reverting to Navan, again in response to local pressure and, perhaps, pride in the possession of the country's sole toponymic palindrome. Similarly, the mellifluous *Rineanna* airport became ambiguous Shannon in response to international aviation exigencies; while Mostrim (Edgeworthstown) and Rath Luirc (Charleville) enjoyed what might be described as virtual existence in the pages of CIÉ railway timetables before somebody finally admitted that the new-old names were not going to find public favour. Muine Bheag, again largely a railway re-creation, seems to hover somewhere in the suburb of Bagenalstown, intermittently asserting its authority. (It is interesting to note *en passant* that Alberto Porlan, in his monumental study, *Los Nombres de Europa* (1998), suggests a Menapian origin for Muine Bheag though his argument, based on the assertion that a city of 'Menapia' existed in the south-east corner of Ireland, is too complex to follow here. (See also Norman Mongan, *The Menapia Quest* [1995]).

Today, even where as the result of a successful reversion an Irish form of a placename is in acknowledged sole use – Dún Laoghaire, Cóbh, Daingean (Offaly), Coill Dubh (Kildare), for example – it more often than not appears on the signposts of the new dispensation in the regressive italics generally employed for the Irish equivalent of an English name on bilingual signs. As Leachlainn Ó Catháin commented (in *The Placenames of Ireland in the Third Millennium* [1992]): 'readers of the Irish-language versions of our signposts would appear to be deemed to be longer-sighted and better-sighted than their English-reading counterparts.' This second-class status is replicated in references to Gaeltacht locations in the English-language media, Oileán Cléire almost invariably appearing as Cape Clear, Árainn as Aran – even Arran! – and so on. Those who genuinely lament the failure to restore – and use – the Irish forms do so against a background of hypocrisy and humbug to which is added a sizeable measure of Nimbyism. By all means restore placenames to their Irish form, but only where it can do no harm to the day-to-day business of living through English.

This attitude is all the more difficult to understand in that reversion would in many instances place no unbearable burden on even the most stubborn monoglot. *Uachtarard,* for instance, is just as pronounceable, recognisable and far more visually appealing than Oughterard; *Cill* would scarcely discomfit its inhabitants or its visitors, while it is no great distance from Tarbert to Tairbeart. On the other hand, of course, there are many instances where such reversions would cause confusion at the best and in many cases severe local indignation at what would be seen as the filching of established identities. And with some justification: few except the adepts would recognise Waterville in An Coireán, Blessington in Baile Coimín, Clonmellon in Ráistin. In a letter to *The Irish Times* (1 Sep. 1999) Dáithí Mac Cárthaigh complained that the work of the Ordnance Survey in the early nineteenth century had reduced placenames 'which had immediate resonance and were rooted in local topography, history and environment' to 'meaningless collections of sounds. Contrast *Cluain Meala* (the meadow of the honey) with *Clonmel*. Contrast *Domhnach Broc* (the Church of the Badgers) with *Donnybrook* … Quite apart from the absurdity of certain Anglicised placenames such as *Gorey* (details?), or *Kilbride* (murder your wife?) the pronunciation problems posed for non-locals, both Irish and overseas … demonstrates that had the Englished versions of Irish placenames never existed there would certainly be no need to invent them!'

For all their apparent eclipse, the Irish originals of placenames maintain a popular resonance, as evidenced by a considerable body of excellent local research and publication. This public concern was demonstrated in a protest in September 1999 over the official equivalent of Knock, County Mayo. The Minister of State for Arts, Heritage, Gaeltacht and the Islands, Éamon Ó Cuiv, responding in the Dáil to **Fine Gael**'s Enda Kenny, warned local authorities that they could not have *carte blanche* to put up signs using any version of placenames in Irish. Kenny had expressed concern that the 'Mhuire' (Mary) had been dropped from 'Cnoc Mhuire' as the official Irish name for Knock though, he said, this was the accepted translation (*sic*) and local tradition for many years. The Minister, in reply, said that his Department had been 'bedevilled' by local authorities putting up any name they wanted and that 'the official forms and procedures will not only be maintained but strengthened to ensure that there is a common, authorised version of all placenames in Irish'. He went on to explain that 'An Cnoc' had been proposed by the Placenames Commission in 1958 on the basis of collected evidence and had been the official form since 1975, but that because of the association with the apparition and possible confusion with, for example, Cnoc na hAille in County Galway, 'I accept that the present modern usage of the Irish form of Knock is now Cnoc Mhuire.'

The continuing identity with and interest in the Irish-language origins of placenames is to a considerable degree attributable to the fact that they are largely, in Alberto Porlan's definition (*op.cit.*) 'connotative' – that is their etymology, with the exception of a few cases, is 'live'. Unlike mainland Europe, Ireland, largely isolated from external linguistic influence from the Celtic invasions to the early modern period, possesses a substantially transparent toponymy, until recently sustained in living speech. This has resulted in a very close identification of people with places: 'The human being is not complete, nor is his world habitable', wrote Porlan, 'if those things which people such a world lack names' – and where those names are apparently identifiable with a local feature, deity, historical figure or legend the sense of unity is reinforced. This does not mean, of course, that there are no traps for the unwary in the establishment of the origins of a particular name, as Joyce was quick to point out: 'It is very dangerous to depend on the etymologies of the people, who are full of imagination, and will often distort a word to meet some fanciful derivation; or they will account for a name by some silly story obviously of recent invention, and so far as the origin of the name is concerned, not worth a moment's consideration.'

Irish-language names are felt to be 'part of what we are', by all sections of the community, and this is evinced by their consistent employment in creating comic or serio-comic images of the country (see panel). While the high incidence in such coinages of the first element 'Bally' (generally though not exclusively <Ir. *baile*, town or townland) is a reflexion of its ubiquitousness (Joyce indexes nearly 200 examples) it is one among several such enjoying a wide dissemination: according to Flann Ó Riain (*The Irish Times,* 24 Jan. 2000) 'there are 1,410 townland names [out of a national total of more than 60,000] having *lios* as the first element, 1,600 having *ráth* and 580 starting with *dún*'. The popularity of 'bally', though, in the perpetuating of the '**Oirish**' image is due not so much to ubiquity as to its slang English usage since the 1840s (though now virtually obsolete) as a euphemism for 'bloody', an adjective itself possibly derived from **Ballyhooly**. Nor is the 'Oirish' image the prerogative of 'bally' and its combinations. As John Banville puts it ('Place Names: the Place' in Tim Pat Coogan (ed.), *Ireland and the Arts* ([1983]), 'If a poet, or perhaps more to the point (let us come clean) a novelist, tries to find or invent – the distinction hardly matters – placenames which shall have a "Hibernophonic plausibility", conforming to Irish, or at least Anglo-Irish, toponymy, he will find himself tending always, helplessly, toward the comic and the infantile, thanks to decisions made 150 years ago by the British

Ordnance Survey. Sometimes, considering all those *Kills* and *Mucks* and *Ballys,* one suspects the Master-General of the Ordnance of a secret sense of humour.'

Oirish Placenames

Bailegangáire; Ballycomequick, *Trad*; **Ballygobackwards**; Ballygullion, *in novels by* **Lynn C. Doyle***;* **Ballyhooly**; Ballykilferret, *in novel by Frank Kelly*; Ballykissangel, *Brit. TV series (aka* Ballykay*);* **Ballymagash**; Ballymagraw; Ballyslapadashmuckery, *in stage sketches by comedian Jack Cruise, 1940s-50s*; Corca Dorcha, *in novel by Flann O'Brien;* Farramore, *in novel 'Bug O'Shea', by Paul Morand*; **Gloccamorra**; **Gumgooly**; **Knackeragua**; Puckoon, *novel by Spike Milligan*; Roscullen, *in 'John Bull's Other Island', George Bernard Shaw.*

If popular etymology is not always to be relied upon, changes in orthography, pronunciation and emphasis over the centuries have combined to obscure meanings and origins. Such factors are, of course, constantly in evidence in any living language, but a contemporary element militating against the survival and/ or revival of Irish-language placenames is the decline in native speakers of Irish combined with a shift in English pronunciation, largely as a result of American influence via the spoken media, which is increasingly placing the stress on the first syllable of a word. Thus one hears the now apparently acceptable *re*search, for example, paralleled, particularly in the case of the so-called **DART** accent, by *Tulla*more, *Rath*mines, *Ban*bridge, etc., whereas the 1989 *Gazetteer of Ireland* indicates in each of these cases the stress on the second syllable.

This development will inevitably have the effect of obscuring if not distorting the etymology of the name and could eventually lead to barbarisms such as *At-Henry* – with which my own mother was confronted when going to work in London in the early years of the last century. Something similar was recorded by Edward MacLysaght in his contribution to Sharon Gmelch's *Irish Life and Traditions* (1986). In July 1905 he was cycling with a cousin in County Galway when overtaken by a car – a rare sight at the time – the driver of which was seeking directions. '"Kindly tell me", said he, "am I on the right road for At-Henry?".' On the other hand the popularity of '**The Fields** ...' will no doubt preserve those particular phonemes; and indeed the number of placenames enshrined in song and generally bearing the traditional emphases is a guarantee of a sort that the inevitable process of phonetic change will not wreak total havoc.

A notable consequence of emigration in large numbers, particularly in the nineteenth century, was the export of placenames to all corners of the world, and of the anglophone world in particular. Some of these, such as Maryborough in Queensland, Australia, perpetuate names now expunged from the domestic map (though there is still a Maryborough Street in Graiguecullen, County Carlow) but the majority enshrine an ascertainable continuity with their origin. In some cases, however – those of some of the many 'Dublins' in the USA (in Arkansas, California, Pennsylvania, Virginia, Alaska, Maryland, New Hampshire and other states) for example – the Irish connection has been lost … even if, in fact, it ever existed. The Dublin in Bucks County, Pennsylvania traces its origin, according to local legend, to an Irish major in the Revolutionary army who opened a tavern, only to have a rival build one right beside it. In due course both properties were bought by a third party and knocked into one, becoming known as the Double Inn … reflecting what *The Irish Times* (12 Feb. 1930) referred to as a 'pidgin etymology … which attributes the origin of the name "Dublin" to a supposed double inn which is said to have been situated in Winctavern street.'

Undoubtedly, as P.W. Joyce realised, such fanciful etymologies and transformations 'were probably made under the influence of a playful humour, aided by a little imagination', citing 'a parish in Antrim called Billy; a townland in the parish of Kinawly, Fermanagh, called Molly; and another, in the parish of Ballinlough, Limerick, with the more ambitious name of Cromwell; but all these sail under false colours, for the first is *bile,* an ancient tree; the second *málaighe,* hill-brows, or braes; and Cromwell is nothing more than *crom-choill,* stooped or sloping wood.' *The Irish Times* article quoted above alludes to the original name of the Dublin suburb of **Ringsend**, deriving it from *Rinn-aun,* 'the point of the tide'. 'Rinn', it suggests, 'means "a miniature promontory" and so Ringsend is a half-Irish, half-English word, meaning "the end of the promontory". One bright etymologist once explained the name by pointing out that at one time there was a line of piles erected near the place, for the mooring of ships, and asserted that "the outermost of these piles, having a ring, was called ring's end, i.e. the end or last of the rings" … Such an attempt at derivation is only comparable to the theory which explains "Donnybrook" as a compound of "dawny", "little", and "brook" (the Dodder) …'

In this context one might well assent to Porlan's assertion that 'la toponimia no es una ciencia. Por no ser, ni siquiera es una disciplina. Se parece más a un immenso depósito de materiales, inanes y saqueables, a un *no man's land* pantanoso recorrido por hombres con antorchas …' ['Toponomy is not a science, nor is it even a discipline. It is more like a huge deposit of useless, expendable material, a boggy no-man's-land traversed by men carrying torches …']

Estates of Chassis

The vast majority of current placenames possess a traceable Irish origin, with in addition many apparently English names, such as Cranfield, Ferns, Longford, etc. being corruptions of the Irish original. The relatively few purely English names, such as Helen's Bay, Arthurstown, Craigavon are of relatively recent provenance, and English is now in most cases preferred in the naming of new features. Industrial estates such as Dublin's Citywest and Park West; the Kilmartin N6 Centre (Athlone); The Millennium Park (Naas); Airside (Swords) or the Lakepoint Retail & Business Park (Mullingar) are rarely accorded Irish equivalents. This is symptomatic of a cultural as well as a linguistic shift which is even more seriously in evidence in the naming of new housing developments. 'Are placenames an integral and precious part of what makes us different?' asked Dick Hogan (*The Irish Times*, 13 Jan. 1993), 'or are they something to be trifled with by the building community in order to put a questionable gloss on modern housing estates? … For some time builders have thought that unless the suffix "downs", "close", "heights", or "court" appeared in granite at the entrance to new housing estates, the general public would be unwilling to get up to their ears in debt to live in them. Some of the modern names are simply laughable, others astonishing for their pomposity or so ill-fitting as to made a body wonder whether or not a massive inferiority complex is at work.' Six years later Hogan returned to the theme (*The Irish Times,* 7 Dec. 1999): 'As our hinterland changes dramatically with the proliferation of housing estates', he wrote, 'usually completed with what the builders perceive to be upwardly mobile British-sounding names, it has become all the more important to record and describe the names given to places by our ancestors. There is an abundance of housing estate names that bear no resemblance to the original placename …'

In his paper *A Future for Irish Placenames* (1992), quoted in both articles by Hogan, Donncadh Ó Corráin castigated 'The purveyors of Tiffany Downs and the like – speculative builders and half-educated property consultants – [who] are in no way qualified to be left with cultural decisions of this significance.' He proceeded to pillory in particular the Cork development rejoicing in the name of 'Tiffany Downs', firstly on the total irrelevance of the 'Tiffany' element and secondly on the well-known (to students of Anglo-Saxon at least) etymological trap hidden in the word 'down' (<OE *dún*, hill,

poss. <Celtic, e.g. Ir. *dún,* Welsh *din,* etc, giving, *en passant,* a new slant to the GAA county slogan 'Up Down!'). Ó Corráin's conclusion was that 'the name giver, then, is a person vainly chasing after grandeur and respectability by using what he feels is fashionable anglicisation, but he falls down because of ignorance. The precious name of his housing estate will cause anybody who knows the English language to laugh at him and his absurd pretensions.'

That such pretensions faded little in the years between Dick Hogan's two comments and after is confirmed by Mary Kenny's examination of 'symbols of Britishness' in Irish public nomenclature (*Irish Independent,* 27 May 2000). She lists some of 'the names being given to new properties and housing estates now springing up all over Ireland. 'Stonewall (Kinsale), The Old Forge (Lucan), Goodtide Harbour (Wexford), Sleepy Hollow (Dublin) ... Analyse the *Irish Independent* property page adverts for new, upwardly mobile estates: Wolseley Village, Hollystown Park, Charnwood, Castle Dawson, Derby Lodge, Priory Lawn, Lakepoint Park, Heathfield, Alderbrook ...' Nor is the phenomenon confined to Dublin and environs. The *Westmeath Examiner* (12 Aug. 2000) criticised 'tacky Westmeath placenames' perpetrated by builders and local authorities, quoting examples such as Sherwood Park, Abbeylands and Ashleigh, concluding that 'the new placenames we give to our streets and housing estates in Westmeath say something about us and our communities and how we see ourselves'.

There is some evidence, however, that what one insensitive commentator described as 'the Downs Syndrome' is beginning to respond to critical treatment (though that specific abomination is still with us – as instanced by the appearance of 'Swords Downs' in Fingal in late 2000). Mary Kenny admitted that 'there are some Irish names favoured – Glasan in Galway, Cluain Mhór near Kells' ... and to her examples might be added Ros na Rí (Navan), Gleann na Rí (Cabinteely, Dublin), Boroimhe (Swords, County Fingal/Dublin), Maeldúin (Dunshaughlin), Dun Eóin (Cork) amongst others. Some of these ventures are, linguistically, more enthusiastic than accurate: the last example omits the *síne fada* on the first element while including it on the second; Togher Páirc (Roundwood, County Wicklow) reverses the conventional word-order; Monastery Heath, County Dublin, offers, complete with a barbarous initial aspiration, the unlikely Irish equivalent Fhraoch na Mainistreach ('Ligean do rud dul sa fhraoch ort' – to let yourself become confused about something), while Crann Mór Cove (Clogher Head, County Louth) creates an unpalatable bilingual mix. An interesting example of creative naming in this context is Tassagard Green, which reverts to the original name for

27

Saggart, County Dublin … described, however, in advertisements as 'Saggart Heritage Village'. 'Village', sadly, has become the gentrified name for what were until recently considered as suburbs; and while real villages fall prey to rural depopulation their place is being usurped by 'instant' agglomerations such as 'Kilminchy Village' (Portlaoise).

If these individual examples of a return to indigenous naming might be seen as straws in the wind, there is more encouraging evidence that some local authorities are beginning to take the matter seriously. A clause in the recent (2000) Limerick Corporation development plan states that 'In the laying out of any area for development, the developer shall, as part of the proposal, agree with the Corporation a scheme for the naming of the area and of the proposed roads and streets therein … Such nomenclature shall be cognisant of local historical and cultural traditions and shall endeavour to maintain a continuity of traditional placenames.' An equally innovative approach was evident in County Tyrone where, according to the *Belfast Telegraph* (22 Jun. 2000) the pupils of St Brigid's Primary School in Altamuskin were invited to suggest a name for a new local housing development. 'Wherever we build, we try to get the local community involved,' said a representative of the developers.

The situation, understandably, is somewhat different in the North, where, though indigenous names abound they are not routinely accompanied by Irish-language equivalents on the signposts, and where they are replaced by such, the motivation is invariably political/sectarian. The case of **Derry/Londonderry** is the obvious example (Foyle books, in a promotional leaflet, settled for compromise in giving its address as '12 Magazine Street L-Derry'); but the naming of the new town of Craigavon was also a political gesture, as was the renaming of **Long Kesh** internment camp, which was built on the site of the former military airfield from which it took its name. When the camp was reconstructed as a prison comprising a complex of **H-blocks**, the British authorities essayed a euphemistic name-change on the model of Windscale/Sellafield but were unsuccessful in erasing the original name from common usage, particularly in Nationalist circles. This sleight-of-hand would seem to hark back to the ancient Egyptians for whom, according to Alberto Porlan (*op. cit.*) there was no difference between the name of a thing and its existence, so that the act of naming is the equivalent of the act of creating. Re-creation, however, usually for cosmetic purposes, rarely achieves this symbiosis.

In the North, the political divide is more sharply evident in selection, perpetuation or replacement of street names which, unlike those of towns or villages, are theoretically susceptible to modification. An example is provided by Camille C. O'Reilly in *The Irish Language in Northern Ireland* (1999): 'Residents of Artillery Flats in the New Lodge area of north Belfast campaigned for many months to have the names of the high-rise blocks of flats changed. Named after the British war heroes and battle victories like Churchill, Dill, Alexander and Templar, the mainly Nationalist residents believe that the names do not reflect the culture and traditions of the area. While a previous campaign in the 1970s was unsuccessful, the Northern Ireland Housing Executive agreed to allow the changes as long as the local community was consulted. The Rename-Our-Flats Committee conducted a survey of residents to decide on names, and these were submitted to the Housing Executive for approval. The names put forward to the Housing Executive are drawn from Irish mythology: *Teach Gráinne, Teach Cúchulainn, Teach na bhFiann, Teach Méabha, Teach Oisín, Teach Eithne* and *Teach Finn.* What was initially heralded as a new era of improved relations between Irish campaigners and government agencies turned sour when the Housing Executive refused the names chosen by residents on the grounds that their "computers only accept the English language" (*Anderstown News,* 23 Sept. 1995).'

The streets where you live

The use of Irish in street signs was prohibited in an amendment to the Public Health and Local Government Act, 1949, after such signs had been erected in the local authority area of Newry & Mourne in 1948; but this was rescinded by the Local Government (Miscellaneous Provisions) (NI) Order of February 1995. In the wake of the Belfast/Good Friday Agreement (choice of title follows largely sectarian lines), Southern politicians, notably the then Foreign Minister, Brian Cowen, expressed themselves as concerned that there should be 'no further evidence of Britishness in the governance of Northern Ireland'. This self-evidently fatuous statement was rightly castigated from an onomastic standpoint by Mary Kenny in the *Irish Independent* article quoted above: 'It is a rum thing, surely, for an Irish Government minister, surrounded, as he is, by symbols of British governance in Dublin, to wish that symbols of Britishness be removed from Belfast. And if he feels so strongly about it, perhaps Mr Cowen should start a campaign, personally, to persuade the Irish people, particularly in the building industry, to stop surrounding their own homes and streets with so many symbols of Britishness. Perhaps he could begin by requesting the hotel opposite Government buildings ... to change its name from Merrion, a name chosen by the Georgian Brits, to, say, the St Colmcille Hotel, or the Roger Casement?'

Mary Kenny pointed to the many Dublin streets, named after titled but forgotten British colonial worthies rather than the English towns they would appear to commemorate, which 'the residents have never sought to change during eighty years of Irish independence' and wondered 'could the problem be psychological, rather than imposed by some imagined form of British oppression? Could those who name hotels, streets and places be influenced by the fact that locations with strong Irish connotations – Seán McDermott Street, James Larkin Road, Ballyfermot Avenue – tend to be more down-market than the names associated with British governance?' In other words, are the old divisions of Irishtown and Englishtown which characterised many urban settlements (Limerick, Athlone *et al.*) still exerting a subliminal influence? 'Even in the Cork of my own youth', wrote Tom McElligott in *Six O'Clock all over Cork* (1992), 'the word "royal" still preceded such well-known establishments as The Oyster Tavern and the Victoria Hotel.'

More localised social snobbery is also observable in the matter of the descriptive component of street names. As McElligott recalled of his childhood in the city: 'At that time we were probably becoming aware of certain gradations in society which accorded a higher ranking to "avenue" than to "street" which, in turn, took precedence over "lane". Much later when I came to understand such matters more clearly, I can remember a successful application to Cork Corporation to change Portney's Lane to Portney's Avenue.' Hence, for example, the recently-built Meadowbrook estate in Ballinasloe, County Galway, which comprises Meadowbrook Gardens, Drive, Close, Lawns and Park … but no Street or Avenue, let alone Lane.

In Cork, according to McElligott, 'Even the names one met with were redolent of the past – Clarence Place, Empress Place, Adelaide Terrace. Names that one might expect to find in a quiet seaside town in the south of England. It seemed that in Ireland, as the hold of the Empire on her subjects weakened, a certain sentimental attachment to imperial links strengthened.' Under the headline 'English street names dismay', the *Leinster Leader* reported on 16 December 1999 the reactions of a Newbridge man returning from England. Seán Farrell 'was amazed and dismayed on a recent visit home to see so many street names of English origin … he noted a general lack of enthusiasm for the choice of street names and in particular the name over the door of the new [Newbridge] hotel, the Eyre Powell. … Mr Farrell went on to cite street names like Eyre, James, John, Edward and George as prime examples of how, on the surface, Droichead Nua resembles many English towns. "I could better sympathise with local feelings if there was a move towards adopting more appropriate street names such as Kildare, O'Connell, or Pearce [*sic*], perhaps in Irish and English", he added.'

The Irish/English division was particularly marked in the plantation towns of Ulster, largely established between 1609 and 1641. In Armagh, an earlier foundation, 54 per cent of the town's Catholics, according to a 1770 census, lived in three streets – Callen, Irish and Castle; while six streets – Market, Little Meeting, Church, English, Scotch and New – were predominantly Protestant. 'As place names scattered over a country give a clue to its history', wrote D.J. Owen in his *History of Belfast* (1921), 'so do street names in a town to a large extent perpetuate the memory of personages and events associated with its origin and early development. Of course, in a period of rapid expansion, when streets are being laid in great numbers, the system of nomenclature is necessarily often arbitrary or haphazard, names being affixed from motives of convenience. It will be found that the older roads in a town have been named for a definite reason, and the tendency to rename old streets is to be deplored.'

Apart from a flurry of renaming on the achievement of 26-county independence which installed some national heroes – and a few heroines – in the place of former British identities, there was little momentum for the process on a national scale; though what was done sometimes had unexpected consequences. 'After the establishment of the State in 1922', wrote the Joycean authority David Norris (*The Irish Times*, 2 Aug. 1995) '... the new government changed many of the [Dublin] street names which had been associated with James Joyce. Great Britain Street, for example, the site of Joyce's first short story *The Sisters*, was renamed Parnell Street after the hero of Joyce's youth.' Though many cities and towns acquired their Parnell thoroughfares, in the matter of the honouring of native sons – or, rarely, daughters – there is no comparison with, for example, the multitude of streets, avenues and squares named for Jean Jaurès or Général Le Clerc in France; nor does native usage favour the commemoration of historic dates on the model of Rome's Via Vente Settembre [20 September] or Santiago's Avenida Diez de Julio [10 July]. Even de Valera, the salient national figure of his time, is sparsely celebrated: strangely there is nothing in his name in the capital to equate with Collins or Griffith Avenues, honouring his ideological opponents. The general reluctance to commemorate more recent political figures was due in no short measure to the bitter legacy of the Civil War and the fear on the part of the relevant authorities of dividing communities, a hesitation which had not been apparent in the matter of earlier and less

31

controversial individuals; thus Connolly, Sarah Curran, Davis, Davitt, Devoy, Emmet, Lord Edward (Fitzgerald), Larkin, Seán MacDermott, Mellowes, Grace O'Malley, O'Connell, O'Rahilly, Parnell, Pearse, Plunkett, Sarsfield, Wolfe Tone all featured in the 1995 Dublin street directory.

Such names are, however, numerically far outclassed in the same listing by the names of saints – some 86 in all from Agnes via Aubyn, Brock, Canice, Eithne, Gaetien, Ita, Maelruan, Mary, Michan, Mura, Patrick, Ronan to Ultan and Vincent – and this religious preponderance would apply to virtually every urban centre with the exception of the largely Protestant regions of the North. Most, but not all the saints thus invoked are Irish, and *Streetnames: Guidelines*, published by An Coimisiún Logainmneacha (1992) sounds a note of warning with regard to the rendering of such names into Irish: 'It will be readily appreciated how important it is for the translators to know whether it is a saint or a person of another category, for example, the son or daughter of the builder, who is being commemorated by a street name.'

The broader Christian culture, widely reflected in placenames and those of religious institutions since the earliest times, continues to exert a potent influence in the field of nomenclature: when a project (2000) for a new city in the western counties was announced the suggested name was 'Sacred Heart'. But, as in the case of new urban developments, historical identities are increasingly at risk. '... the Church of Ireland in its years of dominance', wrote Donnchadh Ó Corráin (*op.cit.*), '... clung to the historical names of parishes and very often of patrons. The leaders of the Catholic Church abandoned the historical parish names in many instances, turned their backs on traditional Irish saints, and tended to give patrons of the universal church to their parish churches ... Here there is damage to the cultural fabric of Irish Christianity that needs to be repaired.'

As in the case of political naming, religious usage has not been without its controversies. Hubert Butler, in his essay 'Naming a Street', wrote of his native Kilkenny: '... not long ago the residents of Asylum Road informed the corporation that they would like the name of their street changed. The corporation discussed it at great length and two names were suggested, Nuncio Street and Berkeley Street. For the Papal Nuncio had recently visited the town and his name had been inscribed on the roll of freemen; Bishop Berkeley, the philosopher, had been born near the town and, like Swift and Congreve, educated at Kilkenny College.' The suggestions provoked a spate of letters to the local press. 'The liveliest of the letter-writers', said Butler, 'argued: "Philosophy is all very well for the gentry, but for the working class people of Upper Patrick Street the Faith of Our Fathers and a reasonable rent for the new council houses are more to the purpose. And why should a Protestant bishop be commemorated in Kilkenny when the Blessed Oliver Plunkett would certainly not get a street named after him in Belfast?" The street was without more ado called "Nuncio Street".'

The letter-writer was probably right about the Belfast of the time (1950s) since in the North there had been until recently an emphasis in street-naming on British associations (Britannia Street, Larne), Great War and other imperial battles and (mostly aristocratic) pillars of the British establishment. In many cases, however, these latter were individuals exercising a powerful local hegemony. That Belfast, according to D.J. Owen (*op.cit.*), 'grew up in close association with the Chichester and Donegall family is abundantly clear when we consider that their names came to be directly attached to so many thoroughfares and places, such as Donegall Street, Donegall Place ... and Chichester Street. Arthur Street and Ann Street are not such obvious cases, but the origin of those names is apparent when it is borne in mind that several of the men of the Donegall family were called Arthur, and that Ann was a favourite name among their women.' He then lists Waring (Waring Street), Pottinger (Pottinger's Entry) and Cunningham (Cunningham Row) amongst other influential families in the city's history for whom streets have been named.

The practice of naming streets, and indeed whole towns, after local landed families was, of course, widespread throughout the island – Edgeworthstown (Mostrim, < *Meathas Troim*, in spite of the CIÉ timetables' best efforts, did not succeed in ousting it), Sherlockstown, Stratford ... 'This town, which is of recent origin', wrote Samuel Lewis in his *Topographical Dictionary of Ireland* (1837), 'owes its origin to Edward, late Earl of Aldborough, who, towards the close of the last century, conferred upon it his family name, Stratford, and distinguished it from other places of that name by the adjunct which described its situation on the Slaney.' Newmarket-on-Fergus, named after the English racing location, followed the same pattern. Street names equally paid due deference, particularly in the case of early modern Dublin, where, according to M'Cready (1892) no fewer than 24 kings and queens, 56 lords lieutenant and 96 property owners and members of the nobility and their families were thus memorialised. South William Street commemorated, however, not the conquering **King Billy** but its only begetter, one William Williams, who laid it out in 1676, apparently resisting the temptation to name it South William Williams Street. A number of other developers of the time similarly sought to eternalise themselves: William Hendrick, John Russell, Frederick Jebb (Frederick Street, which M'Cready posited might have been named for Frederick the Great of Prussia), Henry Aston (Aston's Quay) … It would be a brave, or foolhardy, developer who would seek similarly to implant his name on a contemporary housing development.

Mediaeval Galway, in common with Dublin and elsewhere, featured the simplest of descriptive street-names, many of which survive. Hardiman's *History of the Town and County of Galway* (1820) refers to 'Back-street (which street was so called from its backward situation) … Middle-street (so named from its central situation) … Shop-street (so called because in this street the first shops were opened) … High-street (a street so termed from its high or elevated situation).' The 1812 census listed only a handful of proper names among 'The streets of the town, &c in the parish of St Nicholas': Dominick Street, Mooney's-lane, Murray's Lane, William Street ….' but the mediaeval lanes that linked the 14 principal streets were named for some of the traditional 'Tribes' of Galway: Bodkin, Blake, Kirwan.

The ubiquitous 'High Street', following British practice, became the general term to denote the centre of urban trading. 'The oldest road in a village or town is frequently called High Street, the place generally originating on the high road', D. J. Owen suggested (*op.cit.*). 'This, as we know is true of Belfast, its High Street having been the first street of any kind there.' If this is also true of Dublin, Irish practice has preferred in some instances Main Street (Clara, County Offaly, Dingle, County Kerry, *et al.*), echoing American rather than British nomenclature … and Dublin's High Street was indeed known as Main Street in the latter part of the Middle Ages. Significantly, High Streets (Portadown, Omagh) are more common in the Ulster towns, and the dichotomy assumed tragic significance at the time of the Omagh bombing of September 1998 when a warning phoned to Ulster Television spoke of a bomb near the Courthouse on Main Street. There is no Main Street in Omagh: the Courthouse stands on High Street.

As with placenames, so street names in the wider world reflect the presence of the Irish diaspora. Nor is this solely a phenomenon of anglophone territories: Paris has its Rue des Irlandais and Avenue Mac-Mahon, Madrid, Ceuta and Melilla their Calle **O'Donnell**, Havana its Calle **O'Reilly**, Santiago de Chile its Avenida General O'Higgins amongst the many towns and cities which commemorate the Irish who have done their respective adopted states some service. Of more recent reference is Bobby Sands Street in Tehran, Iran, named after the IRA hunger-striker (d.1981). As Patsy McGarry explained (*The Irish*

Times, 6 Jan. 2001), '… when people discover you are Irish, his is the name they respond to with "Sahid Bobby Sands" (the Martyr Bobby Sands) as he is known. There is no higher honour among Iranians.'

Irish street names, for obvious reasons, abound in the United States and throughout the former British empire, though in the latter case they have in many instances been replaced by native names: New Delhi's Connaught Circus, Hong Kong's Connaught Road Central are, however, examples of Irish names deriving from British titles rather than the original location itself. For equally obvious reasons probably the greatest concentration of Irish street names outside the country is to be found in London where, as Kevin O'Sullivan observed in *The Irish Times* (18 Jan. 2000), one of the oldest streets in the City area is Ireland Yard, where Shakespeare bought a house in 1612. The four provinces are all represented more than once, 'while Connaught (*sic*) comes out on top with four Avenues, a Drive, two Gardens, a House, a Lane, a Mews, a Place, no fewer than 15 Roads, a Square, a Street and a Way!' – a plethora which, once again, must be attributed to the eponymous Dukes rather than the western province *per se*.

Only eighteen counties, however, in O'Sullivan's estimation, are commemorated. On the other hand 'the London streets named after Irish towns are too numerous to list here, but the following is a small selection: two Carysfort Roads, Celbridge Mews, Doneraile Street, Dunleary Court, Granard Avenue and Road … Tarbert Road and Walk. Pride of place must go to Ranelagh …' – which, of course, was a London name before being translated to the Dublin suburb – latterly termed a 'village'. O'Sullivan lists a clutch of personal names 'of the Irish developers, local government councillors and their ilk' as well as those of the Irish more widely acknowledged – Goldsmith, Shaw, Orpen, Barnardo, Balfe, Stanford and Shackleton among them. It is not surprising that these latter all flourished in the era before independence, when they would have been regarded as British: it is unlikely that London streets of the future will carry the names of Joyce, Beckett, de Valera, Collins or Adams – and certainly not Bobby Sands.

If our domestic streetnaming, proceeding from mediaeval simplicity through colonial deference to entrepreneurial barbarity, has exhibited little in the way of innovative humour (with rare exceptions: see **Keasers Lane**), there is more evidence of native wit in the naming, or rather nicknaming, of monuments, statues and other street features. There is, or was, the **Black Man** in Belfast, for example, but Dublin has been in the forefront of irreverent nicknaming since Nelson on his Pillar was dubbed 'the onehandled adulterer'. However, innovative naming, as in the case of **The Meeting of the Waters**, **Tonehenge** or **The Tomb of the Unknown Gurrier**, has of late given way to a predictable and by now insipid formulation on the basis of two rhyming nouns: the **Floozie in the Jacuzzi**, the Tart with the Cart. The proposal to erect a **Monument of Light** on the site of Nelson Pillar provoked a spate of suggestions along these predictable lines for the nicknaming of what had already become known as The Spike: the Pin in the Bin, the Spire in the Mire (allusions to the pervasive litter); the Hypo from the Corpo; the Light in the Blight; the Jab in the Slab; the Lampstand in Clampland; the Stiletto in the Ghetto, A Stiffy by the Liffey, and very many others on descending levels of creative aptitude.

The onomastic ramifications of an urban feature as yet in embryo – the proposed ambitious Metro system – were the subject of speculation by Mary Kenny (*Irish Independent*, 19 Aug. 2000). 'What are they going to be called?' she wondered. 'I sincerely hope we are not about to adhere to the prosaic notion of calling each Dublin metro stop by its existing placename: Drimnagh, Kimmage, Harold's Cross, Ranelagh, Stillorgan, etc. This would show an appalling lack of imagination: it would also be missing a unique opportunity to underline Dublin's status as a major city of culture and history. Consider the wonderful names given to the Paris Metro ...'

Taking several leaves out of Gérard Roland's *Stations de Métro: Le Dictionnaire des 366 Stations* (1986) she discussed the Parisian practice in detail, concluding '... thus do all aspects of history and culture mingle together in the Parisian Metro station names. And this, I most strongly advise, should be the model for Dublin ... Clontarf, for example, could be called Clontarf-Brian Boru. Wicklow [Street] might be Wicklow-Parnell. Sandycove should obviously be James Joyce – does not **Ulysses** begin there? ... This might give character to neutralised, nowhere-land placenames like "Cherry Orchard" or "Quarryvale".'

Though some of her proposals – Islands of Saints and Scholars, Exiles of Erin, Constance Markiewicz – do not exactly come trippingly off the tongue and would surely invite irreverent demotic modification, it is to be hoped that, if ever the Metro is built as planned, the opportunity will not be forfeited for applying names which are not only imaginative, but imaginative in two languages. While new developments, as has been seen, are increasingly named in English only, public bilingualism in the matter of existing names is, it would appear, being steadily eroded. Ennis, County Clare is among the many locations to opt for street names in English only; and as a letter-writer to *The Irish Times,* Leen Vandommele (8 May 2000) expressed it: 'To my regret, I notice that with the introduction of new Bus Éireann buses in Galway City, all of the notices in the Irish language have disappeared ... Why don't the Irish flaunt their language, like the Basques and Catalans do?'

House and home

A modest flaunting in the matter of house-names is still observable, dating in many instances from the enthusiastic era of the Gaelic Revival. The practice of house naming goes back to ancient Babylon and was not unknown in early Ireland. 'Brian Borumha's palace of Kincora', wrote P.W. Joyce, 'was built on a hill in the present town of Killaloe, and it is repeatedly mentioned in the Annals, by the name of *Ceann-coradh* [Kincora], the head or hill of the weir ...' This adoption of a toponomic as a more personal identification was still evident nearly a millennium later in Taylor and Skinner's *Maps of the Roads of Ireland* (1778) in which the properties of the landed gentry exhibit names derived very largely from townlands, geographical features or the names of their proprietors (Cullinagh; Mount Callan; Fort Singleton, Mount Phillips).

With the ending of the Penal laws and the rise of a property-owning Catholic middle class, house names assumed a wider social significance. As Mary Gold put it (*The Times* (London), 22 July 2000): 'House names can speak volumes, which is why we all want one in the first place. It is one of those early claims to being a member of the middle class. There have even been complaints to newspapers, including this august organ, that people living in houses which only have numbers are less likely to have their letters published and are more likely to be convicted of crimes.' In the Irish context, Kevin Whelan observed: 'The newer social pretensions were symbolised by the assigning of a name to the farm, usually the townland one – like "Johnstown House" or "Ballymore House". Wealthy farmers were now sandwiched between a "mister" in front of the name and an "esq." at the back.' (Kevin Whelan, 'An Underground Gentry?' in J.S. Donnelly jr. & Kerby Miller, *Irish Popular Culture 1650-1850* [1999]).

The Gaelic Revival, as has been said, produced its crop of Irish-language names, many within a religious context: Árd Mhuire, Réalt na Mara, and a plethora of saints' names, a preference which, though less evident, still continues. Recently, estate agents were reporting, according to Mark Keenan (*Sunday Tribune*, 21 Nov. 1999), 'that modern Irish house names tend to fall into a handful of set categories. They are either inspired by old Irish history (Tara, **Tír na nÓg**), religion (Santa Maria, St Anthony, Shalom), trees (Oak Wood, the Grove) and homely hopes (Journey's End). There is also a very strong tendency among those born outside a city to use the names of their home townlands (Dromin, Shillelagh, Strangford). Period homes will often simply reflect their historic use: the Old Rectory, the Glebe House, the Mill House and the Cooperage; while Guest Houses will use their names to sell their virtues: Sea View, Hill View, Lake View.'

The commercial advantages, in the view of estate agent Margaret Short, quoted by Keenan, are not confined to guest houses: 'Certainly a relevant name can be a plus for non-estate type houses. It gives a home an identity of its own and of course, it must be said that there is an element of snobbery involved in having an address which stands apart from the rest. I would say that a relevant name, used in brochures and advertising, will certainly add more interest to a home and if this brings more viewers and better offers, then perhaps a name can effect value in an indirect way. ... A unique house which visibly stands apart from the rest deserves more than 6B Whatever Road. If we advise a name, we also advise clients to go for something relevant.'

While pleasure-boat owners frequently indulge in dismaying humour in the matter of names (*Idle Vice, Moonquake, Sea Shebeen, Sailors Not, Tassella* [?< *tasse eile,* another cup of tea]) house names still tend to be embalmed in exiguous inverted commas and to reflect an innate conservatism – or perhaps just a lack of imagination, conditioned by a shrewd awareness of commercial priorities. As Mary Gold advised: 'Do not be tempted to give your house a name that is too quirky; estate agents have discovered that names such as The Shambles or Spider's Cottage can actually deter buyers.' Though she quotes with approval 'Holy See View, the home of a priest in East London, and a houseboat on the Avon and Kennet Canal called Sir Osis of the River'. Seán Beecher, on the other hand (*The Story of Cork* [1971]), withholds his approval from those who 'conceive the most plebeian of anagrams: Larkit, Larry and Kitty; Chrisdoney, Christine and Donal, etc.' A romantic interlude, he suggests, 'may influence others and many the house has been called after the honeymoon haven of a couple. On occasions this may prove an embarrassment as was the case of the couple who, having spent their honeymoon in Spain, called their house Bordello ...'

3

All the Oes and the Mackes

'RÉFLÉCHISSEZ UN INSTANT', suggested Jean Bacon in his Preface to Pierre le Rouzic's *Un Prénom pour la Vie* (1978): 'Think for a moment. Of all the words which, during your whole life, will be uttered concerning you and which will be directed towards you as an appeal or request, a reproach or a challenge, a whisper or a caress, none will come more frequently to the lips than your surname.' Your name, he continues with a certain Gallic emphasis, 'is your identity, your registration; your first name is you in the intimacy of the family, in the warmth of comradeship, *dans les élans de l'amour.*'

Clan-names, deriving from illustrious ancestors, historical or mytho-historical, were in use in Ireland from a remote period – Uí Néill, des-cendants of Niall of the Nine Hostages; Eoghanacht from Eoghan Mór and Dál gCais from Cormac Cas – but, as Patrick Woulfe points out (*Sloinnte Gaedheal is Gall* [1923]), these 'were ordinarily used in the plural and as a common designation of the whole clan. For the individual the single name was the rule.' The patronymic, both in Ireland and in its wider European context, evolved from the necessity, in an increasingly corporate society, to distinguish between individuals in a manner other than the earlier practice of bestowing a nickname reflecting a personal characteristic. These names, orig-inally transparent in that they exhibited a clear signification or description, would rapidly lose such characteristics. Woulfe instances the case of the name Dubhghiolla, or 'black youth': 'As originally employed, it was without doubt

39

a nickname descriptive of the person on whom it was first imposed. But if Dubhghiolla lived long enough, there came a time when he was no longer a "black youth" but a grey-haired old man.' This progressive loss of transparency thus had the effect of transmuting the nickname into the hereditary patronymic, henceforward the property of the family rather than the individual.

Ireland, according to Edward MacLysaght, the authority on family nomenclature, was one of the earliest countries to evolve a system of hereditary surnames; though his predecessor, Patrick Woulfe, advances a stronger claim: 'It is a remarkable fact, though so far as I am aware hitherto unnoticed, that Ireland was the first country after the fall of the Western Empire to adopt hereditary surnames'. However, he dismisses the once commonly held view that the practice had been established by Brian Boirimhe/Boru in the eleventh century. This theory had also been accepted by the English poet, landlord and intermittent Hibernophobe Edmund Spenser, who, in his *View of the Present State of Ireland*, written in the 1590s, urged the extinction of the by then well-established clan names: 'I also wishe, all the Oes and the mackes which the heads of the septs have taken to their names to be utterly forbidden and extinguished, for that same being an old manner (as some sayth) first made by O'brien for the strengtheninge of the Irishe, the abrogating thereof will as much enfeeble them.' No stronger tribute, albeit grudging, could be paid to the potency of the patronymic.

Woulfe suggests that fixed patronymics antedated Brian Boroimhe, instancing Ó Cléirigh as in use from the mid-ninth century. In due course the practice became general of prefixing 'Mac' to the father's first name or 'O' to that of a grandfather or earlier ancestor, this method of surname-creation being subsequently broadened to include the similar prefixing of a descriptive word or nickname. This development sometimes resulted in the dropping of the 'Mac' or 'O', as in the case of Caomhánach (Kavanagh), the name having been adopted, MacLysaght suggests, from its first bearer having been fostered by a successor of St Caomhán. Once established, the sources and methodology of our nomenclature, what Medbh Ruane (*The Irish Times*, 2 Aug. 1999) described as 'the awful straitjacket of having such a homogenous ancestry' remained essentially unaltered and unchallenged until the arrival of the Anglo-Normans.

These twelfth-century adventurers brought with them, together with a formidable array of other invasive attributes, a new concept of personal nomenclature. Most obviously, of course, this was couched in a new language, establishing that bilingualism which has been both the curse and the blessing of the country ever since. The Anglo-Norman system, of relatively recent establishment compared with that of the Gaelic, employed the prefix 'fitz' [<OFr. *filzs,* son] as the equivalent of 'Mac'; 'de' to denote locality, as in Hugh de Lacy – many of the invaders having arrived with only single names – and 'le', descriptive of trade or occupation, as in Thomas le Clerc. As their influence and control extended over the subsequent centuries it became a cornerstone of administrative policy to induce, by persuasion or otherwise, conformity with both their language and their system of nomenclature; thus in 1465 it was enacted by the Statute of 5 Edward IV that every Irishman resident within the **Pale,** which then comprised the counties of Dublin, Meath, Louth and Kildare, should 'take to him an English surname of one towne, as Sutton, Chester, Trim, Skryne, Corke, Kinsale'; or colour, as white, blacke, browne; or art of science, as smith or carpenter; or office, as cooke, butler; and that he and his issue shall use this name under payne of forfeyting of his goods yearely till the premises be done ...' That this ordnance was more honoured in the breach was evidenced by Spenser's outburst against the 'Oes and the mackes' a little over a century later.

As the Normans became, in the familiar phrase, 'more Irish than the Irish' their patronymics accordingly assumed, in some instances but by no means all, vernacular forms involving the substitution of 'mac' for 'fitz' and prefixing it to an Irish version of an ancestral first name: Woulfe cites the Birmingham family which assumed the name Mac Fheórais after an antecendent Piers or Peter. For the native Irish the pressure remained to conform to the English practice, but this did not really make a serious impression until the old Gaelic order was destroyed at the battle of Kinsale (1601). Thereafter the socio-political inducement to adopt an English name or at the least to abjure the 'O' or 'Mac' prefix became acute and was to remain so with the defeats of 1690 and the coming of the Penal Laws.

In spite of this tendency it was still possible, well into the eighteenth century, to identify an individual's religion and politics from the name he or she bore. As the anonymous *Dialogue between a Protestant and a Papist* (1752) expressed it: 'the acts relating to purchases made or leases taken by papists are so eluded by perjuries, trusts in Protestant names, and other contrivances that they are of little significance.' The evidence was not, however, conclusive, many of those bearers of English names who had arrived with Cromwell in particular marrying into Irish communities and adopting the majority religion. In addition there were accretions of other nationalities – especially the Dutch with the Williamite forces – who left a legacy, notable amongst whom was the Van Homrigh family of Swiftian association.

The Gaelic homogeneity was further diluted by the arrival, in 1709, of a large body of refugee families from the Palatinate country of the Rhine. These were themselves of mixed ethnic origin, as Patrick J. O'Connor, in *People Make Places* (1989) explains: 'Judging from the spread of Irish Palatine names alone, it is apparent that the Rhine country acted as a gathering ground for people of diverse origins. … The range is well illustrated, for example, by Jacob Teske's (Teskey) family which ultimately betrays a Slavic origin, Philippus Hofman's which reaches back to old Danish origins, Johan Dolmetsch's (Dolmege, Delmege) which descends from Tolmacz, an old Hungarian name, Hans Martin Müller's (Miller) which derives from Holland, and that of the brothers Michael and Christopher Schweitzer (Switzer) which in its anglicised form remains true to its Swiss origins. To these may be added a significant sprinkle of the bearers of Huguenot names who had fled France following the Revocation of the Edict of Nantes in 1695 … Such families included those headed by Johan David Geyer (Guier), Hans Jurg Glaser (Glazier), Adam Fisel (Fitzelle), Johan Adam Lieger (Legear) and Adam Cornelius (Corneille) … All these names mingled easily with those of German origin which constituted the great majority.'

These and more recent immigrations have nevertheless done little to alter the position as stated by MacLysaght in the sixth edition (1985) of *The Surnames of Ireland* that 'The majority of the surnames borne by Irish people of today are of Irish origin even in Ulster …' The team roll-call for the 2000 GAA Football Final between Kerry and Galway served to support this assertion. As far as Kerry were concerned, the only name (not including substitutes) which would appear to be of non-Gaelic origin were Russell [<OFr. *rossel*, a red-haired person] which, according to MacLysaght, is on record in Ireland since the Norman invasion. Hassett, according to the same authority, is Ó hAiseadha, a sept of Thomond, and the rest – O'Keeffe, Moynihan, McCarthy, Ó Sé, O'Sullivan, Daly, MacGearailt, Kennelly, Ó Cinnéide, Crowley, are unambiguous in their origin. The Galway team – McNamara, Meehan, Fahy, Divilly, de Paor, Walsh, Ó Domhnaill, Joyce, Donnellan, Savage, Clancy and Finnegan – exhibited a similar consistency, only Savage (planted in the Ards peninsula, County Down in 1177), de Paor and MacGearailt suggesting a Norman origin, however remote.

It might be asserted that the GAA is a special case, in the same way that, particularly in the nineteenth century, family names became associated with specific trades or professions. In her contribution, 'Economic and Social Structures of Cork', in David Harkness and Mary O'Dowd (eds): *The Town in Ireland* (1981), Maura Murphy states that 'Much of the city's coachmaking business was in the hands of the Busbys, Eddens, Johnsons, Julians and Williams; the coopering trade displayed such names as Codys, Cronins, Deyos, Drinans, Hickeys and Hollands; cabinetmaking was linked with the Coxs, Dees, Lesters and Notts; and so on … as early as the 1830s the problem of "illegal apprentices" was a major worry to all the city's trade societies. Perhaps this incursion of trades by those not traditionally connected with them accounts in part for the great variety of surnames appearing in the ranks of masters and employers from the 1840s onwards. In the ranks of the coopers, for instance, the old traditional and largely Protestant names – Bath, Burgess, Cottrell, Fair, Paine – were disappearing, to be replaced by others, obviously Catholic.' The same was evident in other trades embodying a strong hereditary principle – effectively a 'closed shop' – such as printing.

The homogeneity represented by the GAA football teams is currently in the process of modification – there is the evidence not only of the telephone directories but of the country's recent transformation into a net importer rather than exporter of its population and a haven, however unwelcoming, for a diversity of refugees. The effect on the national nomenclature will, however, only gradually become significant, taking its place beside that other relatively minimal adjustment represented by the increasing number of women retaining their maiden names after marriage, if only for professional or career purposes. The smaller number who use both their own and their partner's surnames reflects the Spanish practice under which the revolutionary Che Guevara was properly known as Guevara y Lynch – the latter, his mother's name, signifying an Irish connection. These aberrations aside, the fundamentals of Irish patronymics have effectively remained unvaried since the coming of the Os and the Macs.

But Ó or O'? Mac, Mc or M'? The divergences in the orthography of prefixes remained through the period of their widespread annulment to their partial restoration under the influence of the late nineteenth century Gaelic Revival, the guiding principle of which, in the words of D.P. Moran, was that 'The Gael must be the element that absorbs'. As MacLysaght pointed out, however, the recovery of the traditional prefix was often based upon a shaky foundation: 'Chevalier O'Gorman, who should have known better, "resumed" the O, whereas his family was formerly MacGorman. The former Premier of Ireland, John Costelloe [*sic*], was officially described in documents in the Irish language as *Ó Coisdealbha* with the prefix O, instead of the correct Mac.' Equally hit-and-miss was the process of re-Gaelicisation, or Gaelisation pure and simple, of the entire patronymic.

The long process of anglicisation of surnames over the centuries was in no way systematic. Simple attempts to produce a phonetic equivalent, as in Brannagh [<Breathnach] existed side by side with a translated version [Walsh, i.e. Welsh]; while such transparent translations such as Rabbit – later gentrified as Rabbitt or Rabitte – of Ó Conaonaigh, Ó Cuinnín, Ó Cuinneáin, etc., all <*coinín*, rabbit, were counterbalanced by pseudo-translations, as in the case of Duane, anglicised as Kidney [Ir. *duán*]. By the time that interest in the restoration of Gaelic forms was developing, many derivations had become either opaque or anomalous, as, for example in the case of Green, an English surname in Ireland of its own right but which had also come to stand as the anglicised form of names such as Ó hUaithnín, Uaithne [<Ir. *uaine*, vivid green], Mac Glaisin [<Ir. *glas*, grey-green] and several others. Thus the individual anxious to assume or re-assume a Gaelic identity was frequently on uncertain ground. The scabrous jest concerning one James Handcock who emerged from the process as Manus Ó Tuthail is mirrored in real life by the instance of the **Fianna Fáil** minister, P.J. Little, bearer of an unequivocally English name, who emerged as Pádraig Mac Caoilte [?<Ir *caoile,* narrowness, slenderness, sparseness, narrowness of mind … (Dinneen)]. And Fianna Fáil, it would seem, have remained victims of such linguistic vagaries, if contrarywise. According to the *Sunday Business Post* (2 Jul. 2000) a document submitted to the Moriarty Tribunal bore three signatures in Irish: Cathal Ó hEochaidh [Charles Haughey], Eoghan Mac Gearailt and Padraig Ó Floinn [Padraig Flynn, see **Pee**]. 'For those with short memories', the paper commented, 'Eoghan Mac Gearailt is the FF Renaissance Man of the early 1980s, former finance minister Gene Fitzgerald. The official record of the tribunal bizarrely gives the Irish (*sic*) version of his name as "Owen McGarrity". Jesus wept.'

'Once perceived as the tongue of the poor and uneducated', wrote Dan Barry in the *New York Times* (25 Jul. 2000), '… Gaelic is coming to represent the self-confidence born of recent economic and cultural success. … Pubs and shops are rechristening themselves with Irish names. Men once known as Patrick now call themselves Padraig (pronounced POH-rig). …' Possibly [and see chapter 4], but it is not so very long since those assuming Gaelicised names were viewed with more than a degree of cynicism and hilarity by the anglophone populace, amounting to suspicion and mistrust in the case of those who were perceived to be anxious to acquire a Gaelic name as a political or cultural disguise, as in the case of John Stephenson, an Englishman who assumed command of the IRA under the name Seán Mac Stiofáin, or Alfred Willmore, who transmuted himself into the theatrical impresario Micheál MacLiammóir. Retranslation, or reducing a Gaelic pretender to the anglophone ranks, was not uncommon, if at times confusing; as in the case of the broadcaster Liam Ó Murchú who was scarcely recognisable when reinvented by his occasional detractors as Bill Murphy. On the other hand his Cork colleague, advised for professional purposes to assume a Gaelicised identity, remained unassailably Donnacha Ó Dúlaing.

In the political sphere the somewhat bizarre practice of binominalism has been institutionalised since the foundation of the State, the (often fanciful) Gaelic equivalent being paraded along with the obligatory *cúpla focal* on official and semi-official occasions. Such linguistic bilocation is extended, at appropriate times, to commercial enterprises: a poster commemorating the first Dáil (1919) and published in the same year bore the printer's imprint of MacLiam Eartnaill, almost disguising the mildly Ascendancy firm of Wilson Hartnell. It became the practice of the Abbey Theatre under the directorship of Earnán de Blaghd (whose name appeared nevertheless in English only on the programmes as Ernest Blythe), to insist on the actors and actresses performing under the Gaelic form of their names, exceptions being made in the case of those with an international reputation such as Harry Brogan or Eileen Crowe. By the 1960s, however, this perverse requirement had been abandoned.

An echo of the archetypical railway crossing-keeper with one gate open, half-expecting a train, this frequently inconsistent manifestation of bi-lingualism represented a nod in the direction of the Revival while keeping one foot firmly in Anglo-Ireland. It predictably failed to impress the lately-departed colonisers, who not infrequently continued to refuse to recognise the Gaelic version of a name on travel and other documents, in court proceedings involving the Irish in Britain, or, in the same vein, to process mail passing through that country bearing an Irish-language address. Irish patronymics, whether in the original or anglicised, had in any case had a long history of providing a source of amusement in the neighbouring island, most markedly in the popular drama of the seventeenth to nineteenth centuries which, in creating the stage-Irishman [see panel], endowed him not only with the perceived comic characteristics of the race, but with a name to match. And it should be noted, *en passant*, that a sizeable number of the creators of such stereotypes were themselves of the nation they were satirising. This onomastic facetiousness did not entirely disappear with the somewhat grudging abandonment of the stage-Irishman, who survived, albeit under less exotic appellations, at least until the drama of Shaw ('Tim Haffigan, Sir, at your service. The top of the mornin' to you, Misther Broadbent').

English amusement when confronted with Irish surnames was rooted in an inability to pronounce them correctly, as documented in Isaac Jackman's eighteenth century play *The **Milesian***, where a character observes of Captain Corneilus O'Gollagher, 'we must all take care to pronounce his name properly; I never saw him out of humour but once, and that was when a gentleman call'd him Gallager; you must endeavour to pronounce it as they do in Ireland – Gallagher.' With the widening of the Irish diaspora such 'mispronunciations' are now common, if not always phonetically unacceptable: 'It used to grate on my ears to hear the good old Clare name O'Dea pronounced as O'Dee', wrote Edward MacLysaght [in Sharon Gmelch, *Irish Life and Traditions* (1986)], 'and, to go further afield, the two syllables of Maher reduced to Mar, almost Mah. When an American calls Minogue Minnogew, we laugh at him. But the laugh is against ourselves when we fault his MahOney for that is much nearer to the original Irish *Mathúna* than the "correct" way we pronounce it now with stress on the first syllable and the second almost muted.' Flann Ó Riain (*The Irish Times*, 21 Aug. 2000) made the same point: 'The accuracy of the sound representation of Irish place-names in their anglicised forms varies. In the case of a surname, this is frequently further distorted when the bearer emigrates. Surprising then when one finds that the "emigrated" name is closer to the original Irish than the variety of forms found at home' – and he cites the case of an Australian called Creenaun, a form closer to the original Ó Crionán than the anglicisation Crennan.

Stage Oirish

Barney O'Liffy – *Thomas Hurlstone, 'Just in Time.'* Callaghan O'Brallaghan (Sir) – *Charles Macklin, 'Love à la Mode.'* Cornelius O'Gollagher (Capt.) – *Isaac Jackman, 'The Milesian.'* Dennis, Donnell, Dermock and Patrick – *Ben Jonson, 'Irish Masque at Court'.* Dermot O'Leinster – *William O'Brien, 'The Duel.'* Feezil Macafarty (Sir) – *George Powell, 'A Very Good Wife.'* Larry O'Hoolagan – *T. G. Rodwell, 'More Blunders than One.'* Lucius O'Trigger – *R.B. Sheridan, 'The Rivals.'* Mac Tawdry – *John Mottley, 'The Craftsman.'* Mack Shane –

Anon. 'Sir John Oldcastle.' Macmorris (Capt.) – *Shakespeare, 'Henry V.'* Maghloghan Moor – *John Breval, 'The Play is the Plot.'* O'Blunder – *Moses Mandez, 'The Double Disappointment'/Thomas Sheridan, 'The Honest Irishman.'* O'Dogherty/Diggerty – *Charles Macklin, 'The True-Born Irishman.'* Oclabber (Lieut.) [<Ir. *clábar*, mud] – *Tobias Smollett, 'The Reprisal.'* Teg. *Robert Howard – 'The Committee.'* Tegue O'Divelly – *Robert Shadwell, 'The Lancashire Witches'/'The Amorous Bigotte.'* Thady MacBrogue – *John O'Keefe, 'The She-Gallant.'* Thady O'Blarney – *W. C. Oulton, 'Botheration.'* Torlough Rauwer Macahone – *George Farquhar, 'The Stage Coach.'* Wild Murtogh – *John Buckstone, 'The Green Bushes.'*

A handful of epoynms – Lynch, Boycott, Murphy – have entered the language as verbs or common nouns while some foreign names have been facetiously 'Irishised': World War II, for example, saw the transmogrifaction of the Russian general Timoshenko into Tim O'Shenko. The 'O' prefix in particular offers the opportunity for such logomachy, as **Myles na gCopaleen**'s character 'Silent O'Moyle', engendered by the Thomas Moore poem.

The faces and the names

If the study of surnames is generally subject to normal scholarly rigour, that of personal appellations is marked by the incidence of theory and speculation ranging from the plausible to the patently eccentric. There would appear to be a common agreement, however, that forenames and their bestowal should be the matter of serious evaluation. Is it not absurd to leave the choice of a name to chance when, as Jean Bacon (*op.cit.*) put it, 'one considers the lengthy research and expensive market studies necessary to produce a brand name to launch a new product? *Le destin d'un enfant aurait-il moins de valeur que la réussite d'une lessive?*'

The belief that the choice of a personal name can influence a child's future, for better or worse, is not a new phenomenon, though it has become widely popularised in recent times. 'Names themselves, and the giving of them', wrote Donnacha Ó Corráin and Fidelma Maguire in *Gaelic Personal Names* (1981) 'if we may judge from early literature and folk-tradition alike, have always been a matter of lively interest both to their bearers and to those who gave them.' Medb Ruane (*The Irish Times*, 2 Aug.1999) codifies the contemporary approach: 'Names predict lifestyles. They're a noose around your neck or a magic-carpet ride to Hollywood stardom or the presidency.

Names are brands that carry you … through a multitude of virtual and actual futures. Names are history and poetry and accent and allegiances rolled into one.'

They are also, in popular belief, becoming ineradicably 'part of what you are'. 'Every Liam I know is a Liam and every Joe I know is a Joe', wrote Paddy Murray (*Sunday Tribune,* 18 July 1999) 'It's an extraordinary thing, but the Liams look like Liams and the Joes look like Joes. I don't know a single Liam who looks like a Peregrine or a single Peregrine who looks like a Joe. You see, I believe that perhaps the most important, most formative moment in a person's life is the moment they are given a name. While there are obvious exceptions to the rule, it has to be said that, in the main, people look and behave like the names they are given. They end up in jobs that suit their names. … Names have shaped history. I sometimes think the Second World War could have been averted if only Hitler's parents had called him Trevor … I am convinced our history would have been a lot different if Pádraig Pearse's mother had christened him Alistair. And Éamonn de Valera would not have had any impact on this country if his father had stuck with family tradition and called him Pedro.'

An increasing level of academic research into personal names would seem to provide some validation of this belief in a symbiosis between name and vocation. James Bruning, a psychologist at Ohio University has, according to the *New Scientist* (London) (24 June 2000), 'dedicated 20 years to the study of first names. His work suggests that when people seek employment, the name really can determine the job.' The research as quoted, which involved matching 'masculine' and 'feminine' names (of both sexes) with 'the probability of success of applicants seeking work in such supposedly masculine fields as computer programming or construction work, or supposedly feminine jobs such as hairstylist or day-care worker' is not, however, on the face of it particularly convincing – no more than that conducted by another US Department of Psychology (at the University of California in San Diego) which, as reported by Raj Persaud in *The Independent on Sunday* (London) (13 Feb. 2000) 'reveals that what your initials spell significantly affects longevity. Dr Nicholas Christenfeld and colleagues used computers to examine almost four million death certificates from between 1969 and 1995, and found that men with initials which spelled negative words (e.g. DIE or PIG) died an average of almost three years earlier than those whose initials spelled neutral words, or nothing in particular. Conversely, men with positive initials (e.g. ACE or VIP) live for almost four and a half years longer.'

Slightly less threatening, perhaps, is the common use of initials as a replacement for a full name (see **Tay Pay**). Thomas F. O'Higgins (*A Double Life* [1996]) records, for example, that 'Timothy Daniel Sullivan was better known as T.D. Sullivan. It was common practice among the Sullivans and their marriage relations, the Healys, and indeed many of their colleagues in public life, to refer to one another by the initials of their Christian names … T.D. was for many years a member of parliament, as was his brother A.M. …' A single initial can also come to stand for a full name (see **Pee**) (though in this case it takes on virtually the character of a nickname) or be appended to a first name, as in the instance of the politician Michael D. (Higgins).

Whether or not current academic investigations, as exemplified above, may be said to constitute the lunatic fringe of nominative determinism, the fact remains that there is an abiding popular belief in the role of the personal name as a significant influence on the life of its bearer, and that the choice of name should not therefore be a matter of random selection. The extremes of this belief are represented by Pierre le Rouzic's theory (*op. cit.*) that if, 'between two or three in the afternoon' a pregnant woman 'listens' to her unborn child and quietly pronounces the intended name of the child a 'resonance' will inform her as to whether or not the choice is right. From this, taking 79 key names to each of which some 5,000 others are associated, he constructs a methodology of naming based on this resonance and on a complex associative structure involving zodiacal correspondences and much more besides. While many will not be prepared to follow le Ruzic all the way through this attributative labyrinth, some will nevertheless continue to believe that the bestowal of the 'wrong' personal name can materially injure an offspring's prospects. Or, as Murray put it, 'You are unlikely to get a Paddy Murray governing the Falklands. You will certainly never see a Liam there. Diarmuids are out. Séamusses need not apply.'

This, albeit humorous, suggestion that Irish names remain unacceptable in the British colonial context reflects their widespread abandonment in the eighteenth and nineteenth centuries as a consequence of the eclipse of the Irish language and the subsequent political and social pressures to conform to the English norm. With the Celtic Revival the indigenous names began once more to acquire a wider currency, if only among the more nationally-minded. With the achievement of 26-county independence the popularity of Gaelic names continued to gain ground, though those that are in general use today represent only a tiny fraction of the twelve thousand represented in the early literature. Thousands of these, according to Ó Corráin and Maguire (*op.cit.*), fell out of fashion at a very early period, the range being further narrowed in the late Middle Ages with English becoming the dominant vernacular. Though some of these early personal names were less than attractive, according to Flann Ó Riain (*The Irish Times*, 27 Mar. 2000) 'by and large they were complimentary. Whereas on the one hand we had *Banbhán*, "a piglet, a sucking-pig" and *Cinnéide* (Kennedy), "ugly-headed, rough-headed", on the other there was *Caomhnait*, "beautiful girl", *Caoinleán*, "beautiful shape", *Caointiarn*, "gentle lady".'

The Revival, however, tended to favour those names which were either already accessible through the re-telling of Gaelic literature, such as Diarmuid, Gráinne, Aoife, or those with popular religious associations. If such devotional names had for long been a distinctive feature of name choice, in the first half of the twentieth century, according to Ita Eames (*The Irish Times*, 28 Dec. 1999), 'Irish parents … chose many new and often colourful religious names for their children. For boys, Damien, Camillus and Eustatius were added to already established saints' names like Alphonsus, Aloysius and Ambrose. For girls, the canonisation in the 1920s of Joan of Arc, Thérèse of Lisieux and Bernadette of Lourdes ensured a marked increase in the use of their names. While Goretti, Majella and Cabrini (surnames of saints) were later additions, Gemma and Jacinta were probably among the most popular religious names in the 1940s and 1950s.' After the canonisation of Blessed Gemma Galgani in 1940, according to Mary Kenny (*Irish Independent*, 24 June 2000), 'there was a great fashion for Gemmas. Bernadette was made a saint in 1933 and for two or three generations we had lots of Bernies. There was much devotion, in Ireland, to Blessed Martin de Porres, a black South American … and many little boys were thus called Martin.'

One devotional name, however, proliferated across social and religious boundaries. 'I was very glad to see – in a survey of popular names', confessed Mary Kenny, 'that the name Mary has dropped to an all-time low. Mary is now well to the bottom of the most frequently-chosen 40 names given to baby girls all over Europe … I mean no disrespect when I say that I have intensely disliked being called Mary from the word go. It never suited me – Marys should be good girls, not wild little minxes – and from early childhood I considered it incredibly unimaginative of my parents to name me such … But all they could think of when I came along was boring old Mary, the name shared by half the women in the country at the time.' Devotion to Mary, wrote Ita Eames, 'ensured that names associated with her life and attributes enjoyed a steady popularity, e.g. Carmel from her title of Our Lady of Mount Carmel, Dolores as Mother of Sorrows and Loretta from the Italian town of

Loreto which lays claim to the house of the Holy Family. There was, too, the custom of giving the name of Mary to boys as second or third names, a practice which seems to have been discontinued by the 1970s, as was, for the most part, the use of devotional names generally.'

Somewhat surprisingly, the practice of naming boys after the pre-eminent saint, Patrick, proves to be of relatively recent origin. According to Woulfe (*op.cit.*) until the Anglo-Norman invasion the personal names in use in Ireland were almost exclusively Celtic. 'The Irish had been very slow in adopting either Scriptural names or the Latin and Greek names of saints. The few Norse names that had come in as a result of the invasions of the Northmen scarcely affected the Celtic character of our nomenclature. The nomenclature of the Anglo-Normans, on the other hand, was partly Teutonic, partly Scriptural and saintly ... Of names common to the Irish and Anglo-Normans, there were none. To take a name that afterwards found favour with both peoples, we had no Patricks except among the Norsemen in the cities. So that at the period of invasion and for several centuries after, a man's name was an absolute guide to his nationality. Every Donald, every Dermott, was an Irishman, every Robert, every William, a Norman or Englishman.'

If the incidence of indigenous names continued to increase, on the other hand, according to Ita Eames, 'the top names chosen for middle-class Irish children in the first half of the century reflected a community holding to the old values and traditions and resisting any great change. For girls, Mary was by far the most popular name in the period, and with Elizabeth, Margaret and Anne, it dominated the list into the 1950s.' Eames' research was based, it should be noted, solely on names as recorded in *The Irish Times*, reflecting the preferences of what was then still a largely Protestant readership. Excluding the North, where the religio-political divide continues to manifest itself in the choice of personal names (Willie John versus Gerard or Martin) such a distinction is now barely apparent; and even in Ulster it is no longer axiomatic that every Dermot is a Catholic and ever Robert a Protestant. 'Once', as Medb Ruane [*op.cit.*] put it, 'there were Catholic names and Protestant names; Deirdre versus Daphne, so to speak, and you could tell more in five minutes from a person's name than from almost anything else about them.' It would be difficult, nowadays, to diagnose such sectarian differences in the choice of Chloe, Darren, Jason, Megan or Dylan.

As with so many other aspects of present-day living, name-choice has undergone, and continues to undergo, a cultural shift. Chloe, Medb Ruane suggested, 'is now the new Bridget. Just as Marian dated the birth year of babies from in or around 1951 (the Marian Year), and as John Paul dates a generation born after the Pope's visit – which tells us something about how Irish people celebrated it – Chloe will forever condemn its bearer to a certain time and place when Ireland dropped both fada and umlaut to instead embrace a home counties ethos where all "nice" girls sound like they come from Surrey. …'

Chloe, indeed, appeared at number one in the list of the most popular girls' names in 1998 compiled by the Central Statistics Office – the first time that such an analysis was undertaken. Of the top ten boys' names, Conor and Seán were followed by the non-indigenous Jack, James, Adam, Aaron, Dylan, David, Michael and Daniel, though the survey noted regional variations, Seán heading the list in Dublin and the West. Of the girls' names, Chloe was followed by Ciara, Sarah, Aoife, Emma, Niamh, Rachel, Megan, Rebecca and Lauren, with Ciara proving more popular in the midlands. The following year Chloe and Conor both retained their first position. In 2000 Chloe and Conor gave way to Aoife and Jack. Professor John Brewer, of the School of Sociology and Social Policy at Queen's University, Belfast, commenting on the 1998 census, suggested that 'In Ireland the names fit with what we know about Irish society – the growing secularisation, growing urbanisation and increased confidence in identity … Because people have more confidence in their ethnic identity, there is not the same need to express it in an Irish name.'

His opinion was challenged by Terry Moylan, writing to *The Irish Times* (10 Aug. 1999): 'It seems to be more likely that Irish people are rushing to abandon their ethnic identity and accepting as a replacement whatever the Anglo–American entertainment industry serves up to them. Rupert Murdoch will turn out to have had more impact on the Irish identity than Davis, Hyde and Pearse.' Ita Eames' analysis based on the 1901 Census and subsequent *Irish Times* birth announcements would suggest, however, that the use of Gaelic names showed a steady increase through the twentieth century. Kathleen, Eileen, Bridget, Nora and Patrick, most common at the beginning of the 1900s, were followed by Patricia, **Sheila**, Eithne, Deirdre, Maeve, Desmond, Brendan, Kevin, Brian and Dermot. By mid-century popular names also included Liam, Seán, Barry, Geraldine, Fionnuala, Sinéad and Catriona, to be followed post-1950s by names such as Aisling, Aoife, Ciara, Orla, Niamh, Conor, Liam, Eoghan, Oisín and Rory. The latter, the more common anglicisation of the Gaelic Ruaridhe/Ruairí, indicated a practice that has produced the visually unlovely Ashling, Neev and other equally awkward phoneticisations. By the end of the century, nevertheless, some 180 Irish names in all forms were in common use, a significant increase from the 27 recorded in 1901.

Whatever about the domestic popularity of traditional names they would seem to constitute a significant invisible export. While their incidence could be predicted in anglophone territories with ethnic Irish populations their popularity has been by no means confined to these areas. Among Pierre le Rouzic's 1200 *prénoms satellites* are listed Brendan, Brigitte, Cathel, Cathleen, Fiacre, Finnian, Fursy, Gael, Gaelig, Gall, Gavin, Kavan, Kévin, Kiéran, Kilian, Kiliane, Killian and Killien ... some, it must be admitted, without honour in their own country.

More generally, the choice of a personal name could be said to have acquired increased importance with the contemporary practice of employing it without benefit of patronymic in all but the most formal of social contexts. It must now, for better or worse, express all its bearer's individuality – a condition likely to ensure an increasing diversity. As Mary Kenny expressed it: 'Little girls today who are given such names as Page, Scarlett, Tara and Sorrel will at least find that when their name is called out by a friend in O'Connell Street forty women do not turn their heads simultaneously.'

One field in which, rather remarkably, the personal name has not supplanted the surname is that of sport. For some reason sportsmen are almost invariably referred to, both in the media and amongst themselves, by the patronymic plus endearment suffix – usually *-ie, -o'* or *-er*. While British practice favours the first two of this trio, no doubt on account of a general inability or unwillingness to pronounce a final *r* (and compare the Aust. Bazza <Barry; Shazza <Sharon), the *-er* suffix is common in Ireland, both in the sporting context and more widely (see **Croker**, for example) where it assumes the condition of a nickname. On the subject of the Republic's soccer team Tom Humphries wrote (*The Irish Times,* 27 Mar. 1995) 'Is it any wonder that the old game is in the mire this season when the most imaginative nickname attaches to Jack Charlton. Big Jack they call him. Phew ... What's more he's lucky. The trend suggested that he might have ended up being called Jacksey or Charltony. The Irish squad ... have failed to provide any example for those toiling away in the lower leagues. Quinny? Aldo? Cas? Keaney? Babbsey? No lads. No. No. No.'

'Rugby', Humphries continues, 'hasn't contributed much to the field and contents itself by applying the soccer method of adding an "r", a "y" or an "o" to the end of a name. Doyler, Wardy, Springer and Quinner.' However, the GAA, in his opinion, 'has catered for most tastes in the matter of nicknames.

53

Aeroplane O'Shea, Bomber Liston and Sparrow O'Loughlin all seem to reflect a preoccupation with airborne flight … There have been other notables though. Snitchy Ferguson, Buster Leaney, Tiger Lynne, Spoofer McNicholl. The current undisputed champion is Bingo O'Driscoll of Annascaul. Persistent enquiries have failed to provide any clues as to the origins of that one.'

'We are a great people for nicknames', alleged an anonymous writer in *The Irish Times* (15 Nov. 1929), 'seeming to prefer the soubriquet above the Christian name. In country parts it is often necessary to give these additional styles in order to distinguish men of the same Christian and family name. I know of a spot where there reside a Sean Maggie Pat, a Sean Maggie Mick, and a Sean Maggie Rhu. This necessity for discriminating is not always the excuse for a nickname, and other varieties are more piquant. In many districts the parish priest's housekeeper will be Mary the Priest. I know a "Katty the man", so called because she favours men's boots and a caubeen …' The Irish experience was paralleled in Wales where, according to Christie Davies, Professor of Sociology at Reading University (quoted in *Verbatim* [Chicago], Spring 1995) 'It was not unknown for a single community, for instance, to have 10 men called David Jones, largely as a result of the limited choice of surnames, Jones, Williams and Evans, coupled with a passion for biblical Christian names, David, John and Thomas. As a result of this need to distinguish, some very humorous names developed. There was one man who had only two front teeth in the middle and was known as Dai Central Eating …' Evans expressed concern over the breakup of such rural communities and the consequent 'demise of nicknames which were once in widespread use and which many regard as a unique art form'.

From their origins and function as identifiers, nicknames have become in many cases totally opaque in passing from one generation to another, their origins either unknown or forgotten. Even in the present-day context they may usurp the given name almost to the point of complete exclusion. 'There are some people with whom I went to school', wrote Tom Humphries, 'whose real names I have never known. They passed through the clamorous classrooms of our youth answering to nicknames and nothing else.' Conversely, he added, 'There are other characters whose real names are known to me, but in adulthood I cannot bring myself to utter them. I have an old school friend who has left his class nickname behind and successfully rebuilt his life calling himself Tony. To me … he will always be Tiddler.'

Character study

The method, or lack of method, by which writers name their fictional characters is too broad in its scope for full consideration here, involving as it does complex patterns of psychology, strategy and cunning. Why, for instance, did W.B. Yeats, in his early novel *The Speckled Bird*, rename Olive Henderson as Margaret Henderson during the course of the writing? In the same work the naming of the character Maclaglan for the real-life MacGregor Mathers is simple enough, but by what process did the living and breathing Olivia Shakespear take on the onomastic disguise of Harriet St George?

Asking questions like these is frequently as futile as endeavouring to answer them, but there can be more than a passing interest in, for example, the fictional identities that authors bestow upon themselves in the common pursuit of autobiographical fiction. Bernard Shaw appeared as plain Robert Smyth in his novel *Immaturity* (note the syllabic correspondence); Laurence Sterne masqueraded as Yorick, seeing himself, no doubt, as a fellow of infinite jest; Francis Stuart appeared as Amos and Louis in his postwar novels *The Chariot* and *The Flowering Cross*, while Joyce's assumption of the persona of Stephen Dedalus constituted a great deal more than a random choice.

Joyce, of course, paid as much attention to onomastics as to every other branch of learning that was grist to his mill. What was to become the central character of **Ulysses** began life as Alfred H. Hunter, as Richard Ellman (*James Joyce* [revised ed., 1982]) explains: 'Several Dubliners helped Joyce to complete his hero. The first was the man named Hunter ... but in making **Bloom** an advertisement canvasser Joyce had someone else in mind. This man is first mentioned in the story "Grace" under the name of C.P. M'Coy, and is identified there as having been a clerk in the Midland Railway, a canvasser of advertisements for *The Irish Times*. ... These facts all point to M'Coy's actual prototype, Charles Chance ... Chance fitted the description of Bloom, and that Joyce intended to combine him with Hunter is suggested by the juxtaposition of "Charley Chance" with "Mr Hunker" in *Finnegans Wake*.'

The complexity of Joyce's naming of his protagonist did not, clearly, end there. Ellman continues: '"Leopold Bloom" was named with due deliberation. Leopold was the first name of Signorina Popper's father in Trieste. Bloom was the name of two or three families who lived in Dublin when Joyce was young. One Bloom, who was a dentist, had been converted to Catholicism in order to marry a Catholic woman ... Joyce no doubt also knew of another Bloom, who was committed in Wexford in 1910 for the murder of a girl who worked with him in a photographer's shop.'

One is tempted to suggest that the process of naming of fictional characters depends as much upon serendipity as cool calculation. In Flann O'Brien's *At Swim Two Birds*, an assault upon character and characters in more senses than one, 'the inspiration of the name "Trellis"...' wrote Anthony Cronin (*No Laughing Matter* [1989]), 'had a curious origin. In the back garden at Avoca Terrace, there was a 12-foot-high trellis, the function of which was to divide the lawn from the vegetable garden. This tended to be blown down in heavy storms and was more than once a source of contention between the three eldest boys and their father ... they considered the matter in its theoretical aspects and decided there was a better chance of it standing up if it were split into three sections. Needless to say, the trellis when divided had even less chance of remaining erect ...' A man was employed to rebuild it and from the bits and pieces left over from this operation Brian O'Nolan/Flann O'Brien (see **Myles na gCopaleen**] built himself a writing table. 'He wrote the book', said Cronin, '... on this home-made table in the bedroom he shared with his youngest brother Micheál and called one of its key figures Dermot Trellis.'

While many writers attempt to mirror 'real life' in the naming of their characters, eschewing anything that might distract the reader from the larger concerns of the fiction, there are many, like the creator of Dermot Trellis, who seek to embody something more than a factual statement in the creation of verbal identities, a predilection that would seem to transcend both time and literary fashion. Thus O'Casey's Joxer and Fluther are in a direct line of descent from Sheridan's Mr Puff and Oscar Wilde's Ernest; Beckett's relatively straightforward Murphy, Malone and Mercier gave place, across a shift of language, to Krapp, Hamm and the eternally debatable Godot before names of any kind were excised from the canon. The whole business of naming in this context is bound up with the contrapuntal relationship between an author and his characters, as exemplified in *At Swim,* in *Tristram Shandy,* in Pirandello's *Six Characters in Search of an Author* and in many other texts, and is part of the creative unease in the presence of the 'omniscient narrator' approach to the craft of fiction. It is exemplified, as neatly as anywhere, in Ionesco's play *La Cantatrice Chauve* (usually unsatisfactorily translated as *The Bald-Headed Prima-Donna*), in which M. and Mme Smith discuss the death of Bobby Watson. His widow, also Bobby Watson, has been left with two children:

> Mme SMITH. Mais qui prendra soin des enfants? Tu sais bien qu'ils ont un garçon et une fille. Comment s'appellent-ils?

M. SMITH. Bobby et Bobby comme leurs parents. L'oncle de Bobby Watson, le vieux Bobby Watson est riche et il aime le garçon. Il pourrait très bien se charger de l'éducation de Bobby.

Mme. SMITH. Ce serait naturel. Et la tante de Bobby Watson, la vielle Bobby Watson pourrait très bien, à son tour, se charger de l'éducation de Bobby Watson, la fille de Bobby Watson. Comme ça, la maman de Bobby Watson, Bobby, pourrait se remarier. Elle a quelqu'un en vue?

M. SMITH. Oui, un cousin de Bobby Watson.

Mme SMITH. Qui? Bobby Watson?

M. SMITH. De quel Bobby Watson parles-tu?

Mme SMITH. De Bobby Watson, le fils du vieux Bobby Watson l'autre oncle de Bobby Watson, le mort.

M SMITH. Non, ce n'est pas celui-là, c'est un autre. C'est Bobby Watson, le fils de la vielle Bobby Watson la tante de Bobby Watson, le mort …

There is a sense, of course, in which all the characters in a work of fiction wear the same identity – that of the author (in Flaubert's phrase, 'Madame Bovary, c'est moi.') But that is part of a different story.

Pet names

Pangur Bán is dead these thousand years. The little white ninth-century cat who, in Kuno Meyer's translation, 'rejoices with quick leaps/When in his sharp claw sticks a mouse' is probably the best-known – and most loved – of our named domestic animals. In Robin Flower's version: 'I and Pangur Bán, my cat,/'Tis a like task we are at;/Hunting mice is his delight,/Hunting words I sit all night.' If the monk's cat merited a special tribute from his master, the early records, myths and sagas are not deficient in named animals, of both this and the other world.

While the Irish word *cat* is of common European origin, the ultimate source unknown, the language possessed several other synonyms, one of which, *puss*, entered English as a pet-name for the species. As in ancient Egypt and other early civilisations, cats fulfilled both their domestic roles and that of a mystical creature with supernatural attributes – the cat Irusan, for example, was a larger-than-life specimen who lived in a cave on the river Boyne near the prehistoric tumuli and is said to have seized a poet, Senchan, in his jaws and made off with him: his (the poet's) ultimate fate is not re-corded. Three other monstrous, though unnamed, feline specimens, residents of the Cave of Cruachan, guarded the entrance to the Otherworld, while another more domestically-inclined animal bore the name Luchtigern, or mouse-lord.

Dogs, also, had a paw in each world, being subjected to magical shape-changing, as in the case of **Finn McCoul**'s sister, who, in canine guise gave birth to the hounds Bran and Sceolang. Other named dogs include Adhnuall, another of Finn's dogs who was stolen by a son of the king of Britain; Doilín, Fáil Inis, Ailbe, Saidhthe Suaraigne; Mug Eime, the first lapdog to be introduced to Ireland – Dabilla was another. Bulls also merited names: Donn, the famous brown animal which was the cause of the war between queen **Maeve** [Medb] and the men of Ulster; Finnbhennach, Slemuin. Horses (Acéin), sows (Beo) and salmon (Funtain) were also nominally distinguished, albeit less commonly.

While many of these names carried a significance beyond that of a simple domestic convenience – one would have hesitated to employ them to call the animal in question for its dinner – contemporary usage is, with rare exceptions, unclassifiably eclectic. We can learn little from the name of Oliver Goldsmith's horse (Fiddleback), the Joycean **Citizen**'s dog (**Garryowen**), Long Ears the fictional turfcutter's donkey, Síóg [Ir., fairy], the real-life donkey acquired by the 15-year-old Orson Welles on his first and formative visit to Ireland. Pet names by their very nature are inconsequentially bestowed; though there is the occasional insight into a more systematised nomenclature. 'The dogs in the streets of Belfast', wrote Sam Smyth (*Sunday Tribune*, 27 Aug. 2000) 'always had family names. Darkie Smyth and Lucky Armour, both quirky terriers, were next door neighbours on the street in Belfast where this reporter grew up ...' This practice is replicated in recent surveys reported by *Verbatim* (Summer 2000) which 'agree that the most popular names today, such as *Sam* and *Max*, seem to reflect a view of dogs as members of the family, rather than inhabiting the somewhat more distant world of *Spot, Shock, Bounce, Towser* or *Rover*.' In general, however, it is fair to conclude that only animals in their public capacity are named in accord-ance with any accepted norms.

In 1935 the tobacco firm of John Player & Sons inserted into their cigarette packets a series of 50 cards under the title *Famous Irish Greyhounds*. Of these, only a handful – Connaught Lamb, Mah-a-boucaill [Ir. *maith an buachaill!*, good lad!], **Master McGrath, Mick the Miller** (by Glorious Event – Na Boc Lei [Ir. *ná bac léi,* let her alone]), Queen of the Suir, Sairshea [?<Ir. *saoirse*, freedom], The **Long Fellow** II were of recognisably Irish provenance. There was otherwise a strong emphasis on the meat industry: Beef Cutlet, Cutlet's Turn, Floating Cutlet, Future Cutlet, Mutton Cutlet, Stylish Cutlet – a predilection which was again to manifest itself in the 1990s in the naming of racehorses, though in this case with the emphasis on the pig: Slaney Bacon, Slaney Rasher *et al.* barely concealed the connection with a Wexford meat processing company.

The prevailing Bord na gCon [greyhound racing authority] regulations governing the naming of greyhounds prohibit the use of copyright names, together with 'the names of living persons and well-known, famous or notorious people', thus limiting their exploitation for commercial advantage. Foreign names must be accompanied by a translation, made-up names by an explanation where they have no evident meaning, and names 'with vulgar meaning, profanities or suggestive names are debarred and also are names likely to give offence' – though this latter category would appear to lay itself open to wide interpretation. No initials, no names ending in numerals, and a maximum of three words or sixteen letters – inclusive of spacing and punctuation – in all; nor can a name be re-allotted if it has been borne by a 'famous dog' or is similar in pronunciation to one already in use. Given what some might regard as the draconian nature of these regulations the current naming of greyhounds exhibits a remarkable degree of resilience and invention, with local interests and associations playing a significant part. For a different class of canine, the Irish Kennel Club Ltd permits names of 24 letters including spaces, though debarring the titles 'Champion' or 'Winner' as well as duplicate names.

On Wednesday 26 August 1751 the Thirty Pounds Plate at Bellewstown, County Meath was contested, according to *Faulkner's Dublin Journal*, by 'Mr Burrass's Mare Sprightly Peggy, Mr Walpole's Horse Signior Guadagni, Mr Fitzgerald's Gelding Welcome, and Mr Langan's Horse Irish Beau, which was won by the former.' Nowadays Mr Walpole would need to seek the consent of Signior Guadagni, a castrato singer very recently arrived to perform in Dublin, to name a horse after him: the Turf Club insists that no names of persons or companies may be used without this formality. It also bans numerals – an Arkle II, for example, may not come under starter's orders – and in other respects its rules are in general similar to those applied to greyhounds. Increasingly common, however, are multi-word names compacted into one: Tobeornotobe; Youllneverwalkalone, which are now apparently acceptable, if posing space problems for the bookies' boards.

They order these matters differently in France, where all the horses in a given race (with few exceptions) have names beginning with the same initial letter. Here, those (and there are not a few) who pledge their support to animals of both species, horse and hound, on the basis of the names they bear may at least comfort themselves that the rules in each case, though restrictive, continue to allow ample scope for appealing, if not always rewarding, novelty.

Noms de Plume: Pseudonyms of Irish Writers

Irish writers who habitually or occasionally wrote under a pseudonym. English *names simply rendered in their Irish versions or vv. − i.e. John Whelan/Sean O'Faolain − are not included.*

Bax, Arnold (1883-1953): *Dermot O'Byrne*

Blundell, Frances (c1855-1930): *M.E. Francis*

Boyd, Hugh (1746-1794): *Junius*

Brennan, J.N.H (1914-): *John Welcome*

Brophy, R.J. (c1865-?): *R.J. Ray*

Browne, Maurice (1892-1979): *Joseph Brady*

Byrne, John Keyes (1926-): *Hugh Leonard*

Caprani, Vincent (1934-): *Charlotte Massey*

Casey, Elizabeth (1848-1894): *E. Owens Blackburne*

Cox, William Trevor (1928-): *William Trevor*

Davis, Francis (1817-85): *The Belfastman ('The Nation')*

De Blacam, Aodh (1890-1951): *Roddy the Rover*

Doyle, James Warren (1786-1834): ***JKL***

Dunne, Mary (1959-1945): *George Egerton*

Gallagher, Frank (1893-1962): *David Hogan/David O'Neill*

Hannay, James Owen (1865-1950): *George A. Birmingham*

Harbinson, Robert (1928-?): *Robin Bryans*

Hickey, William (1787 or 1788-1875): *Martin Doyle*

Hitchcock, Rex (1892-1950): *Rex Ingram*

Hungerford, Margaret, née Hamilton (1855-1897): *The Duchess*

Hyde, Douglas (1862-1949): *An Craoibhín Aoibhinn*

Kelly, James Plunkett (1920-): *James Plunkett*

Kelly, Mary Eva (c1825-1910): *Eva* (contrib. to '*The Nation*')

Lawler, C.F. (fl. C1810): *Peter Pindar*

Leslie, Mary Isabel (1899-?): *Temple Lane*

Lunel, Arthur Joyce (1888-1957): *Joyce Cary*

Lynd, Robert (1879-1949): *Y.Y.*

MacKenna, Stephen (1872-1934): *Martin Daly*

MacManus, Anna, née Johnston (1866-1911): *Ethna Carbery*

Magee, William Kirkpatrick (1868-1961): *John Eglinton*

Mahony, Frances Sylvester (1804-1866): **Father Prout**

Martin, Violet (1861-1915): *Martin Ross*

Maturin, Charles (1782-1824): *Dennis Jaspar Murphy*

Mayne, Thomas (1818-83): *Capt. Mayne Reid*

Murphy, Arthur (1727-1805): *Charles Ranger*

McCormack, William John (1947-): *Hugh Maxton*

Moore, Thomas (1779-1852): *Thomas Little*

Montgomery, Leslie (1873-1961): **Lynn C. Doyle/Lynn Doyle**

Moran, Michael (1794-1846): **Zozimus**

Ó Grianna, Séamus (1891-1969): *Máire*

Ó Nuallain, Brian (1912-1966)*:* **Myles na Gopaleen/gCopaleen** */Flann O'Brien*

O'Brien, Conor Cruise (1917-): *Donat O'Donnell*

O'Donovan, Michael (1903-1966): *Frank O'Connor*

O'Hara, Kevin (1892-?): *Marten Cumberland*

O'Shea, John Augustus (1840-1905): *The Irish Bohemian*

Pearse, Padraig (1879-1916): *Colm Ó Conaire*

Pollock, John Hackett (1887-1964): *An Philibin*

Reddin, Kenneth (1895-1967): *Kenneth Sarr*

Russell, George (1867-1935): **AE**

Ryan, Frederick (1876-1913): *Irial.* (joint ed., '*Dana*' 1904-5)

Shorter, Dora Sigerson (1866-1918): *Dora Sigerson*

Skrine, Agnes née Higginson (c1870-?): *Moira O'Neil*

Skrine, Mary Nesta (1905-1996): *M.J. Farrell/Molly Keane*

Stephens, James (1882-1950): *James Esse*

Swift, Jonathan (1667-1745): **M.B. Drapier**

Thompson, Arthur (1917-1975): *Francis Clifford*

Varian, Elizabeth (c1830-c1903): *Finola* (contrib. to '*The Nation*')

Waddell, Samuel (1878-1967): *Rutherford Mayne*

Waller, John Francis (1809-1894):
Freke Slingsby

Weldon, John (1890-1963): *Brinsley MacNamara*

Welpy, Eugene (1908-19??): *Mervyn Wall*

Wilde, Jane (1826-1896): *Speranza*

Williams, Richard (1877-1947):
Richard Rowley

Williams, Richard D'Alton (1822-1862): *Shamrock*

Wilson, Robert (1820-1875):
Barney Maglone

Yodaiken, Leslie (1912-1964): *Leslie Daiken*

4

House of Key(e)s

SOMETIME IN THE NINETEEN SIXTIES Bill Watts, a future Provost of Trinity College Dublin, was elected to the presidency of the conservation body then known as The National Trust for Ireland. On its letterhead there appeared, in smaller type and in brackets, the alternative Irish title 'An Taisce', which Dineen defines as 'a store or treasure, a depository, safe or hiding-place; a stake, pledge or guarantee; a term of endearment'. In due course Watts approached my then consultancy partner, Bill Bolger, and myself with a view to giving the organisation a new image – a very modest makeover, be it said, in terms of the vast sums and energies now expended on the same process. We suggested that the current name, a docile copy of the British equivalents, should be replaced by the Irish version. This was advanced with some trepidation in view of the fact that the organisation was then regarded, rightly or wrongly, as the last refuge of the unreconstructed Ascendancy. Watts, however, was enthusiastic, and the new name was visually reinforced by developing the initial 'T' as a distinctive logo. Happily, both name and symbol proved widely acceptable, the former no doubt helped on its way by the liking of the media for one-word labels – even in Irish.

The early nineteenth-century nationalist movement had expressed little interest in the future of the Irish language. Among the leading figures only Thomas Davis was a positive advocate of its preservation whereas O'Connell, a native speaker, had actively encouraged its supplanting by English as the medium of everyday communication. Though specialised bodies such as the

Hiberno-Celtic Society (1818) and the Irish Archaeological Society (1840) were established to study and preserve both the historical and literary heritage, the focus remained largely academic; and it was not until the foundation of the Gaelic League in 1893 that the revival movement effectively entered the public domain.

By then, of course, Irish had ceased to be the language of the streets and the market place for the large majority of the people, so it is not surprising that the move to restore it evoked little enthusiasm in the commercial world and none at all in official circles still under British hegemony. With the coming of 26-county independence, however, the new State, at least on paper, took the language to its bosom, designating its principal offices and office-bearers (Dáil, Uachtarán, **Taoiseach**, **Tánaiste**) in Irish. Some of these were to acquire popular currency while others such as Aire [Minister], **Saorstát**, Seanad [Senate] achieved only partial acceptance. The Garda Síochána, on the other hand, had experienced a brief anglophone existence as the Civic Guards before become generally accepted under its Irish designation. Conditioning factors were: frequency of usage, and ease of pronunciation for the monolingual. But these do not entirely explain why some titles entered the language while others remained on the fringes: as always, language tends to work in its own unpredictable ways.

In the case of government Departments (preferred, on the Australian model, to Ministries) and other less frequently observed organs of State, the sheer cumbrousness of the Irish name – in most cases a literal translation from the English rather than a title coined in its own right – contributed substantially to a deficiency of popular acceptance. The establishment in the 1930s of the new State-sponsored bodies with a legal requirement to follow a bilingual policy in the matter of naming produced mixed results in linguistic terms: while the Electricity Supply Board, one of the first, was never popularly identified under its Irish title of Bord Soláthair an Leictreachais, the organisation which began life as Irish Sea Airways in 1936 became, thanks to the enthusiasm of the Cork County Surveyor Richard O'Connor, **Aer Lingus**, and several other new names were to pass painlessly into the public domain. These included Bord na Móna, the peat authority; Fógra Fáilte, the tourist board [<*fógra,* notice, announcement, advertisement; *fáilte,* welcome] and antecedent of Bord Fáilte; Raidió Éireann (though quickly part-anglicised to Radio); An Gúm, the publishing arm of the Stationery Office – one of the many unashamed institutional borrowings from the British which retained its English-language identity; and Córas Iompair Éireann [Irish

Transport System], an unlikely candidate for acceptance which perhaps struck a chord with the public on account of its somewhat verbose unfamiliarity, carrying its verbal identity into the generally-used acronym CIÉ. Outside the State-sponsored sector, rural organisations such as Macra na Féirme [<*macra*, band of youths; *feirm,* farm] and Muintir na Tíre [people of the country] operated from the outset under Irish-only designations.

More recent examples of exclusively Irish nomenclature include Coillte [wood, forest], the afforestation authority; Dúchas [birthright, heritage], the heritage service; Fás [growth, also acronym of Foras Áiseanna Saothair – Institute of the Facilities of Labour] the employment/training body; and **Luas**, the nascent Dublin rapid-transit system. On the other hand the announcement in November 2000 that An Fórsa Cosanta Áitiúil, the local defence force, was to be renamed the Army Reserve represented a retreat into monolinguistic anonymity; and in the same way that there have always been those who have refused to use the Irish form of personal names, 'translating' them into approximate English equivalents, so some have continued to resist public nomenclature in Irish, insisting, for example, on referring to 'Irish Rail' (**Iarnród Éireann**) and 'the Tourist Board'. It might be surmised that such individuals would rarely be heard to speak of 'Air Fleet' (Aeroflot), Federal Bank (Bundesbank) or the Elysian Fields, the well-known Parisian thoroughfare.

While such mildly perverse opt-outs are perhaps now less common (one rarely, for example, hears 'prime minister' in lieu of **Taoiseach**), they were paralleled by the case of the **Punt** which, though in common usage abroad to designate the pre-Euro Irish currency, failed to find much favour at home, *The Irish Times* in particular steadfastly setting its face against the term even when major financial crises involving the pound sterling led to serious ambiguity. It is difficult to explain why, given a perfectly pronounceable and definitive Irish-language term – far more accessible, for example, than **Tánaiste** – the name failed to enter common usage except in a half-apologetic context.

Perhaps the simplest explanation is that it represented a dying mani-festation of what the Australians know (or knew, until the 2000 Olympics) as the Cultural Cringe, a phenomenon which otherwise would seem to be less in evidence in the face of a growing commercial, if not demotic, use of Irish (see below). The development in some areas of official nomenclature has seen a partnership between the two languages [**Operation Oíche/Samhradh**, Nollaig, Éirgrid – the State company managing the electricity grid; **eircom**] which, if not appealing to the purists, at least indicates that those responsible believe the deployment of the first official language in this manner to be increasingly acceptable. It is an interesting departure which nevertheless sits side-by-side with a generally dismal approach to the bestowal of governmental and other civic names and titles, evinced by examples such as the lamentable **BMW** (which would seem to be designed, incidentally, to inhibit the use of any Irish-language equivalent) and the tendency to settle for lengthy descriptions rather than titles in the naming of government Departments. 'Department of Social, Community and Family Affairs'; 'Justice, Equality and Law Reform' (one might have hazarded that the last-named was implicit in the first two elements); 'Health and Children' (men/women need not apply?); and the crowning glory 'Arts, Heritage, Gaeltacht and the Islands' – and whatever you're having yourself.

It seems a far and nostalgic cry to the days of the Departments of Health, Industry and Commerce, Agriculture (now 'Agriculture, Food and Rural Development' – trying to please everybody and satisfying nobody). Only such stalwarts as the Departments of the **Taoiseach** (predictably), and Defence retain a simple one-word designation (Ministers of War having been euphemistically banished from the world's cabinet rooms though the activity remains as popular as ever). The State, having begun with a department of External Affairs (the Commonwealth nomenclature adopted to mollify the reluctantly-disengaging British) belatedly went 'Foreign' in 1971.

The situation has been rather better in the North, where, from the inauguration of government in Stormont, Ulster taciturnity has ensured that Ministries – as they are designated in that jurisdiction – benefited from short, all-encompassing titles such as Home Affairs, Education, Agriculture, a practice which has survived into the administration set up under the Belfast/ Good Friday agreement. The title enjoyed by the head of the administration, that of First Minister, must, however pose some problems for the international translators endeavouring to make the distinction between 'First' and 'Prime'.

Branding ironies

'It's becoming more and more ridiculous. You know the kind of stuff I mean. Jerseys emblazoned with "South Tipperary Ham and Eggs Emporia" or "Opielinski and Bray Hairdressers" or "O'Malley's Chinese Restaurant".' Seán Diffley (*Irish Independent,* 10 June 2000) was expressing a reaction to the phenomenon of brand-worship echoed by the writer Norman Mailer in an interview with David Aaronovitch (*Independent on Sunday* (London), 20 Aug. 2000). Speaking of his youngest son, Mailer said: 'I think it was when he was

13 and he was wearing a shirt one day, a designer shirt, it wasn't Ralph Lauren but it was one of those, and I said, "would you wear a shirt that had Norman Mailer on it?" He said, "Oh Dad, come on," and I said, "You're buying the goddam thing and then you're advertising the guy on top of it." And now, Mailer adds proudly, he's in Washington with the other demonstrators against global capitalism.'

To many of Mailer's generation the idea of walking around as free advertising space for some multinational, national or local commercial concern continues to remain inexplicable, as does the practice of wearing manufacturers' labels outside rather than inside the clothes – something that a short half-century ago would have been considered either vulgar or in bad taste or both. But vulgarity and bad taste are superseded concepts, and global capitalism would seem to have fixated the masses (a handful of demonstrators apart) on the name rather than the product itself, a capitalist synecdoche which appears to be so far only minimally threatened by the forces of reaction. Though critical voices are increasingly being raised, it will be a long time before the *Ding an sich*, the thing in itself, reasserts primacy over its fabricated image. It is a very long way back to the 'procession of white-smocked men', as recorded in James Joyce's **Ulysses,** shuffling through the Dublin streets with the name of the prominent printers and stationers, Hely's, spelt out in 'scarlet letters on their five tall white hats'.

'Like that, see.' Leopold **Bloom** explained to foreman printer Nannetti in the same work of fiction: 'Two crossed keys here. A circle. Then here the name Alexander Keyes, tea, wine and spirit merchant. So on.' In Ireland, as elsewhere, the branding of goods and services began with the promotion of the name of the manufacturer or vendor – a phenomenon which has come full circle with the exploitation of 'designer labels'. It was a slow beginning, inhibited by the political situation and the concomitant lack of industrial development. By the close of the nineteenth century, however, prospects had improved, as reflected in the views of George Russell (**AE**) in *The Irish Homestead* (21 Apr. 1906). 'We have always held', he wrote, 'that the Gaelic League, by imparting pride and self respect and true love of country to the Irish people, would do a great deal finally to promote an industrial revival. The Gaelic Leaguer has shaken off the melancholy which has withered the faculties of other Irishmen ... and [he] is looking about for things to do, for old native industries to encourage, and new ones to create.'

Just over a decade later, in 1917, the first issue of the *Dublin Chamber of Commerce Year Book* was listing a total of 337 classes of goods manufactured in the city. These ranged from account books to zinc goods and included: artesian well-boring appliances; buoys; deformity apparatuses; feathers; gunpowder; hat racks; ladies' corsets; magnesia; prayer books; river lighters; silver jewellery (Celtic); telescopes; vertical bar railings and whiskey. Among the brand names featured were *Reducine*, 'the great remedy for lameness in horses'; *Shamrock Stout* (Watkins, Jameson, Pim & Co.); *Bullet* collars (Edward D. McCrea & Sons); *D.C.L.* yeast (Distillers' Co. Ltd) and *Rock* underwear (Blackrock Hosiery Co.). The majority of firms, however, promoted their goods under their own name – Lalor's Altar Candles; Coleman's Waterproof Covers, Sacks; D'Arcy's Dublin Stout; Murray's Fluid Magnesia. The advantage of a distinctive brandname as a marketing tool was yet to be fully recognised.

The introduction by the Irish Parliament of stamp duties on newspapers (1774) later extended to a tax on advertising which was raised to a punitive level of one shilling per advertisement in 1784. These taxes, which were not fully repealed until the 1850s, had an inhibiting effect on the promotion of such commercial products as then existed. Amongst these were tobacco and cigarettes, which from the early 1800s were marketed under brandnames publicised not so much in the public prints as at the point of sale, on packaging and showcards. The Belfast firm of Murray, Sons & Co. promoted Hall Mark, Pineapple and Special Crown cigarettes. Goodbody of Tullamore (1848-) offered a wide range of named brands including 'Furze Blossom Navy Cut', 'Golden Flake', 'Light Brigade' and 'Primrose'; while Tom Gallaher, A **Derry** man who founded his firm in 1857, was rapidly successful with his 'Honeydew' and 'Wrestler' tobaccos ('the best for smoking or chewing') and 'Gold Plate', 'Golden Spangled', 'Day Star' and 'Windfall' cigarette brands. The tobacco manufacturers' choice of names, with few exceptions, involved no specific Irish identity, though Goodbody sold 'Eblana' flake and 'Donore Castle' cigarettes while Murray's 'Erinmore' [<Ir. *mór*, big, great, large] tobaccos were to become very widely known and appreciated.

In this regard, however, it must be noted that the majority of manu- facturing businesses of any size were, during this early period and effectively up to the early 1950s, controlled by those of a Protestant/Unionist orientation who were slow to identify with or adopt the overt symbols of nationalism as expressive of a Gaelic-Irish identity. This factor contributed to the retention of 'neutral' individual or commercial names and abbreviations or acronyms thereof on the part of all sections of the business community: 'L.C.F.' (Limerick Clothing Factory) garments; 'D.C.L.' (Distillers' Co. Ltd) yeast; 'J.J.& S. (John Jameson & Sons) whiskey; 'Hiltonia' matresses; '**Mi-Wadi**'

(Mineral Water Distributors] soft drinks and other acronyms such as 'Smyco' clothing (Smyths of Balbriggan) and 'GYE' (**Guinness** Yeast Extract, a cousin of the Australian national symbol 'Vegemite'). Others based on the trading identity of the firms involved included 'Willwood' (Williams & Woods, jam manufacturers) and 'O'Dearest' (O'Dea & Co., mattresses) while some businesses favoured quasi-descriptive brands such as 'Perfect' cream separators; 'Science' polishes; 'Stedfast' shoes. Few of these verbal stratagems could be said to exhibit a discernible Irish identity.

It was not for sectarian political reasons, however, that the Dundalk firm of P.J. Carroll opted for a Scottish image for its 'Sweet Afton' cigarettes (1919-) complete with verbal/visual evocations of Robbie Burns: this was a rare early example of a product aimed specifically at an export market in which, Carrolls clearly believed, an Irish image would serve no commercial purpose. In identifying such an outlet they were, however, one of the few exceptions amongst manufacturers who, in the years of the Economic War with Britain and up to and including World War II, were largely confined to a limited domestic market and who thus looked no further than this in the naming of their products or services. In cases where a specifically national nomenclature was favoured the choice was most frequently restricted to those conventional terms and symbols that had been popularised in the political and cultural spheres. 'Shamrock', 'Emerald', 'Erin', 'Hibernian', 'Eblana' and 'National' brands proliferated, with the associated visual symbolism drawn from what later was to be satirised as 'sunburstry' − round towers, wolf-hounds, harp-twanging maidens and a proliferation of Celtic interlacing.

If such choices now seem embarrassingly naïve in the light of our con-temporary multinationalism it must be observed that more than a handful of these early devisings survived and prospered into the post-war period and the new economic dispensation. Examples include 'Mick McQuaid' tobacco, named after a character in a late nineteenth-century magazine serial; 'Paddy' whiskey (originally **'Paddy Flaherty'**, commemorating a very successful salesman of the product); New Ireland Insurance; 'National' brand under-wear; 'Gaelite' neon signs; 'Emerald' household flour, 'Irel' coffee essence (1913-) and a substantial array of Shamrock, Celtic and Hibernian brands still extending over a wide range of present-day products and services; while, of course, 'Irish' this and 'Irish' that abounded, in many cases monuments to the now happily evaporating national inferiority complex and an example of branding at its most unimaginative in simply tacking the adjective on to an existing − generally British-inspired − product or service.

Placenames figured strongly amongst the early brands, reflecting the fact that they were employed by small businesses catering primarily for local markets. Balbriggan hosiery, dating from the mid-nineteenth century, was an exception in that it was perhaps the first Irish brand to achieve a generic identity and a dictionary definition; it was followed by a host of location-based names such as 'Bushmills' and '**Tullamore Dew**' whiskey; 'Dripsey' and 'Blarney' tweeds; 'Cork' gin; 'Belleek' china and many others, not a few of which were to achieve brand-recognition in wider markets. And while topomony remains a constant resource for products and services destined chiefly for the domestic market, several companies or organisations trading internationally on a large scale also continue to brand their products in this way: examples are Kerry (dairy products, see **Kerrygold**); Kilbeggan whiskey; (the revival of an old brandname, the product being currently distilled else-where) and Waterford (glass, etc.) another revival of an eighteenth-century generic name which in turn has found its imitators in Cavan Crystal; Dublin Crystal; Tyrone Crystal and several other similar undertakings. County names have also been favoured by bottled water producers (Tipperary, Roscommon and many others) even though the modern precursor in the field (1983-) opted for the County Down local name Ballygowan, reflecting the entre-preneur's origins rather than the source of the product (Newcastle West, County Limerick).

In the issue of *The Irish Homestead* for 23 December 1916 its publisher, **AE**, had written: 'We must say that we do not like the idea of calling a cheese made in Ireland "Irish cheddar", any more than we would like to see butter sold in the markets as Siberian Irish, or foreign tobacco rolled up and sold as Turkish "Banba" cigarettes … In our opinion it would be much better to have the Irish trade mark on what we produce from the very start.' In fact, as Diane Duane pointed out in a letter to *The Irish Times* (31 Mar. 1999), a mediaeval work, *The Vision of MacConglainne,* contains 'numerous references to native Irish cheeses, some of them mentioned by name – like maethal, a big round pressed cheese similar to modern Gouda (elsewhere in the literature someone is described as having "a rear end that looked like a couple of half-maethals rubbing together"); táth, a cooked pressed sour-curd cheese, apparently something like mozarella; grúth, a "cottage" cheese; and milseán, a mascarpone-like cream/curd cheese.'

87 Ways to Say Cheese
past and present

Abbey; Adare; Aherlow; Ardrahan; Ardsallagh; Avonmore; Ballingeary; Ballyblue; Bandon Vale; Bartelink; Baylough; Beal Lodge; Bellingham; Blarney; Boilie; Brekish Dairy; Cáis Bán; Cáis Cleire; Cáis na Rí; Calvita; Cahill's Farm; Caora; Capparoe; Carrigbyrne; Carrigaline; Carrowholly; Cashel; Chetwynd; Claire Coogan's; Cooleeney; Coolea; Cooneen; Corlea; Corleggy; Cliffony; Cratloe Hills; Creeshla; Crimlin; Croghan; Crozier; Cuilmore; Delo; Desmond; Dubliner; Dunbarra; Dunbeacon; Durrus; Gabriel; Galtee; Glandór; Glen-o-Sheen; Golden Vale; Gubbeen; Inagh; Irish Blue; Kerry; Killorglin; Kilmeaden; Kilshanny; Knockalara; Knockanore; Lavistown; Liathmore; Maughnaclea; Milleens; Míne Gabhair; Mary Morrin's; Munster; Murragh; Oisín; Old Ardagh; Old Charleville; Ring; Round Tower; Regato; Ryefield; St Brendan; St Killian; St Martin; St Tola; Shannon; Tara; Three Counties; Tipperary; Waterville; West Cork; Whitethorn.

Whether or not the modern Irish cheese industry was aware of these antecedents, it would appear to have taken **AE**'s strictures to heart (see panel), though again one might question the pervading reluctance to utilise Irish-language names. Why should a cheese from an Irish-speaking area have chosen to call itself 'Ring' rather than the perfectly-pronounceable 'Rinn', for example: the French find it neither necessary nor desirable to market one of their major cheeses in anglophone territories as 'Bishop's Bridge' ...

Research by the Irish Seed Savers' Association, devoted to the preservation of threatened indigenous fruit and vegetable strains, has focused attention on named apple varieties. These include Abraham; Aherne Beauty; Blood of the Boyne; Burlington; Buttermilk Russet; Clack-Melon; Codrum Seedling; Davy Apple; Dunkitt; Kilkenny Codlin; Killeagh Seedling; Lady's Beauty; No Surrender; Osborne; Red Kane; Striped Sax; Sweet William; Tom Chestnut; Tommy; Tullaroan Brandy and White Crofton. Resurrected potato varieties include Arran Victory, Irish Queen and Skerry Champion as well as the Lumper, the most common pre-Famine variety, while in Wexford an enterprising farmer has retitled the familiar British Queens as Carne Queens and Dungarvan Queens.

In 1932 a **Fianna Fáil** government replaced the Cumann na nGaedheal administration which had held power since independence and the tentative moves which had already taken place towards the introduction of comprehensive tariffs on imported goods became a policy-driven reality with the appointment of Seán Lemass as Minister for Industry and Commerce. The result was a radical change in the industrial scene with the development of new industries and new consumer products. Many of these were, however, established with foreign – largely British – participation and thus tended to trade on established names and identities. In some instances the new import replacement products exemplified the adage that imitation is the sincerest form of flattery: 'T.D.' Sauce, for example, was both in substance and image modelled on the British 'H.P.' (Houses of Parliament) version.

Few of these new entrepreneurs ventured, in establishing a brandname, into the risky territory of the Irish language. One exception was 'Solus', applied to light bulbs manufactured in Bray, County Wicklow; while the label on 'Locke's Kilbeggan Uisce Beatha Irish Whiskey' backed the linguistic horse both ways. There were occasional examples of phoneticisation of Irish names, of which possibly the most prominent was **Tintawn,** a sisal carpeting. This somewhat unappealing practice has persisted, current examples including 'ShinAwil Productions Ltd [<Ir. *sin a bhfuil,* that's it]; 'Shomera' [<Ir. *seomra,* room] home offices, 'the word for extra room' and 'Stira' loft ladders [<Ir. *staighre,* stair(s)]. Occasionally the use of Irish created pitfalls for the unwary. Discussing the creation of brandnames (*The Irish Times,* 9 Oct. 2000), Olive Keogh instanced 'a small Irish company [which] decided to launch a new perfume on the US market. The perfume was aimed at the Irish diaspora, so it was given an Irish name which seemed like a clever marketing ploy. It wasn't. The name [*Sidhe Gaoth,* anglicised as Shee Gwee] translated as "fairy wind" and not surprisingly the perfume failed to become a sweet-smelling success on the US market.'

Such miscalculations have, not, however, inhibited a continuing, if fitful employment of Irish-language brand or trade names amongst recent examples of which may be cited 'Amárach [tomorrow] Consultancy'; 'Ceirníní Cladaigh' [<Claddagh, County Galway] recording company; 'An Cosantóir' [defender, protector], defence forces journal; 'Eilís Óg' knitwear (Belfast); **'Fadó'**; 'Fiacla' [pl. of *fiacail,* tooth], toothpaste; 'Fódhla' [<mythological figure], Dub. printers; 'Galántas' [style, finery] native gold jewellery; 'Rí Rá' [see **Ree Raw**], Dub. nightclub; **'Slán Abhaile'** [safe home], taxi service; 'tusa' [you], banking facility. One might wonder, however, at the reaction of

those literate in both national languages when confronted with the name of a Dublin knickers shop: is 'Focal' an Irish noun or an English adjective?

Even nomenclature unequivocally English in language is not, however, immune from the semantic banana-skin, as the well-known example of **Irish Mist** attests. In the post-**Pfizer** world the crane hire firm formerly operating from Raheny, Dublin would speedily remove 'O'Leary Erection, Ltd' from its letterhead: in the same vein, the name of the composer of the signature tune to the popular RTÉ radio programme *Sunday Miscellany* – Samuel Scheidt – is rarely given over the air. It is not, of course, simply an Irish predicament: a car model, the 'Nova', was a failure on the Spanish market because it translated as 'no go', while the French soft drink 'Pschitt' and Sweden's 'Krapp' toilet paper have encountered their problems in Irish and other anglophone markets. And, to return closer to home, it might be instructive to be a fly on a French village wall when one of the vehicles of the Irish haulage company bearing the prominent title 'Con Transport' trundles past.

If there are few Irish organisations with brandnames which could be said to be truly multinational, many will be aware of the backlash against the exploitation of sweatshop labour by some of the global names as exemplified by Naomi Klein's book *No Logo* (2000): 'The branding formula leaves corporations wide open to the most obvious tactic in the activist arsenal: bringing a brand's production secrets crashing into its marketing image.' In such instances a change of name may be the only way out ('only the name has been changed to protect the guilty') but this is a procedure full of risks, as the examples of **eircom** and **Diageo** might suggest. The advent of what to most people was the new Christian Millennium on 1 January 2000 provided a case in point: considering 'What to do if you are stuck in the 20th century' (*The Irish Times*, 31 Jan. 2000) Pól Ó Conghaile commented that 'tampering with a brand purely because it contains some reference to a particular date may be akin to tossing the baby out with the bath water. Take 20th Century Designs, for example – at first glance a company on a collision course with the millennium branding bug. "My name basically describes the stuff I sell", Ms Janet Doyle, who owns the company, explains. Her Liberties, Dublin-based business deals in furniture, lighting and glassware dating from the turn of the century to the 1960s.' Others, however, were not so sanguine: 20th Century Plastics (Swords, Co. Dublin) changed its name to Centis Ireland, though Martin Donoghue of Beyond 2000, a Dublin computer retailer, concluded, according to Ó Conghaile, that 'we're just growing into our name. Before the millennium we weren't at our full namesake (*sic*), if you follow me. Several people have asked us about it, but they've also said, "Now your name actually makes sense!"'

But the old question, what's in a name? invites no easy answer. 'People often attach great significance to the intrinsic meaning of words', said Damian O'Malley of O'Malley and Hogan, specialists in brandnaming, 'but very often the meaning disappears once the name is out there. For example, parents agonise over naming a child but once the decision is reached, that child couldn't be called anything else. So names are not always important for the reasons we think they are.' They remain commercially important, nevertheless, and nowhere more than in the rapidly expanding sphere of e-business and the Internet. The development of domain names has sparked off bitter disputes, international scandals (see **bertieahern.com**] and legal actions, with coveted names changing hands for large fortunes. Some live in hope. Mark Brennock (*The Irish Times*, 13 Apr. 2000) reported that 'two Galway schoolboys have become the latest political cybersquatters, registering a Website in the name of Ms Mary Banotti MEP and offering to sell it to the former presidential candidate. Ms Banotti said last night she had no intention of buying the site in her name.'

With the exponential proliferation of websites and the availability of a distinctive name becoming in consequence ever more circumscribed, Irish identities and the unique resources of the Irish language are increasingly exploited. It is, indeed, all about identity: 'Irish people can now purchase a domain name with an .irl.com suffix from Irish company Business Media Ireland,' *The Irish Times* reported on 21 July 2000: 'The company said that IRL is a recognised abbreviation for Ireland and gives a geographical context to Irish domain names ...' Following complaints to the IE Domain Registry that body announced on 25 February 2000 that it was proposing policy changes which would 'permit artists, authors, performing artists etc. who demonstrably trade under their personal names to qualify for the appropriate .ie domain name' – the use of personal names having been until then excluded. *Jamesjoyce.com* had, however, been registered as far back as 1996 by Kitty O'Shea's of Paris (see panel) while Phoenix Data systems of Connecticut has, it is reported, registered *gobshite.com*. The governing legislation, both national and international, remains both complex and controversial. As Denis Kelleher (*The Irish Times,* 25 Oct.1999) put it: 'One of the most important questions in an Irish context is whether or not a domain name can be defined as "property". If domain names are property then the rights of their owners are protected by the Constitution.' Meanwhile the web had opened up a whole new area of Irish nomenclature with highly interesting ramifications.

Inn jokes

The English traveller Fynes Moryson, visiting Dublin in the early 1600s, observed that 'ale hath vent in every house in the town every day in the week, and every hour in the day, and every minute in the hour'. By 1672 it was estimated that there were 1,180 pubs in the city, a figure that would have been proportionately equalled in other urban centres such as Cork, Waterford or Galway. Many of these establishments were retail brewers, selling their own product on the premises, a practice which, given the slow development of the brewing industry in Ireland in comparison with elsewhere in Europe, was to continue well into the eighteenth century.

These taverns most frequently traded under the name of the proprietor, a practice that remained dominant until the latter years of the twentieth century. As Elizabeth Malcolm observed ('The Rise of the Pub', in J.S. Donnelly jr. & Kirby Miller (eds), *Irish Popular Culture 1650-1850* [1999]): 'Irish breweries showed little inclination to involve themselves directly in the retail trade. Irish pubs therefore remained as small independent businesses. Drink palaces did appear in the major cities, most notably the Crown Liquor Saloon in Belfast and the Irish House, the Long Hall, Ryan's and Lynch's in Dublin, but these were far from typical Irish pubs. Unlike English pubs, few Irish ones were purpose-built; many were converted houses or shops, and their fittings were strictly functional. Also, unlike English pubs, many went by the name of the present or past publican, emphasising the fact that one individual ran the house.'

The exception was the southern part of the country, where the rivalry between two Cork breweries in particular (Beamish & Crawford and Murphy's) and the desire to prevent **Guinness** from encroaching on their territory prompted them to acquire 'tied', or brewery-owned houses dealing only, or largely, in their own products. As a result many of these premises operated under names other than that of the tenant: as late as 1959 Murphy's built and operated 'The Tory Top' (Ballyphehane); 'The Orchard' (Ballinlough); 'The Outpost' (Bishopstown) and 'Deanrock House' (Togher) – all in the expanding Cork city area. **Guinness**, interestingly, followed this trend: in the 1960s in Cork it owned, through a subsidiary, 'The Marlboro''; 'The Market'; 'The Mountain' and 'The Top of the Hill'. Taverns trading under non-proprietorial names had, of course, been a feature of towns and cities at least since 'The

Brazen Head' opened its doors in Dublin's Bridge Street in 1613 (or, as a sign over the door claims, in 1198). Such names in the Dublin of the mid-nineteenth century included the 'Trinity Tavern'; the 'Light House Tavern'; the 'Golden Bridge Tavern'; the 'Fox Tavern' and many others.

While proprietorial names remained the rule in the smaller centres of population, by 1976 *A Guide to Dublin Pubs* (Leo J. Mooney, ed.) listed only some 20 such among a total entry of over 90 – the majority bearing names such as 'The Auld Dubliner'; The Bark Kitchen'; 'The Hideway'; 'The Horse and Tram'; 'The Harp'; 'The Oval'; 'The Scotch House'; 'The Stag's Head' and 'The Van Gogh'. Since then, personal names have staged a modest return in the guise of historical, political, literary and other prominent personages: '**Bird Flanagan**' (Dublin); 'Bugler Doyle's' (commemorating a World War I hero); 'Chester Beatty's' (Ashford); 'The Dean Swift' (Dublin); 'Durty Nellie's' (Bunratty, cleaned-up version of Dirty Nelly, former owner); 'Ginger Man' (<novel by J.P. Donleavy, Dublin); '**Kruger's**'; 'Molly Malone' (Kilcoole); 'Peadar O'Donnell's' [writer], Derry; 'Isolde's Tower' [legendary figure], Dublin; 'Jenny Watt's' (Bangor); '**John Hewitt**' (Belfast); 'John Tyndall' (Carlow, after the scientist); 'Kyteler's Inn' (Kilkenny, after a local witch); 'Mother Red Cap's' (<character in Walter Scott novel; Dublin); 'Phil the Fluter' (Borrisoleigh, after Percy French ballad); 'Ronald Reagan' (Ballyporeen, with which village he claimed ancestral connections); 'Sarah Curran' (Rathfarnham); 'Seán Lemass' (Ringabella, County Cork); 'Silken Thomas' (Kildare) constitute no more than a random sample in this category.

Under the influence of rising economic standards and consequently changing markets the trend in pub-naming in recent years has been towards the eccentric and exotic, 'international' in emphasis. In spite of this, animals of all shapes and sizes continue to feature widely (see panel), a predilection which can claim respectable historical antecedents. Cats in particular find favour on the model of French examples such as the 'Le Chat qui Pelote'; 'Au Chat Botté' and the 'Chat qui Fume'. Thus 'The Black Cat' (Kilkenny); the long-established 'Cat and Cage' (Dublin); 'The Cat and Bagpipes' (Tobar, County Offaly), 'The Cat Dragged Inn' (Dublin) and, quite simply, The **Cats** (not Kilkenny as might be expected, but Cappoquin, County Waterford). Not all such felines, however, are what they seem: 'The Cat and Fiddle' (Portumna) reveals itself both as an importation and a corruption of *Caton Fidèle*, after an erstwhile loyal governor of Calais under English occupation.

'The Cat Dragged Inn' is also one of the more felicitious specimens of a legion of puns on the word 'Inn' which include 'Barge Inn' (Robertstown,

County Kildare); 'Dew Drop Inn' (Kill; Laghey); 'Drift Inn' (Buncrana); 'Drop Inn' (Shercock); 'Inn Moderation (Athboy); 'Foot Inn' (Bansha; Burnfoot); 'Half Way Inn' (Enniskillen); 'Igoe Inn' (Ballybrack, County Dublin; Doonbeg, County Clare); 'Inn Between' (Killarney); 'Inn on the Liffey'/'Out on the Liffey' (Dublin); 'Park Inn' (Portlaoise); 'Step Inn' (Carlow; Magherafelt; Stepaside); 'Swan Inn' (Ballivor); 'Turn Inn' (Derrinturn); 'Wander Inn' (Johnstown, Waterford); 'Weigh Inn' (Omagh).

Animalcoholics
pub names avian, mammalian and reptilian

'The Blackbird' (Ballycotton); 'The Black Horse' (Cavan); 'The Bleeding Horse' (Dublin); 'The Blue Bull' (Sneem); 'The Boar's Head' (Kanturk < *ceann tuirc*, the head or hill of the boar); 'The Crocodile Lounge' (Carnew); 'The Crowing Cock' (Castlebellingham); 'The Dolphin' (Edgeworthstown]; 'Donkey Broke Loose' (Cork city); 'The Drunken Duck' (Carrowtrasna); 'The Elk Bar' (Toomebridge); 'The Fighting Cock' (Birr); 'The Goat' (County Dublin); 'The Green Lizard' (Dublin and elsewhere); 'The Greyhound Bar' (Dublin and many others); 'Hair o' the Dog' (Moville); 'The Horse and Hound' (Ceannanus, which also boasts (2000) the 'Mad Cow Bar'); 'Mallard Bar' (Ballinamallard); 'The Lame Duck' (Clonlara, County Clare); 'The Muckey [*sic*] Duck' (Ballymagovern, County Meath); 'The Nightingale' (Scariff); 'The Oyster' (Dunfanaghy); 'The Pheasant' (Craigavon; Drogheda); 'The Pickled Pig' (Ballinderry; Bray); 'The **Red Cow**' (Dublin); 'The Red Setter' (Castlemahon); 'The Rusty Mackerel' (Teelin, County Donegal); 'The Sea Horse' (Tramore); 'Shoot the Crowes' (Sligo); 'The Snooty Pig' (Tipperary); 'The Squealing Pig' (Monaghan); 'Three Jolly Pigeons' (Lissoy, County Westmeath); 'The Unicorn' (Dooradoyle, Limerick); 'The White Dove' (Cootehill); 'The White Horse' (Dublin); 'Wicked Wolf' (Blackrock, County Dublin); 'The Woodpecker' (Ashford).

Except in the case of the north-eastern counties, heraldic designations were never to form a significant aspect of pub nomenclature as was common elsewhere ('The Red Lion', England; 'Le Lion d'Or', France). The reason was at least in part socio-political, since such titles inevitably derived from the arms or family name of the local landlord or other symbols of an imposed authority: indeed the whole art or science of heraldry was slow to gain wide popular acceptance. W. M. Thackeray *(Irish Sketch Book* [1843]) remarks that 'In the time of the rebellion the landlord of this Royal Oak, a great character in these parts [County Carlow] was a fierce United Irishman.' Names such as 'The Conyingham Arms' (Slane), and 'Donegall Arms' (Belfast), reflect the 'Big House' connection while a few, such as the 'Urlingford Arms' (Urlingford) and 'The Leinster Arms' (Maynooth), draw on a wider heraldic resource.

The absence of inn-signs until the modern period, when their incidence nevertheless remains spasmodic, may perhaps also be attributed to a deficiency of appropriately-skilled craftsmen in rural areas; though against this must be set the proliferation of signs exhibited by printers and publishers (often one and the same) in the Dublin of the eighteenth and nineteenth centuries. Among these were to be found 'Milton's Head'; 'Parrot'; 'Pope's Head' (the poet, not the pontiff); (all fl. 1738) as well as 'Cicero's Head'; 'Erasmus Head'; 'Homer Head'; 'The Leather Bottle'; 'Shakespeare's Head'; 'Swift's Head'; 'Virgil's Head', all at one time to be found in the city's Dame Street; and **'Dr Hay's Head'** in Bridge Street. Of the latter Thomas Wall writes: 'Like so many others of its time the actual sign of Dr Hay's head ... has long ago been destroyed. But what may be a faithful copy of it, enclosed in an oval frame with floral decorations, so characteristic of shop signs of the period, survives in the engraved portrait of Hay which Wogan sometimes used as a frontispiece to the various works of the bishop.' The semiotics of pub and shop signs is, however, a subject beyond the scope of the present enquiry.

Irish-language pub names are relatively uncommon outside the surviving Gaeltacht areas, with the exception the case of those displaying the name of the owner. Non-proprietorial examples include 'An Bhróg' [the shoe] (Cork); 'An Spailpín Fánach' [migratory labourer] (Cork); 'An Teach Beag' [the little house] (Bantry); 'Cloch Bán' [*sic*] [black rock] (Clonroche); 'Cois na hAbhna' [beside the river] (Mountshannon); 'Crannóg' [box-like structure; pulpit; rostrum; crow's nest; hopper; winding-frame; lake-dwelling] (Waterford); 'Cruiscín Lán' [full jug] (Courttown Harbour); not a few examples of 'Seanachaí', variously spelt (Killaloe, Kinsale); 'Sibín' [shebeen] (Tipperary); 'Teach Dolmain' [Dolmen house] (Carlow); **'Tír na nÓg'** (Kilrush). Bilingual nomenclature occurs rarely, though Paris has, or had, a pub known as 'Tigh Johnny' [Johnny's house.]

> ## Pubs of Paris
> *past and present; not necessarily under Irish management*
>
> Art O'Leary's; Le Bistrot Irlandais; Carr's; Le Caveau Montpensier; Celtic Connections; Cogan's Irish Café; Le Connemara; Connolly's Corner; Coolin; Corcoran's; The Cruiskeen Lawn; Finnegan's; Finnegans Wake; The Flann O'Brien [see **Myles na gCopaleen**]; **Kitty O'Shea's**; Le Galway; Le Goblet d'Argent (Tony's); **Guinness** Tavern; Hurling Pub; Irlandais; The James Joyce Pub; The James **Ulysses**; Kildare Irish Pub; Molly Malone; Mulligan's; Murphy's House; O'Brien's; The Oscar Wilde; O'Sullivan's; Quigley's Point; The Quiet Man; Shamrock; Shannon Pub; Stolly's Stone Bar; Le Sweeney's; Le Tabac MacMahon; Tigh Johnny; The **Wild Geese**.

The worldwide dissemination of the Irish pub concept – there are currently examples in virtually every country where the consumption of alcohol is permitted – has added another dimension to the onomastics of this branch of human endeavour. Early examples favoured either the tradition of personal nomenclature (Mooney's, Britain) or the established national eschatology (Blarney Stone, US) but vigorous expansion into non-anglophone territories has created a more adventurous approach and a more comprehensive plundering of the store of national icons, literary and cultural in particular ('The Wilde Irish', Tallin, Lithuania).

The close association of inns with the development of coach transport in the eighteenth and nineteenth centuries is recalled in the present-day names of 'coaching inns', some of questionable authenticity, among them 'The **Bianconi** Bar' (Kildysart); 'The Coachman's Inn' (County Dublin); 'The Horse and Coach' (Ballylynan); 'The Old Turn Pike Inn' (Newcastlewest). The coming of the railways perpetuated the link between travelling and refreshment, with 'Railway Bars' a feature of virtually every town or village to which the network at its peak extended. Many of these remain in centres for which the railway is now no more than a fading memory ('Platform 1' [Armagh]); even 'The Signal Box' (in railway-linked Ballybrophy) has seen its namesake virtually eclipsed by the modern technology of Centralised Train Control (CTC).

Sea and canal transport predated trains, and pubs with waterway or maritime associations include 'The Anchor Inn' (Vicarstown – on the Grand Canal – and many others); 'The Ferryboat Inn' (Kildysart); 'The Sailing Cot'

(The Faythe, Waterford); 'The Schooner' (Gorey); 'The Trawler Man' (Moville) and many a 'Yacht' (Dublin, Wexford). Aviation features less widely, though the 'Viscount' and 'Comet' in north Dublin commemorate aircraft types now vanished from the skies and, in the case of the former, once a staple of the **Aer Lingus** fleet.

Name this ship

Transport *per se* is a rich and fascinating exemplar of the naming process and its idiosyncrasies. Ships have, or course, carried names from the earliest times with private preference very largely dictating the choice until the establishment of national and commercial fleets. In the context of organised sea services between Ireland and Britain the fact that the earliest of these were British-owned and operated did not, however, entirely obviate the use of Irish names – the fleet of Government Mail Steamers, for example (1823-47) included *Banshee, St Patrick* and *St Columba*. With the development of indigenous shipping interests from the middle of the nineteenth century their fleets understandably tended to reflect the national identity: between 1851 and 1897 the vessels of the City of Dublin Steam Packet Co. bore the names *Ireland, Eblana* and those of the four provinces – the latter subsequently featuring on ships of many companies, either alone or in combination (*Ulster Prince, Ulster Monarch* of the Belfast Steamship Co. in the 1930s).

When the latter company transferred its vessels *Heroic, Patriotic* and *Graphic* to the Dublin-Liverpool service in the early 1930s they were renamed *Lady Connaught, Lady Leinster* and *Lady Munster,* adding to a long list of 'Ladys' on Irish-British routes which included at one time or another *Lady Betty Balfour; Lady Elsie; Lady Limerick* (and several other counties); *Lady Hudson-Kinahan* (which plied between Dublin and London in the 1890s) as well as *Lady of the Lake* (which operated a passenger service on the Shannon).

There were many vessels named *Blarney, Emerald Isle, Erin, Hibernia, Innisfallen,* **Kathleen Mavourneen**; *Killarney, St Patrick, Shamrock* and *Shannon* together with slightly more original variations on the national theme: **Brian Boru**/*Brian Boroimhe; Cathir-na-Gallimhe (sic)* (Galway Harbour Commissioners' tender, 1930s); *Menapia* (commemorating the Belgian tribe that colonised Ireland at the time of Julius Caesar); *Nora Creina* (Waterford & Bristol Steam Navigation Co.'s first vessel (1826); *O'Connell* and many more.

When a service of passage-boats was inaugurated on the Grand Canal in 1780 they were initially identified only by numbers. Subsequently, however, they were named, most commonly after the directors of the operating company and sundry Lords Lieutenant and their ladies. Among the first vessels so christened were *Duchess of Leinster; Duke of Leinster; Emily Lady Cloncurry; Joseph Hubard; Richard Griffin; William Digges la Touche; Pomeroy* (Arthur Pomeroy MP, subsequently Viscount Harberton of Carbury).

Apart from the Irish-owned services already referred to, the next major maritime development involving a consistent naming policy was the belated creation, early in the **Emergency** years (1941), of Irish Shipping Ltd, a deep-sea fleet initially formed from the acquisition of neutral vessels which had sought refuge in Irish ports. Thus the Greek *Vassilios Destounis*, the first of these, became *Irish Poplar*, and the tree theme was followed thereafter with *Elm, Beech, Hazel, Pine, Willow* and others, with some names transferring to second and subsequent vessels. The closure of the company in 1984, a shameful act of political chicanery, marked the end of the country's brief experience as a deep-sea maritime nation.

World War II also found Ireland without a navy, with the exception of the **Muirchú** and a couple of other insignificant small craft. Some secondhand motor torpedo boats were hastily acquired from the British (1939) but these did not carry names. With the ending of hostilities a small fleet was steadily created, both through purchase and building, all vessels carrying the names of legendary female figures such as *Cliona*, **Maeve**, *Macha* (corvettes) and *Deirdre, Aoife, Aisling, Emer, Eithne Orla* and **Róisín.** In January 2001 it was announced that Ross Casey, a Dublin schoolboy, had been successful in a competition to name a new vessel then building. He chose the winning name, *Niamh*, after his younger sister. His other sister, Orla, already shared her name with another naval ship.

The first organised terrestrial transport was provided by the stage and mail coaches, a network of services which expanded rapidly in the eighteenth and nineteenth centuries and survived, together with canal transport, until well into the railway age as an enduring tradition. Paul Durcan, in *Birth of a Coachman*, wrote of the new-born child: 'His father and grandfather before him were coachmen' and that he 'Will one day be coachman of the Cork to Dublin route,/... In full command of one of our famous coaches/–*Wonder, Perseverance, Diligence* or *Lightning*' ...

As competition developed on major routes coaches adopted names promoting their particular service (*Skibbereen Industry;* **Skibbereen Perseverance**); *Cock of the North* (Dub.-Newry, and its rival *Old Cock*); *Fair Trader* (**Derry**-Enniskillen). In his history of *The Great Northern Railway (Ireland)* (1944) Kevin Murray lists some of the vehicles operating northwards out of Dublin before the opening of the Dublin and Drogheda Railway in 1844: 'The public vehicles were classified as Coaches, Caravans, Cars and Omnibuses. The first group, connecting Dublin with Belfast, Armagh, Derry, Newry, Omagh, etc. included the mail coaches, whose time, 3h. 20m., was the fastest between Dublin and Drogheda; the ordinary coaches might occupy four to five hours. These ran seven, six or three days a week and included such romantic vehicles as the "Wellington", the "Fair-Trader" (obviously a popular name), the "Lark", the "Shareholder", the "Wonder" and (no doubt a competitor) the "No Wonder".'

In 1827 coach services from Cork included *The Cork and Dublin Commercial Union Car* (for commercial travellers); *The Youghal Regulator; The Bandon Diligence; The Macroom Car* and *The Lady of the Lake Coach* (for Killarney via Millstreet). In the 1940s, long after the last regular coach service had trundled along the turnpikes the *Shamrock* clip-clopped its way from Limerick to Adare, complete with red-coated coachman and post-horn, a colourful if brief palliative to those who had been deprived by the **Emergency** fuel shortages of the horseless carriage. Not everyone, however, was impressed. 'I do not suppose there is a decent man within the four walls of Ireland', wrote **Myles na gCopaleen**, 'who has not been annoyed by this stage-coach gag ... Colourful? Every time I hear the word "colourful" I reach for my revolver.'

With the coming of the railways the practice of naming would seem to have transferred as a matter of course to the prime-mover of this new form of locomotion, and subsequently to the train services themselves, the *Irish Mail*, which has run between London and Holyhead since 1 August 1848, being the oldest named train in the world. Ireland's pioneer railway, the Dublin & Kingstown, was inaugurated on 17 December 1834, the first train being hauled, predictably, by a locomotive named *Hibernia*. 'It had been decided', wrote K. A. Murray (*Ireland's First Railway* [1981]), 'that the D&KR engines should have names without numbers. Those by Forrester were *Dublin, Kingstown* and *Vauxhall*, thus honouring the termini of the line and the place of origin of the engines; the Sharp locomotives were *Hibernia, Britannia* and *Manchester*.'

As the railway mania spread and lines reached all parts of the island the practice of naming, at least in the case of the larger express locomotives, retained favour and was to continue to the end of the steam era in the 1960s and even beyond, since successive Northern Ireland railway authorities have continued to name their diesel locomotives (*Great Northern, Northern Counties* and *Belfast & Co Down* after former railway companies) and multiple units (*The Boys Brigade, Glenshane, Glenariff, Sir Myles Humphries*). With the introduction of the '201' class of locomotive on **Iarnród Éireann** services (1994) names, in this case of rivers and in both national languages, reappeared south of the Border. Until this development, however, no Southern locomotives had carried names since the introduction of the *Maeve* and her two sister engines in 1939.

Locomotive naming, as with passenger ships, was a sentimental gesture but one based on hard marketing realities: giving a large and handsome (and in most cases immaculately maintained) express engine a name awoke a chord in the travelling public and to some degree personalised the service offered. As *The Glensman* (Cushendall, County Antrim), commented in September 1932: 'Lovers of things historic in Northern Ireland and County Antrim in particular, will be pleased at the names chosen by the LMS-NCC [London Midland & Scottish-Northern Counties Committee] for their passenger locomotives … many will have noticed the names on the "splashers" of the engines recalling scenes and legends of long ago. The names are in four classes: "County", "Castle", "Glen" and "Mountain". In the "County" class we have: Antrim, Donegal, Tyrone, Londonderry, and Down. In the "Mountain" class, "Slemish", "Trostan", "Knocagh", "Ben Madigan" and "Slievegallion". What a vista of the past the names in the "Castle" class recall: "Glenarm", "Carra", "Dunluce", "Dunananie", "Lisanoure", "Slanes", "Olderfleet", and "Carrickfergus", to mention but a few. And the glamour of the Glens is recalled when we see such well-known names as Glenariff, Glendun, Glenshesk, and Glenaan. Many people hardly know that these places exist and more than one have had a knowledge of their native land enlarged …'

The Dublin-based Great Southern & Western Railway (1843-1925) was less enthusiastic about names, as K.A. Murray and D.B. McNeill's eponymous history explains: 'A few of the very earliest locomotives were named, after animals and birds, but within a short time the names were removed and the system adopted of giving numbers only, to engines in the regular stock. Only five of these ever carried names; Nos. 301-4 were called *Victoria, Lord Roberts, St Patrick,* and *Princess Ena,* but their nameplates were taken off in 1907. The large 4-4-0 No. 341 was named after the chairman, Sir William Goulding.' (Ireland's railway management, it need hardly be said, was at this time almost exclusively Protestant and firmly unionist.)

Smaller railways in most cases settled for names with local associations, as in the case of the little Clogher Valley Railway, which named its six locomotives after villages, rivers, and parishes on its route: *Caledon; Errigal* (<the parish of Errigal Keerogue); *Blackwater, Fury* (river); *Colebrooke* and *Erne*. The last name was popular in the north of the country: another *Erne* was still active at the closure of the County Donegal Railways (1959). A *Lough Erne* ran on the Sligo, Leitrim & Northern Counties (see **Slow, Lazy and Never Comfortable**) together with *Lough Melvin* and *Lurganboy*, while the West Clare's steam stock carried names such as *Kilrush* and *Slieve Callan*, though these were subsequently removed. None of the diesels which functioned in the last days of this storied line was considered fit to carry cast-iron or brass nameplates, in common with this impersonal form of motive power on other lines.

Because of generally slow speeds and short distances, named trains have been a rarity and the names themselves, with the possible exception of the enduring **Enterprise,** showed little imagination. The GS&WR introduced an American Mail in 1859 between Dublin and Cóbh (then a major transatlantic port) and a 'Killarney Express' to cater for the burgeoning tourist traffic (1898); In the following century the Belfast & Co. Down ran a 'Golfers' Express' from the city to Newcastle; the Great Northern operated a 'Bundoran Express' to that seaside town; while in the 1950s CIÉ introduced the *Sláinte* and the *Cú na Mara* [hound of the sea], of which the latter survives, though with minimal publicity, on a train on the Dublin-Galway service.

Ghost Trains
Some 88 railways were named but never built, among them:

Ballyclare, Ligoniel & Belfast Junction Rly; Bawnboy & Maguiresbridge Rly; Belfast and Hollywood Atmospheric Rly; Celbridge, Clane & Donadea Light Rly; Dublin & Armagh Inland Rly; Dublin Grand Junction Rly; Dublin Metropolitan Rly; Grand Atlantic Rly; Grand County Down Rly; Great Central Irish Rly; Irish East & West Rly; Leinster & Ulster Rly; Mullingar & Kells Rly; Munster Steam Tramway; Roscommon Central Light Rly; South Mayo Rly; Strabane, Raphoe & Convoy Rly; Tyrone Steam Tramways; Ulster & Connaught Light Rly; Westport & North Mayo Rly.

If today's privately-operated buses are content to carry nothing more than the name of the company or individual involved, the pioneer years of this form of transport saw names applied with a degree of enthusiasm and invention similar to that which was involved in the titling of stage coaches. 'In the early days of the traffic', *The Irish Times* commented on 30 January 1931, 'owners were content to accept such names as "Pioneer" or "Pirate", and they were rapidly followed by "The Blue Lion", "The Red Line", "The White Line" … and many others of a similar kind. Then we had the roses, red and white, with such names as "Silver Queen", "The General" and "The Major". More recently there has been a run on the calendar of saints for bus names…' (the long-established St Kevin's service between Dublin and Glendalough is a relic of this tendency). With the increase in private participation in road transport and service marks such as 'Aercoach' beginning to appear, the naming of bus services may be about to experience a modest revival.

Aviation nomenclature began effectively with Richard Crosbie's 'Grand Air Balloon and Flying Barge', in which he ascended from Ranelagh Gardens, Dublin, on 19 January 1785, but when Harry Ferguson made the first successful aeroplane flight in Ireland near Hillsborough, County Down, on 31 December 1909 his pioneer machine carried no name. Lilian Bland, who built the first biplane in the country in 1910, named it, hopefully, *Mayfly*: it did. The machines of the first domestic airline, Iona National Airways (1930) did not boast names: the fuselage carried the title 'Iona National Air Taxis and Flying School'. In February 1932 Manco Scally, an amateur aviator, set off to fly to Ceylon [Sri Lanka] in his aircraft *Shamrocket* but died in the attempt. During the same decade a machine of original design, named *Spirit of Erin* – foreshadowing the Ryanair fleet-names – was exhibited in Dublin but members of the Army Air Corps identified it as the reconstructed wreckage of a crashed aircraft and its promoter was not heard of again.

The Air Corps' first machine, nicknamed **The Big Fella**, was not, in common with normal military practice, to be followed by other aircraft carrying individual names, either formal or informal. It was not until the Government became involved in civil aviation with the establishment of **Aer Lingus** that naming became a regular feature of aviation. That company's first aircraft was named *Iolar* [Ir., eagle] followed by *Éire, Iolar II* and *Sasana* [England]. In 1945 the policy was adopted of naming the growing post-war fleet after Irish saints, the aircraft bearing the name in both languages and the fleet thus sanctified benefiting from an annual blessing. This naming policy has continued to the present, most by now having been re-allocated several times. The independent airline Ryanair follows widespread international policy in naming aircraft after destinations served in the form *The Spirit of …*

which format was also reflected in the title of its inflight magazine, *Spirit of Europe*.

That, of course, is not the end of the story. Theatres, wards, cows, clothes-horses, typefaces, interfaces, office blocks, office-bearers, chest freezers, foot warmers, chat shows, chat lines, butterflies, salmon flies, food outlets fast and slow … we live, inextricably, in a nominate landscape. The novelist Anne Enright, like most of us, learned this in early childhood: 'What do you call sky, except sky, what do you call a doll, except doll, or, at a push, Dolly? The capital letter makes all the difference, and I think I sort of knew this.'

PART TWO

THE DICTIONARY

A

AE [pseud.]. George W. Russell (1867-1935), poet, painter, mystic, economist, journalist & editor. **1977** Robert Bernard Davis, *George William Russell ("AE")*: 'In 1888, Russell adopted his famous pseudonym ... For a time, he used AEON as his pseudonym, but when a compositor was unable to decipher his signature he printed it as "AE-?" Russell thereafter omitted the dash and the question mark and, adopting the first two letters, was known by them for the rest of his life.'

Aerin [<Ir. *aer*, air + *Erin*]. **2000** *Irish Air Letter*, Mar: 'This is the name selected by the proposed new Irish domestic airline being set up by comedian Brendan O'Carroll. The initial plans involved the use of Bae146s, but it is believed that 50-seat turboprops are now being proposed.' See also **Aer Lingus.**

Aer Lingus [corrupt. of Ir. *Aer Loingeas,* air fleet; cf. Rus. *Aeroflot,* Span. *Aeronaves de Mejico,* etc.]. National airline (1936-). **1986** Bernard Share, *The Flight of the Iolar*: '... it is difficult not to suspect the involvement [in the choice of name] of Seán Ó hUadhaigh who appeared on the first Aer Lingus letterhead with the explanatory qualification "formerly John K. Woods...".' Hence: **Aer Árann** airline; **AerFi** aircraft leasing; **Aerin** [q.v.]; **Aer Rianta** airport management; **Aer Turas** charter airline; **TransAer** charter airline.

Affane Cherry [< R. Affane, Co. Waterford, trib. of the Blackwater].

Fruit grown by Mr ? Power on eponymous property. **1835** (1st pub. 1999) Robert Graham, *The Irish Journals of Robert Graham of Redgorton:* 'It is said to be here that Sir Walter Raleigh first introduced a fine species of cherry which he brought from the Canary islands and which has become domesticated in this neighbourhood and flourished throughout the country under the name of the "Affane cherry".'

Alice Daly [*fl*. Early C19]. Noted butter-maker. Hence: **the real Alie/ Ally Daly** Something par excellence. **1916** James Joyce, *A Portrait of the Artist as a Young Man:* 'Stephen looked at the plump turkey ... he remembered the man's voice when he had said "Take that one, sir. That's the real Ally Daly".'

Allo see **Broadwater**

Altan [music]. Trad. band. **2000** Fintan Vallely, *Sunday Tribune,* 12 Mar: 'The band spend much of their lives on the road ... A long way this from the origin of their title – Loch Altan, a tiny lake hanging between the parishes of Gaoth Dobhair and Cloghaneely in north west Donegal.'

American note [politic.]. US demand for an end to Ir. neutrality. **1975** John A. Murphy, *Ireland in the Twentieth Century:* 'A real sense of crisis developed in February 1944 when both the American and British ministers demanded the removal of German and Japanese diplomats from Dublin ... The "American note", as it was popularly and correctly called (for the final danger to neutrality seemed to emanate from the American rather than the British side), ignored the fact that a radio transmitter in the German legation had long since been removed ...'

American Wake [<destination]. Farewell celebration for departing emigrants, C19-20. **1996** Leslie Matson, *Méiní, The Blasket Nurse:* 'in all probability they would never see their home and people again. On the island there would have been an "American Wake" on the eve of departure …'

Amicable Literary Society/Amicable Society, the [Civic body]. **1820** James Hardiman, *The History of the Town and County of Galway:* 'On the 16th of November, 1791, the Amicable Literary Society was formed in Galway by some of the most respectable individuals of both persuasions, for the purpose of acquiring and disseminating useful information on the important subjects of agriculture, commerce, science, &c.'

Anacreon Moore [nickname]. Thomas Moore (1779-1852) **1895** E. Cobham Brewer, *A Dictionary of Phrase and Fable* (new ed.): '… called "Anacreon Moore" because the character of his poetry resembles that of Anacreon, the Greek poet of love and wine.'

Andytown [nickname]. Andersontown, Belfast, suburb with strong republican orientation. **2000** Deaglán de Bréadún, *Irish Times,* 21 Dec: 'Women from "Andytown" singing on the [Belfast] train; some of the younger passengers took exception, because there was no let-up throughout the journey. I loved it.'

Angels of Monasterevin [<?]. **Irish Brigade** in Spanish Civil War, 1936-9. **1941** Sean O'Faolain, *An Irish Journey:* '"On the contrary," said a young man who had been in the IRA, "what was wrong with the IRA, it made all promotions depend on piety! A Holy Bloody War, that's what they made of it. A Holy Bloody War! Like O'Duffy's

Angels of Monstarevan [*sic*]. Fightin' for Christ in Spain.'

Anglo-Celt [politic.]. Aust. Designation signifying (1) diversity of allegiance. **1987** Patrick O'Farrell, *The Irish in Australia:* 'There were those to whom being Irish was a secondary allegiance. Australian-born E.W. O'Sullivan adopted the term Anglo-Celt to compound his loyalties.' (2) As a replacement for the term 'Anglo-Saxon' to identify Ir. element in Aust. social make-up.

An Lár [Ir. ibid., the middle, centre]. City centre, esp. Dub., first popularised on bus indication scrolls, 1966. **1995** Mícheál Ó Riain, *On the Move:* 'A minor controversy arose over a newly devised phrase, "An Lár", for town and city centres but it rapidly achieved acceptance. Another controversy arose about the scrolls having been manufactured in England …' **2000** Lise Hand, *Sunday Tribune,* 13 Feb: 'At the Brown Thomas International Fashion show in the Point Theatre on Friday night, a variety of famous faces confessed to having left their hearts in the vicinity of An Lar.'

Anna Liffey/Livia [<Ir. *Abhainn na Life;* personific. of Wicklow/Kildare/Dub. river]. **1988** S. Conlin and J. De Courcy (eds), *Anna Liffey: the River of Dublin:* 'The name of the river is Alyffy, Amliffy, Amplifee, Ampnlyffy, Analiffey, Aneliffe, Anilffy, Anylyffe, Annaliffe, Anna Liffey, Annaliffy, Annylyffy, Anneliffi, Anneylyffe, Anne lyffy, Annlyffy. Antlyffie, Auenelith, Aunlyffe, Avanalith, Avanlith, Aveneliffy, Avenelit, Aveenelith, Avenesliz, Avenliffey, Avenlithe, Avenlyf, Aveyn Liffy, Avon Liffey, Liffe, Liffee, Lybinum, Lyffye, River of Dublin, Ruirteach, Ruirtech.' Hence: **2000** John Daly, *Irish Independent,* 3 Jun: 'After a lifetime of arias for

international applause, Bernadette Greevy is presently engaged in her own version of bringing it all back home – the Anna Livia International Opera Festival.' See also **Liffy**

Aonach Tailteann [Ir., assembly of Tailteann, latterly Teltown]. Tailteann Games, revived 1924. **1928** E.J. Gwynn, *Leabhar Tailteann:* 'Aonach Tailteann is a revival in modern form of a very ancient institution. It is perhaps two thousand years since such games were first held at Teltown and at other places …'

Aosdána [Ir. *idem*, poets of the tribe]. Academy of artists (1983-). **2000** Robert O'Byrne, *Irish Times,* 29 Mar: '… for the general public, in so far as Aosdána is known at all, it is seen as the body giving some members a tax-free income. That money is called the "cnuas"…'

Ape, the [nickname]. Thomas Fitzgerald (C13). **1824** Thomas Crofton Croker, *Researches in the South of Ireland:* '… a name bestowed on him in consequence of the tradition that a tame baboon, or ape, at his father's castle in Tralee, had snatched him from his cradle …'

Apostle of Temperance Fr Theobald Mathew (1790-1856). Advocate of total abstinence from alcohol. **1972** Diarmaid Ó Muirithe, *A Seat Behind the Coachman:* 'Many of the travellers … considered whiskey public enemy number one. The Reverend Theobald Matthew, the Apostle of Temperance, became therefore, in their eyes, a man even greater than O'Connell – a virtual miracle worker.'

Argue and Phibbs [business name, Teeling St., Sligo]. **1981** Adrian MacLoughlin, *Streets of Ireland:* 'Look to the left of this and see the name of a firm of solicitors arched in gold letters on a pane, Argue and Phibbs. Their successors in the firm have different names, but nobody would attempt to erase a title like that.'

Arlo [<Ir. *Eatharlaí*, Aherlow]. **1594** Edmund Spenser, *Two Cantos of Mutabilite:* 'That was, to weet, upon the highest heights/Of Arlo-hill (who knows not Arlo-hill?)/That is the highest head in all men's sights …' **1911** P.W. Joyce, *The Wonders of Ireland:* 'The mountain mass that culminates in Galtymore is Arlo-hill, on which the meeting of the gods was held; but the name Arlo was applied to the hill only by Spenser himself, who borrowed it from the adjacent valley [Glen of Aherlow] …'

Army Comrades' Association Forerunner of **Blueshirt** movement. **1967** T. Desmond Williams, 'De Valera in Power', in Francis Mac Manus (ed.), *The Years of the Great Test 1926-39:* '[General] O'Duffy joined the pre-existing Army Comrades' Association almost immediately. This group had been founded in 1931-2 for the purpose of maintaining free speech on the streets against IRA extremists. He was accepted as their leader on July 20th [1933].'

Aschcled [<Ir. *Átha Cliath*, Dublin]. **1847** Joseph Haydn, *Dictionary of Dates* (4th ed.): 'DUBLIN. This city, anciently called Aschcled, built A.D. 140.'

Asher's Irish Potatoes [brandname]. Sweets. **2000** Quentin Fottrell, *Irish Times,* 14 Oct: 'Asher's Irish Potatoes, another eCandy [Marketplace] offering, are unlikely to make it big here. Described as "a soft coconut confection, delightfully sweetened and rolled in cinnamon", they sound delicious, nevertheless. They also illustrate the cultural significance of sweets.'

Assembly's College [nickname]. Presbyterian College, Belfast. **1921** D.J. Owen, *History of Belfast:* 'The **Magee** College was eventually built at Londonderry, and the Presbyterian General Assembly raised funds for a Divinity College of their own in Belfast, this latter, under the name of "The Assembly's College", being formally opened ... four years after the inauguration of the Queen's College [1849].'

Assembs, the [nickname]. Meeting room/theatre/cinema, Cork. **1970** Pádraig Mac Póilín, *Cork Holly Bough:* 'a famous Cork cinema of yesteryear, the Assembly Rooms – or as it was in the vernacular, the "Assembs".'

Athens of Ireland [nickname]. (1) Belfast. **1921** D.J. Owen, *History of Belfast:* '... in the eighteenth century the intellectual activities of the town, and not its commercialism, earned for it the name of the "Athens of Ireland", or the **"Northern Athens"**, a term which, if not actually coined by John Lawless, the editor of "The Irishman", was much used by him, and must have originated in his time.' See also **Athens of the North**. (2) Cork city. **1975** Davis & Mary Coakley, *Wit and Wine:* 'At this period [early C19] Cork had so many literary men that the city became known as "the Athens of Ireland".'

Athens of the North [nickname]. Belfast. **2000** Pól Ó Muirí, *Irish Times,* 14 Jun: 'After 30 years of violence it is hard to credit that Belfast was once known as the Athens of the North ...' See also **Athens of Ireland**; **Northern Athens**

Athlone [Áth Luain, town]. Hence [media]. Radio transmitter. **1936** A.Z., *Irish Radio News,* 24 Oct: 'A few evenings ago, while tuned to the Dublin transmitter, the Announcer informed me, in common, no doubt, with thousands of other listeners, that I was listening to "Radio Ata Luain [*sic*]". Now this, I maintain, was a very silly thing for him to do, because I knew that it wasn't the Athlone transmitter to which I was listening ... It does not seem to be appreciated that the Athlone transmitter, with all its power and with all its up-to-dateness, is nothing more than a relay station.'

Atmospheric Road [Dalkey, Co Bhaile Átha Cliath/Dublin, <Kingstown (Dun Laoghaire)-Dalkey Atmospheric Railway (1844-54) worked by compressed air]. **1981** K.A. Murray, *Ireland's First Railway:* 'Nobody thought of preserving any memorial of the notable Irish railway experiment. At present, only the slightest indications of the Atmospheric are to be discovered along its route.'

Atty Hayes [*fl.* C18]. Hence: **as old as Atty Hayes's goat** [catchphrase]. Very old. **1966** *Irish Times*, 6 May: 'To be as old as Atty Hayes's goat is still, in Cork, an indication of great antiquity and recalls an animal beloved of the father of Sir Henry Brown Hayes, who built Vernon Mount [Corraghconway, near Douglas] in 1780.'

Aubrian [river; lit.] **1590/6** Edmund Spenser, *The Faerie Queene:* 'There was the **Liffy** rolling down the lea;/The sandy Slane, the stony Aubrian ...' **1911** P.W. Joyce, *The Wonders of Ireland:* 'Although I have made a very diligent search in every available direction, I have failed to discover the river Spenser meant by "The stony Aubrian", the only one in his whole catalogue that remains unidentified ... From the place it occupies in the catalogue ... it may be inferred that it is somewhere in South Munster, and that it is itself a considerable river.'

Auld Sod/Ould Sod [affectionate/ derog.] Ireland. **2000** Cole Moreton, *Independent on Sunday* (London), 19 Mar: 'The old pattern – emigrants returning to the Auld Sod to mark Paddy's Day – was now reversed. "Ireland is so rich now that we come over here [New York] to celebrate properly", said Myles ...' **1999** Lavinia Greacen, *J.G. Farrell:* '"I find I'm very dissatisfied with you," he had remarked at the start of a trip to Killarney ... and he continued to needle without let-up, sneering, "Oh God, the ould sod! Let's make a postcard of it," if she made the mistake of admiring a view.'

Auliana Dublin. **1847** Joseph Haydn, *Dictionary of Dates* (4th ed.): 'It obtained its present name from Alpinus, a lord or chief among the Irish, whose daughter,

Auliana, having been drowned at the ford where now the Whitworth-bridge is built, he changed the name to Auliana ...'

Auxies [nickname]. Auxiliary division of Royal Ir. Constabulary, recruited from Brit. ex-army officers. **1975** Séamus de Burca, *Dublin Historical Record,* Mar: 'Peadar [Kearney] was ordered to get up and dress. The Auxie remarked on the fresh wound on his cheek and sneered at the terse explanation of how he came by it.'

Awbeg see **Mulla**

Awniduff [river; lit.]. **1590/96** Edmund Spenser, *The Faerie Queene:* 'Swift Awniduff which of the English man/Is cal'de Blackwater ...' **1911** P.W. Joyce, *The Wonders of Ireland:* '[it] has been wrongly set down as the Munster Blackwater, whereas it is really the northern Blackwater, flowing between the counties of Armagh and Derry, and falling into the south-west corner of Lough Neagh ...'

B

Baby Power [<John Power & Sons, whiskey distillers; nickname]. Popular small bottle of Power's Gold Label whiskey. **1989** Hugh Leonard, *Out After Dark:* 'I peered behind one of the shelves [of Parsons bookshop] and was in time to see him [Patrick Kavanagh] draining a Baby Power as fast as it would empty.'

BAC [acronym, <Baile Átha Cliath]. Dublin, esp. Dub. government in IRA perception. **1998** Fergus Finlay, *Snakes and Ladders:* 'There were things about the letter I didn't understand. What did BAC mean, for instance? It was explained to me that BAC was short for Baile Átha Cliath, and was the Provo's way of referring to the Irish government.'

Back Lane parliament [nickname]. Catholic convention (1792) formed to seek abolition of remaining penal laws. **1999** *History Ireland,* Spring: 'The original Convention, dubbed the "Back Lane Parliament" by its detractors, met in the same place [Tailors' Hall, Dub.] on 3-6 December 1792, to organise the Catholics of the country ...'

Bagmen [<Ir. *Fir Bolg,* bag men; derog.]. Poss. representing pre-Goidelic population of Ire., who during their enslavement in Thrace were made to carry bags of earth from fertile valleys. Hence **1936** Oliver St John Gogarty, *As I was going down Sackville Street:* '"The Bagmen are up. Don't let the little Firbolgs get you on your way home. The Bagmen broke out before in this country, but we always put them back in their places, and we'll have to do it again".'

Bailegangáire [Ir. *baile gan gáire,* town without a laugh; lit.]. Title of play by Tom Murphy. **1987** Fintan O'Toole, review in *The Irish Review* (Belfast), No 2: 'In *Bailegangáire* ... the overall shape of the play is that of a particular body of Irish folklore – stories about the origin of the names of individuals and of places.'

Balbriggan [Baile Brigín, Co. Átha Cliath/Dublin; but see p.17]. Generic term for hosiery first manufactured 1780 by Smyth & Co. (C19). **1998** Bruce Arnold, *Jack Yeats:* 'He [Yeats] chose Morley's pure wool under-wear for winter, but sea island singlets in summer; he wore Callaghan's Wool Pants, and also "Balbriggan Longpants"...'

Ballroom of Romance [short story title, <William Trevor, *The Distant Past*]. Hence any rural dance-hall of the 1950s-60s. **2000** Dick Hogan, *Irish Times,* 11 Jul: 'The disused dance hall in Waterville, Co. Kerry, once a ballroom of romance, has metamorphosed into the Ballroom of Imagination and Desire ...'

Ballydung [media]. Fictitious midland village. **2000** Catherine Foley, *Irish Times,* 4 Nov: 'Enigmatic TV presenters Podge and Rodge are happy to answer personal questions at their inaugural press conference ... The two brothers from Ballydung in the midlands, speaking over a specially-constructed counter, deny reports that they plan to move to Hollywood in the US ...'

Ballygobackwards Epitome of rural backwater from urban perspective. **1997** John Boland, *Irish Times,* 7 Jun: 'Alas, the asking price of £16,000 was a thousand more than I could come up with at the time. Nowadays you wouldn't get a lean-to in Ballygobackwards for that price.'

Ballyhoo Village near Screen, Co. Loch Garman/Wexford. Hence (?) [*idem*] US sl: colourful or raucous advertising/publicity; cf. Cuban sl. *darse balijú*, give oneself importance.

Ballyhooly [Baile Átha Ubhla]. Village near Fermoy, Co. Chorcaí/Cork, formerly notorious for faction fights. (1, derog.) Epitome of rural backwater from urban perspective. **1976** Edna O'Brien, *Mother Ireland:* 'One [man] said that he hoped I was not called **Sheila** or Oona or Moura or anything Ballyhooly like that.' (2, derog.) Bad trouble.

Ballymagash [derog.]. Fictitious village, created by RTÉ TV series *Hall's Pictorial Weekly*, 1970s, satirising rural life. **1998** Eamon Dillon, *Leinster Leader* (Naas), 19 Feb: "We are here to do business for the town [Newbridge], not for two individuals to clash", he said. "Unless sanity comes now I won't sit here. This has gone worse than Ballymagash", he exclaimed.' **2000** Nell McCafferty, *Sunday Tribune,* 9 Jan: 'There is nothing for it, if you live in Ballymagash, but window-shop via the Irish internet, then get on that awful train to Dublin … Retail therapy, my eye.' Hence: **1994** K.S. Daly, *Ireland, an Encyclopaedia for the Bewildered:* 'Also a slang word for the drug hashish.'

Ballymagraw [media]. Fictitious village. As featured in NI radio programme. **1936** *Irish Radio News*, 17 Oct: 'Monday October 19. 6.20 "The Ballymagraw Gazette" (Second Edition). An Ulster Review. Book by Ruddick Millar, with Sketches by Harry S. Gibson and Music by Dudley Hare.'

Ballymena [An Baile Meánach, Co. Aontroma/Antrim; town]. Hence: **Ballymena anthem** [<pun on 'mean'].

1981 John Pepper, *John Pepper's Ulster-English Dictionary:* 'ironic Co. Antrim description of "What's in it for me?" "Ast him to lenn ye a haun [hand] and you'll soon hear him at the Ballymena anthem".'

Baltinglass [Bealach Conglais, Co. Chill Mhantáin/Wicklow; town]. Hence **Battle of Baltinglass** [nickname]. Confrontation occasioned by dispute over appointment of postmistress (1950). **2000** Dermot Bolger, *Irish Times*, 1 Jul: 'Nobody, for example, has been moved to compose a ballad about Justice Hugh O'Flaherty's appointment to match the immortal lines from *The Battle of Baltinglass:* "There were brenguns and Sten-guns and whippet tanks galore/As the battle raged up and down from pub to gen'ral store".'

Baluba [<Katangan tribe, former Belgian Congo]. Term of generalised contempt, <Ir army service there with the UN (1960)]. **1984** Fergal Tobin, *The Best of Decades:* 'The word "Baluba" passed into Irish colloquial speech as a synonym for barbarism, savagery, or plain oafishness.'

Banagher [Beannchar, Co. Uíbh Fháilí/Offaly, town; also **Banagher Glen**, Roe Valley, Co. Dhoire/Derry]. Hence [catchphrase] **that beats/bangs Banagher** Said of something exceeding the norm. **1895** E. Cobham Brewer, *A Dictionary of Phrase and Fable* (new ed.): 'Wonderfully inconsistent and absurd − exceedingly ridiculous. Banagher is a town in Ireland, on the Shannon, in King's County … When a member [of parliament] spoke of a family borough where every voter was a man employed by the lord, it was not unusual to reply, "Well, that beats Banagher".' **1987** Ruth Delaney, *By*

Shannon Shores: 'Before leaving Banagher I will risk the anger of its people by disputing that the expression "that bates Banagher" is associated with this place. Oswell Blakeston in his exploration of Ulster *Thank You Now* says that the expression "That bates Banagher and Banagher bates the band" related to the village of Banagher, near Dungiven, in Co. Londonderry ... Beneath the tomb of one of the O'Heney family in Banagher Old Church can be found sand which, according to legend, has magic properties. If it is thrown at you by a member of the O'Heney family it "beats the band", bringing you good fortune ...'

BANANA [acronym]. **1999** Liam Reid, *Sunday Tribune,* 30 May: 'Nearly 20 years ago, Bob Geldof ... caused uproar when he christened Ireland a "Banana Republic" ... Now the term BANANA has taken on a different meaning – Build Absolutely Nothing Anywhere Near Anything.'

Bandit Country [nickname, derog.]. South Armagh in the perception of Brit. govt. and army (1975-). **1999** Merlyn Rees, NI Sec., quoted in Toby Harnden, *'Bandit Country':* 'It was a conscious decision to use that term, to try and show people who knew nothing about it the nature of it, that South Armagh was different. When I would go down there to Crossmaglen, I'd get out of the helicopter on a GAA field and run to the police station, which was heavily fortified. For my money, that's bandit country.'

Bang Bang [nickname]. Tommy Dudley, (d.1981) Dub. street character. **1981** *Irish Independent,* 12 Jan: 'He was an institution in Dublin during his lifetime. He carried a huge jail key with

him around the city, mockingly pointing it at strangers and shouting "Bang Bang".'

Banks, de/the [abbrev.]. 'The Banks of My Own Lovely Lee' (words & music, J.C.S Hanahan), unofficial Cork anthem. Hence [*idem*] The Lee/Cork city. **1995** Arthur McAdoo, *Cork Holly Bough:* 'if I caught an early train, I was home by the "Banks" in the early hours of the following morning.'

Banner County/Banner, The [nickname, <support displayed at **monster meeting** (1828) for nomination of Daniel O'Connell as parliamentary candidate]. Co. Clare, esp. its representative GAA teams. **2000** Eamon Falvey, *RTE News,* 21 Jun: 'The people of Clare have been absorbing the news that Jer Loughnane is no longer boss of The Banner.'

Baoithín [typog.]. Typeface adapted (1932) for printing modern Irish from Victor Hammer's *Hammerschrift.* **1992** Colm Ó Lochlainn, quoted in Dermot McGuinne, *Irish Type Design:* '...I called the type Baoithín, for **Colm Cille's** last written words were "Reliqua scribat Baitenus". Let Baoithín (his disciple at Iona) write the rest, just as I had designed "the rest" for Victor Hammer.'

Barlow [<John Barlow, C19 Dublin printer; typog.]. Typeface. **1992** Dermot McGuinne, *Irish Type Design:* '... the **Parker** type, due to its size and proportions, was a "paper hungry" face. Partly for this reason, it lost its appeal for text use. This prompted the development of a distinctly different typeface generally referred to as the Barlow type, named after the printer first to use this unusual face. This fount was prepared in 1808 ...'

Barracka [<Barrack (street name) + endearment suffix; Cork]. Band. **1971** Seán Beecher, *The Story of Cork:* 'The "Barracka" competed in London for the championship of the "British" Isles and were successful. The members were informed that Queen Victoria would present the trophy but it was expected that the band should play the British National Anthem. The band refused ...'

Bartell D'Arcy [lit.]. Character in James Joyce's works based on tenor Barton McGuckin, who also features under his real name. **1914** James Joyce, *Dubliners,* 'The Dead': '"O", exclaimed Mary Jane. "It's Bartell D'Arcy singing, and he wouldn't sing all the night. O, I'll get him to sing a song before he goes.' **1952** 'Quidnunc', *Irish Times,* 9 Jan: 'A distinguished Galway savant goes a little farther towards clearing the meaning of the passage quoted from "Ulysses." "Ah, what McGuckin", is not an expression of appreciation, rather the reverse! He writes: "It is clear that one of the company of drinkers in the Ormond Hotel has interjected: 'What about McGuckin?' implying that McGuckin was not a patch on Joe Maas".'

Bass [brandname]. Imported Brit. beer stigmatised by nationalists as symptomatic of economic imperialism. **1935** *Republican Congress,* 29 Jun: 'Instead of raising the economic war into an assertion of the nation's sovereignty, I.R.A. leaders tried to develop it into a squabble over Bass bottles in public houses.' Subsequently identified as preferred beverage of **Bertie Ahern**, **Taoiseach** (1997-). **1999** *Sunday Tribune,* 5 Dec: 'Ireland's most famous Bass drinker, Bertie Ahern, is known to abstain from drink for the month of November, so Bass sent a giant can to Leinster House to remind him that he only had a few hours left until he could again enjoy a tipple.'

Batchelor's [brandname]. Canned food manufacturers, Dublin. Hence, by attraction, **Batchelors** (*sic*) **Walk** Dublin, etc. **1930** *Irish Times,* 2 May: '... though there may be many dames in Dame street, Batchelor's Walk has no monopoly any more than Lad lane or Lady lane.' **1989** John Gleeson, *The Book of Irish Lists and Trivia:* 'Chart toppers, Ireland's only singles to make No. 1 in Britain ... 2. The Batchelors with *DIANE* ...' See also **Beany and Barney**

Beany and Barney [advt.] Cartoon characters employed to advertise **Batchelor's** beans. **1998** Fiona Looney, *Sunday Tribune,* 7 Jun: '...edibles like pesto and pancetta are filling our presses and tins of pulses that have not been scrutinised first by Barney and Beany are hanging around our larders.' **2001** Brian Cronin and Dermot Quinn, in Derek Garvey (ed.), *A Century of Irish Ads:* 'They started out life as a couple of "stick" characters on the tin until Brian Cronin ... recognised the possibilities of exploiting them. A national press campaign got under way to find catch names for the characters (Brian, himself, had come up with the names Beany and Barney before the competition was launched!).'

Bear and Ragged Staff, the [hostelry, Celbridge, Co. Chill Dara/Kildare]. **1999** Michele Guinness, *The Guinness Spirit:* '... when the old Archbishop of Cashel died in 1752 he left £100 to his faithful retainer, Richard Guinness, whose delicious home-made black brew had made the old ecclesiastic a favourite host with the local gentry. Richard became the proprietor of the Bear and

Ragged Staff in Celbridge and established its reputation as a popular coaching stop.'

Beaten Docket, the [Belfast]. Pub. **1997** Ciaran Carson, *The Star Factory:* 'A "beaten docket" is Belfast parlance for a betting-slip that has passed its sell-by date; so it is appropriate that a public house not two doors away from a book-maker's (Crown Turf Accountants) should be so called.'

Beaufort Scale [<Francis Beaufort, b. Navan, Co. na Mí/Meath (1774)]. Meterological measure. **1999** Rachael Furmston, in W.J. McCormack (ed.), *The Blackwell Companion to Modern Irish Culture:* 'He was appointed hydrographer of the Admiralty in 1829, a post he held for 26 years. He is probably best remembered for his table for estimating the force of wind at sea – the Beaufort Scale.'

Beehive, the [Falls Road., Belfast]. Pub. **1987** Marcus Patton, *Belfast, an Illustrated Yearbook:* 'Some time before 1870 one William Willis managed a hostelry called the Beehive Tavern on this site, but it was not until Hugh McKeown took over the business about 1887 that the present building was erected …'

Bel Éire [< Fr. *Bel Air,* cf. *gens de bel air,* fashionable people]. Dub. residential area. **1997** *Irish Times,* 31 Oct: 'Dún Laoghaire Rathdown Co. Council has moved to restrict development at so-called "Bel Éire", the fashionable coastal strip around Killiney and Dalkey, in south Co. Dublin'.

Belfast [Béal Feirste, city]. **1997** Ciaran Carson, *The Star Factory:* 'The most satisfactory translation of Belfast, according to Deirdre Flanagan [see Bibliog.] is "approach to the ford"… She then draws our attention to numerous sources which corroborate her assertion that the name of Belfast derives from the ford or sand-bank in the River Lagan. *En route,* she quotes some interesting sixteenth-century mutations: "Belferside, Bealefarst … Belfarst, Kellefarst (*sic*), Bellfarste, Bellfaste, Belfaste, Belferst, Belfirst, Belfyrst, Belfarst, Befersyth, Besertt, Belfast"…'
Hence (1) [*idem*]. [milit.]. **(HMS) Belfast** Brit. cruiser (1936-). **1971** Oliver M. Smith, *HMS Belfast:* 'The *Belfast* was to be built by Harland and Wolff in the capital of Northern Ireland … The keel of the *Belfast* was laid on Thursday, December 10th 1936, the memorable day that King Edward VIII … gave up his throne and prepared to leave England.' (2) [*idem*]. [aviation]. Heavylift aircraft. **2000** *Irish Air Letter,* Dec: Transmeridian had been pursuing the acquisition of a number of ex-RAF Short Belfasts to complement the CL-44-O *Guppy,* to carry outside cargo, and TAC Heavylift was formed as a separate subsidiary …' (3) [colloq.] **Belfast Confetti** Bricks, etc. used as ammunition in sectarian riots. **1997** Ciaran Carson, *The Star Factory:* 'The hicker [half-brick] is one ingredient of Belfast Confetti, which originally referred to a not-so-welcome shower of shipyard-workers' bolts and rivets and later, by extension, to any *ad hoc* compendium of hand-launched missiles …' See **Dockyard Confetti**.

Bell's Inequalities [<John Bell (1928-90). **2000** William Reville, *Irish Times,* 14 Dec: 'Born in Belfast … He developed a set of equations called Bell's Inequalities that are of fundamental importance in quantum physics.'

bertieahern.com [website]. **2000** Catherine Cleary, *Sunday Tribune,* 26

Mar: 'Some of Ireland's top politicians and celebrities, including the **Taoiseach**, have had their names purchased by Internet users who have registered them as websites. A spokesman for Bertie Ahern yesterday condemned the bertieahern.com homepage which displays lurid pornographic photographs.' See also **Teflon Taoiseach**.

Bertie Bowl see **eircom**

Bessbrook see **Richardson**

Bessy Bell & Mary Gray [<? Walter Scott, *Minstrelsy of the Scottish Border* (1802)]. Hills on each side of A5 near Newtownstewart, Co. Thír Eoghain/ Tyrone. **1999** Robert Graham, *The Irish Journals of Robert Graham of Redgorton, 1835-1838:* 'I can get no authentic information as to the origin of these names tho' they all consider them to have taken their names from some traditional story similar in its principal feature to the tradition we have in the parish of Methven [Scot.]. One man who gave me most detail had the rashness to say that Mary Gray was buried at Newton Stewart [*sic*], but I did not get this confirmed by any body there.'

Bian see **Bianconi**

Bianconi, Charles (1786-1875) Transport entrepreneur. Hence (1) **Bian** Long car drawn by four horses introduced by him in 1815. **1962** M. O'C Bianconi & S.J. Watson, *Bianconi, King of the Irish Roads:* 'It proved too difficult for the country people to say "Bianconi cars", so they simply called them "Bians" ... ' (2) [tradename] **Bistro Bianconi**. Italian restaurant, Sligo. (3) **Bryan Coony** [anglicisation]. **1954** Constantia Maxwell, *The Stranger in Ireland:* '... he moved again, this time to

Clonmel, and here he took a corner house in what was then Johnson Street, becoming known as "Bryan Coony", or "Bryan of the Corner".' See also **King of the Roads**.

BIC [acronym]. Political institution. **1999** Deaglán de Bréadún, *Irish Times,* 18 Dec: 'The British-Irish Council is known as "BIC" for short, which makes it sound like a particular make of ball-point pen, but the original title, "Council of the Isles", was rejected as too unionist ... Mr Trimble was skating on thin ice yesterday when ... he referred to the BIC members as being part of the "British Isles" ... A press release from the British Cabinet Office was more tactful, merely referring to the BIC as a gathering of representatives of "all the islands".'

Bickerstaffe, Isaac [?prop. name & pseudonym]. **1973** T.J. Walsh, *Opera in Dublin 1705-1797:* 'The libretto [for *Thomas and Sally*] is the earliest extant work by the well known Irish dramatist, Isaac Bickerstaffe [b.1735] ... That his name – Isaac Bickerstaffe – was assumed cannot be entirely outruled for the same name had earlier been used as a pseudonym both by Sir Richard Steele and Dean Swift.'

Biddy see **Brigid**

Biddy Early White witch, Co. An Chláir/Clare (d.1874). Hence [*idem*]. Pub/ brewery. **2000** Breda Shannon, *Ireland of the Welcomes,* 'A Special Brew': 'In 1995, a publican called Peadar Garvey equipped his thriving business with a small brewery. He called it "Biddy Early's", in memory of that county's infamous nineteenth-century witch, who was reputed to have a magic bottle that could either cause or cure many ills.'

Bidet Mulligan see **Mrs Mulligan**

Big Beggarman [nickname]. Daniel O'Connell, politician & statesman (1775-1847). **1921** D.J. Owen, *History of Belfast:* 'A still larger body of people traversed the town shouting and yelling ... The shibboleths of the night [of 19 Jan 1841] among the mob were "To hell with the Pope", "To hell with the Big Beggarman (O'Connell) and his tail", "Down with rebellious Repeal".' See also **Liberator, the**.

Big Bertha [< large WW1 howitzer; agric.]. **1994** K.S. Daly, *Ireland, an Encyclopaedia for the Bewildered:* 'Until the end of 1993 when she died, the oldest cow in the world, at 49 years, was Big Bertha who lived on the farm of Jerome O'Leary near Kenmare in Co. Kerry.'

Big Fella/Fellow, the [nickname]. Michael Collins (1890-1922) revolutionary leader & politician. **1990** Tim Pat Coogan, *Michael Collins:* 'women of his own class found him "cheeky", his "Big Fellow" sobriquet indicating swollen-headedness as much as height, just under six feet.' Hence: [*idem;* nickname]. Martynside Type A Mk 2, first aircraft of Irish Air Corps (1922). **Nd(1980s)** Liam M. Skinner and Tom Cranitch, *Ireland and World Aviation:* 'Flown to Croydon it was held in readiness lest the Anglo-Irish Treaty negotiations broke down and a fast getaway to Ireland or France was necessary. General Michael Collins who was amongst the delegation had at that time the princely sum of £10,000 on his head.'

Big Noise [nickname]. James Larkin, labour leader and revolutionary (1876-1947). **1921-3** Anon. (?Ir. Transport & General Workers' Union), leaflet: 'Is Larkin a Liar? Here is his Birth Certificate ... Larkin swore in Court that he was born in Ireland. Ask "Big Noise" which is true.'

Billie [nickname]. **1911** Wills' cigarette card series, *Regimental Pets:* '"Billie", a Brindled Bull-dog, is pet of the Royal Irish Rifles. He wears two medals for the war in South Africa. He is at present in disgrace, having recently bitten a boy, and has to submit to the indignity of a muzzle.'

Billy Boys [nickname, <King William III of Eng., pop. **King Billy**]. Members of Orange Order and similar Loyalist orgs. **1997** Susan McKay, *Sunday Tribune,* 9 Feb: 'There was no ignoring them last night. "We are, we are, we are the Billy Boys", they roared, "Up to our necks in **Fenian** blood".'

Billy in the Bowl [nickname]. C19 Dub. street character. **1913** James Collins, *Life in Old Dublin:* 'This character used to ply his calling between the quiet streets of Stoneybatter and the Green Lanes of Grangegorman. He was nicknamed "Billy in the Bowl", having been introduced into the world with only a head, body and arms. When he grew up he conveyed himself along in a large bowl fortified by iron, in which he was embedded.'

Bird Flanagan, The [nickname]. Early C20 Dub. eccentric. **1974** Éamonn Mac Thomáis, *Me Jewel and Darlin' Dublin:* '"The Bird Flanagan" got his name from the time he went to a fancy dress ball dressed as a bird. When he didn't win a prize, he went up onto the stage where the judge sat, laid an egg, and threw it at the judge.'

Bish, the [nickname]. St Joseph's College, Galway. **1998** James Lydon,

Irish Times, 24 Sep: 'You know, I think there were people who wouldn't know what school you were referring to if you said St Joseph's – it was "The Bish" and was run by the Patrician Brothers.'

Black and Tans/Tans [nickname, <hounds of a Co. Limerick hunt; owing to their black/khaki uniforms]. Former Brit. army troops reinforcing the Royal Irish Constabulary in War of Independence (1920). **1922** Anon., *Tales of the RIC* [Royal Irish Constabulary]: 'The magic words "Black and Tan" have the same effect on an Irish crowd as the name of Cromwell during a previous period of Irish history …' Hence **1994** K.S. Daly, *Ireland, an Encyclopaedia for the Bewildered:* 'Nowadays the name given to an alcoholic drink combining **Guinness** stout and Smithwicks ale.' See also **Blackthorn**

Black Bush [<Bushmills (Distillery), Co. Aontroma/Antrim; brandname]. Whiskey. **1999** Jim Dunne, *Irish Times,* 26 Jul: 'Irish Distillers has ordered an associate company in Britain to withdraw "an extremely inappropriate" promotion for Black Bush whiskey. A spokesman for Irish Distillers said the promotion drew an unacceptable connection between the whiskey's brand name and pubic hair.'

Blackfeet [nickname]. Members of the **Ribbonmen** opposed to the Catholic priesthood.

Black Man/Blacks [<Orange organisation (1797)]. Member of Imperial Grand Black Chapter of the British Commonwealth. **1966** Robert Harbinson, *No Surrender:* 'To us Belfast boys, the Black men we looked for in the [12 July] procession were not negroes, but the most respected holders

of the highest rank within the hierarchy of the Order. Purple men followed them in precedence …' **1999** Ferghal McGarry, *Irish Politics and the Spanish Civil War:* 'The meetings of the 'Blacks' … during their annual marches on the last weekend of August 1936 provide an interesting sample of unionist response to Spain. (2) **Black Man, the** [nickname, <colour of statue]. Frederick Richard, Earl of Belfast. **1983** J.C. Beckett *et al.*, *Belfast, the Making of the City:* 'His death of scarlatina at Naples in 1853 was a dreadful blow to his father. In Belfast a statue – the original "Black Man" – was erected to him in College Square East, in front of the Academical Institution.' Hence **Black North** N. Ire. as perceived by Southern Catholics. **2000** Róisín Ingle, *Irish Times,* 27 Dec: 'While known to some cynical southerners as the capital of the Black North, Belfast in 2000 offered proof that Dublin isn't the only city that can be heaven.'

Black Oath, the [nickname]. Political strategem (1630s). **1921** D.J. Owen, *History of Belfast,* '… insult was added to injury when he [Lord Strafford] intimated his intention to require all the Scots in Ulster to take what became known as the "Black Oath", which involved their swearing that they would yield fidelity and obedience to the King, and that they disapproved of the rebellion which had taken place in Scotland.'

Blacks see **Black Man**

Black Santa [nickname]. Jack Shearer, Dean of Belfast (d.2001). **2001** Monika Unsworth, *Irish Times,* 15 Jan: 'The dean, who was known throughout the North for his tireless charity work, in particular his annual pre-Christmas sitouts in front of the city's St Anne's

Cathedral as "Black Santa", had been planning to retire in May.'

Blacksmith of Ballinalee, the [nickname]. Seán MacEoin, soldier (1893-1973). **1988** Henry Boylan, *A Dictionary of Irish Biography* (2nd ed.): Became known as "The Blacksmith of Balinalee" after holding the village of Ballinalee, Co. Longford against superior Brit. forces in February 1921.' **2001** Ella Shanahan, *Irish Times*, 26 Jan: 'Born in Ballinalee in Co. Longford ("my father was a friend of 'the Blacksmith' and a farmer"), Mr [John] Hourican is the second of 13 children.'

Blacksmith's money [numismatics]. **1979** Patrick Finn, *Irish Coin Values:* 'It is now thought that this coinage was struck by Royalists at Kilkenny in 1649, but it has been attributed previously to the Confederated Catholics. It is so-called because of its very crude style ...'

Blackthorn [cocktail, USA]. **2000** Jim DeRogatis, *Let It Blurt:* '... Peter Myers, non-chagrined as always, calmly asked what he was having. "I'm in a black mood," Lester [Bangs] announced with a hint of menace. "I mean a really black mood. What should I have?" ... He proceeded to run through the gamut of every black elixir that he and Myers could name, including shots of Johnnie Walker Black Label, **Black and Tan**, a Blackthorn (Irish whiskey, dry vermouth, Pernod and bitters) ...'

Black Tom [nickname, <his ungracious ways and 'black looks']. Thomas Butler, 10th Earl of Ormond, Lord Deputy of Ireland, succeeded his father 28 Oct 1546. **1890** Emily Lawless, *With Essex in Ireland:* 'He being very stately in apparel, and erect in port ... yet with a dark, dour, and menacing look upon his face, so that all who met his gaze seemed to quake before the same.'

Black Velvet [trade name]. **Guinness** and Champagne cocktail, created in Brooks's Club, London (1861). **1999** Michele Guinness, *The Guinness Spirit:* '... on the day that Prince Albert, the Prince Consort died, the wine steward announced with due solemnity that even the champagne would be in mourning, and added a touch of Guinness.'

Black 47 [<1847, worst year of Great Famine]. **1972** Diarmaid Ó Muirithe, *A Seat behind the Coachman:* 'William Bennett spent six weeks touring the country when the famine was at its worst. This is his account of Belmullet, county Mayo, written in March of the year the people afterwards called "Black 47" ...'

Blarney [An Bhlarna, Co. Chorcaí/ Cork]. Hence (1) [<Blarney Castle]. Loquacious eloquence. **1948** *Cork Examiner,* 21 Sept: 'History has it that the word "blarney" ... originated when one of the Carthy clan found one thousand and one excuses for not surrendering his castle to Queen Elizabeth [of Eng.]'s troops, Elizabeth finally exclaiming impatiently that she had had enough of Blarney.' (2) **Blarney Stone** Stone in castle wall which, when kissed, is said to convey such eloquence. Hence [*idem*]. Chain of new York pubs.

Blayney's Bloodhounds [nickname]. **1895** E. Cobham Brewer, *Dictionary of Phrase and Fable* (new ed.): 'The old 89th Foot; so called because of their unerring certainty, and untiring perseverance in hunting down the Irish rebels in 1798, when the corps was commanded by Lord Blayney.'

Blind Billy [nickname]. C19 Limerick hangman. Hence: **Blind Billy's bargain**. Illusory bargain. **1910** P.W. Joyce, *English as We Speak it in Ireland:* '… on one particular occasion he flatly refused to do his work unless he got £50 down on the nail: so the high sheriff had to agree and the hangman put the money in his pocket. When all was over the sheriff refused point-blank to send the usual escort without a fee of £50 down …'

Bloody O'Reilly [nickname]. Alexander O'Reilly (1722-1794). Irishman in the service of Spain. **2000** Susan Wilkinson, *Irish Times,* 7 Jul: 'Although he is known in New Orleans, where he arrived in 1769 to quell a revolt against the then governor, Antonio de Ulloa, following the Spanish annexation of Louisana, as "Bloody O'Reilly", many of his policies as governor of Louisiana were decidedly liberal for the times.' Hence: **Calle O'Reilly**, Havana, Cuba. **2000** R. Buckley, *Irish Times,* 29 May: 'In the middle of old Havana there is a street named "Calle O'Reilly". A plaque on the wall in Spanish, Gaelic and English says "two island nations on the same sea of hope and struggle, Cuba and Ireland".'

Bloody Sunday [nickname]. (1) Dub., 31 Aug. 1913. <Rioting and casualties after meeting during Lockout. **2000** Dermot Keogh, *Irish Times,* 18 Nov: '[James] Larkin, of course, continues to harangue the masses as a bronze statue in O'Connell Street − once the scene of the infamous baton-charge that followed the labour leader's appearance on the balcony of a hotel almost facing the General Post Office on "Bloody Sunday" 1913. (2) Dub., 21 Nov 1920. 14 Brit. secret service agents killed by an IRA unit, subseq. avenged by Brit. milit. firing on GAA crowd in Croke

Park. [see **Croker**]. **1990** Tim Pat Coogan, *Michael Collins:* 'The account given to the [Brit.] Cabinet of the events of Bloody Sunday … makes one wonder how much the Government was kept informed by the military of what was really happening in Ireland.' (3) **Derry**, 30 Jan 1972. 13 civil rights demonstrators killed by Brit. troops. **1984** Bruce Arnold, *What Kind of Country:* 'Events such as Bloody Sunday, and the **H-Block** hunger strikes, can raise ancient animosities and provoke apparent hatreds …'

Bloom, Leopold [lit.]. Central character in James Joyce's novel *Ulysses* (1922). Hence **Bloomophile**; **Bloomsday** 16 June, day on which (1904) the action of the novel was set, celebrated in Dub. since c1954. **2000** Katie Donovan, *Irish Times,* 16 Jun: 'Bloomophiles take note: today's the day for the straw boater, the battered copy of *Ulysses* (to show everyone how many times you've read it) and indulging your passion for all things Joycean.' **2000** Miriam Lord, *Irish Independent,* 17 Jun: 'A couple of days ago, a colleague was despatched to the streets of Dublin to find out if citizens were aware that Bloomsday was almost upon them … The following exchange took place with one particular Einstein: "Do you know what day tomorrow is?" "Yeah. It's a Friday." "Do you know when Bloomsday is going to happen?" "Bloo-ims-day? Sure, nobody knows dat. Bloo-ims-day? Dat's de end of de world".'

Bluebell [nickname]. Margaret Kelly. **2000** Lara Marlowe, *Irish Times,* 11 Nov: 'She was a sickly child when early in the last century a Dr O'Connor in Dublin exclaimed one day, "You're my little Bluebell!" The name stuck, and Margaret Kelly made it famous, though she was also known simply as Miss. Nearly 70 years after she led the first Bluebell Girls at the Folies Bergère, Miss Bluebell was awarded the French Legion of Honour ...'

Blue Blouses [nickname, <colour of uniform]. Female members/supporters of **Blueshirts**. **1995** Éamon Kelly, *The Apprentice:* 'These followers of General O'Duffy ... were dressed in their military type shirts and were accompanied by their women, the blue blouses as we called them.'

Blue Flu [nickname, <colour of Garda uniform; first heard on a Garda radio resource reported by *Irish Independent*]. Strike action under the guise of sick leave. **1998** Jim Cusack, *Irish Times,* 25 Apr: 'It will be the first serious industrial action by members of the force. Under the 1928 Garda Síochána Act, officers are forbidden to strike. The "sickness" ruse, already nicknamed "blue flu", is an attempt to circumvent the anti-strike clause.' **1998** *Sunday Tribune*, 3 May: '**Bertie Ahern** is fully aware that widespread public resentment at the Garda "blue flu" could rapidly change to unreasoning rage against the Government.' See also **Choo-choo flu**

Blueland [military]. Imaginary independent State for the purposes of largest military exercise ever undertaken in Ireland. **1999** Donal MacCarron, *Step Together!:* 'On the 1st September 1942, the Army of Blueland, a small democratic state with its northern border on the River Blackwater in **Munster**, was warned that its neighbour, Redland, an aggressive totalitarian country, had declared war. The country's other neighbours, Brownland on the East and Greenland on the West, remained neutral ...'

Blue Raincoat Theatre Company Sligo. **2000** Ian Kilroy, *Irish Times,* 8 Jul: 'It was in this climate of possibility that [Malcolm] Hamilton and Niall Henry set up the company in 1991 ... taking its name from the song by Leonard Cohen.'

Blueshirt [nickname, <uniform]. Fascist political movement (Apr. 1933-). Hence [derog.] **Fine Gael** party and members thereof; those espousing right-wing views. **2000** Conor Cruise O'Brien [see **Cruiser**], *Irish Independent*, 24 Jun: 'Mr [John] Bruton is a successful and prosperous farmer, from a Fine Gael family. For some political thinkers this combination makes Bruton a rancher and a Blueshirt.'

B-man/B-Special [<division of force in 'A' full-time), 'B' (local) and 'C' (emergency) units]. Part-time member of the **Ulster** Special Constabulary (est'd 1920). **1969** Bernadette Devlin, *The Price of my Soul:* 'Most of the Protestant men in our district were B men, or Specials – members of the civilian militia in Northern Ireland which was formed to fight the IRA.'

BMW [acronym]. Border Midlands and Western Region. **2000** Brendan Glacken, *Irish Times,* 11 May: '... the midlands are those flat bits with nondescript towns and pointless "traffic-calming" zones which slow up your journey from Dublin ... to the real Ireland. The new designation, the ironic (as opposed to iconic) BMW, only accentuates the region's reputation as the anonymous bit in the middle between the border and the west.'

Bob and Joan [Cork, nickname]. Statues. **1971** Seán Beecher, *The Story of Cork:* 'Outside the gate of "The Green Coat School" were two lead statues,

familiarly known as "Bob and Joan" …
When the building was being demol-
ished, the authorities … had them
removed to Shandon Steeple … "Bob
and Joan" were to add a new phrase to
the patois of the north side of the city as
courting couples, desirous of privacy,
were accustomed to dally in the sec-
luded laneway flanking Skiddy's and so
"Bob and Joan" took on a different
meaning.'

Bobel Loth [<first letters of early Ir.
alphabet]. **1992** Dermot McGuinne,
Irish Type Design: '… the Irish alphabet
… did not begin with a, b, c, but in one
form with b, l, f, from which it received
the name of *Bobel-loth*, or alternatively
with b, l, n, after which it was called
Beth-luis-nin. John O'Donovan points
out in the introduction to his grammar
that "Each of the letters of the Bobel-
loth alphabet took its name from one of
the masters who taught at the great
schools under Fenius Farsaidh, and in
the Beth-luis-nion alphabet each letter
was named after some tree, for what
reason we know not".'

Bogland [nickname, derog.] Ireland
beyond the **Pale**. **1999** Ross O'Carroll-
Kelly, *Sunday Tribune*, 21 Nov: 'He
goes: "I'm asking you how would you
know you are approaching one [a
pedestrian crossing] when it's dark." I'm
like, "Sorry, I've answered your spa
question. Jesus Christ, we're in the middle of Bogland. How many pedestrian
crossings do you see in an average day
anyway?".' See **Bogman**

Bogman Countryman; urban term of
contempt – see **Bogland**. Hence (1)
Bogman's Ball [Connemara]. **2000**
Lorna Siggins, *Irish Times,* 21 Oct:
'Songs, poems and stories have been
written about it since 1959, when the

first Bogman's Ball was held to mark the
saving of the turf. Although a much
more sophisticated society is no longer
so dependent on the fuel, the celebration has continued every year.' (2)
Bogmen [politic.] C19 agrarian society.
1999 Toby Harnden, *'Bandit Country'*:
'Made up of members of the **Ribbon**
society, the Bogmen and the Rednecks,
the [Irish Patriotic] brotherhood was
believed to have been inspired by
Patrick Burns, a visiting American …'

Bolg an tSolair [<Ir. *bolg an tsoláthair*.
corpus. miscellany]. Journal, pub. Belfast
(1795) by *Northern Star*, newspaper of
United Irishmen. First Eng. language
magazine to use Ir. language title.

Bomb Alley [nickname]. Dub. streets
from South Great George's St. to
Portobello Bridge. **2000** John Moran,
Irish Times, 8 May: 'In the earlier part of
the last century the area was notorious
for violent political unrest … Then the
area was dubbed "Bomb Alley" and "the
Dardanelles" because of the attacks on
British army vehicles on their way from
the city centre to Portobello barracks.'

Bombay Deserter [nickname]. Dub.
street character. **1940** Robert Gahan,
Dublin Historical Record, 'Some Old
Street Characters of Dublin': 'The nickname is a deserved one, for this hero
actually achieved the remarkable feat of
deserting from his [British] army unit
while stationed in India; it is a long way
from Bombay to Dublin, but the news
somehow reached the city that the
Indian Army had had its strength reduced
by one, and that one our character.'

Bonham see **Brooke**

Bono [stage name]. Paul Hewson, lead
singer with **U2**. **1993** Dave Bowler &

Bryan Dray, *U2:* 'To the outside world Lypton Village's most important contribution to Paul Hewson was to name him Bonovox, the name of a hearing aid shop on Dublin's O'Connell Street, something with which he wasn't entirely happy until he later realised that it made a reasonable Latin approximation of the term "good voice"!'

Boolean algebra [<George Boole (1815-1864). **2000** William Reville, *Irish Times,* 14 Dec: 'Was the first Professor of Mathematics in Queen's College Cork … Boole, sometimes called the father of computer science, developed his system of Boolean algebra while in Cork.'

Borey Dancers [<Borealis]. The Aurora Borealis. **1999** Diarmaid Ó Muirithe, *Irish Times,* 6 Mar: 'In a fascinating introduction to the poems she [Nuala Ní Dhomhnaill] tells us about speaking to the Kerry folklorist, Dr Joe Daly, about local words for the phenomenon … Dr Daly told her that the usual term used by the people in his young days was *The Borey Dancers.* A lovely conceit this is …'

Botany Bay [<First Australian penal settlement (1788)]. Residential square, Trinity Coll. Dub. **1936** Oliver St John Gogarty, *As I was going down Sackville Street:* '"If the Botany Bay quad was justifiably called after the Penal settlements more than one hundred years ago, what should they call it now?" "It ought to be the first object for clearance by the College Society for demolition of the slums".' **1946** Constantia Maxwell, *A History of Trinity College, Dublin 1591-1892:* 'Botany Bay to the north of the Library Square grew out slowly as an offshoot from the square … Some say that it got its name from "being poked

into a retired corner", and another explan-ation is that it was humorously called after a convict settlement in Australia where Irish political prisoners had mutinied in 1801, since the residents of the Bay, being further removed from official eyes, were often noisier than other undergraduates.'

Bots, the [abbrev., nickname]. Botanic Gardens, Dub. **2000** Mary Carolan, *Irish Times,* 13 Sep: 'Mr **[Bertie] Ahern** described the gardens, which opened in 1800, as "one of the jewels of Dublin city", and said he had the warmest affection for "the Bots" since his mother brought him there as a child.'

Bottle, the [nickname]. Medicine administered at Foundling Hospital, Dub. (C18). **1913** James Collins, *Life in Old Dublin:* 'The Hospital Nurse deposed when examined on oath by the Committee that a medicine called "The Bottle" was handed round to them all at intervals indiscriminately. She did not know what was in it, but supposed it was a "composing draught", for "the children were easy for an hour or two after taking it".'

Boundary [politic.]. Demarcation between NI and Irish Free State following 1921 Treaty, subseq. 'Border'. Hence: **Boundary Commission**, est'd post-1921 to determine such boundary. **1999** Tony Harnded, *'Bandit Country':* '[Frank] Aiken brought the Civil War to an end on 30 April 1923 … for the next three years, the people of South Armagh were convinced that the Boundary Commission would transfer them from Northern Ireland to the **Free State**.'

Bowl of Light [Dub.] Artefact installed on O'Connell Bridge to mark first **An Tóstal** festival, 1953. **1953 Myles na**

Gopaleen, *Irish Times*, Apr: 'Last Sunday a public-spirited gentleman [Anthony Wilson] put the plastic "flame" of the Bowl of Light on O'Connell Bridge into the River Liffey. Lawlessness? Maybe so, but I am delighted. ' **1953** 'Father Mathew', *TCD, A College Miscellany*, 15 May: 'The Bowl of Light somehow epitomised the occasion; its unveiling was attended by a riot, its violation gave cause for much self-righteous denunciation, while its mechanics led one of our distinguished colleagues [Myles na Gopaleen] to enrich our vocabulary by reinstating the word "Splarge".' See also **Tomb of the Unknown Gurrier**

Boyle Roche, Sir [1743-1807]. Politician noted for his penchant for **Irish Bulls**. Hence (1) **Boyle Balderdash, Sir** [nickname]. **1797** *Memoirs of Mrs Margaret Leeson, Written by Herself, Vol. III:* 'Another day as I was riding in the [Phoenix] Park, with a little diminutive dwarf-looking servant trotting after me, Sir B-- Balderdash accosted me with "yarrow Piggy, what's that behind you?" "My a--e, Sir B--," I said.' (2) **Boyle Roche Bird, the** [fabulous creature]. **2000** Brian Maye, *Irish Times,* 14 Feb: 'His rhetorical question, "How can I be in two places at once unless I were a bird?" gave rise to the expression, "the Boyle Roche bird", a creature that solved the age-old problem of bilocation.'

Boyle's Law [<Robert Boyle, b. Lismore Castle, Co. Phort Láirge/ Waterford (1627)] Law of physics. **1988** Henry Boylan, *A Dictionary of Irish Biography* (2nd ed.): 'His first experiments on the properties of air were published in 1660, and in answer to criticism he enunciated the famous Boyle's Law, that the volume of gas varies inversely as the pressure.'

Brandy Pad [nickname, <pad/padroad <OE *paeth,* footway]. Smuggling route, C19-20. **1990** Mick Matthews, quoted in Walter Love, *The Time of Our Lives:* 'The Brandy Pad was the smugglers' route through the [Mourne] mountains. They'd have loaded up in Kilkeel off the boats and come up the Pad to Hilltown ...'

Breo [Ir. idem, brand, torch; glow; brandname]. Beer. **2000** Christine Doherty, *Sunday Business Post,* 29 Oct: 'Guinness Ireland has confirmed that Breo, its wheat beer that cost close to £5 million to develop, is to be withdrawn ... Breo – which means "glow" in ancient Irish – was seen by many as GI's last great hope ...'

Brian Boroimhe/Boroma/Boru High-King of Ireland (C11). Hence [brandname]. Vodka. **2000** Paul O'Kane, *Sunday Tribune:* 'Boru, which was launched in September 1998, now has a 10% share of the fast growing Irish vodka market, and claims to be the second-biggest brand in Dublin.'

Brigid/Brigit [personal name, <Ir. Brighid; Bríd; Celt. *★Brigentí*]. Hence: (1) [USA]. Name applied in gen. to Ir. domestics. **2000** Joe Lee, *Sunday Tribune*, 16 Apr: 'The "Brigids" had to learn how to assert their independence and not become mere shadows ... It would be many a long year before all the Brigids would acquire a name of their own.' (2) **Auld Biddy** [dimin., derog.]. **2000** Rosita Boland, *Irish Times*, 22 Apr: 'Biddy [Byrne, character in TV soap], as we all know from several million years of experience, isn't the sunniest lady in the land ... In fact, Biddy does the cranky cross thing so well that it's hard to remember which came first: Biddy from *Glenroe* or the

expression "Auld Biddy", so Siamese twin-like do they now appear to be entwined.'

Broadwater [**Munster** Blackwater]. **C17** Gerard Boate, *Natural History of Ireland:* 'The two chief rivers of Munster are Sure and Broadwater ... The other [Broadwater] passeth by Lismore and falleth into the sea by Youghal.'

Brogue about [<Ir. *bróg,* shoe]. Wake game, C19. **1999** Gearóid Ó Crualaoich, '"The Merry Wake"', in J.S. Donnelly jr. & Kerby Miller (eds), *Irish Popular Culture 1650-1850:* '"Brogue about" is regarded as the best and most popular game of all. For this all the men sit around on the kitchen floor in a circle with their legs pulled up to them. An old shoe is passed around the circle under the raised knees, and someone is prevailed on to stand in the middle of the circle to try to intercept the shoe in its passage.' Also known as **Faic** [Ir., 'stick', <stick used to harry contestants] and **Hurry the Brogue**.

Brooke [<Charlotte Brooke, 1740-93, author of *Reliques of Irish Poetry* (1789); typog.]. Ir. lang. typeface, used to print *Reliques.* **1992** Dermot McGuinne, *Irish Type Design:* 'A typeface influenced in a major way by the Paris [Irish] type and generally referred to as the Brooke and sometimes as the Bonham type ... was produced in Dublin in 1787, and as such is the first Irish fount known to have been cut and cast in Ireland.'

Brophys, the [<?, Dub.]. Venereal disease. **1987** Lar Redmond, *Emerald Square:* 'mercurial ointment (Navy Blue Butter) for the treatment of crabs or their more fearful cousins, "the Brophys", who not alone bit a piece out of your balls but ran up your arse to eat it.'

Brownland see **Blueland**

Broy Harriers [<Eamonn Broy, Garda Commissioner; nickname]. Members of the Garda Síochána nominated by **Fianna Fáil** and recruited by Broy in the 1930s. **1996** Katie Donovan, *Irish Times,* 9 Nov: 'The real Ned Broy, incidentally, lived on to found **Dev**'s version of the Special Branch in the 1930s, called the Broy Harriers.'

Brunswick Constitutional Clubs [<Duke of Brunswick]. Political assoc. **1921** D.J. Owen, *History of Belfast:* 'Considerable feeling arose on the Catholic question, and the proceedings of the "Catholic Association" aroused an amount of opposition, one result of which was the founding in various parts of the country of "Brunswick Constitutional Clubs" ... One such club was established in Belfast in September, 1828.'

Bryan Coony see **Bianconi**

B-Special see **B-man**

BT1 [Belfast]. Pub. **2000** Glenn Patterson, *Irish Times*, 1 Apr: '... one recent addition to the city's nightlife is its [Robinson's] refurbished basement bar, named for the city centre's postcode, BT1.'

Bugs Moran [nickname]. Chicago gangster, b. Co. Kerry. **2000** Pól Ó Conghaile, *Irish Independent,* 10 Jun: 'Raised in the Irish shantytown of Kilgubbin on Chicago's Near North Side, Dion O'Bannion and his followers in the North Side Gang, George "Bugs" Moran, Earl "Hymie" Weiss, and Vincent "The Schemer" Drucci were known to the police as an accomplished gang of hijackers, burglars and safe-crackers.'

Bull Island [<North Bull Island, Dublin + US. sl. *bull,* 'trivial, insincere or untruthful talk or writing' (ODMS)]. Satirical RTÉ TV prog. (1999-). **2000** Dick Walsh, *Irish Times,* 1 Apr: 'As for the public, it's reached the point where many can hardly tell the difference between *Bull Island* and a meeting of the Cabinet. Like their predecessors on *Scrap Saturday* and *Hall's Pictorial Weekly,* the islanders have become more convincing than the crowd they imitate.' **2000** Seán MacConnell, *Irish Times,* 3 Aug: 'Ireland is fast becoming the real Bull Island of Europe with a huge expansion in the number of bulls being reared for slaughter and export ...'

Bull's-Eye Day [nickname]. Payment day for Brit. army pensions. **1993** Áine de Courcy in Michael Verdon, *Shawlies, Echo Boys, the Marsh and the Lanes: Old Cork Remembered:* 'Every Wednesday in Ireland was called Bull's-Eye Day because that's when the soldiers got their pensions.'

Bully's Acre [<?]. Three and three-quarter acre cemetery, Kilmainham, Dub. **1907** Samuel A. Ossory Fitzpatrick, *Dublin, a Historical and Topographical Account of the City:* 'Adjoining the [Royal] Hospital is the ancient grave-yard said to have been the burying-place of Prince Murchadh, son of Brian, and other slain at the battle of Clontarf ... The enclosure, formerly known as "Bully's Acre", was used for interments up to 1832 ...'

Bunker, the [nickname]. Anglo-Irish Secretariat, Maryfield, Belfast, set up under Anglo-Irish Agreement, 1985. **1998** Renagh Holohan, *Irish Times,* 12 Dec: 'The Bunker ... has a colourful past ... The dreary two-storey building has no underground bunker, but gained its name from the conditions in which Irish officials had to live for their own safety. For the past 14 years they have stayed indoors, rarely venturing out, even at night ...'

Burke, William [b. Co. Thír Eoghain/ Tyrone (1792), hanged Edinburgh (1828), murderer and body-snatcher]. Hence **burke** [vb.] **1895** E. Cobham Brewer, *A Dictionary of Phrase and Fable* (new ed.): 'To murder by placing something over the mouth of the person attacked to prevent his giving alarm.'

Burton books [<name of publisher]. Cheap reprints of schoolbooks. **1968** P.J. Dowling, *The Hedge Schools of Ireland:* '[William] Carleton is particularly critical of the reading books used by school children ... Most of them were probably the cheap reprints issued at Dublin, Limerick and Cork, and known as the "Burton Books" or "sixpenny books".

Butcher's Apron [nickname, derog.]. Brit. Union flag. **1999** Toby Harnden, *'Bandit Country':* 'An Irish tricolour was hoisted to the top of the [Crossmaglen] Markethouse in defiance of the Union flag – soon to become known to locals as "the Butcher's Apron" – flying from the RUC station.'

C

Cadenus [nickname, self-bestowed]. Jonathan Swift (1667-1745), Dean of St Patrick's Cathedral, Dub. **1962** Sybil Le Brocquy, *Cadenus:* 'Since the available evidence would seem to show that this poem was written for Esther Van Homrigh *before* Swift became a dean, the use of the anagram *Cadenus* for *Decanus* has caused a great deal of speculation. A possible explanation may be that this name – specially invented by Swift for intimate use between himself and the girl for whom he also invented the name **Vanessa** – had a totally different derivation. The Oxford Dictionary gives a XVII Century meaning of the word *Cad*, as *a familiar spirit* … Swift's handwriting was not always very legible, and his *V* might have been easily misread as U by a stranger. If this mistake had been made, their secret name may, in reality, have been an anagram of *Cad Es Vn* i.e. *The familiar spirit of Esther Van (Homrigh).*'

Cake Dance Rural festival. **1983** Theodora Fitzgibbon, *Irish Traditional Food:* 'Cakes were often baked for special festivals. There were Cake Dances for instance, and an account exists of one in County Mayo near Newport where the cake was placed on a pole and each dancer paid to join the dance. Whoever paid most and danced most got the cake.'

Calamity Avenue [Luimneach/ Limerick]. **1981** Adrian MacLoughlin, *Streets of Ireland:* '… we eventually come to a junction with Blackboy Road, which is a continuation of Mulgrave St.,

unkindly referred to at times by Limerick people as "Misery Row" or "Calamity Avenue" since it contains a prison, a cemetery and two hospitals, one of them for psychiatric cases.'

Captain Moonlite [Aust., *nom de guerre*]. Andrew George Scott, bushranger. **1987** Patrick O'Farrell, *The Irish in Australia:* 'Certainly the Irish were among bushranging's big names and those that have attracted the fame of balladry – Donohue, Doolan, Henry Power, Captain Moonlite …'

Caravat [nickname, <Ir. *carabhat*, cravat]. One of two hostile agrarian factions (early C19). **1824** R.H. Ryland, *The History, Topography and Antiquities of the County and City of Waterford:* 'The following extract from a report of a trial … at Clonmel in the year 1811, will give the reader some explanation of the names by which these formidable factions were distinguished … Q. Why were they called Caravats? A. A man of the name of Hanly was hanged: he was prosecuted by the **Shanavests** and Paudeen Car said he would not leave the place of execution till he saw the *caravat* about the fellow's neck. …'

Carder [nickname]. Revolutionary assoc. (late C18). **1824** Thomas Crofton Croker, *Researches in the South of Ireland:* 'In the Central Counties, the Carders … (a name derived from their inhuman practice of inflicting punishment on the naked back with a wool-card) were in great measure inflamed by a desire to punish informers …'

Carrantuohill [Ir. *Carrán-tuthail*, Ire.'s highest mountain]. Hence [music] Trad. band. **2000** Ian Kilroy, *Irish Times,* 3 May: '… in Poland, Zbigniew Seyda and friends, otherwise known as

Carrantouhill, have been thrashing out reels and jigs since 1987. It seems that no matter where you go you might hear a slow air on the wind. In Sweden that air might be played by *Blackthorn,* in Germany by *The Hibernians,* or in Denmark by *Ashplant.*'

Carson's Army [politic., <Edward Carson (1854-1935), unionist leader]. **2000** Stephen Collins, *Sunday Tribune,* 6 Feb: 'The illegal UVF [Ulster Volunteer Force], founded in 1912 to resist **Home Rule**, was known as Carson's army. In 1981, [Ian] Paisley launched his "Carson trail" of rallies ...'

Castlebar [Caisleán an Bharraigh, Co. Mhaigh Eo/Mayo, town]. Hence **Castlebar Races** [nickname]. Battle between French-Irish forces and Brit. garrison, 27 Aug. 1798. **1988** John Cooney (ed.), *The Irish-French Alliance:* 'Assisted by the several thousand untrained but enthusiastic Irish volunteers, [General] Humbert defeated superior English forces at Castlebar ... So spectacular was the English defeat, that this battle is known in history as "the Castlebar Races".'

Castle Catholic [<Dub. Castle, former seat of Brit. rule; nickname, derog.]. One who evinces sycophantically pro-Brit. sympathies and seeks to profit therefrom. **1938** He [Robert Peel] began in Ireland a policy that many of his successors developed and copied – the formation of a class that became known as "renegade Catholics" or, in mockery of their affected half-English accents, "Cawstle Catholics".' See also **Peel's Brimstone**

Castle money [<Dub. Castle, former seat of Brit. rule]. Money paid out to informers. **1966** Patrick J. Flanagan, *The*

Cavan & Leitrim Railway: 'Dissension was fostered by a flow of money to informers ... to some, "Castle money" was always acceptable.'

Castle Rackrent [lit.]. Novel (1800) by Maria Edgeworth (1767-1849). Hence any ruinous estate. **1849** Samuel Ferguson, *Inheritor and Economist: a Poem:* 'So shall we speedily the land behold/Once more exchangeable for British gold;/And in its Castle-Rack-Rent mansions see/A bran-new Cheesmonger propriet'ry.' **1887** D.M. Craik, *An Unknown Country:* 'There are landlords and landlords. No doubt Ireland has suffered cruelly from the worst type of that order, who, generation after generation, lived recklessly, ruinously, in their castle Rackrents ...'

Castlereagh RUC interrogation centre, Belfast. **2000** Renagh Holohan, *Irish Times,* 5 Feb: 'Until the current deadlock, relations between the previously warring factions in the **North** were getting increasingly familiar. Witness this week's jibe in the Assembly at Martin McGuinness from DUP member Sammy Wilson who told the Minister for Education that he was allowed to answer questions now – he wasn't in Castlereagh ...'

Castletown [Baile an Chaisleán, Co. na hIarmhí/Westmeath]. **2000** *Sunday Tribune,* 9 Apr: 'If prizes were being given out for GAA teams with the longest names, Castletown-Finea-Coole-Whitehall would surely be in the running. But the extended title belies the volume of players available to the north Westmeath club.'

Catacombs, the [nickname, Dub.]. Large rambling basement of Georgian house in Fitzwilliam St., resort (1940s/

early '50s) of literary coterie. **1976** Anthony Cronin, *Dead as Doornails:* 'Most of this company assembled in McDaid's [pub] every day … and almost every night the entire assemblage moved on to the Catacombs.'

Cathedral Quarter [Belfast]. Urban development. **2000** Róisín Ingle, *Irish Times*, 27 Apr: '… St Anne's Cathedral looms large over the district where life is being breathed back into Belfast's inner-city. Laganside Corporation … has named it "the Cathedral Quarter". For those looking for a neat analogy, it has also become known as Belfast's Temple Bar.'

Cathleen/ Caitlín/ Kathleen Ní Houlihan Legendary personification of Ire., latterly ironic. **1950** *Irish Times,* 16 Aug: '… one of us spotted an old tinker woman with a sheaf of broadsheets. She had a face like Kathleen Ní Houlihan after the mortgage on the **four green fields** had been foreclosed.' **1973** Noël Conway, *The Bloods:* 'They, like the rest of the Army they had helped to train, were neutral, serving the most ungrateful Lady in Irish history – Cathleen ní Houlihan.'

Catholic Sourface *see* **Sourface**

Cathy Barry [<?]. Incompetent individual. **1999** James Healy, *Leinster Leader*, 24 Jun: '"That hedge looks like Cathy Barry tried to fix it", he [my Grandad] told me once, as we did a bit of fencing down the fields. Cathy Barry, whoever she was, apparently never did anything right. "You are going round by Moll Watson's", he commented when I chose a particularly out of the way route home on the tractor. Who the heck was Moll Watson?'

Cats, the [<**Kilkenny Cats**, nickname]. Kilkenny Gaelic football/Hurling teams; Kilkenny citizens. **2000** Headline, *Westmeath Examiner* (Mullingar), 3 Jun: 'Westmeath Minor footballers crush the "Cats".' **2000** *Kilkenny People,* 17 May: 'The Cats are bracing themselves for a Titanic struggle. They aim to defeat the bureaucrats who want to wipe or 400 years of the city's history.' Hence: **Cat Laughs** (1) Comedy festival. **2000** Ian O'Doherty, *Irish Independent*, 3 Jun: 'When more than 30,000 laugh-hungry punters descended on the usually sleepy Kilkenny last year for the Murphy's Cat Laughs festival, it was the largest crowd ever to gather for a comedy event in the country.' (2) Pub. **2000** Caroline Allen, *Stage Left:* (Carlow/Naas): 'A new addition this year will be "Kitty Flicks" … where comedy films starring a variety of Irish comedians will be screened in the chilled-out atmosphere of the Mousetrap, over the Cat Laughs pub.'

Celtic Snail see **Celtic Tiger**. **2001** Headline, *Sunday Tribune*, 28 Jan: 'CELTIC SNAIL COMES HOME TO ROOST.'

Celtic Tiger [coined, poss. by Dub. banker David McWilliams, on analogy of 'Asian Tiger'. **2000** *Irish Independent,* 14 Oct: 'There is argument over whether McWilliams … invented the phrase "Celtic Tiger", although he did make it popular' – but see **Emerald Tiger**]. Booming Ir. economy (c1996-). **2000** Oliver O'Connor, *Irish Times,* 2 Jun: 'We are all too familiar now with the attributes of the Celtic Tiger – downside, underside, backside, soft belly, claws, paws, teeth, tail, eyes, ears, cubs, offspring, growls and purrs, footprints, stalking and shadow … The metaphor of the Celtic Tiger serves not to clarify an idea, if it ever did, but to mish and mash what could be useful discussions.' **2000** *Irish Independent,* 1 Jul: 'Measured over the long term by international standards, the Celtic Tiger looks more like a mangy old moggy.' **2000** Deasún Breathnach, *Irish Times,* 17 Jul: 'Some appear to believe that the term Celtic Tiger represents a recent attempt to create a racialist symbol for Ireland. It can be revealed now, however, that it is nothing of the sort … All we have to do is to look at the word *ceilteach* in modern Irish. It means "secretive", with-holding" (Ó Donaill, 1977: 217). The same source, for *ceilt,* gives "concealment; and, significantly, *níl ceilt ar bith ann,* "he can't keep a secret" … The word can be traced back to Old Irish, *ceilid,* "hides, conceals"… Ayae! Brown envelopes, black plastic bags, confusing entries in accounts, widespread abhorrence of **DIRT** by obsessively hygienic persons in high places. So now the secret is out. It's part of what we are.' Hence [brandname]. **2000** Lorna Siggins, *Irish Times,* 29 May: 'Mr Staunton has already drawn up a business plan which identifies the market in Ireland and Europe for four domestic fuel products suitable for smoke-controlled areas – Dubrite, comprising 40 per cent peat, 25 per cent petroleum coke, 25 per cent anthracite and a binder … and Celtic Tiger, similar to Dubrite but specially packaged for niche markets.' Hence **Celtic Snail** [politic.]. Adv't promotion for **Fine Gael** party (2000). **2000** John Moran, *Irish Times,* 7 Dec: 'The advertising undertaken by Fine Gael recently exemplifies the growing detachment of politics from reality. "Eradicate the Celtic Snail. We'll grab it by the horns" – or some such nonsense, accompanied by a grotesque image of a green snail. Is it a joke?'

Celtic Twilight, the [< W.B. Yeats's

book title, *idem.* (1893)]. Literary movement. **1979** Robert Hogan, *Dictionary of Irish Literature:* '… it became a not entirely appropriate tag to describe the ferment of Irish literary activity in the 1890s and for a few years afterwards. The description called up a vision of the mournful, the moody, and the mystical which was, and perhaps even still is, one romantic way of viewing Ireland.' **1939** *Irish Times,* 29 Sep: 'Statements in the Dáil about the black-out, or the new "Celtic Twilight", as it has been called by somebody with a happy sense of the fitness of things, have left the public as much in the dark as ever.' **1999** Ian Jack, *Independent on Sunday* (London), 26 Sep: 'In Cameron's film [of the **Titanic**], the armies that clashed on that calm North Atlantic night represented youth and age, new and old … To be young and new was to have, as your soundtrack, the ghastly Celtic Twilight pastiche of James Horner's music.'

Ceoltóirí Chualann [Ir., musicians of Cuala]. Trad. music group. **1981** Gerard Victory, 'Ó Riada on Radio', in Bernard Harris and Grattan Freyer (eds), *The Achievement of Seán Ó Riada:* 'The result was a hectic few years until his death in 1971 in which he created a stream of splendid traditional records performed by his ensemble Ceoltóirí Chualann …, Cuala being the old name for South County Dublin – a tribute to the birthplace of his new ideas at his earlier home in Stillorgan.' See also **Cuala Press**

Chalk Sunday [nickname]. First Sunday in Lent, during which no marriages were celebrated. **1986** Padraic O'Farrell, *'Tell me, Sean O'Farrell':* 'It was called Chalk Sunday in some places because single people were marked with chalk by some joker – usually kneeling behind the person at mass.' See also **Cock Tuesday**

Chas Mahal [play on *Taj Mahal*; nickname]. Government Buildings, Dub., as restored (1990) under the aegis of Charles J. Haughey as **Taoiseach**. **2000** Olivia Doyle, *Sunday Tribune*, 6 Feb: 'But the former **Fianna Fáil** chief won praise for the imposing government edifice on Merrion Square, dubbed the "Chas Mahal", some of the plaudits coming from the most unlikely quarters.'

Cherryvalley [Belfast]. **1983** *John Pepper's Illustrated Encyclopaedia of Ulster Knowledge*: 'Belfast suburb associated with ostentatious speech, due mainly to the way in which Belfast comedian James Young used it as a vehicle for poking fun at people who spoke with a marble in their mouths.'

Cherrywood [Dublin]. Planned 'instant' village. **1999** Mark Keenan, *Sunday Tribune*, 7 Nov: 'The concept of an "instant village" was first promoted in Dublin almost 10 years ago when Monarch properties tabled such a scheme for Cherrywood …The original plan was derailed because of planning objections …'

Chicago May [nickname]. May Duignan, b. Co. Longford (1871). **1999** Seán Mac Connell, *Irish Times,* 19 Aug: 'She … left home in June 1890, travelling to New York via London later that year. She moved to Chicago in 1894 … By the time she returned to New York, she had become known as "Chicago May", because of her notorious behaviour involving prostitution, blackmail and robbery. She was one of the first people to use photography as a method of blackmail.'

Chief, the [politic.] Charles Stuart Parnell (1846-91). **1954** Oliver St John Gogarty, *It Isn't That Time of Year At All:* 'My father died in the same year as Parnell. I had seen crowds assembled to hear "The Chief" speak from a house about eight doors above ours …'

Chieftains, The [stage name (1963-)]. Trad. music group. **1987** Bill Meek, *Paddy Moloney and the Chieftains:* '… John Montague, himself a director of Claddagh, was to recall: "We named them after a book of mine which had just appeared." Such indeed was the case. The book in question was *Death of a Chieftain* which is perhaps ironical in that the naming of the group had rather more to do with *birth*.'

Cholesterol Coast [nickname]. Coast of Co. Aontroma/Antrim. **1994** Michael Palin, *Great Railway Journeys:* 'Along these fine, languid headlands and wide bays are dotted a string of hotels and guest houses whose preferences for breakfast delicacies like the **Ulster Fry** have earned this stretch the name of the Cholesterol Coast.'

Choo-choo flu [nonce term; indust.]. Strike action under the guise of sick leave: see **Blue flu**. **1998** Frank Kilfeather, *Irish Times,* 23 Nov: 'Despite talks in Dublin yesterday … the [locomotive] drivers are determined to go ahead with their unofficial action. It is not known what support the "choo-choo flu" – as it is being called – will get …'

Christian [attrib.] Horse perceived to possess human qualities. **2000** Diarmaid Ó Muirithe, *Irish Times,* 15 Apr: '… the late Ned Cash once described a child's pony he wanted to sell me as "an absolute Christian gentleman". I have often heard horsemen from Wexford and Wicklow speak of their horses as Christians.'

Christie [<James Christie, Dub. printer and typefounder (*fl.* 1815). Typeface]. **1992** Dermot McGuinne, *Irish Type Design:* 'The Christie type, while some of its individual capital sorts seem awkward and ill-conceived ... nonetheless appears striking in body setting ...'

Churchman [Ulster]. Adherent of the Church of Ireland. **1913** Alexander Irvine, *My Lady of the Chimney Corner:* 'Ye know, no doubt, Anna, that Misther Gwynn is a Churchman an' I'm a Presbyterian.'

Citizen, the (1) [media]. Revolutionary journal. **1987** Richard Davis, *The Young Ireland Movement:* '[Thomas] Davis revealed his anti-imperialism by contending that Britain's alien civilisation had ruined the natives of India. He developed this theme in a number of articles in *The Citizen,* a little magazine owned by W.E. Hudson and controlled by Thomas Wallis and other members of the "**Hist**" set.' (2) [nickname]. **1954** Oliver St John Gogarty, *It Isn't That Time of Year At All:* 'The time at the Royal [Univ.] was not altogether lost. I met a less disciplined class of student in the Aula Maxima: '"Citizen" Elwood, James Joyce, Cosgrove ... John Elwood [was] called the Citizen to ridicule his advanced views.' Hence [lit.]: **1922** James Joyce, *Ulysses:* 'So we turned into Barney Kiernan's and there sure enough was the citizen up in the corner having a great confab with himself and the bloody mangy mongrel, **Garryowen**, and he waiting for what the sky would drop in the way of drink.'

City Music [Dub.] Municipal band. **1930** *Irish Times,* 8 Mar: 'Two hundred

years have elapsed since Lewis Layfield, an English actor, was appointed as "major hautboy" of the City Music by the Corporation of Dublin ...The Dublin Corporation Band is much older than that, but is not specifically referred to as such till June, 1561 ... when "the Mayor and his bretheren, with the city music, attended the Lord Deputy and Council to Thomas's Court by torchlight".'

City of Dreadful Knights [<poem by James Thomson (1834-82), *The City of Dreadful Night*; nickname]. Dublin. **1967** Terence de Vere White, in Francis Mac Manus (ed.), *The Years of the Great Test 1926-39:* 'The survivor of Protestant ascendancy, unlike his sporting coreligionists in the country, was a quiet living and industrious fellow. It was not by such as he that Dublin won its title, the City of Dreadful Knights.'

City of the Broken/Violated Treaty [Treaty of Limerick, 1691]. Limerick. **1930** *Irish Times,* 22 Aug: 'Many of the quaint old sayings about Irish places seem to be dying out. We have even forgotten the meaning of many of them. Some, like "The City of the Tribes" [Galway], "The City of the Violated Treaty", "The County of Short Grass" [Kildare] and "Tyrone of the Bushes" explain themselves ...'

Civic Guard Police force. **2000** Conor Brady, *Irish Times,* 19 Feb: 'Between March and August 1922, the long-familiar bottle-green uniform of the Royal Irish Constabulary disappeared from 26 of Ireland's 32 counties. In the Free State the RIC was replaced by the Civic Guard, quickly re-titled as An Garda Síochána.'

Clare [Co. an Chláir] Hence (1) **Clare hearse** [nickname]. Ten of clubs. **1991**

John B. Keane, *Love Bites and Other Stories*: 'Fortunes are told by the casting of cards and beware if you fall foul of the ace of spades or the ten of clubs! The latter used to be called the "Clare hearse" when I was a gorsoon.' (2) **Lark in the Clare air** (play on song title *The Lark in the Clear Air*). Merriman Summer School (<Brian Merriman, (1747–1805) poet, his location and reputation) **1997** Dick Hogan, *Irish Times,* 2 Sept: '… there are many claims of being in at the start of the Merriman, otherwise known as the "lark in the Clare air."'

Cleburne, Patrick [soldier (–1864)]. Hence **2000** M.E. Synon, *Irish Independent,* 20 Aug: 'My congratulations to the Bandon/Macroom committee of the Cork County Council for their decision to name the new interchange at Ovens after a hero of the American south – Major General Patrick Roynane Cleburne, Corkman and Confederate soldier … Of course, some of the Cork County councillors were grizzling because Cleburne had served in the British army before immigrating (*sic*) to Tennessee. How odd that one hears just such councillors going on, at other times, about "embracing both traditions on this island".'

Clonakilty [Cloich na Coillte, town]. Hence (1) **Clonakilty-God-Help-Us** [<euphem. for large workhouse for sick poor; nickname]. **1993** William Trevor, *Excursions in the Real World*: 'yellow furniture vans … carted our possessions off, westward through Cork itself and through the town people called Clonakilty-God-Help-Us.' (2) **Clonakilty Wrastler** [brandname] Stout. **1999** Brian McCarthy, *Irish Times*, 28 Sep: 'It was to this beautiful spot [Castlefreke] in 1890 that the ninth Lord Carbery brought a

young bride … A torchlit procession to the castle was organised by the parish priest, the schoolmaster and other worthies. "Clonakilty Wrastler" porter was poured …'

Coal Quay, The [pronun. 'Kay']. Cornmarket St., Cork, site of a traditional market. **1881** *Shaw's Tourists' Picturesque Guide*: 'this is a part of the city amusing enough to strangers, yet far too unfashionable for the respectable citizens to take much interest in … coal is not sold within its precincts.' **1967** Seán Jennett, *Munster*: 'At the end of St Patrick's Street is the Coal Quay, where there is a kind of "flea market" that may or may not provide bargains but certainly offers colour and interest.'

Cock Tuesday [nickname]. Shrove Tuesday. **1938** Seumas Macmanus, *The Rocky Road to Dublin*: 'Cock Tuesday, the eve of Lent, was then the great day of the year for marriages.' See also **Chalk Sunday**

Coffey Still [<Aeneas Coffey (b.Dub. c1780)]. Distillation apparatus. **1980** Malachy Magee, *1000 Years of Irish Whiskey*: 'Coffey was not first in the field with the new type of still. Several versions were introduced in the quest of perfecting a method of producing pure spirit in a continuous stream, but it was the Irishman who made the breakthrough with his improved design. Indeed the original Coffey still remains basically unchanged today …'

Cois Cluana [Eng. 'Meadowside'; streetname, Belfast]. **1999** Camille C. O'Reilly, *The Irish Language in Northern Ireland*: 'A street off the Shaws Road which runs through the Irish-speaking area was the centre of a naming controversy for over a decade. Members of the

Shaws Road community have been trying since the early 1980s to have the
street named in Irish. The first name
they chose, *Cois Cluana*, was rejected by
the city council because it was in Irish.
For it to be accepted, it would have to
be Anglicized. The residents posted a
sign anyway.'

Colcannon [<Ir. *cál ceannan* <*cál ceann
fhionn,* white-headed cabbage]. Dish
made from cabbage, potatoes, leeks,
milk and seasoning. **1983** Theoroda
Fitzgibbon, *Irish Traditional Food:* 'This
is traditionally eaten in Ireland at
Hallowe'en or All Hallows' Day,
October 31st [1 Nov.] …. Colcannon at
Hallowe'en used to contain a plain gold
ring, a sixpence, a thimble or button:
the ring meant marriage within the year
for the person who found it, the sixpence meant wealth, the thimble spin-
sterhood and the button bachelorhood.'
Hence: **Colcannon Club** [London].
1875 *The Athenaeum* [London], 20 Jan:
'About 1774 Isaac Sparks, the Irish
comedian, founded in Long Acre a
Colcannon Club.'

Colette [<Colette Farmer, RTÉ TV
Late Late Show production assistant].
Hence [catchphrase] **Roll it there,
Colette**. **2000** Frank McNally, *Irish
Times*, 9 Feb: '… three television sets
were installed in the courtroom for the
possible viewing of the chair's *Late Late*
appearances. "One for everyone in the
audience", exaggerated plaintiff's coun-
sel, Gerry Danaher, who may have been
looking forward to saying "Roll it there,
Colette", too.'

Colleen Bawn [Ir. *cailín bán,* fair-haired
girl; lit.]. Eily O'Grady, heroine of
Gerald Griffin's novel *The Collegians*
(1829) based on actual murder case.
1997 Seamus Deane, *Strange Country:*

'Even the fact that she has two names,
one in phonetically rendered Irish, the
other in English, establishes her as a
person who summarises in her name a
historical process, a transition between
folk origin and social respectability.'
Hence (1) **The Colleen Bawn** [lit.].
Play by Dion Boucicault (1820 or 22-
1890). **1979** Robert Hogan (ed.),
Dictionary of Irish Literature: 'With his
play *The Colleen Bawn* (1860), he had
discovered what was perhaps his most
moving theatrical genre, the Irish play.'
(2) [maritime]. Passenger vessel. **1992**
John de Courcy Ireland, *Ireland's
Maritime Heritage:* 'Drogheda [Steam
Packet Co.]'s graceful *Colleen Bawn* of
1862 was the first ship on the Irish Sea
to provide sleeping accommodation for
ordinary passengers.'

Colleen Kisses [brandname]. Confectionery. **1999** Delia Gallaher, *Irish
Times,* 25 May: 'In those days the
"Colleen Kisses" (peppermint lumps)
were made by hand. I was fascinated to
see a man pulling a brown sugar mixture
off a roller. After a few years the
[**Urney**] factory also caught fire.'

Colles Fracture [<Abraham Colles
(1773-1843)]. Medical condition. **1989**
John Gleeson, *The Book of Irish Lists and
Trivia:* 'A fracture of the lower end of
the radius causing backward and out-
ward displacement of the wrist and
hand, is named after the Irish surgeon …
who first described it in 1814.'

Collop Monday [<Sc. *Collop,* slice of
meat, bacon & eggs; Ulster]. Day before
Shrove Tuesday, when bacon & eggs
were traditional fare.

**Colmcille/Colm Cille/Colum Cille,
St** [b. Donegal, 6th cent.]. **1964**
John Irvine, *A Treasury of Irish Saints:*

'Colmcille, called Columba, the latin-
ized version of his name, by the Scots.
Originally baptized by the name of Colm
(The Dove) and later, to distinguish
him from other Saints of that name,
Colm-Cille, from the great number of
monastic cells (called by the Irish
"Killes") of which he was the founder.'
Hence (1) **Colum Cille** Typeface,
designed by Colm Ó Lochlainn. **1992**
Dermot McGuinne, *Irish Type Design:*
"I [Ó Lochlainn] wish that the type
should be called COLUM CILLE as he
is, par excellence, the patron of Irish
scribes." Following this instruction the
Monotype records include an entry
dated 20 February 1935: "To be known
in future as Colum Cille." (2) **St
Colmcille** Aer Lingus Douglas DC3,
registered EI-ACE (27 Feb 1946).

Confederation of Kilkenny see
Kilkenny

Congested Districts Board [politic.].
Govt. land distribution agency (est'd
1900). **2000** Harry McGee, *Sunday
Tribune,* 23 Jul: 'Even in 1994, when I
met the Ó Guithín brothers in Dún
Chaoin … the only English they were
comfortable with were words for which
there is really no Irish like "dole" and
the "Congested Districts Board" …'

Connemara [<Ir. *Conmaicne-mara*, the
descendants of Conmac who lived by
the sea (P.W. Joyce)]. Region W. of
Loughs Con and Mask. Hence (1) *idem.*
[transport]. Imperial Airways (UK)
flying-boat destined for inauguration of
transatlantic service through Foynes.
1939 *Meccano Magazine* (Liverpool),
Aug: 'The tanks of this aircraft were [19
June] being refilled from a barge in
readiness for a test flight by night when
there was an explosion and fire broke
out on the barge. Flames quickly spread

to the flying boat … and the *Connemara*
finally sank.' (2) *idem.* Whiskey.
'Connemara Single Peated Malt Irish
Whiskey.' (3) **Connemara Chaos**
[astronomy] **2000** Tom Humphries,
Irish Times, 11 Mar: 'He [Randy Tuft]
discovered a fault line the size of the San
Andreas fault on the planet Jupiter. A
family interest in Ireland and Celtic
mythology has led to him christening
various areas with Celtic or Irish names.
The most interesting part of the planet is
now known to those who study it as
Connemara Chaos.' (4) **Connemara
Visitors** [geolog.] **2000** Leo Daly, *Ireland
of the Welcomes,* 'Island Cenotaphs', May-
Jun: '… the island's [Inis Mór] burial
relics of today and yesterday are of
the same native limestone … which were
deposited by the ice floes from
Connemara on their journey seawards,
and aptly named "Connemara Visitors".'
(5) **Connemara 4** [<analogy of **Dublin
4**]. **2000** Ian Kilroy, *Irish Times,* 6 May:
'This once-sleepy Gaeltacht village [An
Spidéal] is now preoccupied by spiralling
property prices and traffic congestion,
earning it the dubious distinction of
being dubbed "Connemara 4".'

Connolly, James [1868-1916] Founder
of Irish Citizen Army and commander
in the GPO during Easter Week 1916].
Hence (1) **Connolly Association**
[Aust.] Political faction. **1987** Patrick
O'Farrell, *The Irish in Australia:* 'The
new-born Irish generation … derived its
Irishness from militant nationalism or
socialism: a typical expression was its
formation in Melbourne, in 1964, of a
Connolly Association, on the British
model …' (2) **Connolly Column** [mis-
nomer] **1999** Fearghal McGarry, *Irish
Politics and the Spanish Civil War:*
'Notwithstanding the widespread
acceptance of another myth, that of the
"Connolly Column", there was no Irish

company in the International Brigades. Frank Ryan was merely the most senior officer in the Brigades rather than the "Commander of the James Connolly Section".' (3) **Connolly Station** [Dub., (1966-)]. **1995** Mícheál Ó Riain, *On the Move:* '… the committee adopted a proposal … that the Republic's main railway stations be renamed to commemorate the sixteen who were executed after the Rising … The selection of Connolly for Amiens Street station arose from the nearness of that station to James Connolly's 1916 headquarters in Liberty Hall.'

Constitution Room [**Shelbourne** Hotel, Dub.]. **2001** *Irish Times,* 20 Jan: 'The constitution of The Irish **Free State** was framed in one of its public rooms, known now as the "Constitution Room". Who knows what it might become in the future; perhaps the "Regency Room" or the "Savoy Room".'

Continuity IRA [<Irish Republican Army, paramilitary group]. **2000** Jim Cusack, *Irish Times,* 7 Feb: 'The group calling itself the Continuity IRA is thought most likely to be behind the bomb plot. This group is the paramilitary wing of Republican Sinn Féin, the party which broke from Sinn Féin in 1986. The Continuity IRA has existed since about 1991 …'

Corno di Bassetto [basset horn; nom de plume]. George Bernard Shaw (1856-1950) **1981** Dan H. Lawrence (ed.): *Shaw's Music:* 'It was not until February 1889 that Shaw replaced [E. Belfort] Bax completely and, in need of a pseudonym, created his *alter ego*. Corno di Bassetto, after months of anonymity, made his presence known to readers of The Star on 15 February …'

Corrigan's button [medic.]. **1999** W. J. McCormack (ed.), *The Blackwell Companion to Modern Irish Culture:* '[Sir Dominic] Corrigan, the first Catholic to play a leading role in the College of Physicians, described aortic incompetence and popularised "Corrigan's button" to apply counter-irritation.'

Country 'n' Irish [music]. **1984** Ciarán Moran, *The Crane Bag: Media and Popular Culture,* 'The Advertising Agency View of Ireland: Conservative Mono-Culture': '… the rural section prefers a hybrid musical style of American country and western crossed with native musical influences to produce "Country 'n' Irish" provided by groups called "The Nevada", "The Indians", "Doc Carroll" and "T.R. Dallas".' **2000** Kevin Courtney, *Irish Times,* 18 Apr: 'Country 'n' Irish was a unique, rather grotesque hybrid … but it became the music which defined rural Irish culture during the **Gaybo** era … In recent years, the **Celtic Tiger** has swept Country 'n' Irish under the **bogland,** but now the genre is threatening to resurface and reclaim its rightful place in the Irish *zeitgeist*.'

Court of Piepowder [legal, <Lat. *curia pedis pulverisati*]. Mediaeval legal instrument. **1333** *Charter of Edward III of Eng:* 'And we have granted to the Sovereign, Burgesses and Commons [of Kinsale] that they may hold one market on Wednesday and another on Saturday, and hold fairs in the town … and that the Sovereign be clerk and governor of the market and a Court of Piepowder by reason of the market and fairs aforesaid.' **1986** Patrick Logan, *Fair Day:* 'The person who presided over this court might be the chief magistrate of the town or someone appointed by him, and any disputes which arose during the

fair about prices, the quality of the goods or goods which were mislaid or stolen, were tried before the Court of Piepowder.'

Cows Lane/Lána na Bó [Dub.]. New street officially opened March 2001. **2001** Margery Long, *Irish Times*, 9 Mar: 'One is entitled to expect a little more from a Cabinet Minister than that he should promote illiteracy in two languages, as Mr Noel Dempsey does in your front-page photograph of March 7th. An apostrophe would not go amiss in "Cows Lane" and the Irish version should read "Lána na mBó". As a retired teacher, I feel ashamed.'

Craoibhín, An [Ir., little branch, < *An Craoibhín Aoibhinn*, the delightful little branch; pen-name]. Douglas Hyde (1860-1949], scholar and first President of Ire. **1949** *Irish Press*: 'During the greater part of the struggle [for independence], Douglas Hyde's was the guiding hand and his the biggest influence. The younger Gaels looked up to him as men look up to a prophet. "An Craoibhín" – the "Little Branch" – was the name that they called him affectionately ...'

Croker [abbrev., <Archbishop Croke (1842-1902), strong supporter of Gaelic games; nickname]. Croke Park, Dub., National Gaelic Athletic Assoc. headquarters. **2001** Tom Humphries, *Irish Times*, 19 Mar: 'A fraction of the **Bertie Bowl** would finish Croker AND save the Leaving Cert AND stop this awful demonisation of teachers.'

Crooked Mice [drama]. Theatre group. **1999** *Leinster Leader* (Naas), 25 Nov: 'Newbridge's innovative Crooked House Theatre Co. are launching another year of exciting young people's theatre and drama. Crooked Mice, the young

people's arm of Crooked House Theatre Co., will be running theatre and drama classes every Saturday ...'

Croppy [<short-cropped hair favoured by 1798 insurgents, on model of French revolution; nickname]. Rebel; Catholic (Ulster, derog.). **C1798** Pop. ballad: 'We'll fight for our country, our king and our crown,/And make all the traitors and croppies lie down ...'

Cross see **XMG**

Crotty's [Kilrush/Cill Rois, Co. an Chláir/Clare]. Pub. **2000** Jennifer O'Connell, *Sunday Business Post,* 11 Jun: 'One of west Clare's musical landmarks since the 1920s, this establishment borrows its name from the area's most celebrated, though now sadly demised, landlady. Elizabeth Crotty was as "quiet and unassuming a woman" as you're ever likely to find, or so a plaque on the wall informs the curious (though they weren't the first words which came to mind when we perused the framed sepia photographs of the blousy septuagenarian wielding her trademark concertina).'

Cruiser, the [nickname]. Conor Cruise O'Brien, diplomat, politician, academic and historian. **2000** 'Sadbh', *Irish Times,* 16 Sep: 'Sadbh would dearly love to be in Boston University on October 7th to hear Conor Cruise O'Brien speak on the fascinating topic, "How to Recapture Selective Memories". The Cruiser is addressing a conference on autobiography, biography and memoir ...'

Crum, the [nickname]. Crumlin Rd. jail, Belfast (closed 1994). **1999** Danny Morrison, *Irish Times*, 28 Jun: 'When I was young, certain people would be pointed out in whispered reverence as having been "on the [prison] ship", or "in the Crum". They were few in number, always men ...'

Cuala Press [<see **Ceoltóirí Chualann**; tradename (1908–46)]. Printers/publishers, formerly Dun Emer Press (1903). **1979** Robert Hogan (ed.): *Dictionary of Irish Literature:* 'In 1908 ... the Yeats sisters left the Dun Emer Industries and, as Cuala Industries, continued the embroidery and hand printing. The first book from the Cuala Press ... was finished in October 1908.'

Cuddens see **Foorins**

Cuirm [Ir.*idem,* 'a kind of ale formerly used by the Irish; drink in general' (Dinneen); brandname]. Beer. **2000** Breda Shannon, *Ireland of the Welcomes,* 'A Special Brew', May–Jun: '... the Greek physician Dioscorides, in the first century AD, reported that the Irish drank *Curmi* or *Coirm* ... St Patrick liked his *Coirm*, and kept the brewer Mescan at his monastery. Indeed, one of a range of beers brewed in Co. Carlow is named *Cuirm*.'

Culinso [Kinsale/Cionn tSáile, Co. Chorcaí/Cork]. Pub. **1981** Adrian MacLoughlin, *Streets of Ireland:* '... in a yard behind the fish market site is a charming inn with dormer windows, now known as the Hole-in-the-Wall but formerly the Culinso, corruption of "cuilin seo" in Irish, "this little corner".'

Cullaville/Culloville [Baile Mhic Cullach, Cos. Ard Mhacha/Armagh; Lú/Louth]. **1999** Tony Harnden, *'Bandit Country':* 'The eccentricities of the border remained. The settlement on the southernmost extremity of Northern Ireland was split in two; it was called Cullaville north of the border and Culloville to the south.'

Cullum's Cups [<John Edward Cullum, superintendent of Valentia Observatory, 1875–1915; nickname]. Base for electrical anemometer. **2001** Brendan McWilliams, *Irish Times,* 11 Jan: 'High on Killbeg Hill on Valentia Island, Co. Kerry, is a strange concrete structure, a landmark known locally as "Cullum's Cups".'

Cunningham Acre [<Sc. Gael. *Cuinneag,* milk pail + OE *ham,* village; family name]. Land measure. **1999** Flann Ó Riain, *Irish Times,* 9 Aug: '... it is interesting to recall the variety of measurements of area that existed in Ireland in times past. There was the *gníomh,* anglicised gneeve, the *ceathrú,* anglicised carrow, *baile biathach,* anglicised ballybetagh etc., the polls in Cavan and the tates in Fermanagh. There was the statute acre, the "plantation" acre, the English acre and the Cunningham acre ... The Cunningham perch of south-west Scotland is sometimes thought to have originated in Gaelic Ireland.'

Cursiter see **Thesiger**

Cú Uladh [Ir. idem, Hound of Ulster]. Cúchulainn, mythical hero. Hence [brandname]. Bus service. **1995** Mícheál Ó Riain, *On the Move:* 'On 27 November 1961 the Cú Uladh, the name given to the first [CIÉ] express bus, took off from Busáras without a conductor. Quickly, it was a success.'

Cyber Plains Housing estate. **2000** John Meagher, *Irish Independent,* 1 Jul: 'The [Leixlip] landscape has altered dramatically – not just by gleaming computer factories and the construction cranes that punctuate the skyline. The very name of the 200-house Cyber Plains indicates that its residents are probably workers in the IT sector.'

D

Dagenham Yank [<location of Ford motor factory, Dagenham, UK; nickname]. Workers in the Cork Ford factory who transferred to Dagenham (1930s). **1993** Michael Verdon, *Shawlies, Echo Boys, the Marsh and the Lanes, Old Cork Remembered:* 'Leaving behind a skeleton workforce the American employer moves the greater part of its operation to Dagenham ... Most of the foundry workers move with the company. These Corkmen become known as "Dagenham Yanks".'

Daily Bulletin see **Limerick Soviet**

Dakota [Dub.]. Pub. **2000** Willie Dillon, *Irish Independent,* 11 Nov: 'Dakota, on the site of an old clothing warehouse in South William Street, has been there since last May. A conscious decision was made to omit the definite article from Dakota. Has the name anything to do with John Lennon (who was shot dead outside the Dakota building in New York?). "A few people have said that," says Ciaran [McCabe], dismissing any macabre Lennon connection. "It's a destination – 'I'm going to Dakota.' It rolls off the tongue easily".'

Damer, Joseph (1630-1720) Miserly Dub. banker. Hence [derog.] **As rich as Damer**. **1930** *Irish Times,* 26 Apr: 'The simile "as rich as Damer" has been used for over two hundred years in Ireland, and derives its origin from the richest, meanest and most unscrupulous Shylock banker that modern times have produced.'

Damn Slow and Easy see **Dirty, Slow and Easy**

Danoli [sport]. Racehorse. **2000** Paul O'Meara, *Leinster Leader* (Naas), 7 Sep: 'Now a twelve year old, Danoli was one of the greatest of all National Hunt horses when he was trained in County Carlow by Tom Foley for owner Dan O'Neill, after whom he was named.'

Dardanelles see **Bomb Alley**

Dargan's Island [Belfast, 1849-]. **1921** D.J. Owen, *History of Belfast:* 'During its formation the materials from the excavations [of the Queen Victoria Channel] were deposited on the eastern side so as to form an island, which acted as a training bank for the river. This island became known as "Dargan's Island" from the name of the contractor, William Dargan ... Afterwards it was called "Queen's Island".'

Dark Rosaleen see **Róisín Dubh**

DART [acronym]. Dublin Area Rapid Transit, electrified rail system. **1984** Frank McDonald, *Irish Times,* 20 Feb: '"We picked DART after brainstorming through literally hundreds of names in three groups – hi-tech, contrived and descriptive", said Mr [Cartan] Finegan. "After testing them out on people, we found that words like 'speed' and 'line' in names like Speedway or Bayline had a drugs connotation. Finally, we settled on DART because it seemed to say everything".' **1995** Mícheál Ó Riain, *On the Move:* 'He [John Wilson] told the House of his failure in having an Irish language name applied to DART and of his irritation when finding that it was just a variation on BART (Bay Area Rapid Transit) when he visited San Francisco. The similarity between BART and

DART was hardly accidental ... The DART name, however, was tested for public reaction against a number of other names, e.g. Metra, Greenline, Rapidlink, Cityline, though no Irish language name ... was tested in the sample.' Hence **DART/DORT Accent**. Perceived manner of speech of southside Dub., gen. derog. **1992** Nuala O'Faolain, *Irish Times,* 28 Sep: 'The teacher said that the pupils of Dublin southside all-Irish schools speak Irish in this "**Roadwatch**" accent. Or call it a DART accent. Connoisseurs say that it is found along the line of the DART, becoming even more pronounced the nearer it gets to Glenageary.' **1999** Frank McNally, *Irish Times*, 26 Jun: 'So let me say again that the key element of DART-speak – the bit that attacks the nervous system of listeners in the same way as the sound of fingernails scratching a blackboard – is the sound that occurs twice in the word "southbound" and four times in the phrase "how now brown cow?".'

Davis Escape Chamber [<submarine escape apparatus]. Pub offering refuge to illicit drinkers. **1941** Sean O'Faolain, *An Irish Journey:* 'I had one such night with a group of men in my hotel. They began by complaining bitterly that the screw was being turned on the local public-houses and that the Davis Escape Chambers, as my friend described the pubs which evade the licensing laws, were becoming fewer and fewer.'

Dea [nickname, <?]. *Dublin University Magazine.* (1833-77). **1940** *Irish Times*, 18 Mar: 'Some magazines of last century were better known by a catchword than, perhaps, by their actual title. Blackwood's was "Mag," Frazer's was "Regina" and the Dublin University Magazine became known as "Dea".'

Dead Woman's Hill [Cork]. **1992** Tom McElligott, *Six O'Clock all over Cork:* 'As children we loved especially the Tivoli-Blackrock route ... the tram groaned its way up Dead Woman's Hill before speeding down to Ballintemple and Blackrock. Dead Woman's Hill owes its name to the morgue of a private mental hospital, Lindville, which existed at the foot of that hill.'

Dear Summer [nickname]. The summer of 1818, when the cost of living rose in the aftermath of the Napoleonic wars. **1938** Seumas MacManus, *The Rocky Road to **Dublin**:* 'I went to Mickey's funeral myself ... That was the second winter before Waterloo – and five before the Dear Summer.'

Defenders [politic.]. Agrarian Cath. secret soc., founded in response to Prot. **Peep o' Day Boys** (1780s). **1999** Tony Harnden, *'Bandit Country'*: 'A document found in the possession of a suspected Defender leader arrested near Jonesborough – founded early in the 18th century by Colonel Roth Jones – had been signed by 51 Defenders at Drumbanagher in County Monaghan and was dated 24 April 1789.'

De Paper [nickname, <alleged inability of Corkonians to pronounce dental fricative]. *Cork Examiner* newspaper, renamed *The Examiner* (1996) and *The Irish Examiner* (2000). **2000** Michael Clifford, *Sunday Tribune*, 5 May: 'The holier than thou tone of the advertisement must sound ironic to some of the more dyed in the wool readers of de paper ...'

Derry/Londonderry [Doire, city & Co.]. **2000** Raymond Whitaker, *Independent on Sunday* (London), 2 Apr: 'The first dilemma is what to call the place. For nationalists it is Derry … for unionists it is Londonderry, the "London" having been added when large tracts of land were granted to London livery companies during the 17th century. Gerry Anderson … used to call it "Derry-stroke-Londonderry", which evolved into "**Stroke City**"' See also **Free Derry Corner**

Desperate, Mrs see **Maud Gone Mad**

Dev [nickname]. Éamon de Valera (1882-1975), revolutionary and statesman. **1993** Tim Pat Coogan, *Dev: Long Fellow, Long Shadow:* 'It was in Rockwell [College] that he was first christened "Dev" – by one of the other teachers on the staff, Tom O'Donnell.'

Devil's Own, the [nickname, < bravery in Peninsular War (1809-14)]. Ir. regiment in Brit. army. **2000** *De Burca Rare Books Catalogue,* Spring: 'The Connaught Rangers, the "Devil's Own", the "Gallant Fighting 88th", was raised in 1793 by Colonel the Honorable John Thomas de Burgh, later 13th Earl of Clanricarde.'

Diageo [brandname]. Multinational org. (1) **1999** Michele Guinness, *The Guinness Spirit:* 'For years the family resisted any suggestions of changing the firm's name … Thanks to yet another major merger – this time with Grand Metropolitan – the company name of Guinness has given way to Diageo, pronounceable in the days of the multinationals in any language. The word means "through" and "earth", and for its creation Guinness paid an advertising company £250,000. But … no one, for the forseeable future, will ever nip out for a pint of Diageo.' (2) **1999** Sandra Burke, *Irish Times,* 20 Sep: 'Diageo … is difficult to pronounce, hard to remember and has no clear connection with anything.' See also **Guinness**; **Uncle Arthur**.

Dingle [An Daingean/Daingean Uí Chúis, Co. Chiarraí/Kerry; town]. Hence (1) **Dingle pie** [gastronomy]. **1893** Theodora Fitzgibbon, *Irish Traditional Food:* 'Mutton pies – *Pióga caoireola.* These pies, also called "Dingle pies", and somewhat like the Cornish pasty, are traditional in Co. Kerry and are still sold in Dingle and every August at Puck Fair [see **King Puck**] in Killorglin.' (2) **Dingley-Cooch/Cootch** [nickname]. Unimaginable location, <its remoteness, as in **send to Dingley-Cooch** Send to Coventry.

DIRT [acronym]. Deposit Interest Retention Tax; notoriously not deducted nor remitted to Revenue Commiss-ioners by major financial institutions and others (1980s-90s). Hence many punning references. See **Celtic Tiger** (Breathnach).

Dirty Shirts [nickname]. Royal **Munster** Fusiliers, Ir. regiment of Brit. army. **1998** Tom Dooley, *History Ireland,* Spring: 'The Munsters' nickname, the "Dirty Shirts", by which they became popularly and famously known, has been attributed to comments by General Lake at the siege of Bhurtpore in 1805. But it more probably dates from the Indian Mutiny …'

Dirty, Slow and Easy/Damn Slow and Easy [nickname, <initials]. Dublin & South Eastern Railway (1907-25). **1996** Anthony Cronin, *Samuel Beckett, The Last Modernist:* 'The line by which they travelled was the DSER … known, though not in earshot of the children, as the "Damn Slow and Easy" Railway because of its frequent stops and delays.'

Divil's bedpost, the [nickname, <Hiberno-Eng. pronoun. of 'devil';]. Playing card. **2000** Diarmaid Ó Muirithe, *Irish Times,* 30 Sep: 'I used to play cards in Kilkenny long ago; around Glenmore I heard the four of clubs spoken of as *the divil's bedpost*, the unluckiest card in the pack.'

Dockyard confetti [<Harland & Wolff shipyard, Belfast]. Metal detritus used as ammunition. **1999** Tony Harnden, *'Bandit Country'*: 'Around the explosives had been packed "dockyard confetti" – jagged metal, nails and bolts – designed to kill and maim members of an Army patrol returning to Bessbrook Mill.' See **Belfast Confetti**

Dodo [nickname]. Adelaide Mary Guinness (1844-1916), wife of 1st Earl of **Iveagh**. **1999** Michele Guinness, *The Guinness Spirit:* 'Edward Cecil Guinness ... the power behind the Brewery, married his cousin Adelaide Mary ... Although "Dodo", as she was known, was three years older than her groom ... her mother was not at all pleased with the match.'

Doggett's Coat and Badge [<Thomas Doggett, travelling actor, b. Dub. c1660]. **1895** E. Cobham Brewer, *A Dictionary of Phrase and Fable* [new ed.]: 'The first prize in the Thames rowing-match, given on the 1st of August every year. So called from Thomas Doggett, an actor of Drury Lane, who signalised the accession of George I to the throne by giving a waterman's coat and badge to the winner of the race.'

Dolan's ass [<?]. Time-server, sychophant. **1961** Frank O'Connor, *An Only Child:* 'My fight for Irish freedom was of the same order as my fight for other sorts of freedom. Still like Dolan's ass, I

went a bit of the way with everybody.' Similarly, Billy Harran's dog; Lanna Macree's dog; **Lanty McHale's dog**; O'Brien's dog.

Doll's House [nickname]. Sheriff's house, Cork city. **1971** Seán Beecher, *The Story of Cork:* 'The Sheriff's house was familiarly known as the "Doll's House" and was a beautifully symmetrical structure ... The "Doll's House was featured in Frank O'Connor's *The Saint and Mary Kate* and Donal Giltinan's *Goldfish in the Sun.*'

Dolocher [*Recte* **Olocher**]. Suicide in Black Dog prison, Dub., alleged to have taken the form of a black pig. **1939** P.J. McCall, *Dublin Historical Record,* 'In the Shadow of Christ Church', Dec: '... a woman came before the magistrates and made oath that she saw the Dolocher (by which name it afterwards went) in Christchurch Lane – that it made a bite at her with its tusks, and that she fled and left her cloak with the monster.'

Donegal Red [agric.]. Cattle breed. **1986** Patrick Logan, *Fair Day:* 'There were some other native Irish breeds, all of which appear to have died out. These included the Donegal Red and the Irish Dun, and I used to hear old men speak of a breed which they called the "Yellow Polly". These were said to have been particularly good milkers.'

Don 'n' Nelly [advt. characters, < 'Donnelly' (sausages). 1950s-]. **2000** Lise Hand, *Sunday Tribune,* 20 Feb: 'an imaginative neon sign can be a jolly presence on a drab boulevard ... And most grizzled **Dubs** [see **Dublin**] over the age of 30 fondly remember the Donnelly's Sausages neon pan-and-flying food illumination on Westmoreland St.'

Doras [Ir. *idem*, door; tradename]. Directory of Irish and Irish-related websites (1996–). **2000** Advt: 'Doras Abú. Abú is the Irish term for excellence [lit. for ever!] or fantastic and each week the Doras team selects a site of the week from the Doras Directory at its Doras Abú.'

Dracula [lit.]. Character in eponymous novel by Bram Stoker (1847-1912). Hence [joc.]. **2000** Seán Moran, *Irish Times*, 5 Jul: 'Did you know how Bram Stoker got the idea for Dracula? He was a theatre manager and picked up the idea when travelling in the midlands, scouting out good venues. He was told Offaly [GAA] teams are never dead, undead if you like, and the name Dracula is a derivation of the Irish droch cúl, in English a jammy goal – the count's traditional means of cheating death.'

Drapier, the/M.B. Drapier [nom de plume]. Employed by Jonathan Swift in *A Letter to the Shop-Keepers, Tradesmen, Farmers, and Common-People of Ireland concerning the Brass Half-Pence coined by Mr Woods* ... (1724). **1724** The Lord Lieutenant and Council of Ireland, *A Proclamation*, 27 Oct: 'Whereas a Wicked and Malicious Pamphlet, Intituled, *A Letter to the whole People of* Ireland, *by* M.B. *Drapier, Author of the Letter to the Shopkeepers,* &c ... in which are contained several Seditious and Scandalous Paragraphs highly Reflecting upon His Majesty and His Ministers ... We the Lord Lieutenant and Council do hereby Publish and Declare, That in Order to Discover the Author of the said Seditious Pamphlet, We will give the necessary orders for the Payment of Three Hundred Pounds *Sterling* ...' See also **Wood's Halfpence**

Dr Hay's Head [<Dr George Hay, C18 Scottish Cath. bishop]. Shop sign used by Pat Wogan, bookseller & printer, Bridge St. Dub., late C18. **1958** Thomas Wall, *The Sign of Dr Hay's Head:* 'Dr Hay's Head over Wogan's shop was in some respects a sign of the times and a symbol of the Catholic revival which came in the late decades of the eighteenth century.'

Drum [poss.<military patronage (C18); nickname]. Cork city social assembly. **1824** Thomas Crofton Croker, *Researches in the South of Ireland:* 'there were weekly meetings termed Drums, which are said to have been extremely sociable and agreeable ...'

Drumm Battery Train [<Dr James Drumm, scientist & inventor]. Innovative transport powered by high voltage rechargeable batteries, Dublin & South Eastern Rly., (1922-50). **1932** 'The Watchman', *The Glensman* (Cushendall, Co. Antrim), Apr: 'Quite the most interesting feature of the Irish **Free State** Patents Office Journal for February is the fact that it discloses at last the secret of the Drumm invention ...'

Dublin [Baile Átha Cliath, city & Co.]. Hence (1) **Dublin Man** Archetypical citizen, form preferred by cognoscenti to **Dubliner**, both now gen. replaced by **Dub**. (also denoting member of Royal Dublin Fusiliers, former Brit. army regiment). **1977** Flann O'Brien (**Myles na gCopaleen**), *The Hair of the Dogma:* '"Ah yes", he says ... "The two of them was buried in the same grave." If you are yourself even one-eighth a true Dublin Man, your reaction will be instantaneous. You will say: "Pairdin?".' (2) **Dublin South/Dublin North** [<mutual rivalry/contempt of communities north and south of the Liffey]. **2000** Seán O'Driscoll, *Sunday Tribune*, 6 Feb: 'Visitors to Glasnevin [cemetery]

might be surprised to see signposts for "Dublin South" and "Dublin North" which are marked out for workers to find their way around, not as an indication of after-life snobbery.' (3) **Dublin 4** [<southside postal district]. **1999** Eddie Holt, *Irish Times*, 16 Oct: 'In its idiomatically pejorative meaning, "Dublin 4" suggests a state of mind which thinks it is the mind of the state or, at least, ought to be. Hence the legitimate and generally healthy criticisms the term attracts. But nobody pretends that the geographical district is utterly synonymous with the mindset suggested by the cliché.'

Duke of Tralee [nickname]. Roger Brosnahan. **1981** Adrian MacLoughlin, *Streets of Ireland:* 'Tralee was the birthplace of Roger Brosnahan (1881-1945) who became a celebrated baseball player in America, was known as the "Duke of Tralee" and introduced the use of shinguards in 1907.'

Dunbar see **Hamlet**

Dunphy's Corner [Dub.] **1955** J.L.J. Hughes, *Dublin Historical Record,* 'Dublin Street Names', Sep: 'The present Doyle's Corner at Phibsborough I knew as Dunphy's Corner. If a person was asked to explain a morning's absence from work he might reply that he had gone round Dunphy's Corner, meaning that he had attended a funeral to Glasnevin Cemetery.'

Durationist [nickname]. Individual enlisting in Defence Forces for the duration of the **Emergency**. **1991** John P. Duggan, *A History of the Irish Army:* 'On 7 June 1940 the government declared that a state of emergency existed. The Defence Forces Act was amended to authorise the enlistment of personnel for the duration of the Emergency ("Durationists" or "**E-men**"].'

Dust, the [nickname]. Stonemasons. **1966** Séamus Murphy, *Stone Mad:* the right to have beer at 11 o'clock in the morning ... is still held by the "Dust".'

Dustin [Hofmann] [media]. TV turkey puppet created by John Morrison; subseq. (1990s) ubiquitous in the role of a national watchbird. **1999** Frank McNally, *Irish Times*, 28 Dec: 'Cynicism about politics affects the presidential elections in November, when the veteran turkey, Dustin, wins more than half the votes cast. His election is eventually overruled on the grounds that, though old for a turkey, he is not the 35 years of age required by the Constitution.' **2000** Ronan McCabe, quoted *Irish Times,* 23 Dec: '"He says what other people think", McCabe muses. "You can't really react to a turkey, or you'll look like a bigger plank than people already say you are. **Zig and Zag** were always good on music and pop culture. Dustin on sport and politics."'

Dutch Billy [nickname, <William, prince of Orange, later William III of Eng.]. Dub. house style with curvilinear gables. **1991** Douglas Bennett, *Encyclopaedia of Dublin:* 'In about 1670 a housing development began in the area [the Coombe] with houses known as Dutch Billies with their gables facing the street.'

Dyke, de/the [nickname, abbrev.] The Mardyke, Cork thoroughfare (1719). **1992** Tom McElligott, *Six O'Clock all over Cork:* '... we imagined India as being governed exclusively by Pres [Presentation College] boys who talked of Delhi as if it was an extension of "de Dyke"...'

Dyker [nickname, <Klondyke, he having claimed to have dug for gold in the Yukon]. 'Dr' Jeremiah Healy, Cork city character. **1971** Seán Beecher, *The Story of Cork:* 'The principal plank in the "Dyker"'s [election] campaign was that a toilet should be erected for the ladies in the centre of the city ... "The nations of Europe are frantically rearming. They are spending millions of pounds on arsenals – and all I ask is one urinal".'

E

Earl of Cork [nickname]. William Carleton (1794-1869). **1972** Eric Partridge, *Dictionary of Historical Slang:* 'Called the Earl of Cork, because he's the poorest nobleman in Ireland.'

Early, Biddy see **Biddy Early**

Easter house [Ulster]. Children's playhouse. **1996** C.I. Macafee (ed.), *A Concise Ulster Dictionary:* 'playhouse made of branches, sacks, etc. where children boil eggs at Easter.'

Easter Lily [*Lilium longiflorum, et al.*]. Worn by post-1916 republicans to commemorate the Rising and thus referred to. **1944** 'Puss' (M.J.F. Mathews), *T.C.D.,* 9 Mar., 'Moryah': 'You can quote me every one of Emmet's speeches?/And you never stigmatise the G.A.A?/So you wear an Easter Lily/And you blew up Good **King Billy** ...'

Easterling [nautical]. **1945** Anthony T. Lawlor, *Irish Maritime Survey:* '... a seaman or ship from Scandinavia, the Baltic, Germany or the Low Countries. It is an old term, and in this country has sometimes been applied to a person from Great Britain.'

e-blana [<Eblana, name for Dublin first used by Egypt. geographer Ptolemy (C2); media]. Internet provider. **2000** Advt: 'e-blana. We map your world; you see the future.'

Echo boys [nickname, Cork]. Young street sellers of *Evening Echo* newspaper. **1975** S.F. Pettit, *This City of Cork:* 'To these traditional cries there came another towards the end of the [19th] century when the "Echo" boys spilled onto the streets in the late afternoon.'

Edge, the see **the Edge**

Effernock Manor *see* **Effin**

Effin [Eifinn, Co. Luimní/Limerick; village]. Source of translingual ribaldry (cf. Intercourse, Penna., USA). **1999** Kathryn Holmquist, *Irish Times*, 20 Sep: 'The *Limerick Leader* chose its words carefully when it reported that e.coli had forced the closure of a local water system: 'Effin water off.' Cf. also in this regard **Effernock Manor** [housing development] Trim, Co. Meath.

Eglinton see **HMS Gannet**

Eighty-Two Club [<?]. Political club. **1987** Richard Davis, *The Young Ireland Movement:* 'Early 1845 saw the inauguration of a new organisation ... The Eighty-Two Club, intended as an élitist auxiliary of the Repeal Association, provided a centre for the "intelligence, rank and wealth" of Repeal and attracted super-class sympathisers ...'

eircom [brandname, <*Éire* + *(Tele)com*]. Communications co., formerly Telecom Éireann. **1999** Sandra Burke, *Irish Times,* 20 Sep: 'The word eircom ...was a clever choice. It signifies both Irishness and the transformation from a phone company to a communications group ... Apparently, many Europeans had difficulty pronouncing Éireann while some Americans assumed Telecom Éireann was an Iranian phone company.' Hence **Eircom Park** Projected soccer stadium. **2000** Frank McDonald, *The Construction of Dublin:* 'Bernard O'Byrne ... who had been a member of the steering committee for the **Taoiseach's** "Abbotstown Albatross" project, otherwise known as the "**Bertie Bowl**", made it clear that it would be going ahead with its own 45,000-seater Eircom Park scheme ... (The name was a payoff for eircom, who pledged £11 million to the project.)'

Éirí na Gréine [Ir., sunrise]. Japanese band. **2000** Ian Kilroy, *Irish Times*, 3 May: 'An example of the internationalisation of Irish traditional music is a band such as Éirí na Gréine. The name might suggest a hardcore traditional outfit, but when you discover that one of the principal players is named Takeshi Yasui you may be a little taken aback ... But Irish music has even filtered down to the Japanese provinces, with bands such as the Nagoya-based Irish traditional group The Rising Pints.'

EJ-10 [brandname, <Eddie Jordan, Formula One team manager]. Energy drink. **2000** Paul O'Kane, *Sunday Tribune*, 26 Nov: 'The energy drink is likely to be the first in a range of Jordan branded items as Eddie and his backer attempt to capitalise on the popularity of his team.'

Electron [physics]. Invariable charge of negative electricity. **1994** K.S. Daly, *Ireland, an Encyclopaedia for the Bewildered:* 'The first use of the word "electron" in its present meaning is attributed to Irishman George Johnstone Stoney in 1891.'

El Paso [nickname]. Dundalk, Co. Lú/Louth. **2000** Frank McNally, *Irish Times,* 16 Dec: 'Residents saw the [Clinton] visit as a formal end to the bad old days during which, as a local person reminded our reporter, the town was known as "El Paso", especially in the

North. There was a geographical contradiction in this because the Republic as a whole used to be referred to in the North as "Mexico", partly on account of it being south of the border, and partly because of its poverty in the eyes of the *gringos* who lived north of the Forkhill customs post.'

E-man [nickname]. Volunteer for military service during the **Emergency**. **1996** Deasún Breathnach, *Irish Times*, 1 Apr: 'Volunteers after the declaration [of war] were known as E (for Emergency) men. I became one of them.' See also **Durationist**

Emerald Isle [attrib., <green landscape]. (1) Ireland, latterly ironic; first employed by William Drennan (1754–1820) in 'When Erin first Rose': 'Nor one feeling of vengeance presume to defile/The cause of the men of the Emerald Isle.' **2000** Frank McNally, *Irish Times*, 29 Jan: 'But our physical landscape is fast changing. Specifically, Ireland is in danger of losing the title "Emerald Isle", a reputation which rested on its possession – prior to joining the EEC – of "40 shades of green". Intensive farming and increased use of fertiliser had reduced this to about 15 shades of green at the latest count.' (2) Montserrat, W. Indies. **1985** Norman Mongan, *CARA*, Mar./Apl: '... the first thing that catches the eye is the big green shamrock that adorns the airport building. "Welcome to the Emerald Isle of the Caribbean" ...'

Emerald Tiger [econ., <Far East 'Tiger Economy' model, coined by US magazine *Newsweek*, Dec, 1996, superseded by **Celtic Tiger**]. Ir. economy thus perceived. **1996** Fintan O'Toole, *Irish Times,* 28 Dec: 'What *Newsweek* magazine described as ... the Emerald Tiger

... was not so much on the prowl as on the razzle-dazzle.'

Emergency, the World War II, 1939-45. **1983** Robert Fisk, *In Time of War*: 'De Valera introduced legislation to amend article 28 of the Irish Constitution, allowing the Dáil to declare a state of emergency even though Éire was neutral. Thus 'the Emergency' came into existence, a legally accurate but nonetheless euphemistic description for what, north of the border, was about to become the Second World War.'

Emergency Man [<?] **1895** E. Cobham Brewer, *A Dictionary of Phrase and Fable* (new ed.): 'One engaged for some special service, as in Irish eviction'. **1883** Lord Rossmore, *Orange proclamation* (Derry), 16 Oct: 'They [the **Invincibles** and Land Leaguers] declare that you're as ready to obey them as their dupes in the south, but we will show them, as did the Tyrone men, that they are liars and slanderers. Boycott and Emergencymen to the front, and down with Parnell and rebellion!' **1999** Kathy Sheridan, *Irish Times,* 7 Aug: '[William] Simpson, smart and dapper, was an "emergencyman" or property defence protector for big landowners – a deeply unpopular breed subject to constant attack and local boycott ...'

Enable Ireland [State body]. Provider of services to the physically disabled. **2000** Elaine Larkin, *Irish Times,* 27 Oct: 'It is the day before the official opening of the centre and the name change from Cerebral Palsy Ireland to Enable Ireland ... He [Michael Cummins] gives two reasons behind the change of name. "People felt that the name shouldn't be disability-specific – only 30 per cent of the client base had cerebral palsy ... The whole language of disabilities is an ever-changing process".'

Enterprise [transport]. (1) Bus service. **1969** Patrick Flanagan, *Transport in Ireland 1880-1910*: 'As early as 1905 there was quite a fleet ... of assorted charabancs operating on the direct route between Bangor and Donaghadee. Each vehicle gloried in a name – "Enterprise", "Invincible", "Reliance" and so on.' (2) Inter-city rail service. **1987/88** W.T. Scott, *Five Foot Three* (Belfast), 'The Enterprise': 'The Great Northern Railway made a commendable, if unsuccessful, attempt to recover from World War II and the Enterprise was one of the moves to recovery. The inaugural train left Belfast at 10.30 am on 11 August 1947 headed by No. 83 "Eagle"...'

Enya [stage name]. Eithne Ní Bhraonáin, singer. Hence **Enyanomics** [nonce word]. Economic phenomenon. **1999** Fintan O'Toole, *Irish Times*, 23 Nov: 'A country that used to be admired, not least for the alleged authenticity of its culture, has now given the world a new word for the virtual economy – Enyanomics, named after the Irish new age singer who had sold millions of CDs around the world without ever giving a live concert.'

Erin [<dat. of Ir. *Éire*, Ireland]. *Idem.* **1807** T. Comerford: *The History of Ireland (4th ed.):* 'The natives call this island Erin; from which the names Ierna, Juverna, Iouernia, Overnia, and Hibernia (see **Hibernian Archipelago**) are plainly derived. The Britons styled it Yverdon; the Romans, Hibernia; and the Saxons, Iren-landt, i.e. the country of Iren or Erin.' **1996** Joep Leerssen, *Mere Irish and Fíor-Ghael:* '[Under pre-Union Irish Patriotism] a national ideal of Ireland, embracing Protestant Anglo-Irish and Catholic Gaels alike, had come into being. A new word was even coined to describe this newly-imagined nation:

the neologism *Erin* came into vogue around this time ...' Hence: (1) **Erin Foods** [brandname]. **1996** Fintan O'Toole, *The Ex-Isle of Erin:* '... he [Michael Costello] tried to create an aggressively commercial but socially progressive food processing company called Erin Foods (Erin means, simply, Ireland and the symbolism was intentional – Costello saw the company as a national metaphor) ...' (2) **Erinox** [brandname]. Beef cube, à la 'Oxo'. **1951** Advt., *Wolfe Tone Annual:* 'I just turn towards the shelf – and I'm smiling to myself -/For I always store a tin or two of CLOVER./ And just beside them in a box/I keep a packet of ERINOX.' *See* **Garryowen**. (3) **2RN** [media]. Radio call-sign (1926-). **2001** John Bowman, RTÉ radio, 'Bowman at 8.30', Jan. 1: 'The call sign had been agreed internationally and 2RN was chosen because it rendered phonetically the last three syllables of *Come Back to Erin*'.

Erse [early Sc. variation of *Irish*]. Scots Gallic and more usually Irish; now gen. derog. **1999** Renagh Holohan, *Irish Times,* 16 Oct: 'Arthur Quinlan ... remembers [Herbert] Morrison's stopover here after the second World War. The British foreign secretary arrived at Foynes by flying boat ... and was escorted indoors by the airport manager, Col Patrick Maher. "What language is that?", he asked pointing to a sign in Irish. *Eirse* [sic] said his British civil servants. Oh yes, said Morrison, *Arse*. His entourage tittered at his great wit.'

Euthymol [brandname, poss. <Gk. *euthymy*) cheerfulness of mind (OED) + Lat. *olium*, oil]. Toothpaste. **2000** Éibhir Mulqueen, *Irish Times,* 13 May: 'Further north is the birthplace of Euthymol toothpaste, "a scientific dental preparation" invented by the Moynan brothers in the chemical plant founded outside Nenagh in 1924.'

Exhibition Expositor and Advertiser, The [media]. Journal of Irish Industrial Exhibition, Dub. (1853). **1993** Nancy Netzer, in Adele M. Dalsimer (ed.), *Visualising Ireland:* '... the *Exhibition Expositor* described [Queen] Victoria and Albert's visits to the exhibition and especially their call on **Dargan** at home as "amongst the most important incidents in its history, and deserving of a permanent record in the annals of this country".'

Ex-Pat [nickname, play on expatriate]. Academic emigrant. **1999** Neil Mackay, *Sunday Tribune,* 11 Apr: 'Scottish student life teems with Northern Irish. They call first years "ex-Pats". The bus-run from Glasgow is known as the "Paddy wagon" ...'

Extermination, the Term for eviction employed by C19 nationalist press. **1901** *The Poems of R.D. Williams:* poem title.

F

Fadó [Ir., long ago.] Hence (1) Dub. restaurant. **2000** Tom Doorley, *Sunday Tribune*, 2 Jul: 'Fadó, apart from being a traditional way of starting a story and a form of Portugese lamentation, is a joint venture between Dublin Corporation and a catering company.' **2000** Chris Heaney, *Irish Times*, 28 Oct: 'It must be said that the name doesn't do it any favours. "Fadó" may be a punchy two-syllable title, but when I first heard the name I had visions of a Bunratty Castle olde-style mediaeval "feast" complete with mead, tranches of mutton and all the attendant palaver.' (2) Pub company. **2000** *Sunday Tribune*, 24 Sep: 'Fadó, the Atlanta-based Irish pub company, has managed to pick up a couple of new pubs from American brewpub company Ram International … Apparently Ram wasn't particularly looking to sell the two pubs, based in downtown Seattle and both named **Tír na nÓg** …'

Faic see **Brogue about**

Faithful/Faithful County [nickname]. Co. Uíbh Fháilí/Offaly, esp. as applied to its GAA teams. **1982** Vivienne Clarke, *Leinster Gaelic Games Annual*: 'The title of the "Faithful County" generally attri-buted to Bob O'Keeffe, an Association President in the mid-Thirties, dates only from the Golden Jubilee era [1980s] and was no doubt prompted by his observations of the efforts of a small county to achieve some measure of success in both codes [hurling/football] …' **2000** *Irish Independent*, 5 Aug: '**Rebels** primed to stifle the Faithful backlash.'

False Men see **Fir Bréaga**

FAT DAD [acronym]. The six counties of NI. **1994** K.S. Daly, *Ireland, an Encyclopaedia for the Bewildered*: 'Acronym for the six counties of Ulster under British rule, Fermanagh, Antrim, Tyrone, Derry, Armagh, Down.'

Father Prout [nom de plume; lit.]. Francis Sylvester Mahony (1804-66). **2000** *Irish Times*, 1 Jul: 'When Mahony began his career in journalism he chose as his pseudonym that of a lately deceased Fr Prout, parish priest of Watergrasshill near Cork.'

Father Trendy [media]. Populist cleric created for TV by humorist/actor Dermot Morgan on model of journalist Fr Brian Darcy (1980s). Hence **Father Trendyism/Trendiness** Banal tabloid religion for the unthinking. **1995** Eddie Holt, *Irish Times*, 6 Nov: 'Dr Daly … was furious that the authority of the conservative church was being challenged. His rigidity exposed the safe, cosmetic, functional unction of three decades of Father Trendiness.'

Faugh-a-Ballagh [<Ir. *fág an bealach*, clear the way]. (1) [nickname]. Coach. **1939** *Irish Times*, 19 Mar: '**Bianconi** started with a small jaunting car, increasing to the big lumbering four-wheeler coach. The light-going coaches were known as "Faugh-a-Ballagh" (clear the way), the next size the **Massy-Dawsons**, and the heaviest the **Finn McCouls**. The drivers of these coaches wore great frieze **ulsters** to defy the weather …'

Favourite (1)[transport]. **1959** *The Irish Times*, 8 Jun: 'In 1859 there were four horse-drawn omnibus routes in the Dublin area. The "Favourite" omnibuses, starting from Nelson Pillar, served

133

Ranelagh and Clonskea, a second service of the same name ran from Nelson Pillar to Sandymount, while a third ran to Roundtown or Terenure ...' (2) [brandname] Soap. **1928** Advt., *Leabhar Tailteann:* 'The Favourite Soap. A Pure Household Soap in Tablets, recommended by Sir Charles Cameron, C.B., M.D. Manufactured only by Dixon & Co., The Erne Soap and Candle Works, Dublin.'

FBI [acronym, Savannah, Georgia, USA]. The native Irish. **2000** Margaret O'Brien, *Avenue*, Feb: 'Jerry [Hogan] introduces me to the Savannah interpretation of FBI – it stands for "Foreign Born Irishperson". While you might be forgiven for believing that label applies to himself – it doesn't, it's the descriptor reserved for those of us actually born in Ireland ...'

Feinaiglian Institution, the [<Prof. Von Feinaigle]. Eccentric Dub. C19 school (1813-c33) located in Aldborough House. **1930** *Irish Times,* 26 Sep: '... the professor, having acquired the premises for one eighth of their original cost, founded the Feinaiglian Institution, which lasted about twenty years. He is chiefly remembered as having devised a system of memorising dates which consisted in changing the figures of the date into the letters of the alphabet corresponding to them in their numerical order. These letters were then twisted into a word, to be somehow associated with the date to be remembered.' Hence [?] **finagle** [Ir. & US sl.] Fix, contrive, arrange by dubious means.

Fenian [adj. & n., <Ir. *na Fianna*] Legendary warrior-band led by Fionn Mac Cumhaill/**Finn McCoul**. Hence (1) Member of Fenian Brotherhood, revolutionary organisation founded

New York 1859. **1910** John Denvir, *The Life Story of an Old Rebel:* 'The trials in 1859, following the arrests in connection with the **Phoenix** movement ... were the first public manifestations of what developed into the great organisation known in America as the Fenian Brotherhood, and, on this side of the Atlantic, as the IRB, or Irish Revolutionary Brotherhood'; (2) [*idem, derog.,* Ulster] Catholics/Nationalists. **1913** Alexander Irvine, *My Lady of the Chimney Corner:* '"Anthrim's a purty good place fur pigs to live in," he told the travellers. "Ye see, pigs is naither Fenians nor Orangemen.' (3) **Fenian-lover** [derog., Ulster]. Protestant/Unionist 'soft' on Catholics/Nationalists. **2000** David McKittrick, *Irish Independent*, 27 May: 'The last time David Trimble addressed the Ulster Unionist Council ... the jeers and heckles directed against him included a number of calls of "Fenian-lover". The accusation of being prepared to consort with Catholics is one of the most primeval and one of the most potent in the loyalist lexicon.' (4) **Fenian Ram** [naut.]. Submarine commissioned by US Fenians from John Holland (b. Liscannor, Co. Clare, 1841). **1983** Ray Hardie, *Sunday Press*, 13 Nov: '... the committee commissioned him to build a second submarine, one that in the words of Holland's brother Michael would "undoubtedly destroy English naval supremacy". It was dubbed the FENIAN RAM by a reporter from the New York Sun.'

Fiacre, St [Ir. *Fiachra*]. **1895** E. Cobham Brewer, *A Dictionary of Phrase and Fable* (new ed.): 'A French cab or hackney coach. So called from the Hotel de St Fiacre, Paris, where the first station of these coaches was established by M. Sauvage, about 1650.' **1964** John

Irivine, *A Treasury of Irish Saints:* 'St Fiacre is claimed by both the Scots and the Irish as their countryman. He crossed to Gaul early in the sixth century ... The Paris cabs took the name of "fiacres" from having started from a house with a statue of this Saint over the doorway.' Hence **Aer Lingus** EI-AKG Friendship 100 *St Fiacra/Fiachra* (registered 10 Sep. 1957).

Fianna Fáil [Ir. *idem*, Soldiers of Ireland, aka **Soldiers of Destiny**;] (1) [media]. Revolutionary journal (1914). **2001** Whyte's (Dub.) catalogue, *The Eclectic Collector Sale,* 15 Jan: 'A Journal for Militant Ireland ed. by Terence McSwiney, Co. Cork ... Its title was the first use in modern times of the term "Fianna Fáil" which MacSwiney borrowcd from Gaclic mythology.' (2) Political party (1926-). Hence **Fianna Fáilers**, members/supporters of F.F. **1998** Fergus Finlay, *Snakes and Ladders:* '... Dick [Spring] even joked at one point that we should consider putting an ad in the newspapers, using the job description and saying "Fianna Fáilers need not apply".'

Fibber McGee [<?]. Curse. **1997** Neil Francis, *Sunday Tribune,* 10 Aug: 'The money from participation in the European [rugby] Competition is well worth the effort. So why play the inter-pro series at all, since nobody gives a Fibber McGee about winning it?'

Field, the [Ulster]. Venue for Orange gatherings on the **Twelfth**. **1993** Muriel Breen, *Liquorice All-sorts, A Girl Growing Up:* '"If you're good," Mumper said, "and if it's a nice day, we'll all go to "the Field on the 12th of July". "What's 'the Field'?" I asked her, puzzled. "It's a wonderful picnic", she said, "run by the Orange Order".'

Fields of Athenry, the [town, Co. na Gaillimhe/Galway]. Ballad sung esp. on international sporting occasions. **2000** Frank McNally, *Irish Times,* 19 Aug: 'Even in these days, when optimism is official Government policy ... some of the old tradition lingers. It's no coincidence that the favourite chant of Irish soccer supporters is a song about how lonely it is around the fields of Athenry – and how low-lying and generally miserable those poxy, rain-sodden fields are.'

Fifteen Acres, the [**Phoenix Park**, Dub.]. Large open area. **1907** Samuel A. Ossory Fitzpatrick, *Dublin:* 'On the left of the main road is the fine review ground, curiously designated the "Fifteen" acres, its area being some 200, where formerly many notable duels were fought.'

Fifteenth Night 15 Aug., feast of the Assumption, celebrated by Belfast Catholics with bonfires. **1997** Ciaran Carson, *The Star Factory:* '... we threw out our old horsehair-stuffed, hide-covered sofa, and half-dismantled it with a hatchet before dragging it off to the place of immolation where, on the Fifteenth Night, it would be assumed as smoke into the heavens ...'

Finbarr/Fin Barre, St Patron saint of Cork. **1999** Pádraig Ó Riain, *Irish Times,* 26 Oct: '... since 1977, I have been publishing books and articles to show that what travelled along the river Lee was not the saint but his legend. In fact, the saint never set foot in Cork, or in any other of the many churches associated with his name and legend ...' **2000** Dick Hogan, *Irish Times,* 1 Feb: 'How would you spell it? St Fin Barre's or St Finbarr's? In one Christian tradition it is the former, in the other, the latter ... the present and wonderful edifice of St Fin Barre's Church of Ireland Cathedral [is] nowadays as much a part of Cork's skyline as anything else that links the city to its roots.' Hence (1) [tradename]. Brewery. **1997** Diarmuid Ó Drisceoil & Donal Ó Drisceoil, *The Murphy's Story:* 'Abbot's Brewery had been established in 1805 and originally brewed a sweet table beer called "Abbot's Beer". It was taken over in 1861 by Sir John Arnott & Co. Ltd … and renamed St Fin Barre's Brewery on account of its location, on Fitton Street, now Sharman Crawford Street, near St Fin Barre's Cathedral.' (2) **Barrs, the** [abbrev., sport; nickname] Hurling team (1876-). See **Rancher**

Fine Gael [Ir. *fine*, family/racial group]. Political party (1933-). Hence **Fine Gaeler** [nickname] Member/supporter of that party. **2000** Pat Leahy, *Sunday Business Post,* 25 Jun: '"Whatever happens from here on in, it's a great day for us," said one senior Fine Gaeler as the results of the first complete tallies … were digested around the hall.'

Finian, Sts [Ir. *Finnén;* Finnén, bishop of Moville; Finnén, abbot of Clonard, amongst others]. Hence (1) [aviation]. **Aer Lingus** Friendship 100 *St Finian* (registered 10 Sep 1957); (2) [brandname]. **2000** Breda Shannon, *Ireland of the Welcomes*, 'A Special Brew', May-Jun: 'The Celtic Brewing Company in Enfield Co. Meath began life in 1997 … Dean McGuinness borrowed from monastic brewing tradition by naming his beers after a local saint, St Finian. There is *Finian's Irish Red Ale* and *Finian's Original Gold … Finian's Premier Lager* was recently launched both on the English and Irish market.'

Finn McCoul/Mac Cool [<Ir. *Fionn Mac Cumhail,* the fair one, son of

Cumhal] Legendary hero. Hence (1) [nickname]. **1993** Thomas P. O'Neill in Kevin B. Nowlan (ed.), *Travel and Transport in Ireland:* 'Thus **Bianconi** developed his four wheel cars. The longest of these were to be known as "Finn McCools" after the legendary Irish giant.' See **Bianconi**; **Faugh-a-Ballagh**; **Massey-Dawson**

Finn Varra Maa [poss. <Ir. *Fionnbhara Maighe*, Finbarr of the Plain]. **1996** Fintan O'Toole, *The Ex-Isle of Erin*: 'For Christmas 1917, the **Irish Ireland** movement produced T.H. Nally's *Finn Varra Maa – The Irish Santa Claus* at the Theatre Royal … Instead of Santa, true Irish children were to expect a visit from Finn Varra Maa. Finn would come down the chimney at midnight and leave toys made by fairies. But he would live the rest of the year, not in the alien North Pole, but in **Connemara**.'

Finucane, Marian Radio chat-show host (1990s-). Hence **Finucanisation** [nonce word]. Reduction of debate to populist level. **1999** Diarmuid Doyle, *Sunday Tribune,* 12 Dec: 'The debate over [Charlie] McCreevy's proposals highlighted many things, not least of which was the Finucanisation of Irish discourse.'

Fir Bréaga [Ir., *recte fir bréige*, false men; archaeology]. Standing stones. **1975** Peter Somerville-Large, *The Coast of West Cork:* 'Fir Bréaga is a general term for standing stones. Throughout the country many are known as False Men, possibly an indication of phallic association.'

Fire Away Flanagan [<his learning to ride a pig; nickname]. Employee on Pallas estate, E. Galway, appointed whip of the hounds by 9th Earl of Westmeath. **1999** Lorna Siggins, *Irish Times,* 3 May:

'... any youngster in the area who displayed wild characteristics was named after him ... "Fire Away" let out the dogs one moonlit night after a fox had been bothering them. Both he and Nugent [9th Earl] gave chase on their horses as far as Duniry. Sadly, "Fire Away"'s horse fell at a wall and he was badly crushed.'

Fitzgerald-Kenny's Cows [nickname]. Detectives acquitted of assault on IRA man T.J. Ryan (1929). **1993** Tim Pat Coogan, *Dev, Long Fellow, Long Shadow:* 'the police said his injuries had been caused by being "kicked by a cow". The Minister for Justice, [James] Fitzgerald-Kenny ... said that he accepted their explanation; as a result the detectives were known from that time onwards as "Fitzgerald-Kenny's Cows".'

Fizz [acronym, Belfast]. **1997** Ciaran Carson, *The Star Factory:* 'In about 1973, I worked in Central Belfast as a clerk in a branch of the Civil Service, Family Income Supplements, known as Fizz.'

Flecknoe, Richard (c1600–c1678). Putative priest and indifferent poet. Hence **MacFlecknoe**, caricature of same by Eng. poet John Dryden ('Reigned without dispute/Through all the realms of nonsense absolute').

Flood's Ligament [<Valentine Flood; medic.]. **1983** John F. Fleetwood, *The History of Medicine in Ireland*: 'In his brief appearance on the Dublin medical scene, Valentine Flood (1800–47) left his name to a ligament in the shoulder, "Flood's ligament", which helps to preserve the integrity of the joint.'

Floozie in the Jacuzzi, the [nickname]. Monument in O'Connell St., Dub., representing the river **Liffey**. **1993**

Vincent Caprani, *The Berlitz Travellers* [sic] *Guide to Ireland:* 'a 1988 Millennium presentation to the city – by well-known local businessman Michael Smurfit – is an elongated female figure ... reclining in a bubbling fountain; the wags quickly christened it "the floozie in the jacuzzi". Aka **The Hoor in the Sewer**. See also **Mrs Mulligan**

Florencecourt yew see **Irish yew**

Flue with a/the view [nickname]. Observation platform, Smithfield, Dub. **2000** Denis Carroll, *Irish Times*, 18 Mar: 'Sir, As a nickname for the observation tower on top of the Jameson Distillery chimney, may I suggest "the flue with the view"?'

Flying column [milit.]. Mobile volunteer unit, War of Independence (1919–21). **1949** Tom Barry, *Guerilla Days in Ireland:* 'After only one week of collective training, this Flying Column of intelligent and courageous fighters was fit to meet an equal number of soldiers from any regular army in the world, and hold its own in battle, if not in barrack-yard ceremonial.'

Flying Irishman see **Master MacGrath**

Foorins [<Ir. *fuairéan*, guillemot, nickname]. Inhabitants of Rathlin Is./ Reachlainn, Co. Aontroma/Antrim. **2000** Róisín Ingle, *Irish Times*, 29 Aug: 'Those from the lower end of Rathlin are known by the other end as *foorins*, local Irish for sea birds. Upper Enders ... also sniffily refer to the Lower Enders as *cuddens*, or small fry.'

Foreigner [agric.]. Ovine blow-ins. **1998** Con Costello, *Leinster Leader* (Naas), 30 Jul: '"Foreigners" was the term used to describe sheep from Wicklow which were grazed on the Curragh sward, according to a witness appearing before the Curragh Commission in 1886.'

Fortnight [media]. Belfast magazine (1970-). **2001** John Horgan, *Irish Media: a Critical History Since 1922*: 'The name *Fortnight* was chosen because it was the only option, among many others considered, which was totally free of any sectarian or political undertones.' See also **Lá**

Forty-Coats [nickname]. Common name for city street habitués. Hence (1) **1983** *John Pepper's Illustrated Encyclopaedia of Ulster Knowledge:* 'Down the years Belfast has produced ... "Forty Coats", so called because he went out with at least four or five ragged coats to keep him warm.' (2) **1993** Áine de Courcy in Michael Verdon, *Shawlies, Echo Boys, the Marsh and the Lanes, Old Cork Remembered:* 'If you have a picture in your mind of Father Christmas, white whiskers, pink skin, big bushy eyebrows and a shock of white hair, that was *Forty-Coats*. He got his name because he had a coat and another old coat pinned over it.' Also **Johnny Forty-Coats** [Dub.]. **1995** Patrick Boland, *Tales from a City Farmyard:* 'I remember him walking along the street with a sack slung over his back, and a few kids running after him shouting out: "Johnny Forty Coats" as if the poor devil didn't know his name, or the number of garments he had on.'

Forty-Five Club Cork debating society (C19). **1964** Richard Hayward, *Munster and the City of Cork:* 'The best known of these societies ... was the famous *Forty-Five Club*, a name that arose from the circumstance that every new member, upon initiation, was bound to honour forty-five toasts in forty-five glasses of punch!'

Four Green Fields The four provinces, esp. in relation to the reclamation and reintegration of Ulster into an all-Ireland state. **1966** James Plunkett in J.W. Boyle (ed.), *Leaders and Workers:* '"God Save Ireland" was the slogan of the middle class nationalist who dreamed of restoring to **Kathleen Ni Houlihan** her four green fields.'

Foursquare Laundry [Belfast]. Brit. army covert operation. **2000** Will Self, *Independent on Sunday* (London), 29 May: 'Army intelligence ran "the Foursquare Laundry" which picked up laundry for forensic analysis from Nationalist areas ...'

Fox and the Goose, the [Ulster]. Game of noughts and crosses. **1966** Florence Mary McDowell, *Other Days Around Me:* 'Sometimes, slates and slate pencils were brought out for the playing of "The Fox and the Goose".'

Foxy Jack [nickname]. John MacBride (1865-1916), 1916 leader and member of Irish Brigade in Anglo-Boer War (1899). **1999** Giles Foden, *Irish Times,* 23 Oct: 'They must have made quite a pair: Foxy Jack, as MacBride was known – "swashbuckling miles gloriosus" as Roger Casement ... would later call him, and the cowboy-hat-wearing [John] Blake ...'

Fraughan Sunday [<Ir. *fraochán,* bilberry]. **1983** Theodora Fitzgibbon, *Irish Traditional Food:* 'Fraughan Sunday was a great day in the past and took place on the nearest Sunday to August 1st, also called Lammas Sunday. Being the first fruit to ripen, and also the occasion for the digging of the new potatoes, it was a festival in many ways with many attractions.'

Free Derry Corner Nationalist redoubt est. prior to **Bloody Sunday** (3). **2001** Dick Grogan, *Irish Times,* 23 Jan: '"The orders I heard given to the soldiers were to take up firing positions, identify targets and fire", the witness said. The soldiers immediately started to fire south, towards the crowd at Free Derry Corner.' See also **Derry/Londonderry**

French fiddle. Harmonica/mouth organ. **1968** Austin Clarke, *A Penny in the Clouds:* 'the men rowed on one side of the boat, while I played treasonable music on the mouth-organ, or, as it is called here [Donegal], a "French fiddle".'

Freney [nickname, <James Freney, C18 highwayman]. One-eyed individual. **1847** John Edward Walsh, *Ireland Sixty Years Ago:* 'Those who saw and conversed with him described him as a mean-looking fellow, pitted with the small-pox, and blind of an eye, when Freney became a *soubriquet* for all persons who had lost an eye.'

Friendly Brothers of St Patrick Benevolent society, founded Athenry, Co. Galway. **1763** *Fundamental Laws, Statues and Constitutions:* 'The ancient and most benevolent ORDER of the FRIENDLY BROTHERS, consisteth of an unlimited Number of Members, distinguished by the Word FRIENDLY inserted between their Christian and Sirnames: who, in honour of Ireland, where this ORDER was first instituted, and hath long flourished, have put themselves under the Patronage of St Patrick; and are therefore styled THE FRIENDLY BROTHERS OF SAINT PATRICK.' **1936** Oliver St John Gogarty, *As I was going down Sackville Street:* 'Well, of all the places I have drifted into … Friendly Brothers! Now

had they called it **"The Sick and Indigent Roomkeepers' Society"** it would at least have had the advantage of a magnificent if somewhat pretentious title.'

Fringes [Dub.] **1847** John Edward Walsh, *Ireland Sixty Years Ago:* 'To guard themselves from encroachment, the citizens from time immemorial perambulated the boundaries of their chartered district every third year, and this was termed "riding the franchises", corrupted into "riding the fringes".'

Frying Pan, the [trade name]. C18 Dub. publishing house. **2000** Flann Ó Riain, *Irish Times,* 26 Jun: 'Samuel Wheatley (d.1771) was at Salutation Alley, opposite Crane Lane, Cork Hill, and later at the Frying Pan, Anglesea Street, opposite Cope Street.'

Fumbally Lane [Dub.] **1955** J.L.J. Hughes, *Dublin Historical Record,* 'Dublin Street Names', Sep: 'The facts are that Wilson's *Dublin Directory* has Bumbailiff's Lane for this street until 1789 when the name changed to Fumbailie's Lane. The spelling became Fumbally in 1834 which took away from the previous similarity of sound.'

Fungie [nickname, <fisherman's nickname for bearded colleague]. Dolphin resident in Dingle Bay, Co. Kerry (1983-). **1991** Seán Mannion, *Ireland's Friendly Dolphin:* 'the dolphin's escapades at sea soon became such a talking point in the town that one day a visitor asked if it had a name. Not wishing to disappoint the enquirer, a Dingle citizen thought one up. "Fungie", he said.'

Furphy, Joseph Son of emigrant from Armagh to Aust. (1840). **2000** Flann Ó Riain, *Irish Times,* 3 Jul: 'His son, Joseph

Furphy, set up a firm in manufacturing water carts and, like farmers of the milk carts now gone, the drivers of the water carts, used all over the country, became known as "furphies", and in turn "furphy" came to mean "rumour without foundation, gossip"...' **1992** *Concise Australian National Dictionary:* 'A rumour or false report; an absurd story.'

G

Gallaher's Blues [brandname, < Thomas Gallaher]. Cigarettes manufactured in Belfast (1902-). **1999** W.J. McCormack (ed.), *The Blackwell Companion to Modern Irish Culture:* 'The range included the series Blues, Greens (both untipped) and Reds (tipped). In their distinctive large packet, Blues looked like a set of piano keys and were generally regarded as a symbol of working-class prosperity before becoming a sign of cultural authenticity.'

Galloping Hogan (the) [nickname]. Michael (?) Hogan, who poss. entered the service of France/Portugal after the Flight of the Earls. **1990** Robert Shepherd, *Ireland's Fate, The Boyne and After:* 'Tradition has it that Sarsfield had been guided [on the ride to Ballyneety, Co. Limerick (1690)] by the legendary Galloping Hogan, a guerilla-style Irish resistance fighter who knew the terrain intimately.'

Galway [Gaillimh; city and Co.] Hence: (1) **Galway Hooker** [maritime] Trad. sailing craft. Also ribald confusion with US Sl. usage (prostitute). **1999** *Irish Times*, 10 Apr: 'Síle de Valera is certainly putting her stamp on the department by changing its name (from Arts and Culture), its logo (from what has been called "three Galway hookers" to an ogham design) and its location.' (2) **Galway Jury** [legal] An enlightened, independent jury. **1895** E. Cobham Brewer, *A Dictionary of Phrase and Fable* [new ed.]: 'The expression has its birth in certain trials held in Ireland in 1635 upon the right of the king to the counties of Ireland. Leitrim, Roscommon, Sligo and Mayo gave judgement in favour of the Crown, but Galway opposed it ...'

Garbardick [acronym; politics]. **1998** Fergus Finlay, *Snakes and Ladders:* 'The *Sunday World*, another O'Reilly publication, coined an awkward, ugly acronym "Garbardick" – Garret [FitzGerald], Barry [Desmond], and Dick [Spring] – to sum up its disgust at how awful a government it was.'

Garden of Ireland/Garden County [nickname]. (1) Co. Carlow. As thus: **1895** E. Cobham Brewer, *A Dictionary of Phrase and Fable* (new ed.); (2) Co. Wicklow (esp. as applied to GAA teams). **1996** Róisín Ingle, *Sunday Tribune,* 11 Feb: 'The Chinese spy satellite which some experts predicted would plunge to earth somewhere in the Garden of Ireland within the next month may now land in Limerick instead ...'

Garlic/Garland Sunday [nickname]. Last Sunday in July. **1957** E. Estyn Evans, *Irish Folk Ways:* '... Lammas, originally 1st August, now held on Lammas Sunday ... which is also known as Garland, Bilberry or Height Sunday.' See **Fraughan Sunday**

Garrett Reilly (<?) as in **not for the world and Garrett Reilly** [catchphrase]. In no circumstances. Also **the world and Garrett Reilly**. Everyone. **1995** Niall Toibín, *Smile and Be a Villain:* '... and the world and Garrett Reilly knew that while we were at Mass on Sunday, they [Protestants] were in bed with their neighbours' wives reading *The News of the World.*'

Garryowen [Garraí Eoin, district, Limerick city]. **1826-7** Gerard Griffin,

The Collegians: 'The little ruined outlet, which gives its name to one of the most popular songs of **Erin**, is situate on the acclivity of a hill near the city of Limerick ... Tradition has preserved the occasion of its celebrity, and the origin of its name, which appears to be compounded of two Irish words signifying "Owen's garden". A person so-called was the owner, about half a century since, of a cottage, and plot of ground on this spot ...' Hence (1) [lit.] Irascible mongrel found in the company of the **Citizen** in James Joyce's novel *Ulysses*. **1930** Stuart Gilbert, *James Joyce's 'Ulysses':* 'At one moment the dog Garryowen is rechristened Owen Garry ... Garryowen is mentioned as "grandpapa Giltrap's lovely dog Garryowen that almost talked.' (2) [sport] High kick forward, <Garryowen Rugby Football club. (3) [milit.] State of alert. **1996** Jim Cusack, *Irish Times,* 27 Apr: 'The 79th [Lebanon] Battalion members assembled in the camp's square to be addressed by a man with a megaphone who informed them that a state of "Garryowen" was in place – which meant that they must wear flak jackets and helmets at all times outdoors and in unprotected buildings.' (4) [brandname] Tobacco. **1951** Advt., *Wolfe Tone Annual:* 'So pleasant and kindly, so gentle and soothing /Still constant and true after long years have flown /So mild and so mellow, so rich and so fragrant /The Plug of all plugs is my sweet GARRYOWEN!' (one of several versified advts. In this publ., poss. by the publisher, Brian O'Higgins. See **Erin** [4])

Gathering, the Day preceding the first day of Puck Fair, held in August in Killorglin, Co. Chiarraí/Kerry. **1964** Richard Hayward, *Munster and the City of Cork:* 'We had timed our visit very carefully to reach this place on the 9th of August, the day before what is known as *the Gathering,* and as we travelled along we overtook more and more bands of tinkers ...'

Gaybo [nickname, <first name + endearment suffix]. Gabriel (Gay) Byrne (1934-), radio/TV presenter. **2000** *Sunday Tribune,* 9 Apr: 'The Ghost of Gaybo was still haunting RTÉ. And it was causing some people in particular some very sleepless nights.' Hence **Greybo**, ageing entertainer. **2000** Headline, *Sunday Tribune,* 2 Apr: 'The new Greybos. With so much talent around, why do both RTÉ and Today FM use middle-aged men to front their flagship programmes?'

Gaybrick [<Ir. *ar oibrigh sé?* Did it work?; nickname]. Seaside visitor. **1989** Leslie Matson, *CARA,* Mar-Apr: 'Tramore [Co. Waterford] is a favourite destination for visitors from inland areas such as **Tipperary** – at one time they were known as "Gaybricks" because many went boating deliberately to get sea-sick, for their health's sake. Their friends would call to them in Irish "Ar oibrigh sé?".'

General, the (1) [nickname]. John Pentland Mahaffy (1830-1919) Provost, Trinity College Dublin (1914-19). **1935** N.J.D. White, *Some Recollections of Trinity College, Dublin:* 'In my undergraduate days Mahaffy was known as "the General," in consequence of his proficiency in many subjects.' (2) [nickname]. Martin Cahill, Dub. criminal gang boss (murdered 1994). **1995** Padraig Yeates, *Irish Times,* 3 Jun: 'Martin Cahill, The General, Tango One were the various names by which a chubby, balding, shabbily-dressed, middle-aged Dubliner with a benign smile and two families was known to his friends.'

Gentry, the [euphcm.]. Evil fairies. **1960** John O'Donoghue, *In Kerry Long Ago:* "'the Gentry are the people fond of pleasant pastimes, that sell their souls forever to the devil … In return they can have all the pleasures of the world until they die.'

George Brent [stage name]. Actor (1904-79). **1938** Carreras, cigarette card series, *Film Favourites:* 'A romantic young Irishman – George Brent – who at one time or another has been revolutionist, sailor, blacksmith, stoker, diamond miner, and stage star.' **1940** *Irish Times*, 16 Mar: 'Actually he is the son of a Dublin newspaper man, and his real name is Nolan … He drifted to New York, joined a stock company of actors, and adopted the name of Brent for stage purposes.'

George Killian's [brandname]. French beer, publicity for which was based on renamed Wexford former brewer George William **Lett**. **1990** Jean-René Ruttinger, *George Killian, ou l'extraordinare histoire d'un gentleman brasseur irlandais:* 'Avec George William Lett, la bière rousse de Pelforth s'était trouvé un pays, des racines, une tradition, une famille, un père spirituel et nourricier. Quand on sait l'importance que nos contemporains accordent à l'origine de tout ce qui s'ingurgite et leur engouement pour les produits régionaux … cette filiation que nous entendions établir au plus vite apparaîtrait comme une marque indéniable d'authenticité, une garantie de qualité.' [With George William Lett, Pelforth's brown ale found a country, roots, a tradition, a family, a spiritual and cherishing father. When one considers the importance which our contemporaries attach to the origin of everything that is consumed and their infatuation with regional products … that consanguinity which we proposed to establish as quickly as possible would appear as an undeniable brand of authenticity, a guarantee of quality.']

Glacier [brandname; Belfast]. Transparent colour labels for shop windows (1880s-). **1990** W.H. Crawford in Bryan McCabe, *From Linenhall to Loopbridge. The Story of McCaw Stevenson & Orr Ltd. Printers 1876-1990:* 'From this it went on to produce rolls of "Glacier" window decoration able to transform the coldest and dullest windows of an institution into wonders of stained glass.'

GlamorEire [nonce word]. The Ire. of the **Celtic Tiger**. **2000** Medb Ruane, *Irish Times,* 7 Apr: '*TVNow!*'s cultural consensus is … addressing itself to emerging celebrities of this GlamorEire generated by so many busy-busy PR experts.'

Glenroe [Ir. *gleann rua*, red glen; media]. Fanciful location of RTÉ TV series, filmed in Kilcoole, Co. Chill Mhantáin/Wicklow (-2001). **2000** *Irish Times*, 2 Feb: 'The Glenroe Deli restaurant in the Co. Wicklow village of Kilcoole – known to RTÉ viewers as *Glenroe* – is to be sold by auction on February 22nd.' See also **Brigid**

Glimmer man [<glimmer of gas remaining in pipes when supply had been turned off]. Inspector who checked on unauthorised use of domestic gas during 1939-45 **Emergency**. **1978** Bernard Share, *The Emergency:* "'Look out missus, here's the glimmer man!" echoed from street to street as that individual arrived … to lay hands on your jets to see were they still warm.' Hence **The Glimmer Man** (pub), Stoneybatter, Dublin.

Glocamorra/Gloccamorra/Glocka-morra [<Ir. *clocha móra*, many stones]. Fanciful location as featured in the US musical *Finian's Rainbow* (1947), esp. lyric 'How are things in Glocca Morra?'. **1992** Tom McElligott, *Six O'Clock all over Cork:* 'Glocamorra is the name of a townland on the Cork side of Mitchelstown ... A song called "Glocamorra" was popular in the forties especially among Cork exiles in Dagenham ...' Cf. James Stephens, *The Crock of Gold* (1912): 'It so happened that the Leprecauns of Gort na Cloca [*recte* gClocha] Mora were not thankful to the Philosopher for having sent Meehawl MacMurrachu to their field.' **1994** Anne Devlin, *After Easter:* 'HELEN: You'll be taking us to Glockamorra next. MANUS: Glockamorra? Where's that then? HELEN: I've never been there myself – but I'm told it's where Irish Americans go when they die ...'

Golden Vale see **Golden Vein**

Golden Vein [Co. Thiobraid Árann/ Tipperary, <richness of agric. land; aka **Golden Vale**, poss. From assoc. with eponymous popular processed cheese, 1930s-]. **1939** Tourist brochure, *Tipperary, Ireland's Premier County:* 'If you stand on the Rock of Cashel, amid the ruins of fifteen centuries of history, you will see around you the most fertile stretch of land in the world, the famous Golden Vale of Tipperary.' **1954** Oliver St John Gogarty, *It isn't this Time of Year At All:* '"Is it in good heart?" I asked Fanning, the tall tavernkeeper who had in his veins Cromwellian blood, that is the blood of the sour, jar-nosed humbug's troopers who settled in the Golden Vein.'

Goldie Fish [nickname, Cork city]. Gilt salmon weathervane on St Anne's

church, Shandon. **1995** Tom Widger, *Sunday Tribune,* 18 Jun: 'Elsewhere, the increasingly bizarre soap *Under the Goldie Fish* would hardly be complete without a bedouin.'

Gooseberry Fair [Clogher, Co. Thír Eoghain/Tyrone, <fruit ripening time]. **1986** Patrick Logan, *Fair Day:* '... the fair held on 26 July, appears to have been a very special occasion known as the Gooseberry Fair and the Spoilin Fair. This word [<Ir. *spóilín aonaigh*, 'small joint of meat used at a fair (Dinneen)] refers to the tents and bothies put up ... to cook meat for the crowds.'

Gophers [nickname]. Irish-American criminal gang. **2000** Pól Ó Conghaile, *Irish Independent,* 10 Jun: 'Before they achieved notoriety, the Gophers – a 500-strong Irish gang including among its ranks "Happy" Jack Mullraney and "One Lung" Curran – specialised in robbing shops and pool halls and looting the property of the Hudson Railroad.'

GPO [acronym] General Post Office, Dub., specifically as focus of 1916 Rising. See **the Gunman**

Grab All Association [nickname, <play on initials]. Gaelic Athletic Association. **1996** Seán Kilfeather, *Irish Times*, 21 Sep: '"That's typical of the GAA", was the immediate cry. The old "Grab All Association" *canard* was trotted out. "How do they expect people to pay once again for a replay?"'

Grace-card/Grace's card [<Grace family, Courtstown, Kilkenny]. The six of hearts (playing card). **1895** E. Cobham Brewer, *Dictionary of Phrase and Fable* (new ed.): 'At the Revolution of 1688, one of the family of Grace ... equipped at his own expense a regiment

of foot and troop of horse, in the service of King James. William of Orange promised him high honours if he would join the new party, but the indignant Baron wrote on a card, "Tell your master I despise his offer." The card was the six of hearts, and hence the name.'

Granuaile [Ir. *Gráinne Mhaol/Gráinne Umhaill*]. Grace O'Malley (1530–c1600), sea captain and pirate. Hence [maritime] Ship's name. **1999** Lorna Siggins, *Irish Times,* 13 Aug: 'Friday 13th is still dreaded as a date for some. Down in Dublin port some fears have been expressed about the impact of a renaming ceremony on an Irish ship. The vessel, *Granuaile*, is tender ship for the Commissioners of Irish Lights. It is to be renamed *Granuaile II* this morning.'

Graves disease [<Robert James Graves, (b. Dub. 1796), physician]. **1999** W.J. McCormack (ed.), *The Blackwell Companion to Irish Culture:* 'Robert Graves recognised a glandular disorder commonly called "Graves disease" and with his colleague William Stokes … introduced bedside teaching at the Meath Hospital.'

Great Hunger, the [nickname]. Great Famine (1845–50) caused by failure of staple potato crop. **1989** Cormac Ó Gráda, *The Great Irish Famine:* 'the "Great Hunger" has gained wider and more lasting notoriety than most famines. There are several reasons for this.'

Green boats [transport]. C19-20 Cork harbour ferry services. **1992** Tom McElligott, *Six O'Clock all over Cork:* 'It must be borne in mind that even Crosshaven, Cork's nearest seaside resort, was considered to be far from the city in my parents' time, only to be reached on the "Green Boats". These

steamers, so called because of their colour, left the Albert Quay at stated hours for Crosshaven …'

Green Isle [pop. attrib.]. Ireland. **1808ff** Thomas Moore, *Irish Melodies,* 'The Prince's Day': 'He loves the Green Isle, and his love is recorded/In hearts which have suffer'd too much to forget:/And hope shall be crown'd, and attachment rewarded,/And **Erin**'s gay jubilee shine out yet.' **1968 Myles na gCopaleen**, *The Best of Myles:* 'I notice these days that the Green Isle is getting greener. Delightful ulcerations resembling buds pit the branches of our trees, clumpy daffodils can be seen on the upland lawn.'

Greenland see **Blueland**

Green Linnets [nickname, <colour of uniform] Ir. army in **Emergency** period. **1999** Anon, quoted in Donal MacCarron, *Step Together:* 'They [Brit. troops in NI] called us "the Green Linnets" but, I can tell you, those khaki fuckers would have sung a different tune if we ever got to grips with them.'

Green Man, The [trade name, <trad. green dress of gamekeeper (Eng. usage)]. **2000** De Burca Rare Books, *Catalogue 55*, Spring: 'Robert Kinnier was the son of Joshua Kinnear, whose premises were at The Green Man, on the Lower Blind Quay, Fishamble Street [Dublin]. He was in business as early as 1743, and was an extensive publisher of street ballads.'

Greenshirts [< new uniform adopted (Mar. 1936) by National Corporate Party, fascist party aka **Blueshirts**; nickname]. **1999** Ferghal McGarry, *Irish Politics and the Spanish Civil War:* 'The impotent Greenshirt rump and the collapsing Republican Congress/CPI [Communist Party of Ireland] coalition were partly motivated to fight in Spain by their domestic political failures.'

Grey Ghost, the [Civil War (1921-2); nickname]. Armoured rail vehicle. **1963** Martyn White, *Journal of the Irish Railway Record Society,* Spring: 'A small armoured Lancia car, fitted with flanged wheels, and known as "The Grey Ghost", was patrolling the line between Clonmel and Thurles. The **Irregular** forces trapped the vehicle between two overbridges, and a concentrated attack was made on it.'

Grey Man's Path [<?]. Geolog. feature, Ballycastle, Co. Aontroma/Antrim. **1950** Richard Hayward, *Ulster and the City of Belfast:* 'A steep and broken path, *the Grey Man's Path* or *Fir Leith* [*sic*], leads to the beach through a mighty chasm which is bridged at one point by a gigantic fallen column.'

Grey Washer by the Ford see **Washer of the Ford**

Growl [nickname]. Fund-raising organisation launched by Eamon de Valera [see **Dev**] (Nov 1920). **1993** Tim Pat Coogan, *Dev, Long Fellow, Long Shadow:* 'Called the American Association for the Recognition of the Irish Republic (AARIR), appropriately enough it became generally known as Growl.'

GUBU [acronym, derog., coined 1982 by Conor Cruise O'Brien; see **Cruiser**]. **2000** Michael Mulqueen & Walter Ellis, *Independent on Sunday* (London), 2 Jul: '... the **Fine Gael** leader, John Bruton, drew blood when he charged that the Government's recent performance was GUBU – "grotesque, unbelievable, bizarre and unprecedented". The last GUBU charge was made in the Haughey years, when the then **Fianna Fáil** Attorney General was found to be harbouring a murder suspect in his flat.' Hence [Dub. (1999-)] Pub, Capel St. **2000** Frank McDonald, *The Construction of Dublin:* 'Lawlor Briscoe's antique furniture emporium has given way to Zanzibar, a cavernous souk ... Together with the Life bar in the Irish Life Centre, Pravda, GUBU and the Morrison Hotel, it probably qualifies as "one of those southside embassies on the northside" ...'

Guinness [brand name, <Arthur Guinness (1725-1803), founder of the brewing dynasty]. Stout and (formerly) porter; now gen. accepted as the 'wine of the country'. (1) 1999 Michele Guinness, *The Guinness Spirit:* '... when Arthur Guinness quietly adopted the coat of arms of the Magennises of County Down, one of Ireland's oldest and most powerful Catholic clans, no one questioned his right to do so ... How and when the name became Guinness and he a Protestant, no one knew for sure.' (2) **1939** James Joyce, *Finnegans Wake:* '... we have highest gratifications in announcing to pewtewr publikumst of praactician pratusers, genghis is ghoon for you.' (3) **Miranda Guinness** [<Countess of **Iveagh**] [transport]. **1992** John de Courcy Ireland, *Ireland's Maritime Heritage:* '... Arthur Guinness, Son and Company is owned in Britain though for generations its handsome vessels, such as the Clarecastle and the Carrowdore, and more recently vessels like The Lady Patricia and Miranda Guinness, have been watched and admired by Dubliners lying just below Butt Bridge.' See also **Iveagh**; **Uncle Arthur**

Gumgooly [media]. Fictitious village. **2000** Lorna Kernan, *Irish Times,* 'Radio

Highlights', 23 May: 'Gumgooly ... The Richie Beirne/Séamus Calligy series is back ... the lads are both not well and prosperous in this place that lies somewhere along the Roscommon/ Sligo border.'

Gúnagate [<Ir. *gúna*, dress, frock + element of *Watergate*, etc; nonce word]. Employed with ref. to US President Clinton's affair with Monica Lewinski involving semen-stained dress. **1998** Lise Hand, *Sunday Tribune,* 2 Aug: '**Bertie [Ahern]**, busy as usual, is in the throes of planning the schedule for Bill Clinton's visit ... This, of course, assuming the Prez survives his frock shock, or Gúnagate, as it is called in Spiddal.'

Gunman, the [philately]. **1997** Ciaran Carson, *The Star Factory*: 'The 2½d blue-black definitive commemorative of 1941 is known as the Gunman: it depicts a Gulliver-sized Volunteer armed with a bayoneted rifle, poised at his post above a Lilliputian GPO ...'

Gunmoney [numismatics]. Coinage issued by James II (1689-90). **1979** Patrick Finn, *Irish Coin Values:* 'After various expedients to raise funds failed, James established mints at Dublin and Limerick and had issued a "token" coinage of halfcrowns, shillings and sixpences. This coinage commonly called "gunmoney" was struck in brass and base metal from obsolete cannon, church bells etc.'

Gut, the [nickname, Dub.]. **1999** John S. Doyle, *Sunday Tribune*, 17 Oct: '"I am steeped in luck to be living not only in **Dublin 4** but in the *gut* of Dublin 4," said Paul Durcan. The Gut, as **Ringsend**ers call it, is "where the River Dodder and the Grand Canal converge to discharge themselves into the River Liffey".'

Gypsies, the [nickname, Dub.]. Bohemians soccer club. **1996** Emmet Malone, *Irish Times*, 18 Jul: 'at the final whistle, it was the Gypsies who had the greater cause for relief having escaped defeat.'

H

Hadji Bey et Cie [tradename]. Manufacturer and retailer of Turkish Delight, McCurtain St., Cork. The shopfront carried the slogan, 'A good name is worth millions.' **1992** Tom McElligott, *Six O'Clock all over Cork:* 'In 1902 an Armenian named Batmazian who had come to Ireland by way of London first offered "Turkish Delight" for sale. During World War I and after the Turks massacred the British at Gallipoli, he was quick to protest his Armenian nationality to some Munster Fusiliers who tried to attack Cork's "Turkish Shop" ... the shop remained in business until 1971 ...'

Hairy Fairy [nickname, <beard & his interest in mysticism]. George W. Russell ('**AE**'), poet, painter and journalist. **1905** D.P. Moran, *The Philosophy of Irish Ireland:* 'Shoneens; apers of English manners; **Sourface**s; Protestants; **West Britons**; Anglo-Irish; The Hairy Fairy: AE (George Russell).'

Half-in-Half see **Patent**

Half Past Six [nickname]. James Joyce (1882-1941). **1994** Bob Cato and Greg Vitiello, *Joyce Images* (photo caption): 'Joyce with fellow students and faculty at Clongowes Wood School ... Upon his arrival there, he said his age was "Half past six", which became his school nickname.'

Hamar [<Hamar Greenwood, last Chief. Secretary for Ireland under Brit. administration]. Untruth, as in **tell a Hamar**, tell a lie. **1990** Tim Pat Coogan, *Michael Collins:* '... few political figures of the time could have stood over the activities of the next actors to enter the scene [the **Black and Tans**] as did Hamar Greenwood whose name was to pass into Irish folklore – "telling a Hamar" – as a synonym for lying'.

Hamlet [nickname]. **1939** Robert Gahan, *Dublin Historical Record,* 'Some Old Street Characters of Dublin', Dec: 'Probably the most interesting characters of their time were the trio, "Hamlet", "Dunbar" and "Uncle" who performed on the streets of Dublin about 65 years ago. "Hamlet" was so called from his giving of occasional street presentations of himself as the Prince of Denmark ... His real name was O'Brien ... "Dunbar" was a fine smart young fellow, always neat and clean. "Uncle", whose real name is unknown, gained his nickname from singing a song once popular: "Tommy, make room for your Uncle".'

Hanging Gale [legal]. Six months' grace in the payment of rent (C19). **1885** *The Times* (London), 17 Nov: 'We went to collect the rents due the 25th of March, but which, owing to the custom which prevails in Ireland, known as "the hanging gale", are never demanded till the 20th September.'

Ha o tha Thane [Ulster Scots]. President's House. **2000** Frank Millar, *Irish Times,* 19 Oct: 'In the House of Lords next week, Lord Laird will be arguing the Unionist case for the retention of the Royal **Ulster** Constabulary as part of a double-barrelled name for the new "Police Service of Northern Ireland". In the same spirit, he suggests the Garda Síochána will in future double-up as the Hainin Polis. Likewise, the President, Mrs McAleese, could find herself residing at "Aras an Uachtaráin – Ha o tha Thane".'

Harp [<national symbol; nickname, gen. derog.]. Irishman. **1945** Anthony T. Lawlor, *Irish Maritime Survey:* '... a slang term for an Irishman. It is in general use at sea and occurs in old-time chanties (e.g. *Blow boys blow* – "A big thick harp called Patsy Bonner").'

Harry, Lord see **Lord Harry**

Haut-Brion, Château. Bordeaux wine, 1st growth under 1855 classification. **1990** T.P. Whelehan, *The Irish Wines of Bordeaux:* 'In 1926 he [Maurice Healy] was elected to "The Odd Volume"... He subsequently read a paper to that body titled "Irish Wine". The contribution of Ireland to European viticulture was well understood in this distinguished circle. However, Maurice Healy casually suggested a new proposition: that the renowned *premier grand cru*, Haut-Brion, was in fact a corruption of O'Brien .... Unfortunately he did not substantiate it with facts. Research indicates that he could never do so.'

H-block [<shape as viewed from the air]. Prison building, esp. at **Long Kesh**, Belfast. **2000** John O'Farrell, *The Observer* (London), 23 Jul: 'By the late Nineties, cells were open 24 hours a day with the "screws" locked into the "circle" – the bar in the 'H' shape of the [eight] blocks – while prisoners controlled the four wings of each block.'

Hearts of Steel see **Steelboys**

Heaven's Reflex [poet]. Killarney/ Cill Áirne, Co. Chiarraí/Kerry. **Nd** Pop. ballad, 'Killarney': 'Angels fold their wings and rest,/ In that Eden of the West,/Beauty's home, Killarney,/ Heaven's reflex, Killarney.' **1999** Donal Hickey, quoted *Irish Times*, 29 Dec: 'The area [Sliabh Luachra] has its own

beauty – nothing like the so-called Heaven's Reflex or manicured refinement of nearby Killarney, but something more primaeval ...'

Hell, Heaven and Purgatory see **Mardyke**

Hell-of-a-din [nickname]. Sophia Pierce-Evans, b. Co. Limerick 1896; aviatrix. **1999** Jane Falloon, *Throttle Full Open:* 'So much attention did she seek and get when she was flying as Mrs Eliott-Lynn that the press christened her "hell-of-a-din". She married again at the height of her career, and became even more renowned as Lady Heath.'

Hennessy [<Richard Hennessy, b. Co. Cork (c1727); brandname]. Cognac brandy. **1999** L. Cullen, in W.J. McCormack (ed.), *The Blackwell Companion to Modern Irish Culture:* '... his 1798 business, in which he was partnered by his forceful and ambitious son James and another Irishman Samuel Turner, laid the foundations of the present celebrated brandy house.'

Hepenstall [see **Walking Gallows**]. **2001** Richard Marsh, *RTÉ radio*, 'Sunday Miscellany', 25 Feb: 'His name was Edward Hepenstall, though I have only heard of him with the 'm' [Hempenstall] in Wicklow oral tradition.'

Herald [abbrev.] **Evening Herald** newspaper, Dub. **2000** *Irish Times*, 11 Mar: 'For many years "*Herald* and *Mail*" were the traditional cries of newspaper sellers on the capital's streets ... But 1954 brought new, and deadly, competition for the *Mail* in the form of the *Evening Press*.' **1959** N. O'K (Niel O'Kennedy), cartoon caption, *A Book of By-Lines:* one newsboy to another: 'It's "PRESSheralermail" if you're a **Fianna**

Fáil man, and "HERALERMAILpress" if you're **inter-party**.'

Hibernian Archipelago [geog.] **2000** *Sunday Tribune,* 2 Jan: 'As our national confidence soared, at times it seemed as if the term "the British Isles" might be replaced by "the Hibernian Archipelago" yet the most popular girl's name last year was the distinctly unIrish Chloe. Quare times indeed.'

Hibernian Chronicle [media]. First Ir.-American newspaper. **2000** Sue Carter, *Irish Times,* 17 May: 'There is a long tradition of Irish newspapers in America, from the arrival of the *Hibernian Chronicle* in 1810 right through the *Emerald* to the present-day titles.'

Hibs [abbrev/nickname]. (1) [politico-religious org.]. Ancient Order of Hibernians. **1990** Anon., quoted in Robert Shepherd, *Ireland's Fate:* 'Divil the one o' the Hibs walking on the fifteenth [of Aug.] knowed it was **King Billy** was on the drum ye borrowed from the Orange Lodge.' (2) [sport, Dub.] Hibernian soccer club.

High-Cauled Cap Trad. dance. **1928** Risdeard Mac Gabhann, *Leabhar Tailteann:* 'The Round Dances generally are made up of side-step, swing movements, chains and figures. The Four-hand, Eight-hand and Sixteen-hand Reels; the Eight-hand Jig, the High-Cauled Cap, the Muirgheis Reel, the Humours of Bandon are the best known of the Round Dances …'

Hist [abbrev., nickname]. College Historical Soc., TCD. (1770-). **1987** Richard Davis, *The Young Ireland Movement:* 'In June 1840, [Thomas] Davis treated the "Hist" to a full-scale attack on Trinity College itself, though the president had "not, personally, one sad or angry reminiscence of old Trinity".'

HMS Gannet [milit.]. Brit. naval station, Co. Derry. **2000** *Irish Air Letter,* Jul: 'On 01 May 1943 both Eglinton and Maydown were transferred to the Royal Navy … In the usual Navy tradition, Eglinton was given the name of HMS Gannet, and it was primarily used as a base for working up of fighter units.'

Hogan Stand [sport]. Facility at GAA headquarters, Croke Park, Dub. (1959-). **1982** Pádraig Puirséal, *The GAA in its Time:* 'The stand which seats 16,000 was named, like its smaller predecessor, after Seán Hogan, the Tipperary player killed there on **Bloody Sunday** 1920.' See also **Croker**

Holy Farmer [euphem.]. Holy Father. **1922** James Joyce, *Ulysses:* 'by the holy farmer, he never cried crack till he brought him home as drunk as a boiled owl.'

Holy Ground, the (1) [ballad] '… You're the girl I do adore/And still I live in hopes to see/The Holy Ground once more – Fine Girl you are!' **1965** Colm O Lochlainn, *More Irish Street Ballads:* 'Cork men maintain that "The Holy Ground" is the waterfront at Cóbh (Queenstown) but others hold that it is Swansea dockland, and others still that it is part of New York Harbour.' (2) [Dingle/An Daingean, Co. Chiarraí/Kerry. **1992** Liam Mac Mathúna, in *The Placenames of Ireland in the Third Millennium:* 'In Dingle, too, there is a *Bóthar an Uisce* corresponding to *River Lane,* while *Bóthar a' Phúca* and *Holy Ground* are one and the same. *Holy* here is from *hole,* the reference being to the holes in the ground where the tanners used cure animal hides.'

Holy Hour [nickname]. Period of compulsory closing, 14.30-15.30, of licensed premises in principal cities – later limited to Dub. and Cork (1927-1960). Also, by extension, two-hour Sun. afternoon closing under same legislation and other similar. **1995** Frank McNally, *Irish Times,* 15 Aug: 'By 5 a.m. the café has grown quiet … The [Bewley's] staff … start the clean-up operation in advance of the official "holy hour".' **2000** John McManus, *Irish Times,* 7 Jul: 'On Sundays, the closing time will remain 11 p.m. … The "holy hour" from 2 p.m. to 4 p.m. on Sundays also disappears.'

Holy Mary [derog.]. Hypocrite, religious crawthumper (*m.* or *f.*). **1961** Tom Murphy, *A Whistle in the Dark:* MUSH: 'Us? We've no chance. Har? Too much back-handin', too much palm-oil, too many Holy Marys pulling strings …'

Home Rule [polit. movement/philosophy]. **1921** D.J. Owen, *History of Belfast*: '… the matter of self-government for Ireland had come prominently to the front in 1872, when Isaac Butt, the originator of the term "Home Rule", created an Irish Home Rule League.'

Honest Jack Lawless [nickname]. **1837** *Northern Whig* (Belfast), 12 Aug: 'We regret to announce the death of this eloquent and incorruptible Irish patriot … Even the Orange party gave him credit for unflinching integrity, and he was consequently honoured by all with the title of "Honest Jack Lawless".'

Hoods, the [nickname]. Belfast criminals. **1998** Henry McDonald, reviewing Malachi O'Doherty, 'The Trouble with Guns', *Observer* (London), 19 Apr: 'One of the most perceptive passages is when O'Doherty compares the horrific punishments meted out by the IRA to so-called anti-social elements in West Belfast, "the Hoods", as they are locally known, to the violence inflicted on Catholic boys by the Christian Brothers …'

Hook and Eye, the [nickname, <type of centre-buffer railway coupling]. Cork & Muskerry Light Rly. **1977** *Cork Holly Bough:* 'The public usually travelled to the Fair on the "Muskerry Tram", the narrow-gauge steam railway, often referred to as the "Hook and Eye".'

Hoops, the [nickname, <design of strip; sport]. Shamrock Rovers soccer club (Dub.). **1988** Robert Allen, *Magill,* May: 'The thought from many Shamrock Rovers fans of a move to Tolka Park … was unthinkable. "Will Greed Kill the Hoops?" said one of the protest banners.'

Hoor in the Sewer, the see **Floozie in the Jacuzzi**

Humanity Dick/Martin [nickname]. Richard Martin, politician & landowner. **1983** Martin Wallace, *100 Irish Lives:* 'In 1824 he was the founder of the (now Royal) Society for the Prevention of Cruelty to Animals … The Prince Regent (later George IV) nicknamed him "Humanity Dick".'

Hunting Cap [nickname]. Maurice O'Connell (1728-1825), uncle of the **Liberator**. **1972** Maurice R. O'Connell, *The Correspondence of Daniel O'Connell:* '… known as Hunting-Cap because of the cap he wore in order to avoid the cost of a conventional gentleman's hat which was taxed.'

Hurry the Brogue see **Brogue About**

Hyde Park [<Douglas Hyde, 1st President of Ire. on London analogy]. **1938** *Irish Times,* 29 Apr: 'I found myself in an amusing circle the other day at the [Royal Irish] Academy, when they were wondering whether the mansion in the Phoenix Park would be known as *Teac an t-Uachtarain* [*sic*] or *Dun an t-Uachtarain,* [*sic*] but neither the house nor the fort satisfied the wags, who insisted that the "lads" would call it "Hyde Park".'

I

Iarnród Éireann [transport]. State rail company. **1995** Mícheál Ó Riain, *On the Move:* 'Some debate took place both at [CIÉ] board and in the Oireachtas about the names of the three subsidiaries: Iarnród Éireann – Irish Rail; Bus Éireann – Irish Bus; Bus Átha Cliath – Dublin Bus. Speakers, including the minister, were hopeful that the companies would be known by their Irish names, but somehow it was felt that the English forms could not be dispensed with, even though the uncompromising Irish form of Córas Iompair Éireann had not been challenged for forty years.'

I-doubt-it Hall [nickname]. Ballynagarde House, Ballyneety, Co. Limerick. **2000** Flann Ó Riain, *Irish Times,* 25 Sep: 'On his deathbed his clergyman son Robert ended his prayers with the comforting thought that the sick man was going to "a far, far better place". The dying man [Edward Croker] sat up in the bed and viewing his magnificent wondrous demesne through the window, commented "I doubt it", and fell back dead. Ever after the house was known locally as "I-doubt-it Hall".'

Immortal MacGrath see **Master MacGrath**

Inchiquin Money [numismatics]. Non-legal coinage (1642-46). **1979** Patrick Finn, *Irish Coin Values:* '... it has often been suggested that they were struck by order of Lord Inchiquin the Vice-President of **Munster**. However, documentary evidence has now been discovered which demonstrated that they were in fact issued by the Lord Justice of Ireland and furthermore that they were never given the status of legal tender ...'

Independent (Irish) Party [polit.]. Tenant Right Movement (1850s-). **1900** *Leinster Leader,* 13 Jan: 'But what concern, it may be asked, have the woes of the Government and the intentions of its critics for Irishmen? They have a great deal indeed; for, if the policy of the Independent Party is not thwarted by selfish and short-sighted hostility, a united Irish representation will be able to take full advantage of the situation at Westminster.' See also **Irish Brigade**

Inst. [nickname, abbrev.]. Royal Belfast Academical Institution (1810-). **1987** *Belfast, an Illustrated Yearbook:* 'The original drawings for Inst. were by the distinguished architect Sir John Sloane ... One of Belfast's major schools, it gave its name to College Square ...'

Inter-party Government [polit.] Coalition (1948-51). **1995** Mícheál Ó Riain, *On the Move:* 'The general election was held on 4 February 1948; **Fianna Fáil** lost heavily and was replaced in government by an "Inter-party Government", so called because "coalition" was then perceived to be too derogatory a term.'

Invincibles [est'd as 'Irish Invincibles' (1882)]. Secret society. **1922** James Joyce, *Ulysses:* 'I heard that from the head warder that was in Kilmainham when they hanged Joe Brady, the invincible. He told me that when they cut him down after the drop it was standing up in their faces like a poker.'

Ireeshan/Ireeshian [mildly derog.]. Irish speaker. **1995** Niall Tóibín, *Smile and Be a Villain:* 'I will not dwell on the mortifying embarrassment of being an "Ireeshian"'. **1998** Cristóir O'Flynn, *There is an Isle:* 'Granny told us that the Gearys were great Republicans and "Ireeshans" ... that's why they had the name in Irish on the sweets.'

Ireland Inc. [< Incorporated; US legal terminology]. Ire. as a business entity. **2000** Christine Doherty, *Sunday Business Post,* 23 Jul: 'If Ireland Inc. was manifested in a brand, it was **Guinness** – even though the company has always been registered in London.'

Ireland's Eye [mistrans. Of *Inis Ereann,* island of Eria, myth. figure]. Isl. off N. Dub. coast. Hence [media] **1952** B.P. Bowen, *Dublin Historical Record:* 'Dublin Humorous Periodicals of the 19th Century': In January 1874, a new journal, known as Ireland's Eye, was started by Christopher Smyth of 57 Dame Street ... In the first number it is stated that 'the paper is issued for the benefit of the inhabitants of the islet [none], to each of whom free copies will be sent, but a limited number of copies will be sold to people on the mainland.'

Irena [poet]. Personification of Ire. **1590/96** Edmund Spenser, *The Faerie Queene:* 'He now went with him in the new inquest,/Him for to aide, if aide he chaunst to neede,/Against that cruel tyrant, which opprest/The fair Irena with his fould misdeede ...'

Irish [adj. as n., sl.]. Aggression. **1945** Anthony T. Lawlor, *Irish Maritime Survey:* '... very common in seamen's parlance for pugnacity. A hand may speak of "Getting his Irish up".'

Irish ... For racial names and expressions thus prefixed see Bernard Share, *Slanguage, A Dictionary of Slang and Colloquial English in Ireland* (Appendix).

Irish Brigade [milit.]. (1) Irish troops in the service of France (1690-). **1959** John A. Murphy, *Justin MacCarthy, Lord Mountcashel:* 'The Brigade, of which Mountcashel was commander in chief, comprised five regiments of widely differing strength ... In all, the Brigade totalled 5,387 military of every rank.' (2) Irish unit in American Civil War (1861-5). **1998** Simon Winchester, *The Surgeon of Crowthorne:* 'There were around 150,000 Irish soldiers on the Union side in the struggle, many of them subsumed into the Yankee units that happened to recruit where they lived. But there was also a proud assemblage of Irishmen who fought together as a bloc: these were the soldiers of the 2nd Brigade, the Irish Brigade ...' (3) Volunteer force in Spanish Civil War (1936-9). **1999** Fearghal McGarry, *Irish Politics and the Spanish Civil War:* 'Of all the Irish responses to the Spanish Civil War ... the most infamous was the involvement of General Eoin O'Duffy's 700-strong Irish Brigade on the side of General Franco's Nationalist army.' (4) [polit.]. Pressure group. **1988** R.F. Foster, *Modern Ireland 1600-1972:* 'The **Independent Irish Party** was based on an alliance between the Tenant Righters and the so-called Irish Brigade – Irish MPs who had come together against the anti-popery campaign that dominated English politics in 1850-51.'

Irish Bull ['Etymology of an Irish Bull uncertain', Maria Edgeworth, *Essay on Irish Bulls* (1802)]. Self-contradictory proposition containing a manifest contradiction or ludicrous inconsistency. **1796** Sir Boyle Roche, *Speech on threatened*

French invasion: 'Here, perhaps, sirs, the murderous Marshellaw men would break in, cut us to mincemeat, and throw our bleeding heads upon that table, to stare us in the face.'

Irish Cheddar [nickname, milit.]. Explosive used by IRA in War of Independence, (1920s). **1999** Michele Guinness, *The Guinness Spirit:* 'When the Army arrived half an hour later the house was burning, though not enough to make it uninhabitable. Cans of "Irish cheddar", home-made explosives, wired up and planted all over the building, had not had time to explode.'

Irish Club [London]. **1990** Lord Killanin, in Cornelius F. Smith & Bernard Share (eds), *Whigs on the Green:* 'I was instrumental in its foundation and the first president. The Club arose from an amalgam of people from the London Irish Rugby Club, the old Four Provinces Club and the Shamrock Club, which had been founded for Irishmen serving in the British forces during the war.'

Irish Company of White Papers [tradename]. First Ir. paper mill, Dub. **1996** Brian McCarthy, *Irish Times,* 15 Jan: 'In 1690, a Nicholas Duplin requested assistance from the Privy Council, which granted him a warrant for a patent for the "sole making of all types of white writing and printing paper in Ireland". His "Irish Company of White Papers" was, apparently, an ambitious undertaking.'

Irish Danish Blue [<ubiquity of Dan. Blue cheese]. First commercial Irish blue cheese (1960s). **1965** Tom Whisker, *The Harp*, Christmas: 'Oh, yes, I think Guinness and cheese definitely go together. I have just had some **Phoenix**

Barley Wine and if I may call it Irish Danish Blue.'

Irish Dun see **Donegal Red**

Irish Elk [misnomer]. Great Deer (extinct). **1937** Robert Lloyd Praeger, *The Way that I Went:* 'Among the foothills of south Dublin, near the hamlet of Glencullen, is the filled-up lake of Ballybetagh ... This spot has yielded in amazing numbers remains of that splendid animal the Giant Deer or "Irish Elk" – but it is not an elk at all, and its nearest relation is the well-known Fallow Deer.'

Irish Elm [transport]. Vessels of Irish Shipping fleet (1953/68). **1977** Flann O'Brien/**Myles na gCopaleen**, *The Hair of the Dogma:* 'The tree is historically connected with warfare and bloodshed – for example, in the construction of bows and arrows, of ships (for "trade", a fancy name for military imperialism) ... Why do you name your ships the Irish Elm, the Irish Plane, the Irish Larch, and so on? I regard this obsession with trees simply as an archaistic indulgence, a love of the past born of a hatred of the present; it is the same thing as craving to revive ancient languages, customs and dress.'

Irish Examiner [media]. Cork-publ. newspaper. **2000** Roddy O'Sullivan, *Irish Times,* 11 Apr: 'The first edition of the *Irish Examiner*, the new name for the Cork-based national daily newspaper, the *Examiner*, will appear tomorrow. The new title is the second name change for the paper; four years ago, the *Cork Examiner* became the *Examiner*. Executives at the newspaper say they see the change as a "clear and unambiguous message" that they intend to take readers from the *Irish Independent*.' See also **De Paper**

Irish Exile and Freedom's Advocate [media]. First Ir. newspaper in Aust. (1850). **1854** John Mitchel, *Jail Journal:* 'To my utter amazement, I had a letter today from Patrick O'Donoghue, who has been permitted to live in the city of Hobart Town, informing me that he has established a newspaper called the *Irish Exile*, enclosing a copy of the last number, and proposing that *I should join him* in the concern.'

Irish Fear Civil panic following William III's invasion of England (1688). **1990** Robert Shepherd, *Ireland's Fate:* 'On the night of 12/13 December there occurred one of the most extraordinary incidents of the crisis, the so-called "Irish Fear" or "Irish Night". In London in the early hours of Thursday the 13th, "a report was spread all over the town that a great number of Irish" were "got together, that they had burnt Uxbridge and were marching directly to London".'

Irish Ireland [politic.]. Nationalist slogan. **1995** Patrick Maume, *D.P. Moran:* 'Moran had attracted scholarly attention as an aggressive and articulate exponent of a Catholic Gaelic vision of Irish identity, summed up in his slogans "Irish Ireland" and "The Gael must be the element that absorbs".' **1996** Fintan O'Toole, *The Ex-Isle of Erin:* 'The [**Fianna Fáil**] party does not justify itself to the people ... because it is the people, or at least the people who matter, the real Irish people. "This ard-fheis", Mr Haughey told his congregation in 1984, "speaks with the authentic voice of Irish Ireland".' Hence **Irish Irelander** [gen. derog.]. One given to excessive nationalist views. **1945** Sean O'Casey, *Drums Under the Windows:* '... and to Sean the voice was the voice of Eithne Carbery making her moan, though the

Irish Irelanders loved her, and gave her twenty thousand welcomes ... so a generous drop of sleety moisture from a leaden sky lingered on every Irish Ireland cheek, just like a tear at this moment shed, turning Éire into a woman of immemorial moaning ...'

Irish Johnstone [nickname]. John Henry Johnstone (b. Kilkenny 1749), singer. **1973** T.J. Walsh, *Opera in Dublin 1705-1797:* 'In 1783 he was engaged by Thomas Harris, manager of Covent Garden Theatre, at a weekly salary of £16. In time he became famous for his performance of Irish − or, to be more explicit, '**Oirish**' roles, and was soon known as "Irish Johnstone".'

Irish Legion [milit.]. Abortive force raised for service in S. America (1818). **1972** Maurice R. O'Connell (ed.), *The Correspondence of Daniel O'Connell* (Vol II): 'John Devereux ... wrote to Bolívar on his way back to the USA, offering to raise a volunteer force in Ireland for service in Venezuela. Bolívar accepted, and Devereux was back in Ireland at the end of 1818 to organize. His legion reached Venezuela in the latter half of 1819, but Devereux himself did not arrive until June 1820, by which time his legion had mutinied and the greater part had been packed off to Jamaica.'

Irish Loyal and Patriotic Union [polit.]. Loyalist org. (1885-). **2000** De Búrca Rare Books, *Catalogue 56,* Spring: 'The aim of its members, mainly businessmen, landowners and academics, was to oppose Home Rule. They contested five seats at the general election of November 1885, but only one candidate was returned.'

Irish Mist [brandname]. Whiskey liqueur. **1987** Marie O'Halloran, *Irish*

Press, 5 Sep: '"Don't change the name", insisted Karlheinz Hofrichter, of Heinemann the German duty-free importers. "Mist" in German means "dung" but, says Mr Hofrichter, people who buy Irish Mist know that it's a good liqueur.'

Irish pendants [maritime]. Cat's tails. **1945** Anthony T. Lawlor, *Irish Maritime Survey:* '… pieces of line, loose or adrift. Sometimes referred to by our neighbours as "Irish pendants".'

Irish Republican Brotherhood [polit.]. Revolutionary movement. **1968** E.R.R. Green in T.W. Moody (ed.), *The Fenian Movement:* '… a revolutionary organisation was launched in Dublin on St Patrick's Day, 1858 … Apparently the organisation had no definite name at this time; the title Irish Republican Brotherhood came into use much later.'

Irish stew [gastronomy, misnomer?]. **1895** E. Cobham Brewer, *Dictionary of Phrase and Fable* (new ed.): 'A dish that is unknown in Ireland.' **C19** *Dublin street song:* 'For all sorts of bellies there are dainties,/But the best feed, between me and you,/Is some mutton with onions and potatoes,/And three cheers for a real Irish stew.'

Irish Sunday Closing and Saturday Early Closing Campaign Anti-alcohol org. **1899** [media]. Pamphlet title: '*A Message to Ireland. AN ADDRESS GIVEN by the MOST REV. JOHN IRELAND, DD, Archbishop of St Paul, USA, in the Opera House, Cork, On Thursday July 20th 1899. Published by the Irish Sunday Closing and Saturday Early Closing Campaign, National Executive Committee, 4 and 5, Eustace Street, Dublin and 20, Lombard Street, Belfast.'*

Irish Swoop [<Irish Sweep(stakes), sponsors; aviation]. Intending competitor in England-Aust. air race (1934). **1980** Liam Byrne, *History of Aviation in Ireland:* '[James] Fitzmaurice consented to fly the Irish entry, a Bellanca aircraft named the *Irish Swoop*, but only hours before the race was due to begin a row developed over the amount of fuel the aircraft could carry. The final bitter blow came when the *Irish Swoop* was forced to withdraw.'

Irish tandem, as in **drive Irish tandem**, walk, put one's best foot forward. **1889** *The Shamrock,* 16 Feb: 'Ask how a peasant intends to travel to a place forty miles off, and, with an irresistible smile, he answers, "I'll drive Irish tandem" …'

Irish Tenors [< The Three Tenors (Pavarotti, Domingo, Carreras); tradename]. Performing group(s). **2000** Arminta Wallace, *Irish Times,* 13 Oct: 'If it's tenors, it has to be three. Unless, of course, you're talking about "Irish Tenors". At the time of writing Irish tenors appear to be multiplying at a rate that would make rabbits blench … if it isn't "The Irish Tenors", it's "The Three Irish Tenors", or "The Young Irish Tenors". Confused? Don't worry. So is everybody else.'

Irish Transvaal Brigade [milit.]. Body of men fighting on the side of the Boers in Anglo-Boer wars (1890s). **2000** Gerard Siggins, *Sunday Tribune,* 23 Apr: 'The group of Irish soldiers – called the Irish Transvaal Brigade or the Irish corps – was led by [John] MacBride for just a couple of months.'

Irish yew [<origin as a wild sport on mountains near Florencecourt, Co. Fhear Manach/Fermanagh (c1780)]. *Taxus Hibernica.* **1999** Robert Graham,

The Irish Journals of Robert Graham of Redgorton, 1835-1838: 'The bold point which I first noticed is called Gort a Thoal [Gortatole] and in the face of it the original plant of the Florencecourt yew (what passes with us by the name of the Irish yew), grows.'

Iron Lung [nickname, <apparatus formerly employed in treatment of tuberculosis]. Metal cask for draught stout introd. by **Guinness** (1950s-). **1997** Diarmuid Ó Drisceoil & Donal Ó Drisceoil, *The Murphy's Story:* 'Guinness completed the changeover from wood to metal in 1961, and in that year Murphy's bowed to the inevitable and bought in a number of the "iron lungs".'

Iron Throat, the [nickname]. Hospital. **1999** Brian McCarthy, *Irish Times,* 28 Sep: 'The widowed Lady Mary [Carbery] remarried … an ophthalmic surgeon called Kit Sanford, who had built the Cork Eye Ear and Throat Hospital – known locally as "de Iron Trote [phonetic approx. of Cork pronunciation]".'

Irregular [euphem., milit.]. Member of Anti-Treaty force in Civil War (1921-22). **1923** W.B. Yeats, 'Meditations in Time of Civil War': 'An affable Irregular,/A heavily-built Falstaffian man,/Comes cracking jokes of civil war/As though to die by gunshot were/The finest play under the sun.'

Italian Warehouse [tradename]. Dub. grocer's shop. **1936** Oliver St John Gogarty, *As I was Going Down Sackville Street:* '… he had demonstrated with a cutlass before a ham which hung with twenty others on a rail outside one of those shops which are called Italian Warehouses in Dublin. They would be called grocers' shops elsewhere.' Hence **Italian Warehousemen**

Iveagh, Earl of Brit. title conferred on Edward Cecil **Guinness** (1847-1927). **1999** Michele Guinness, *The Guinness Spirit:* 'In opting for the name of Iveagh, he unleashed a barrage of unexpected publicity and controversy. Correspondents in *The Dublin Evening Telegraph* and several other leading national newspapers resented his appropriation of the hereditary title of the aristocratic Magennises of Iveagh.'

J

Jackal, The [nickname]. Terrorist. **1998** *Irish Times*, 5 Jun: 'Robin Jackson, a loyalist killer of the 1970s and 1980s, who was known as "The Jackal", has died of cancer at his home near Lurgan.'

Jack Carvill's [tradename]. Off-licence, Dub. **2000** *Sunday Business Post*, 11 Jun: 'Jack Carvill's on Camden Street, one of Dublin's oldest off-licences, is to be auctioned in June 30 … This is a List 2 building which was mentioned in *Ulysses*.'

Jack Lattin [<John Lattin, Morristown House, Co. Chill Dara/Kildare, who successfully wagered that he would dance home from Dublin changing his steps every furlong]. Hence **I'll make you dance Jack Lattin/Latten,** threat of chastisement. **1922** James Joyce, *Ulysses:* 'I'll make it hot for you! I'll make you dance Jack Latten for that.'

Jack's Army [nickname, <Jack Charlton, manager of Rep. of Ire. soccer team (1986-95)]. Team's followers and supporters. **1995** Paul Kimmage, *Sunday Independent,* 17 Dec: 'Five years ago – on my first major assignment as a sportswriter – the editor of the *Sunday Tribune* … bought me a boat and rail ticket to Sicily and enlisted me in Jack's Army.'

Jack White's [Co. Chill Mhantáin/Wicklow]. Pub, scene of a recent murder. **2000** Kate McMorrow, *Irish Times*, 8 Jun: 'Jack White's pub was a smuggler's inn, named after Jack White who kept a room there. A warrant for his arrest was eventually issued by Lord Shrewsbury [C18 Lord Lieut. of Ire.].'

Jacob's Ulcer [medic.]. **1989** John Gleeson, *The Book of Irish Lists and Trivia:* 'An eye condition discovered by the Maryborough (Portlaoise)-born Irish oculist, Arthur Jacob (1790-1874). Jacob was Professor of Anatomy at the Royal College of Surgeons of Ireland 1826-1869.'

Jacuzzi see **Floozie in the Jacuzzi**

Jailic [pun, <'Gaelic']. Irish acquired in prison, specifically **Long Kesh** (1970s). **1986** Derek Dunne, *Magill*, Apr: 'As the men of the **H-blocks** began to be moved from cell to cell, they were learning from the writing on the wall. For example, the past tense of an Irish verb might be on one wall, the future on another … "Jailic", they called it.'

JAM [acronym]. Junior Assistant Mistress. **1995** Niall Tóibín, *Smile and be a Villain:* '… they were what were called "JAMs", or junior assistant mistresses, who would have had no status whatsoever in law or education …'

James of the Fleeing [nickname]. James II, defeated at the Battle of the Boyne (1690). **1950** Richard Hayward, *Ulster and the City of Belfast:* 'James the Second, *James of the Fleeing*, was a shiftless creature whose lack of tact lost him the English throne, and whose foolish machinations had turned Ulster Protestants against him, to a man, several years before.'

James's St. [street name, Dub., location of **Guinness** brewery]. Hence **James's Street!** [interj., euphem.] Jasus! [Hiberno-Eng. pronun. of 'Jesus']. **1982** Éamonn Mac Thomáis, *Janey Mack Me*

159

Shirt is Black: 'Men who didn't want to curse or use the holy name in vain used the name of James's Street and Jacobs [biscuit factory] instead.'

Jarvey, the [media]. **1952** B.P. Bowen, *Dublin Historical Record*, 'Dublin Humorous periodicals of the 19th Century': 'When R.J. Mecredy was the editor of the Irish Cyclist, one of the contributors of both prose and verse of a humorous character was Percy French. At one time when he was at a loose end, French asked R.J. for a permanent post on the Cyclist. Instead Mecredy asked him to act as editor of a new comic paper to be called The Jarvey ... The Jarvey was launched on January 3rd, 1889 and appears to have run until Christmas 1891 ...'

Jealous Wall, the [Co. na hIarmhí/Westmeath]. Architectural folly. **1981** Leo Daly, *Titles:* 'After the trial which had disposed of Arthur Rochfort [1757], Lord Belvedere turned his full attentions towards his neighbour [and brother], George. Between the two houses of Belvedere and Rochfort he had built a Gothic ruin, since called the "Jealous Wall", which completely blocked the view of one house from the other ... It was described at the time as a silent witness to the past feelings of hatred and malice which the neighbouring brothers shared for each other ...'

Jeanie Johnston [transport]. Sailing vessel. **2000** *Irish Times*, 4 Apr: 'The finishing touches are being put to the carving of Jeanie Johnston, which will be mounted on the prow of the replica Famine vessel of the same name, currently being constructed in Co Kerry ... However, it is still unclear who Jeanie Johnston was. The project historian, Ms Helen O'Carroll, thinks the name might

have something to do with the poetry of Robert Burns.'

Jem/Jembo [cf. *jemmy fellow,* smart, spruce individual (Brit. Sl.)]. Generic Dubliner. **1946** Donagh MacDonagh, *Happy as Larry:* 'when one of them dies [in India]/He's burnt to be buried in style;/Right up on the fire will go Jem ...' **1996** Joe O'Connor, *Sunday Tribune*, 9 Jun: 'I was comin home from de pub wit de war department when sez she to me, Jembo, will we buy de papers?' See also **Dublin**

Jerusalem [nickname]. Thomas 'Buck' Whaley (1766-1800) who, for a wager, travelled to Jerusalem and back in 2 years (1788-9). **1847** John Edward Walsh, *Ireland Sixty Years Ago:* 'to the hour of his death, which occurred recently, he was called "Jerusalem Whaley".'

JKL [<James Kildare & Leighlin; pseudonym]. James W. Boyle, Cath. bishop of Kildare & Leighlin (1786-1834). Hence **JKL Street** [Edenderry, Co. Uibh Fhailí/Offaly]. **1993** Annie Behan in Joe O'Reilly & Sixth Class, *Over the Half Door:* 'I don't remember much about JKL St. We were young when we moved ... In JKL St. we lived where the Bradys live now ...'

Job of Journeywork [dance]. **1928** Risteard Mac Gabhann, *Leabhar Tailteann*, 'Rinnce na h-Éireann': 'There are quite a number of these set-dances, the most generally known being "The Blackbird", "The Job of Journeywork", "St Patrick's Day", "Garden of Daisies", "The Jockey at the Fair", "The Drunken Gauger", Buonaparte's Retreat", "Humours of Bandon", "The Sea Captain", etc.'

John Fanshawe Ellis [nom de plume]. Jane Frances Elgee, Lady Wilde (c1824-

96). **1930** *Irish Times*, 7 Apr: 'Her letters to the ***Nation*** were signed John Fanshawe Ellis, maintaining her initials, and an admirer wishing to meet that gentleman was rather astonished to learn that "he" would be found at Dr Wilde's residence, and more astonished still when the Doctor produced the author as his wife.'

John Hewitt, the [<eponymous poet (1907-87)] Belfast pub. **2000** Glenn Patterson, *Irish Times*, 1 Apr: 'The John Hewitt is named for one of Belfast's most highly regarded poets, who died, aged 79, in 1987 … Michael Longley … remembered what it was like going out for a drink with Hewitt: the elderly poet would always order a half of **Bass** to Michael's pint and if Michael were to suggest a second drink, would ask rather sternly if it wasn't time they were going.'

Johnny down the road [nickname]. Provisional IRA, Belfast. **1999** Oliver Stanton, *Independent on Sunday* (London), 4 Apr: 'A long-time clubber who grew up on a well-known road in Belfast explains: "For years kids were brought up to respect Johnny down the road (the paramilitaries) because he was fighting for his country".'

Johnny Fortycoats see **Forty-Coats**

John Roberts Square see **Red Square**

Josef Locke [stage name]. Joseph McLaughlin (1917-99), singer. **1999** *Irish Times,* 16 Oct: 'His career saw its greatest progression through the 1940s, when the big international stars were prevented from travelling to Dublin … soon Irish stars were topping the bill. Among them, the by-then-named Josef Locke.'

Joy, the [nickname, abbrev.]. Mountjoy prison, Dub. **1940** *Irish Times,* 27 Apr: '"What's it like in Mountjoy?" and "What's hard labour?" are questions frequently asked. First let me say that so far I have had no personal experience! Nevertheless, I can give you some idea of what the ordinary prisoner's day is like in "the Joy".'

Jubilee mutton [<Diamond Jubilee of Britain's Queen Victoria (1897)]. Small quantities of meat distributed to Dublin's poor on that occasion. Hence very little of anything. **1922** James Joyce, ***Ulysses:*** 'Dusty Rhodes. Peep at his wearables. By mighty! What's he got? Jubilee mutton.'

Just Society [politic., abbrev.]. **Fine Gael** election manifesto (1965). **1984** Fergal Tobin, *The Best of Decades, Ireland in the 1960s:* 'Within a week a manifesto was produced. *Towards a Just Society* was a victory for the liberals in the party … [Seán] Lemass was forced to disinter his 1963 pledge of a social policy in order to counter the "Just Society".'

K

Kaiser, the [nickname]. Dermot Desmond, Dub. businessman. **1999** Frank McDonald, *The Construction of Dublin:* '... nobody could deny that Desmond was the quintessential north-side boy made good, with a net worth of several hundred million pounds and a nickname, The Kaiser, to go with his distinctive *fin de siècle* moustache.'

Kate Carney [*recte* **Kearney**, Brit. rhyming sl.] **1948** James Curtis, *The Saturday Book,* 'Why Rhyming Slang?': 'Army: In rhyming slang, this is the *Kate*. A very poor rhyme indeed, but Kate Carney's cottage, one of the sights of the Lakes of Killarney, seems to have impressed itself deeply enough on popular imagination for it to have become synonymous with Army. Kate Carney was also a favourite music hall artist, so perhaps it is from here that the phrase comes.'

Kate Mac [<? nickname]. West Clare Railway (1887-1961). **1990** Edmund Lenihan, *In the Tracks of the West Clare Railway:* 'The West Clare – "Kate Mac" – as it was affectionately known by many Clare people – became one of the mainstays and shapers of the agricultural and social life of its hinterland.'

Kathleen/Cathleen Mavourneen (system) [nickname, <pop. Ballad, 'Kathleen Mavourneen' (1830): 'Oh hast thou forgotten how soon we must sever!/Oh hast thou forgotten this day we must part,/It may be for years and it may be for ever ...']. Payment by instalments; as in 'on the never-never'. **1985**

Máirín Johnston, *Around the Banks of Pimlico:* 'On the Kathleen Mavourneen system (the never-never) the tenement rooms were furnished and the walls elaborately decorated with gold-framed pictures of Pope Pius XII ...'

Kathleen ní Houlihan see **Cathleen/ Caitlín/Kathleen Ní Houlihan**

Keasers Lane [Dub.]. **1577** Richard Stanihurst, in Raphael Holinshed, *The Chronicles of England, Scotland and Ireland:* 'This lane is steepe and slipperie, in which, otherwhyles, they that make more haste than good speede clincke there bummes to the stones. And therefore the ruder sorte, whether it be through corruption of speache, or for that they gyue [give] it a nickname, commonly terme it, not so homely as truly, kiss arse lane.'

Keepers [Agrarian conflict]. **1895** E. Cobham Brewer, *Dictionary of Phrase and Fable* (new ed.): 'A staff of men employed by Irish landlords in 1843, etc., to watch the crops and prevent their being smuggled off during the night. They were resisted by the **Molly Maguires**.'

Kelly's Book [nickname]. Book of Kells, manuscript (C9). **2000** *Irish Times,* 16 May: 'See Kelly's Book without the coach. Taking a trip to Trinity College Dublin may no longer be necessary for those interested in seeing the Book of Kells. Last week a CD-ROM of the entire 680-page manuscript became available ...'

Kelvin Temperature Scale, the [<William Thomson Kelvin, b. Belfast 1824]. Absolute temperature scale (1848). **1989** John Gleeson, *The Book of Irish Lists and Trivia:* 'Kelvin made major

advances in the science of thermo-dynamics and electricity ... and also invented several scientific units, including the Kelvin compass, the Kelvin balance, and the Kelvin tide predictor.'

Kentish fire [<Winchelsea, Kent, England]. Form of political protest. **1835-8** (publ. 1999) *The Irish Journals of Robert Graham of Redgorton:* 'The great attempt of the few oppositionists was to get up what is called the Kentish fire. It is the signal of the orangemen and consists of a quick reiteration of three claps of the hands. It is said to have been invented by Lord Winchelsea and hence the name.'

Kerry [Co. Chiarraí]. Hence (1) **Kerry Blue** [dog breed]. **1953** Candy Novelty Co [UK], card series: 'in Ireland, the original home of the dog, his origin goes back a long time, possibly longer than his first cousin the Irish Terrier, especially in the county of Kerry.' (2) **Kerry Cousins** [<close-knit political families]. As such in general. **1976** T.J. Barrington, *Discovering Kerry:* 'From 1692 to 1800, when the Irish parliament came to an end, there was never a time when the county was not represented by either a Blennerhasset, a Crosbie or a Denny, often by two of them ... These families, and some others, were intermarried again and again, so giving rise to the expression "Kerry cousins".' (3) **Kerrygold** [brandname]. Butter. **1996** Fintan O'Toole, *The Ex-Isle of Erin:* 'It was the wrapping that turned it into money: a name that had, as the marketing reports put it, "a definite Irish sound, with overtones of richness and purity". In Ireland, the name sounded like nonsense, since Kerry was associated with stony mountains, not green pastures.' Hence **1999** Tony Harnden, *'Bandit Country'*: 'As with most of the devices

planted in England in the 1990s, including the Docklands bomb, the IRA codeword used was Kerrygold. This was thought to have been selected in 1989 after a Kent supermarket owner withdrew Kerrygold butter and other Irish goods from sale in protest at the Deal bombing.' (4) **Kerryman joke** Anecdote portraying Kerrymen/women as preternaturally stupid (cf. similar attitude by Canadians to Newfoundlanders, French to Belgians). (5) **Kerry Security** [coll., derog.]. **1811** Capt [Francis] Grose, *A Dictionary of Buckish Slang, University Wit and Pickpocket Eloquence:* 'Bond, pledge, oath and keep the money.' (6) **Kerry Witness** [coll., derog.]. **1972** Eric Partridge, *Dictionary of Historical Slang:* 'One who will swear to anything.'

Kildare [Cill Dara, Co. & town]. Hence (1) **Kildare Place Society** [Dub., <street name] C19 education society. **1999** J.R.R. Adams, 'Swine-Tax and Eat-Him-All Magee', in J.S. Donnelly jr. & Kerby A. Miller (eds), *Irish Popular Culture 1650-1850:* '... the most important organisation of this kind was the Society for the Education of the Poor of Ireland, more commonly known as the Kildare Place Society. This body was founded in 1811 ...' (2) **Kildare Side** [metaphor, <Punchestown racecourse, Naas] Right-hand side. **1985** Máirín Johnston, *Around the Banks of Pimlico:* 'His accordion was strapped under this [cloak] from his shoulders, and on his head he wore a battered slouched hat, cocked on the "Kildare" side ...' **1999** Rose O'Donoghue. *Leinster Leader* (Naas), 22 Apr: '... one of the traders, a hardened biddy who sat at the same stall every year (on the Kildare side, next to the gates) called me and said "Do us a favour, luv. Go up there and put ten bob to win on number five ...".'

Kilkenny [Cill Chainnigh, Co. & city]. Hence (1) [*idem.*] 'An old frize [*sic*] coat' (Grose); (2) **Kilkenny cats**, as in 'fight like Kilkenny cats' [<C17 Hessian soldiers alleged to have tied two cats together by the tails and thrown them over a clothesline to fight]. **1925** E.L. Ahrons, *Railway Magazine* (London), 'Great Southern & Western Railway': '... when they were both at the main platform [at **Limerick Junction**], the two engines faced each other looking like a couple of cats – Kilkenny brand – which, had they been able to waggle their trains, would very likely have sprung at each other.' (3) **Confederation of Kilkenny** [politic.] **1999** Raymond Gillespie, in W.J. McCormack (ed.), *The Blackwell Companion to Modern Irish Culture:* 'The term ... dating from the 1840s, describes the organisation established on 24 October 1642 as an umbrella body for those at war in Ireland. It termed itself the "Confederated Catholics of Ireland" ...' See also **Cats, the**

Killinchy muffler [<Killinchy, Co. an Dúin/Down]. Female embrace. **1998** Margaret McCann, *Irish Times*, 19 Dec: 'The Killinchy men, being cold, slow and useless are given a hoult round the neck to get them closer; muffler as in scarf ...'

Killyman wrackers [<wreckers, Ulster, pronun.]. Yeomanry of Killyman area, Co. Tyrone, who wrecked Catholic houses during the 1798 rising. Hence [*idem*] variety of potato. **1932** *Ulster Hiker* (Cushendall, Co. Antrim), 'The Ulster Dialect', Jun: 'We used to have a variety of potato known as "Killyman Wrackers", and the name originated from a company of Yeomanry!' See also **Yeo**

King Billy [nickname]. William III of Eng., who became icon of Unionism following Battle of the Boyne (1690). His equestrian statue stood in Dublin's College Green until blown up (1929). See **Easter Lily**

Kingdom, the [nickname, esp. in GAA context]. **Kerry. 1996** John B. Keane, *Irish Times,* 4 Apr: '... John Philpot Curran commented adversely that the magistracy of the county of Kerry were so opposed to the laws of the land that they were a law unto themselves, a Kingdom apart ... In fact some Kerrymen say there are only two Kingdoms, the Kingdom of God and the Kingdom of Kerry.' **2000** Keith Barr, *Irish Independent,* 7 Oct: 'Fitzgerald key to the Kingdom. It is more than a little ironic that Maurice Fitzgerald, who could so easily have been the reason Kerry won the All-Ireland [football championship] may turn out to be at the centre of the reason they lose it.'

King of Dalkey [Deilginis, Co. Bhaile Átha Cliath/Dub.]. Notional monarch of Dalkey Island, Dub. Bay. **1847** John Edward Walsh, *Ireland Sixty Years Ago:* 'Among the singular societies which have existed in Ireland within the last sixty years, was the "Kingdom of Dalkey and its Officers". It was then common, in forming associations, serious or convivial, to adopt, instead of the plebeian name of "club", some more high-sounding title.'

King of Spain's Daughter, the [nickname]. Spanish wine. **1617** Fynes Moryson, *An Itinerary Containing His Ten Years' Travel:* 'But when they ["the wild Irish"] come to any market town to sell a cow or a horse, they never return home till they have drunk the price in Spanish wine (which they call the King of Spain's daughter), or in Irish usque-baugh …'

King of the Roads [nickname]. Charles Bianconi (1786-1875), coach transport entrepreneur. **1977** S.F. Pettit, *This City of Cork 1700-1900:* 'Clonmel was to be the centre of the nationwide horse transport enterprise of the "King of the Roads", Charles Bianconi.' See also **Bianconi**

King Puck [<ON *puki,* mischievous demon]. Totemic goat, central feature of annual Puck Fair, Killorglin/Cill Orglan, Co. Chiarraí/Kerry. **1950** *Irish Times,* 16 Aug: 'The general estimate was that 20,000 attended Puck this year. Our personal estimate was that there was one pub to every 500 people, and, as the ceremonies attending King Puck's enthronement seemed to have started a raging thirst in everybody who was present, the necessary quenching was more than somewhat congested.' Hence **Queen of Puck**. **2000** Anne Lucey, *Irish Times,* 11 Aug: 'Sara-Jane Joy (13), this year's Queen of Puck, performed the coronation ceremony at 7.30 pm yesterday. **Gathering** Day …'

King Rat [nickname]. Billy Wright, Loyalist paramilitary (1960-97). **1997** *El País* (Madrid), 28 Dec: 'Rey Rata fundó su propio grupo para-militar, la Fuerza de Voluntarios Lealistas, que se opone al proceso de paz en general …'. [King Rat founded his own paramilitary group, the Loyalist Volunteer Force, which is opposed to the peace process in general]. **1998** David Sharrock, *Irish Times,* 3 Jan: 'A local [Belfast] journalist writing for the *Sunday World* newspaper gave Wright the nickname King Rat … Wright said he hated the name at first but grew to accept its worth.'

Kinsale Fortune [<Kinsale, Ceann tSáile, Co. Chorcaí/Cork; nickname]. **1930** *Irish Times,* 22 Aug: 'Are Dingle boys exceptionally fat as implied in the saying "fat as a Dingle boy"? Have **Mullingar** heifers more beef to the heel than any other heifer? "A Kinsale for-tune", I believe, meant a piano as a bride's dowry …'

Kips, the [<Dan. *Horekippe,* brothel, <*Kippe,* hut, mean alehouse; nickname]. Dub. red-light district. See **Monto**; **Nighttown**

Kitty O'Shea's [<Catherine O'Shea (1845-1921), mistress/wife of Charles Stewart Parnell (see **Uncrowned King of Ireland**); tradename]. Pubs in Dub., Brussels, Paris. **2000** Alison O'Connor, *Irish Times,* 21 Jun: 'Why are they [Ir. pubs in France] so popular? A man well qualified to answer that is Dermot Toolan … who spent eight years man-aging the well-known Kitty O'Shea's pub in Paris before opening his own bar, Bugsy's, just over a year ago …'

Kitty the Hare [<fictional character of travelling woman created by V. O'D Power]. Travelling women in gen. **1987** Lar Redmond, *Emerald Square:* 'I stuck my head out the window. "Kitty the Hare country", I told him. "Why don't you ask the headless coachman when he passes by?"'

Klondyke see **Dyker**

Knackeragua [<*knacker,* itinerant, trav-eller; play on *Nicaragua*]. Rural Ireland beyond the **Pale**, in the perception of **Dublin 4**]. **1999** Ross O'Carroll-Kelly, *Sunday Tribune,* 'Diary of a Schools' Rugby Player': '… and I was in there on, like, Thursday night, late night shopping, like 70 per cent off clothes and shit. There was, like, every skanger in Dublin in there. It was, like, TOTAL Knackeragua. Totally.'

Kruger [<his leadership of a school gang; nickname]. Muiris Kavanagh (1894-1971), film publicist and latterly publican in Dún Chaoin, Co. Kerry. **1988** Henry Boylan, *A Dictionary of Irish Biography* (2nd ed.): At the local school he was leader of the Boer faction and got the nickname "Kruger" by which he was known for the rest of his life.' **1996** Leslie Matson, *Méiní, the Blasket Nurse*: 'That was to be another day. I closed the door behind me and set off through the fields to the road which led north through Ballinaraha to Kruger's.'

Kutu–Kutu/Cutchacutchoo [<?]. Party game. **C1820** *Recollections of Ireland, by a late Professional Gentleman:* 'Kutu–Kutu was the glorious and pre-vailing fun by night … none but married ladies were members of this Kutu-Kutu Club, who had for partners young and old, married and unmarried men. The lady first led off, and crouching on her hunkers, she placed under each knee-cap a hand, and then hopping round the room as best she could, a gentleman followed in her train as speedily as possible, and … overtaking, jostled up against her, when both upset and went sprawling on the floor …'

Kyanise [<John Ward Kyan (1774-1850); vb.]. **1931** *Irish Times*, 10 Feb: 'It is just a century ago since an ingenious Wicklow man … by his discovery of a means of preventing dry-rot in wood, added a new word to the English language. To "Kyanise" timber intended for use in building became a common expression with contractors and masons from 1831 onward.'

L

Lá [Ir., day; media]. Belfast Ir.-language newspaper (1984-). **2001** John Horgan, *Irish Media: a Critical History Since 1922*: 'In 1991 it became a weekly, giving Northern Ireland yet another distinction: it was the only part of the United Kingdom – perhaps the only part of the world – in which there was a weekly publication called "Day" and a monthly one called "**Fortnight**".'

Lads, the [nickname]. Members of an illegal organisation, gen. the IRA in its various versions. **1982** Trevor Danker, *Sunday Independent,* 7 Nov: 'The verses were written the morning after the statue of Sir Hubert Gough in the **Phoenix Park** was dynamited by The Lads on July 23, 1957.'

Lady Betty [pseudonym, Ros Comáin/ Roscommon]. Hangwoman, real name unknown. **1981** Adrian MacLoughlin, *Streets of Ireland:* 'This eighteenth century jail became a lunatic asylum before it fell into disuse about 1822, and has a macabre claim to fame as the place where Ireland's last hangwoman plied her trade, or – as one account puts it with unconscious humour – executed her duties. Executioners used pseudonyms for an obvious reason, and this charming girl went by the title of "Lady Betty".'

Lake County, the [nickname]. Co. na hIarmhí/Westmeath, esp. in GAA context. **1996** *Westmeath Independent,* 14 Jun: 'While Barney's boys might have been full of optimism against Dublin ... there was to be no fairytale ending to the Lake County's campaign of the last months.'

Lambeg [Co. Aontroma/Antrim; village]. Hence [politic]. Ceremonial drum. **1987** Rosemary Evans, *The Visitor's Guide to Northern Ireland:* 'The hamlet gave its name to the big drums which came to Ireland from Holland with the army of William III [1690]. "Lambegs" are seen – and heard – on Orange Lodge parades.'

Lána na Bó [*sic*]. See **Cows Lane** [*sic*].

Lanna Macree Legendary owner of accommodating canine. **1906** William Boyle, *The Eloquent Dempsey:* 'You're like Lanna Macree's dog – piece of the road with everybody.' Similarly endowed dog-owners include Billy Harran, O'Brien, **Lanty McHale**. **1944** James Joyce, *Stephen Hero:* '"Put this in your diary", he said to transcriptive Maurice. "Protestant orthodoxy is like Lanty McHale's dog: it goes a bit of the road with everyone".' See also *Leannamachree*

Lanty McHale see **Lanna Macree**

Lár. An see **An Lár**

Lartigue, the [<Charles François Lartigue, C19 inventor; transport]. Listowel & Ballybunion elevated monorail (1888-1924). **1989** A.T. Newham, *The Listowel & Ballybunion Railway:* 'In June 1889 it was revealed that numerous complaints had arisen concerning the noise of travel on the "Lartigue" (as the railway was popularly known) ...'

Laurence O'Toole, Saint (c1130-80). Archbishop of Dub. Hence (1) Hospital. **1940** *Irish Times,* 29 Apr: 'During the second reading in the Dáil of the Saint Laurence O'Toole Hospital Bill a reporter was heard to remark: "What a name for a hospital! Will we be required to write "St Laurence O'Toole Hospital" in full every time it is in the news? Or can we shorten it to O'Toole? (2) [transport]. Aer Lingus Douglas C-47A, originally registered (26 Nov 1948) as *St Kevin*, subseq. *St Laurence O'Toole, St Fergal, St Declan*.

Law Braw [<Ir. *lá breá*, nice day; mildly derog.]. Student of Irish, esp. in Gaeltacht (Ir.-speaking) areas. **1998** Brian Fallon, *An Age of Innocence*: '... he [**Myles na gCopaleen**] regularly derided the Bicycle Clip Brigade of Gaelgeoirí [enthusiastic Ir.–speakers] the (often Dublin-based) type known in the countryside as Law Braws and Taw Shays ...' See **Tá Sé**

Lay of the Victories, the [Dún na nGall/Donegal]. Folk custom. **1932** 'S.M', *The Glensman* (Cushendall), Feb: 'Among charms, the one in which most implicit faith is put is called the "Lay of the Victories". This is a charm which is to be said three times without stumbling. If the person saying the charm stumbles in the words, then the one for whom the charm is being said is in danger.'

League of Youth [politic.]. Youth movement. **1967** David Thornley in Francis Mac Manus (ed.), *The Years of the Great Test 1926-39*: 'On 21 September [1934] General O'Duffy was induced by the Central Council to resign from Fine Gael. O'Duffy subsequently denied that he had resigned from the Director-Generalship of the youth movement and set up a rival League of Youth and, subsequently, a National Corporative Party. Neither enjoyed any success.'

Leannamachree [see **Lanna Macree**]. **2001** Tom O'Dea, *Irish Times*, 13 Jan:

'Gay Byrne ... must perceive that [*Who Wants to be a*] *Millionaire* is a prefabricated piece of multinational junk television accorded him by vain trendies in RTÉ who take off down the road after every passing caravan, like Leannamachree's dog.'

Leestown [media]. Fictitious village created for TV serial (1964), purportedly in Co. Kilkenny but actually in Co. Meath. **1977** Wesley Burrowes, *The Riordans*: 'Fierce arguments raged about what the programme should be called ... The chosen author, James Douglas, favoured *The Lees of Leestown* and later, *Look at the Lees* ... But someone felt that *Look at the Lees* might be corrupted into *Leak at the Loos* ... I have not been able to discover how they came to be The Riordans.'

Left Bank [<Rive Gauche, Paris, in cultural context]. Right bank of **Liffey**, Dub., esp. Temple Bar area. **2000** Michael Smith, quoted in *Irish Independent*, 27 May: 'Ever since **Riverdance** and Italia '90, we've become a country with all the depth of a colony of DJs. Listen to what they're saying right now on Dublin's Left Bank. "Two Corlsbergs please. How's she cuttin', Mike." Hilarious.' Hence **2000** Frank Kilfeather, *Irish Times,* 12 May: '... Sligo shows all the hallmarks of the **Celtic Tiger** ... with the building of Rockwood Parade, a magnificent example of tasteful construction. This has become the town's Left Bank, or Temple Bar, an area built along the Garavogue river.'

Leprechaun [Ir. *leipreachán*, a pigmy, a sprite, a leprechaun (Dinneen)]. One of the 'little people'. Hence [media] **The Leprechaun** Periodical. **1952** B.P. Bowen, *Dublin Historical Record*, 'Dublin Humorous Periodicals', Mar-May: '... a journal which enlivened the early days of this century, and which by the excellence of its cartoons and drawings set a headline which was a model to later periodicals. The Leprechaun was started in May, 1905, and continued till 1915 (February).' Hence **leprechaunisation** [vb. derog.] Process of degradation of national ethos. **2000** John Boland, *Irish Independent,* 9 Sep: 'B.P. Fallon … snarled that the *Riverdance* mullarky was "no more authentic than Darby O'Gill and the **Little People** or shillelaghs at duty-free … the continuing leprechaunisation of Ireland.'

Letts [tradename]. Enniscorthy brewery. **1981** Adrian Mac Loughlin, *Streets of Ireland:* 'Mill Park Rd goes to the right below the post office. Mill Park brewery was owned by the Letts, its slogan predictably being "Let's drink Letts".' See **George Killian's**

Levellers [<practice of levelling hedges on enclosed land formerly commons]. Agrarian agitators (1740s) subsequently **Whiteboys**. **1973** Dying declaration of Darby Browne, hanged July 1762, quoted in Maureen Wall (T. Desmond Williams [ed.]), *Secret Societies in Ireland:* 'We had all led an honest and laborious life 'till January last, when finding the levellers or Whiteboys in the county of Tipperary, had partly succeeded in redressing some of the grievances they had complained of, by levelling ditches …'

Leviathan (of Parsonstown). 72-inch reflecting telescope built by 3rd Earl of Rosse at Birr Castle, Birr (formerly Parsonstown) Co. Uibh Fháilí/Offaly (1840s). **1971** Patrick Moore, *The Astronomy of Birr Castle:* 'Its tremendous light-grasp, and the excellence of its optics, were no longer in doubt. The

"Leviathan" was capable of doing all that its maker had hoped …' **1996** Bernard Lovell, *Sunday Independent*, 7 Jan: 'Surrounded by one of the great gardens of the western world there is a sleeping giant – the Leviathan of Parsonstown.'

LibDev [nonce word]. **2000** John Waters, *Irish Times,* 16 Oct: 'This is the era of the LibDev, a refinement of the **Dublin 4** Liberal, the term for someone who, while espousing liberal views is happy to live in the slipstream of de Valera's Ireland.' See **Dev**

Liberator, the [nickname]. Daniel O'Connell, politician and statesman (1775-1847) **1980** Brian Friel, *Translations:* 'MÁIRE: I'm talking about Daniel O'Connell. HUGH: Does she mean that little Kerry politician? MÁIRE: I'm talking about the Liberator, Master, as you well know.'

Liffey Valley [Retail complex, Dub.]. **2001** Elaine Larkin, *Irish Times*, 5 Feb: 'Where do you prefer to go shopping in Dublin? Quarryvale? Lucan Town? The Liffey Valley? The Liffey Town? The Liffey Gate? The Liffey Village? West Gate? Liffey West? West Vale? Esker Park? Or Clondalkin Town? … Before even a block was laid, the branding of the centre was a critical factor in the marketing of the sprawling shopping centre and so potential shoppers and local residents were polled on the names. The name Liffey Valley won out over all of the above.'

Liffy [abbrev. <R.Liffey; aviation]. Waystation for navigation purposes. **2000** *Irish Air Letter,* Apr: 'Flights out of Dublin routing via LIFFY, TOLKA or Strumble were subjected to widespread delays from 23 March 2000 because of a

difficulty which arose in respect of restructuring of UK airspace over the Irish Sea.' See also **Anna Liffey**

Lilliburlero [music <Ir. Lile ba léir ó the [orange] lily it were clear ...]. Pop. ballad (1687-). **1990** Robert Shepherd, *Ireland's Fate:* 'The tune "Lilliburlero", which is played before the World News in the BBC Radio World Service, owes its title to the mock Irish refrain of a savage satire, composed when Tyrconnel embarked for Dublin in February 1687 ... and opened with an offensive reference to "Teague"...' See **Taig**

Lilywhites/Lilies [<colour of sports strip; nickname]. Co. Chill Dara/ Kildare GAA teams, and by assoc. Kildare inhabitants. **2000** James Healy, *Leinster Leader* (Naas), 17 Aug: '"Behold the Lilies of the field. They toil not. Neither do they spin." But they sure play one hell of a game of football!' **2000** Joan Walsh, *Leinster Leader:* 'A Naas man is hoping to cruise into the top ten with the Kildare anthem "C'mon Ye Lilywhites".'

Limerick Junction [transport]. (1) Railway centre, not in Limerick but in Co. Thiobraid Árann/Tipperary. See **Kilkenny**. (2) Pub. **2001** Chris Heaney, *Irish Times*, 17 Mar: 'Today, in Irish pubs all over the world – from O'Hara's in Tokyo to The Limerick Junction in Atlanta – pints of stout will be poured, ballads sung and hangovers acquired in celebration of Ireland's favourite Welshman.'

Limerick Soviet [politics]. General strike, 14–24 Apr 1919. **1999** James Kemmy, in W.J. McCormack (ed.), *The Blackwell Companion to Modern Irish Culture:* '... the Trades and Labour Council called a general strike, named a

Soviet by international journalists in the city covering the proposed transatlantic flight by Major Woods. The workers took control of the city, organised the distribution of essentials, and issued their own currency and *Daily Bulletin*.'

Lisnagarvey [Lios na gCearrbhach]. Former name of Lisburn, Co. Aontroma/ Antrim. **1927** Player's cigarette card series, *Irish Place Names:* 'A pamphlet published in 1691 thus sets forth the origin of the name ... "The Fort of the Gamblers": "We marched towards Lisburn, one of the prettiest towns in the North of Ireland. The Irish name is Lisnegarvagh [*sic*] which they tell me signifies 'gamester's mount ...'".' Hence (1) [sport] Hockey club. (2) [media]. Radio transmitter. **1936** A.Z., *Irish Radio News,* 28 Mar: 'Not Lisburn nor Blaris – but Lisnagarvey! That is the title of Northern Ireland's new high-power station, situated some few miles from the town of Lisburn. The choice of name is certain to please the immediate inhabitants, as it is a name with tradition behind it ...'

Little People [euphem.]. Native fairies, latterly iron. **1995** Patsy McGarry, *Irish Times,* 2 June: 'Anyhow, in 1963 if anyone said "There's gold in them thar' hills" they would probably have assumed it belonged to "the little people" and should be left there.'

L.L. Whisky [acronym; brandname]. Whiskey reserved for the Duke of Richmond, Lord-Lieutenant 1807-13. **1895** E. Cobham Brewer, *Dictionary of Phrase and Fable* (new ed.): 'Mr Kinahan being requested to preserve a certain cask of whisky (*sic*] highly approved of by his Excellency ... marked it with the initials L.L. and ever after called this particular quality L.L. whisky.'

Loft, the [<location]. Cork Shakespearean Society. **1992** Tom McElligott, *Six O'Clock all over Cork:* 'Father O'Flynn, who founded it, was for long attached to the Cathedral parish and it was his custom ... to walk down Mulgrave Road. He would stop and talk to those whom he met and inevitably some of them would walk back with him to "the Loft".'

Lola Montez [stage name]. Maria Dolores Eliza Rosanna Gilbert, b. Limerick (1818). **1988** Henry Boylan, *A Dictionary of Irish Biography* (2nd ed): 'After studying dancing for a few months she made a disastrous début in London in 1843 as "Lola Montez, Spanish dancer".'

Long Fella/Fellow, the [<height; nickname]. Eamon de Valera (1882-1975), statesman and politician. **1991** Bob Quinn, *Smokey Hollow:* 'Mrs Toner referred to him as "The Long Fellow" or "The Lanky Oul' Get" or "The Spaniard".' See **Dev**. Also **Long Hoor**: nickname employed by Michael Collins. **1937** Frank O'Connor, *The Big Fellow:* 'But Collins put his foot down at last. "The Long Whoor [*sic*] won't get rid of me as easy as that," he said.'

Long Kesh [Belfast]. Detention centre for political prisoners (1971), renamed The Maze with the building of the **H-Blocks**. **2000** Tom McGurk, *Sunday Business Post,* 30 Jul: 'It was somehow always there. Long Kesh. The two words with which so many sentences over the last 30 years ended. On the streets it was simply known as "the Kesh" – a euphemism that in a word betrayed so much.'

Lord ha' Mercies Clay pipes. **1999** Gearóid Ó Crualaoich, 'The merry Wake', in J.S. Donnelly jr. & Kerby Miller (eds), *Irish Popular Culture 1650-1850:* 'Pieces of hard turf are being smoked on all sides – pipes known as "lord ha' mercies" from the response required on being presented with one on arrival at the wake house.'

Lord Harry, be/by the [euphem. for the Devil]. Mild oath. **1922** James Joyce, *Ulysses:* 'by the Lord Harry green is the grass that grows on the ground.'

Lower Ormeau [<Ormeau (<Fr. *idem*, young elm tree), in townland of Ballynafeigh near Belfast, seat of the Marquis of Donegall]. Belfast district, location of Protestant/Catholic confrontation. **1999** Glenn Patterson, *Irish Times*, 23 Oct: 'More and more imagination seems to be expended on drawing even finer distinctions between the city's constituent parts. Many Belfast people, for instance, will tell you that they have no recollection of a district known as "the Lower Ormeau".'

Luas [Ir. velocity, speed, quickness, quick motion (Dinneen); transport]. Dublin light rail transit system. **2000** Frank McDonald, *The Construction of Dublin:* 'CIÉ's newly appointed chief executive, Michael McDonnell, tore himself away from its boardroom strife to coin the name Luas ... for the proposed tramway network ...'

Lundy [<Robert Lundy, governor of **Derry**, who recommended surrender during the siege of 1689]. Hence traitor to the Prot./Unionist cause. **1988** R.F. Foster, *Modern Ireland 1600-1972:* 'Burned in effigy on every anniversary of the siege: his name became the Unionist synonym for "traitor".'

Lynn C Doyle [pseudonym]. Leslie A. Montgomery (1973-1961), writer. **1985**

Lynn Doyle, *An Ulster Childhood*, publisher's intro: 'His pseudonym was typical of his sense of fun – early in his writing career, he happened to notice a can marked *Linseed Oil* in a grocer's shop, and so "Lynn C Doyle was born. Later he dropped the "C" …'

M

MacAlpin [personal name]. **1895** E. Cobham Brewer, *A Dictionary of Phrase and Fable* (new ed.): 'It is said that the founder of this famous family was named Halfpenny, and lived in Dublin in the 18th century. Having prospered in business, he called himself Mr Halpen. The family, still prospering, dropped the H, and added Mac ...'

McAlpine's Fusilier [<Sir Robert McAlpine & Sons, Brit. building contractors]. Emigrant working in the Brit. construction industry (1950s-); nickname]. **1977** Wesley Burrowes, *The Riordans*: 'He [John Cowley] became, successively, a barman, a McAlpine Fusilier and a porter at St Pancras [London] Station.'

Macktown See **Nighttown**

Mad Dog [nickname]. (1) Vincent Coll (b. Gweedore 1908) gangster, USA. **1999** Ian Kilroy, *Irish Times,* 18 Dec: 'The death of Mad Dog Coll [1932] was something of a milestone. It marked the end of the tradition of Irish gangsters, who lost out to the more organised Jewish gangs and Italian mobsters that were emerging ...' **2000** Con Costello, *Leinster Leader,* 27 Jan: 'Coll's success was recognised when he got the new pseudonym of Mad Dog after fifteen members of an opposing gang were killed within a few months, and he, in attempting to shoot one of the leaders of the gang, killed a five year old child and wounded three other children.' See also **Mick**. (2) [nickname] Johnny Adair, Ulster Freedom Fighter paramilitary.

2000 Roisín Ingle, *Irish Times,* 15 Jul: 'One short stroll, and the presence of the international media assured the name Johnny "Mad Dog" Adair was known all over the world.'

Maeve [Ir. *Meadhbh, Medb*]. Legendary Queen of Connacht. Hence [transport] (1) Locomotive, Queen class, Great Southern Railways. **1982** O.S. Knock, *Irish Steam:* 'Only one locomotive had been completed by the time Great Britain declared war on Nazi Germany, the celebrated No 800 *Maeve*. As completed in 1939 this anglicised version of the name was used, though rendered on the nameplates in **Erse** [*sic*] characters, but it was subsequently changed to *Maedhbh*'. (2) Naval vessel. **1962** Basil Peterson, *Turn of the Tide:* '... in 1946-47 three Flower-class corvettes were purchased from the British Admiralty and commissioned as *L.E. Macha; L.E. Maev* and *L.E. Cliona,* the prefix L.E. standing for *Long Éireannach,* or *Irish Ship,* and the names being those of women famous in Irish mythology.' (3) **Queen Maeve** Champion duck. **2000** *Irish Times,* 21 Dec: 'The **Guinness** *Book of Records* has confirmed that it has accepted a duck egg laid in Belcare, Co. Galway, as the largest in the world. A certificate confirming the record is being sent to Mr Willie and Ms Kitty Costello, who own Queen Maeve, the duck which laid the egg in November 1999.'

Magdalene [<Magdalen Society, mid-C19 charity]. Female inmate. **1979** Peter Somerville-Large, *Dublin:* 'Lady Arabella Denny, descendant of William Petty, founded the Magdalen Society which still offers facilities "for the reception of such unfortunate females as abandoned by their seducers, prefer a life of penitence and virtue to guilt, infamy and prostitution". At their house in Leeson

Street each of these "Magdalenes" was assigned a number ...'

Magee, Rev William C19 Presbyterian minister, Lurgan, Co. Ard Macha/Armagh. Hence **Magee College**, Co. Dhoire/Derry. **1921** D.J. Owen, *History of Belfast:* '... an exceedingly bitter dispute was being waged in connection with the will of Mrs Magee ... by which a sum of £20,000 had been bequeathed for the establishment of a Presbyterian college. The decision as to the site for this college had been left with Mrs Magee's trustees ...' See **Assembly's College**

Magner [brandname]. Cider. **2000** Christine Doherty, *Sunday Business Post:* 'Forget Bulmer's Cider, our American cousins are about to meet Magners Original Irish Cider, the new name for the Clonmel cider in the US ... The Magner name comes from William Magner, a Clonmel man who started making cider in the town in 1937.'

Maiden City [<its withstanding the Jacobite siege (1690); nickname]. **Derry/Londonderry**. **1950** Richard Hayward, *Ulster and the City of Belfast:* 'And even those whose faith and historical background might beget a different set of emotions, could never find it in their hearts to grudge the grand old Maiden City its well-earned and most glorious fame.'

Maid of Erin [<C19 bare-breasted statue by Anthony McAuliffe]. Pub. **2000** Eibhir Mulqueen, *Irish Times,* 4 Mar: 'The modesty of a Maid of Erin's cleavage in Listowel, Co. Kerry, has been lost forever after the valiant efforts of a Clare man to get her covered up.'

Mainland [geog/polit.]. Britain, with particular ref. to Ireland. **1990** Maurice

Craig, *The Elephant and the Polish Question:* '... the exquisitely ludicrous calling an offshore island "the mainland" when it has a perfectly good and accurate name of its own. This seems to have originated in the media about 1972.' **2000** Joe Lee, *Sunday Tribune,* 9 Jan: 'It is a contribution to political discourse of a combination of Ulster unionists and English nationalists who first made the term popular to stress unionist identity as British rather than Irish, with the added bonus of rubbing the noses of Irish nationalists in the dirt by insisting that it was their mainland too, indeed coyly implying that Britain was the "mainland" of the whole island of Ireland.'

Malahide Roar [<Malahide/Mullach Íde, Co. Dublin/Baile Átha Cliath; transport]. Noise produced by trains crossing viaduct. **1989** J.P. O'Dea, *Journal of the Irish Railway Record Society,* 'Amiens Street to Drogheda', Oct: 'The form of its construction resulted in the "Malahide Roar", audible for miles as trains crossed the bridge. After more than 100 years of service, it was replaced in 1967 with pre-stressed concrete beams and stone ballast, and the Roar was heard no longer.'

Mallow [<Ir. *Meala;* Co. Chorcaí/Cork; town]. Hence (1) [politic.] **Mallow Defiance** Repeal meeting at which Daniel O'Connell issued challenge to Brit. govt (11 Jun. 1843). **1880** Charles Gavan Duffy, *Young Ireland:* 'O'Connell left Richmond Prison suffering under a mortal disease ... The slow retreat before the triumphant enemies from the Mallow Defiance to the sentence and the jail had tortured him.' (2) **Rakes of Mallow** Young men about town [C18-19]. **1962** *Official Guide to Mallow:* 'This was the title

which the roistering young blades who frequented Mallow for the spa seasons adopted ... 'The "Rakes" were fortune hunters, gamblers, duellers, drinkers and dancers. Many of them were penniless adventurers, though scions of aristocratic families.' Hence, *idem* [transport] Cork-Mallow coach. **1843** William Mackepeace Thackeray, *The Irish Sketch Book:* '... and in Patrick Street, at three o'clock, when "the Rakes of Mallow" gets under weigh (a cracked old coach with the paint rubbed off, some smart horses, and an exceedingly dingy harness) ...' See also **Allo**

Manahan Peak [Antarctica]. Mountain. **2000** Renagh Holohan, *Irish Times,* 2 Dec: 'A 2000-metre high mountain in Antarctica is to be called after an Irishman, *living*. Manahan Peak, on Ross Island, where Scott spent his first winter, is being named for Donal Manahan, Dean of Science at the University of Southern California, Los Angeles. A biological scientist, Manahan has been 20 years in the US ...'

Man from God Knows Where [nickname, <eponymous poem by Florence Wilson]. Thomas Russell, United Irishman (1767-1803). **1988** Henry Boylan, *A Dictionary of Irish Biography* (2nd ed.): '... tried at Downpatrick for high treason, and hanged there on 21 October 1803. His story is told in a well-known poem "The Man from God Knows Where" by Florence Wilson.'

Manistys [tradename]. Iron foundry, Dundalk. Hence **made in Manistys,** commendatory catchphrase. **1997** Canice O'Mahony, *Journal of the Irish Railway Record Society,* 'Made in Manistys', Oct: Such was the reputation enjoyed by the local foundry ... that the phrase 'Made in Manistys' was familiar to a generation

of Dundalk inhabitants, who used it to describe a person or article they considered could always be depended on.'

Man of the people [nickname]. Daniel O'Connell (1775-1847), statesman. **1832** Prince Hermann Ludwig Heinrich Von Pückler-Muskau, *Tour in England, Ireland and France in 1828 and 1829,* trans. Sarah Austin: 'I am indebted for the great cordiality, I might say enthusiasm, with which I am received here, to my visit to the "man of the people", with whom the curious believe me to be in God-knows-what connection.' See also **Liberator, the**

Maol [<Ir., *bó mhaol,* hornless cow]. Cattle breed. **2000** *Irish Times,* 14 Feb: 'Ireland's rarest breed of cattle has ensured its survival with the birth of a bull calf. The Maol calf – called Fionn Bán – weighed in at 84 lbs at Donal and Margaret Nolan's internationally known rare breeds' farm in Holycross, Co Tipperary ... it was named by the Nolans' daughter Ruth (10) after Fionn Mac Cumhaill.' See **Finn McCoul**

Maoldúin [Ir., 'chief of the fort' (Woulfe, see biblio.) or poss. <Celt. *Duno-maglos* [or *Duno-magros*] 'warrior of the fortress' (O'Corráin & Maguire, see biblio.)]. Housing development. **1999** Flann Ó Riain. *Irish Times,* 8 Nov: 'We always welcome Irish local names on new housing developments, as against snobbish "English" imitations, but we are puzzled at a new housing development in Dunshaughlin, Co. Meath, being named **Maoldúin**.'

Marble City [<occurrence of marble in the area; nickname]. Kilkenny. **2000** Chris Dooley, *Irish Times,* 24 May: 'It's known as the marble city, but Kilkenny may face the prospect of becoming a

mere town … The marble town?
Doesn't quite have the same ring to it.'

Mardyke, the [Cork]. City street. **1971**
Seán Beecher, *The Story of Cork:* 'The
Mardyke was originally known as the
Red House Walk and took this name
from a tea-house or tea-garden in the
vicinity. It was formed in 1720 by
Edward Webber, a city official. It was a
beautiful avenue … flanked by the
famous elm trees and by a stream running along its length. At the eastern city
end, a triple gateway, known as "Hell,
Heaven and Purgatory" all but sealed it
from vehicular traffic.'

Maritime Inscription [<Fr. *Inscription
maritime*, C19 naval service]. Naval
reserve (1940-49). **1962** Basil Peterson,
The Turn of the Tide: 'The Irish
Government, realising that every man
was needed to face possible eventualities,
created a naval reserve force in
September 1940. This force, known as
the Maritime Inscription, was composed
mainly of yachtsmen and fishermen …'

Massey-Dawson Landed family,
Ballynacourty, Co. Thiobraid Árann/
Tipperary. Hence [nickname; transport].
Coach. **1993** Thomas P. O'Neill in
Kevin B. Nowlan (ed.), *Travel and
Transport in Ireland:* 'As the [**Bianconi**]
business grew so too did the cars. They
became longer and longer and soon
four-wheeled vehicles were replacing
two-wheeled ones. The largest of the
two-wheelers were named "Massey
Dawsons" after a popular Tory land-
lord.' See also **Bianconi**; **Faugh-a-
Ballagh**; **Finn McCoul**

Master McGrath [sport]. Greyhound
(whelped 1866), breeder James Galway,
Co. Waterford. **1935** John Player &
Sons, cigarette card series, *Famous Irish*

Greyhounds, no.32: 'Known as "The
Immortal McGrath" and "The Flying
Irishman" this, the most famous greyhound of all time, may be said to have
passed from the realms of coursing into
that of history and romance. He won
the Waterloo Cup three times … losing
only one course during his entire running career.'

Master of the Revels State office. **1973**
T.J. Walsh, *Opera in Dublin 1705-1797:*
'On May 8 of that year [1661], King
Charles II in a royal patent revoked "all
Graunts made to other[s] for representing anything" of a theatrical nature in
Ireland, and provided that (1) John
Ogilby should be granted for life the
office of Master of the Revels in Ireland;
(2) he should be licensed "to build upon
such grounds by him to be purchased …
in Dublin … such Theatre or Theatres as
to him shall seem most fit…".'

Maud Gone Mad [nickname]. Maud
Gonne MacBride (1865-1963), revo-
lutionary. **1993** R.F. Foster, *Paddy & Mr
Punch:* 'Charlotte Despard, Maud
Gonne's companion in arms … is
another [convert]. Dubliners knew
them as "Maud Gonne Mad and Mrs
Desperate".'

Mayor of the Bull Ring [Dublin C18,
<iron ring in the Corn Market to which
bulls for baiting were tied]). Official
elected on May-day for one year, during
which he had authority to punish those
frequenting brothels. **1847** John Edward
Walsh, *Ireland Sixty Years Ago:* 'An officer, called the "Mayor of the bull-ring",
had a singular jurisdiction allowed to
him. He was the guardian of bachelors,
and it was a duty of his office to take
cognizance of their conduct. After the
marriage ceremony, the bridal party
were commonly conducted to the ring

by the "mayor" and his attendants, when a kiss from "his worship" to the bride concluded the ceremony ...'

M.B. Drapier see **Drapier**

Mean Fiddler, The [<commendatory phr. 'he's no mean fiddler']. Irish country music bar, Harlesden, London (1982-). **1999** Vince Power, quoted in *Irish Times,* 26 Aug: 'It seems really obvious now but back then, all you could get was warm pints in shabby tired kind of places. The Mean Fiddler was kind of ahead of its time.' **2001** Annmarie Hourihane, *Sunday Tribune,* 8 Apr: 'The first music venue that he owned was named with an expression ... used in the traditional music circles in County Waterford ... Eighteen years later Vince Power has turned The Mean Fiddler into a brand name.'

Mecklenburgh St [Dub.]. **1979** Peter Somerville-Large, *Dublin:* 'Even in **Monto**'s heyday, the upper end of Mecklenburgh Street, the main thoroughfare for the brothels, had a seedy respectability ... By 1887 Mecklenburgh Street had become Tyrone Street in a vain effort to change its atmosphere by changing its name. Dublin Corporation often tried this tactic. In 1862 murky Park Street behind the University became Lincoln Place, while Upper Mercer Street ... had evolved from French Street, the brothel area that preceded Monto. Notorious Temple Street was renamed Chatterton Street by an angry Corporation after the Rt. Hon. Hedges Eyre Chatterton ... refused to allow the name of Sackville Street to be altered to O'Connell Street. However, it relented and Temple Street became Hill Street.'

Meeting of the Waters [nickname,

<song by Thomas Moore (1779-1852) in praise of eponymous Wicklow beauty spot]. Dub. public urinal, College St., in front of which stood statue of Moore. **1922** James Joyce, *Ulysses:* 'He crossed under Tommy Moore's roguish finger. They did right to put him up over a urinal: meeting of the waters.'

Mé Féiner [<Ir. mé *féin,* I myself]. Self-regarding individual. **1997** Brenda Power, *Sunday Tribune,* 26 Oct: 'Mary McAleese, according to a consensus of columnists and commentators last week, is just too cold, too arrogant, too patronising, too self-satisfied, too much of a "mé-féiner" ... to be a suitable replacement for [President] Mary Robinson.' **1998** *Irish Times,* 31 Oct: 'We measure our time in money terms, Mr [John] Lonergan said. Most of us only get involved in an activity provided we gain materially. Individually, we had allowed ourselves to become "mé féiners".'

Metal Man, the (1) [Sligo]. Maritime marker. **1981** Adrian MacLoughlin, *Streets of Ireland:* 'Also in this part of Sligo is a gigantic statue of a sailor known as the Metal Man, standing on Perch Rock to warn ships of its presence. It was cast in 1819 by John Clark from a design by Thomas Kirk ...' (2) [Waterford]. Monument. **2001** Colman Cassidy, *Irish Times,* 30 May: 'In 1816, some 363 people drowned when the troop transport *Sea Horse* sank in Tramore Bay. The famous Metalman was erected in the bay as a memorial.'

Methody [nickname] (1) Methodist. **1931** Shan F. Bullock, *After Sixty Years:* 'What religion Mr Bean and his family observed I cannot say ... Perhaps they were Methodys, as we called them.' (2) Methodist College, Belfast. **1985** John Boyd, *Out of my Class:* 'Only one scholarship boy from Mountpottinger chose Methody and I assumed that that was because nobody had told him that girls went there.'

Metro Éireann [media]. Multicultural newspaper. **2000** Chinedu Onyejelem, *Irish Times,* 12 Apr: 'Last October, Abel Ugba – like myself, a Nigerian journalist now living and working here – met and decided to work together … We registered Cross Cultures Communications to publish the *Voice* newspaper … In mid-February we announced April 17 as the launch date. We had to change the name to Metro Éireann because we heard that a newspaper called the *Voice* already exists here.'

Mexico see **El Paso**

Michael Kelly's Sauce [<Michael Kelly (b.Cork c1790), composer who became director of music at the Theatre Royal, Drury Lane, London (1822)]. **1983** Theodora Fitzgibbon, *Irish Traditional Food:* 'Serve with crubeens (pig's feet), calf's head, boiled tongue, or tripe … Mix together 1 tablespoon brown sugar, 1 teaspoon each of dry mustard powder and freshly ground black pepper, and stir in 2 tablespoons garlic vinegar. Blend, then gradually mix with 1 cup of melted butter.'

Mick/Micky [nickname, gen. non-Ir. or NI usage, gen. derog.]. Irishman/ Catholic. **1997** Ciaran Carson, *The Star Factory:* '… Michael is more usually associated with Catholics (hence the term "Mickies") who regard St Michael the Archangel as the conductor of the souls of the dead …' Hence (1) **The Mick** [nickname] Vincent Coll, gangster. **2000** Con Costello, *Leinster Leader* (Naas), 27 Jan: 'At the age of nineteen Vincent Coll, alias The Mick, was

charged with the killing of a speakeasy owner who had refused to stock Schultz's beer.' See also **Mad Dog**. (2) **Mickey**, as in **take the Mickey** [sl.]. Deride, taunt. **1984** Liz Curtis, *The Same Old Story:* 'A child said, "Some Irish people come to England to live and some people take the mickey out of them when they speak, so they try to get the accent out." The term "to take the mickey" – "Mickey", like "Paddy" is an old term for an Irish person, testified to the degree to which the view of the Irish as an object of derision is ingrained.' (3)**The Micks** [nickname; milit.] Irish Guards regiment of Brit. army. **2000** Geraldine Comiskey, *Irish Times,* 13 Jan: 'The "Micks", as the Irish Guards are known, have a proud reputation, which includes battle honours in both world wars …'

Mick the Miller [sport]. Champion greyhound. **1931** *The Glensman* (Cushendall), Nov: 'Quite a number of Ballycastle people travelled up to Belfast to see "Mick the Miller", as famous in track racing as **Master McGrath** was on the course.'

Milesian [<Ir. *Mil Espáin,* Spanish soldier) 'a fabulous Spanish king whose sons are said to have conquered Ireland about 1300' (OED)]. (1) Irishman; Irish. **1987** Richard Davis, *The Young Ireland Movement:* '[Michael] Doheny, who, according to John Mitchel, had "a broad, honest Milesian face", was born in 1805 …' Hence [media] **1812–25** *Milesian Magazine or Irish Monthly Gleaner.* (2) Opera. **1973** T.J. Walsh, *Opera in Dublin 1705-1797:* 'Charles Thomas Carter had yet another opera, *The Milesian,* performed in Dublin on February 25 [1783] … No report of the production which was described as "a new musical farce" can be discovered.'

Millie [<(linen) mill worker, nickname]. **1997** Suzanne Breen, *Irish Times,* 28 Oct: 'If they are not viewed as paramilitary groupies they're regarded as "lower-class", says Tina Wallace (19): "People automatically think we are 'millies' – that we all dress cheaply and talk in broad Belfast accents".'

Milly [<Militant Tendency, nickname]. Left-wing political faction. **1988** Fergus Finlay, *Snakes and Ladders:* 'Each "Milly" had to be identified by name, and given an opportunity to choose between their own organisation or the party.'

MIL 2000 Vehicle registration plate. **1999** Jamie Smith, *Irish Times,* 25 Nov: 'A telephone bid of £10,500 secured the glamorous MIL 2000 number plate at an auction in Northern Ireland yesterday. A local number plate dealer is rumoured to have bought it as a millennium present for his wife … A similar style of auction is not possible in the South, where number plates cannot be transferred between vehicles.'

Minor Planet Ireland [astron.]. **1996** Fintan O'Toole, *The Ex-Isle of Erin*: 'In November 1995, the Minor Planet Centre in Cambridge, Massachusetts decided to name Minor Planet 5029, an asteroid recently discovered somewhere between Mars and Jupiter, "Ireland". Minor Planet Ireland is far away and virtually invisible to the naked eye and almost nothing is known about its composition.'

Miranda Guinness see **Guinness**

Misery Row see **Calamity Avenue**

MiWadi [<Mineral Water Distributors, brandname]. Orange drink (1927-). **2000** *Irish Times,* 22 Nov: 'Twenty years ago, MiWadi was so well established that its name was the generic one for any dilutable orange "cordial". To become a "generic" is the dream of every brand. It means than when consumers think of a product category they automatically think of your brand name.'

Mná na hÉireann [Ir. *idem*, women of Ireland] Came into vogue at time of election of Mary Robinson to the Presidency (1990); subsequently often applied iron. to articulate women in general. **1999** Kathy Sheridan, *Irish Times,* 24 Dec: 'Apt, isn't it, that the decade should squeal to a close to the clamour of Mná na hÉireann in full cry? Apt because, after all, it began with their glistening eyes raised to Mary Robinson as she urged them to rock the system.'

Mockey [cf. US underworld sl. *mockie* (adj.), fake, phoney; nickname]. **1998** Catherine Cleary, *Irish Times,* 28 Aug: 'Those selling to undercover gardaí, or mockeys, as they were called when the device was used in the 1980s against heroin dealers, were not arrested on the spot in a "buy-and-bust" operation.'

Model County [<its model farms & first agric. school in Ire. (mid-1850s); nickname, esp. in GAA context]. Loch Garman/Wexford. **1996** Headline, *Irish Times,* 3 Sep: 'Model county greets return of hurling victors.'

Moffett [<James S.D. Moffett, Gen. Manager, Belfast Corporation Tramways; transport]. **1996** James Kilroy, *Irish Trams:* 'In Belfast there was a policy that all new tramcar designs were named after the General Manager responsible for their introduction and that new batch [1919] were known as "Moffetts".'

Molanna [invented name; lit.]. Behanna/

Behenna river, Co. Thiobraid Árann/ Tipperary. **1590/96** Edmund Spenser, *The Faerie Queene:* 'Among the which there was a nymph that hight/Molanna, daughter of old Father **Mole**,/And sister unto **Mulla** faire and bright …' **1911** P.W. Joyce, *The Wonders of Ireland:* 'There are only two streams of any consequence flowing into the Funsheon valley from the Galtys. One of these is the Funcheon itself … The other stream is the Behanna, which rises in "**Arlo**-hill", a little to the west of the summit of Galtymore … This is the Molanna.'

Mole [invented name; lit.]. Mountain range. **1595** Edmund Spenser, *Colin Clouts Come Home Againe:* 'One day (quoth he) I sat (as was my trade)/Under the foot of Mole, that mountain hore,/Keeping my sheepe amongst the cooly shade/Of the green alders by the **Mulla**es shore.' **1911** P.W. Joyce, *The Wonders of Ireland:* '… as **Arlo**-hill in the Galty's is "the highest head in all men's sights of my old father Mole" it is quite plain that by "old father Mole" the poet meant the whole range, including the Galtys and the Ballyhouras.'

Moll Doyle's Daughters [politic.]. Secret agrarian society (C18-19). **1867** Patrick Kennedy, *The Banks of the Boro:* 'Some folk, however, owed him a spite for the taking of the land, and Moll Doyle and her daughters were hired to pay him a visit.' Hence **give s.o. Moll Doyle**, administer a severe reprimand.

Moll Watson *see* **Cathy Barry**

Molly Bán [?<pop. ballad *Molly Bawn* by Samuel Lover (1797-1868). Hence (1) Confusion, panic **1916** Willie Ryan, letter to his brothers: 'They [the Brit. forces] were drawing a cordon round the city [of Dub.] … This caused

"Molly Bawn" with us …' (2) **The times of Molly Bán**, life of leisure/ luxury. **1992** Brian Leyden, *Departures:* '"Why should they get married when Mammy does it all? … They have the times of Molly Bán, with mothers dancing attendance on them".'

Molly Maguires [nickname]. Agrarian movement active in Leitrim, Longford and Roscommon (1843-). **1895** E. Cobham Brewer. *A Dictionary of Phrase and Fable* (new ed.): 'Stout, active young Irishmen, dressed up in women's clothes, blackened faces, and otherwise disguised, to surprise those employed to enforce the payment of rents. Their victims were ducked in bog-holes …' Hence [*idem,* nickname] Followers of political leader John Redmond. **1992** Tom McElligott, *Six O'Clock all over Cork:* 'The bitter political rivalries which had divided the citizens during the elections of 1910 into "O'Brienites", followers of William O'Brien, and "Molly Maguires", followers of John Redmond, were muted during those years only to surface again after the Treaty.'

Molyneux problem [<William Molyneux (1656-98), philosopher and patriot]. Philosophical/scientific thought experiment. **1999** David Berman, in W.J. McCormack (ed.), *The Blackwell Companion to Modern Irish Culture:* 'He asked whether a man blind from birth would upon gaining his sight be able to distinguish (visually) a sphere from a cube. The problem was first published in Locke's *Essay Concerning Human Understanding* (2nd edn, 1694) …'

Momonia [<Ir. *Mumhan,* **Munster**]. As thus. **1808** Thomas Moore, *Irish Melodies:* 'Remember the glories of Brien the brave/Though the days of the hero are o'er,/Though lost to Momonia, and

cold in the grave,/He returns to Kincora no more.'

Monaghan [Ir. *Muineacháin,* Co., barony, parish & town] Hence (1) (term of abuse) Clown, fool. **C.1735** Jonathan Swift, *A Dialogue in Hybernian Stile:* '... I have seen him often riding on a sougawn [straw saddle]. In short he is no better than a spawlpeen, a perfect Monaghan.' (2) [sport]. Snooker shot. **1999** Peter Woods, RTÉ *Sunday Miscellany,* 13 Jun: 'A Cavan man once told me that an "English" is known as a "Monaghan" around Belturbet.'

Monduf [< Mon(ica) Duf(f); Ballaghaderreen, Co. Ros Comáin/ Roscommon; brandname]. Grocery/ household product range. **1999** Mary Gallagher, *Irish Times,* 21 Sep: 'Monica Duff & Co. was also trading in beer, wines, spirits and tobacco, retail and wholesale ... By the 1880s the firm had its own Monduf brand labelling almost every grocery and household product.'

Monks of the Screw, The [<Society formed by Lord Avonmore near Newmarket, UK; screw = corkscrew]. C18 Dublin dining club. **1859** Charles Phillips, *Recollection of Curran and Some of his Contemporaries* (2nd ed.): 'This society was entitled, no doubt very appropriately, *"The Monks of the Screw".* It met on every Saturday during the law term, in a large house in Kevin's Street ... The furniture and regulations of their festive apartment were completely *monkish* ... Curran was installed Grand Prior of the order, and deputed to compose the charter song.'

Monks, the [Limerick]. Christian Brothers' School. **1998** Críostóir O'Flynn, *There is an Isle:* '... we had been warned by our older brothers of the dreadful daily horrors in the "Monks" ...'

Monster meetings [nickname]. Popular manifestations first organised to demand Repeal of the union with Britain by the **Liberator,** Daniel O'Connell, subseq. by Charles Stewart Parnell. **1891** Anne Marie de Bovet, *Three Months' Tour in Ireland:* 'I was lucky enough to be present at one of those grand popular out-of-door meetings which constantly keep alive the spirit of rebellion in Ireland. These "monster meetings", as they are called here, are announced weeks beforehand in all the villages of the adjacent counties, by placards with the three cabalistic letters, I.N.L. – Irish National League ...'

Monthly Asylum for Neglected Biography [subtitle; media]. **2001** Con Costello, *Leinster Leader* (Naas), 11 Jan: 'The history of Castledermot, as told in The Irish Magazine or Monthly Asylum for Neglected Biography for May 1809, is replete with the names of saints and kings.'

Monto [<Montgomery St, Dub., nickname]. C19-20 brothel area. **1979** Peter Somerville-Large, *Dublin:* '"Tyrone Street of the crowded doors/And Faithful Place so infidel" were located west of Amiens Street Station in an area known as Monto after one of its main streets named for Elizabeth Montgomery, who married Luke Gardiner, Lord Mountjoy – a title Joyce failed to make use of in *Ulysses.*' See also **Mecklenburgh Street**

Monument of Light see **Spike, the**

Mother Ireland [personific.] **1976** Edna O'Brien, *Mother Ireland:* 'Countries are either mothers or fathers ... Ireland has always been a woman, a womb, a cave, a cow, a Rosaleen, a sow, a bride, a harlot, and, of course, the gaunt Hag of Beare.' **1999** Aidan Arrowsmith, in Scott Brewster *et al* (eds), *Ireland in Proximity:* 'Here [in Samuel Beckett's *Murphy*], **Cathleen ní Houlihan** or Mother Ireland becomes a literal oppression, but less for Irish women than for the tortured male artist, who must escape at all costs.' See also **Shan Van Vocht**

Mother Machree [<Ir. *mo chroí,* my heart]. Pop. Ir/US ballad by Rida Johnson Young (C19). Hence **Mother Machree-ish,** sentimentally **Oirish.** **1993** John A. Murphy in Seán Dunne (ed.), *The Cork Anthology:* 'At the vulgar end of the spectrum the Irish songs were "stage" or syrupy, or Mother Machree-ish, brought home by returned **Yanks.**'

Mountain Mine Man Engine House [Allihies, Co. Chorchaí/Cork]. Mine building. **2000** Michael Viney, *Irish Times,* 14 Apr: 'The Mountain Mine Man Engine House (to use its full, reso-nant name) is unique in Ireland and one of fewer than 20 built anywhere in the world. Cornish by design, it used a steam engine to hoist miners up and down on steps fixed to a long timber rod.'

Mountjoy [family name]. Gardiner fam-ily, Viscounts Mountjoy (esp. Luke Gardiner (1745-98). Dub. developer). Hence (1) [street names]. Gardiner St., Mountjoy Sq., etc. (2) [transport]. Sailing ship. **1992** John de Courcy Ireland, *Ireland's Maritime Heritage:* 'And there was also, in 1689, the famous episode when the 135 ton **Derry**-owned and, so far as we know, Derry-built, Mountjoy … rammed and broke the Jacobite boom across the Foyle and ended the 105-day long siege of Derry.' See also **Lundy.** (3) Dub. prison. See **Joy, the**

Mount Melleray [<Fr. *St Meillery*]. Cistercian abbey, Co. Phort Láirge/ Waterford. **1999** Robert Graham, *The Irish Journals of Robert Graham of Redgorton, 1835-1838:* 'A great portion of this country belongs to Sir Richard Keane. He has lately bestowed 575 acres of it for one hundred years on an estab-lishment of Trappists, who have rested in this country on the breaking up of the monastery of St Meillery in France.'

Moyne, Lord [family name]. Borne by sons of the Earls of **Iveagh,** e.g. Walter Edward **Guinness** (1880-1944), 1st holder. **1999** Michele Guinness, *The Guinness Spirit:* 'In 1932 he was offered a peerage … In the end he conceded and picked the name Moyne for his title from a map of Loch Corrib, near his uncle Arthur's Ashford estate. It desig-nated a small inlet – and it was plain and short.' Hence [catchphrase]: 'Moyne's a Guinness!'

Mr McGilligan's White Elephant [<Patrick McGilligan, Minister for Industry & Commerce (1924-32)]. The Shannon Hydro-Electric Scheme, which he fostered. **1967** Terence de Vere White, 'Social Life in Ireland 1927-1937', in Francis Mac Manus (ed.), *The Years of the Great Test 1926-39:* '1927 was a significant year in the history of the five year old Irish **Free State.** The Shannon Scheme (Mr McGilligan's White Elephant as an ebullient critic called it even four years later) was launched.'

Mrs Mulligan/Biddy Mulligan [stage name]. Dub. character created by come-dian James Augustine (Jimmy) O'Dea (1899-1965). **1949** *Irish Times,* 23 Dec: '… a link with the past is provided by the appearance of Jimmy O'Dea's first love, Mrs Mulligan, in a new sketch on an old theme – "Mrs Mulligan in the Pawnshop".' **1996** Louis McRedmond (ed.), *Modern Irish Lives*: 'His most famous persona was that of Biddy Mulligan, "The Pride of the Coombe", a role created for him by Harry O'Donovan ...' Hence **Bidet Mulligan** [nickname]. Monument in O'Connell St, Dub., aka 'The **Floozie in the Jacussi'**

Muirchú [Ir, *muir chú,* hound of the sea; transport]. First navy vessel. **1992** John de Courcy Ireland, *Ireland's Maritime Heritage:* 'When the world crisis of summer 1939 occurred, at the very last minute of the eleventh hour an Irish navy (the Marine Service) had to be improvised, made up chiefly of the Dublin built Fishery Patrol Ship Helga renamed Muirchú (which had been used by the British as a gunboat against the 1916 rebels) ...'

Mulchán [Ir., dried, baked curds]. Cheese. **1999** Diane Duane, *Irish Times,* 31 Mar: 'Mulchán, a hard skim milk cheese, was the last of the group mentioned in the *Vision* [*of MacConglainne*] to be made in Ireland in modern times – it was last manufactured in Waterford in 1824, when an English writer ran across it and anglicised its name to "Mullahawn".'

Mulla [invented name, lit.]. Awbeg, tributary of the Blackwater. **1595** Edmund Spenser, *Colin Clouts Come Home Againe:* 'He [Old father **Mole**] had a daughter fresh as floure of May/Which gave that name unto that pleasant vale;/Mulla the daughter of Old Mole so hight/The nimph, which of that water course has charge ...' **1911** P.W. Joyce, *The Wonders of Ireland:* 'The name Mulla, which Spenser took such delight in, is not, and never was, the name of the river; but the poet used it, as elsewhere he used **Arlo** in preference to the true name, on account of its musical sound. Its proper name is Awbeg, little river ...'

Mullingar [An Muileann gCearr, Co. na hIarmhí/Westmeath]. Hence (1) [<local cattle trade, catchphrase] **beef to the heels like a Mullingar heifer,** generally male comment on female with sturdy legs. **C19** Pop. ballad: 'There was an elopement down in Mullingar,/But sad to relate the pair didn't get far,/"Oh fly", said he, "darling, and see how it feels",/But the Mullingar heifer was beef to the heels.' (2) [pub] **Mullingar House** [Co. Bhaile Átha Cliath/Dub.] **2000** Pól Ó Conghaile, *Irish Times,* 10 Jun: 'Mullingar House in Chapelizod was recently gutted and re-roofed by its new owners. The pub features centrally in [James Joyce's] *Finnegans Wake,* where the hero, Humphrey Chimpden Earwicker, is described as its owner.' (3) [gastronomy]. **2001** Gareth Allen, *Irish Times,* 10 Mar: 'They [menu writers] also hold an odd reverence for the provenance of certain comestibles ... If a dish comes with chutney and the chutney happens to be the produce of some industrial unit in Mullingar, then it shall be known as "Mullingar" chutney, as if this was a byword for undisputed excellence and the good name of the chutney mongers of Mullingar was something of proverbial brilliance.'

Mulready Envelope, the [<William Mulready, painter (b. Ennis 1786)] Postal stationery (1840). **1895** E. Cobham Brewer, *A Dictionary of Phrase and Fable* (new ed.): '... an envelope resembling a half-sheet of letter–paper when folded. The space left for the address formed the centre of an ornamental design by Mulready ...'

Munster [<Ir. *An Mhumha* <*Muma,* tribal name + ON *stadr,* a place; or ON, gen. *−s* + Ir. *tír,* land, territory]. One of the 4 (formerly 5) provinces. Hence (1) Cheese. **1999** Diane Duane, *Irish Times,* 31 Mar: 'The Munster cheese one now finds in continental Europe is not named after any monastic establishment there, as might be likely from the name, but after the province. Irish monks away on the Continent in the first millennium AD left more than the poem "Pangur Bán"' (2) **Munster plums** [nickname] Potatoes (Grose, see biblio).

Murphia [<Murphy + Mafia, nickname]. The Ir. diaspora, esp. high-profile professionals in Brit. **1996** Oliver Bennett, *Independent on Sunday* (London), 17 Mar: 'In Britain, the Irish who benefit from such affirmative reinforcement tend to be white collar workers, particularly those who work in high-profile liberal-minded professions: they have been tagged "the Murphia" …'

Myles na gCopaleen [Ir. *Myles na gCapaillín,* Myles of the Little Horses].

Character in novel by Gerald Griffin, *The Collegians* (1829). Hence nom de plume of journalist, novelist and playwright Brian O'Nolan (aka Flann O'Brien) (1911-66), adopted for his satirical column in *The Irish Times* (1940). **1989** Anthony Cronin, *No Laughing Matter:* 'To begin with he called himself "Myles na gCopaleen"… the g before the capital C being the eclipsis which the genitive case demands. At a later stage, when he had begun to cherish the hope that he would make this persona known outside Ireland, he simplified this to Myles na Gopaleen, rather to the regret of some of the *Irish Times* staff who liked the pedantry of the eclipsis in the genitive.'

Myles the Slasher [nickname]. Myles O'Reilly, rebel leader (C17). **1950** Richard Hayward, *Ulster and the City of Belfast:* 'and that famous O'Reilly, *Myles the Slasher,* another great Confederate warrior, came here [to the Franciscan friary, Cavan town] after his death-blow at Finea.'

N

Nancy [nickname]. Gun employed by associates of Robert Emmet (Rising of 1803). **1943** George A. Little, *Malachy Horan Remembers:* 'Three hours I lay bleeding,/My Nancy by my side./'Till early the next morning/I shot G- from Malahide.'

Nancy Hogan Syndicate [sport]. Racehorse-owner. **2000** Cormac MacConnell, *The Examiner* (Cork), 8 Jan: '... the ballad of Nancy Hogan's Goose is the party piece of merry Ennis sportsman Pat Quinn ... And Pat was in great form because he is a member of the syndicate which owns the very good horse Inis Cara ... And the syndicate which owns Inis Cara is called, quite simply, the Nancy Hogan Syndicate. So that's where the name comes from.'

Napoleon's Nose [<similar contour; nickname]. MacArt's Fort, Cave Hill, Belfast. **1950** Richard Hayward, *Ulster and the City of Belfast:* 'From there [the dome of the City Hall] also you will get a more detached impression of that MacArt's Fort which we have just visited, and from its profile you will understand why it is familiarly known to Belfast people as *Napoleon's Nose*.'

Nasdaq [<US stock market index]. Pub. **2000** *Sunday Tribune,* 10 Dec: 'The public house, once the true home of Irish humour, character and merriment, has succumbed to the depths of this despotic **Celtic Tiger** Regime. On Camden Street, in the city of Dublin, a new public house is opening called Nasdaq The Bar. Pass the sick bucket ...

Camden Street is, of course, in Dublin's **Village Quarter**. Pass a fresh bucket ...'

Nasher [nickname]. National Yacht Club, Dún Laoghaire. **2001** Anne Marie Hourihane, *She Moves Through the Boom*: 'There are three old yacht clubs in Dún Laoghaire ... **Prods** in the [Royal] Irish. Rich Catholics in the [Royal St.] George and fun people in the Nasher ... There used to be talk of wife-swapping down in the Nasher ...'

Nation, The [media] Organ of Young Ireland movement, first issued 15 Oct 1842. **1945** J.L. Ahern, *Young Ireland, its Founder and his Circle*: 'As the principal object of the paper was to make Ireland a nation, it was given the name of the "Nation", which would be a fitting prelude to the attempt.' **1992** Brendan O'Cathaoir, *Irish Times,* 14 Oct: Davis christened the *Nation* – a name derived significantly from that of a Parisian newspaper.'

National Corporative Party see **League of Youth**

National League [politic.]. Party founded by Capt. William Redmond (1926). **1967** Kevin B. Nowlan in Francis Mac Manus (ed.), *The Years of the Great Test 1926-39:* 'In the House, from which the **Fianna Fáil** deputies were excluded, [William] Cosgrave was elected President of the Executive Council once more. But the atmosphere was strained, the Labour party was critical of the Government and so was Captain Redmond at the head of his new National League.'

National League of the North [politic.]. Party launched by Joseph Devlin (1928). **1967** David Kennedy in Francis Mac Manus (ed.), *The Years of the*

Great Test 1926-39: 'For about five years after Devlin's entry into the House of Commons there were hopes that better relations would develop between the two parties. He had launched the National League of the North pledged to constitutional opposition.'

National Literary Prize [nickname]. Said to have been gained by a book banned under the Censorship of Publications Act 1929. **1993** Seán Joyce in Michael Verdon, *Shawlies,* **Echo Boys***, the Marsh and the Lanes: Old Cork Remembered:* 'As soon as **Dev** took over you got a whole new attitude to literature. Books that were classics in other countries were suddenly banned here ... The writers used to call that ban the National Literary Prize.'

Navan Man [<Navan, Co. na Mí/ Meath]. Typification of small-town mistrust of outsiders. **1999** Diarmuid Doyle, *Sunday Tribune,* 14 Nov: 'Just what is a Navan man exactly? Is he in the mould of the entertainingly foul-mouthed dimwit caricatured on Today FM each evening? ... Navan Man is a hugely proud individual; he will not take kindly to his small town being clogged up by outsiders who have no commitment to the area, and for whom a move to the town is almost an ironic statement, one which allows them to put on funny accents ...'

Ned of the Hills [aka Éamonn an Chnuic]. C17 outlaw. Hence **The Wicklow Mountains, or The Lad of the Hills** Opera (1796). **1973** T.J. Walsh, *Opera in Dublin 1705-1797:* '[John] O'Keeffe tells us that he got the idea of his opera from "A gold mine discovered in the mountains of Wicklow" and that he "founded the story" on "Ned of the Hills, as he is called in the old legend".'

Neophilosophers Learned society (C18). **1993** Máire de Paor, in Adele M. Dalsimer (ed.), *Visualising Ireland:* 'He [General Vallancey] had been pushing for the foundation of a select committee of antiquarians from the Dublin Society, and finally, in 1772, the society appointed one to enquire into "the antient state of arts, literature and antiquities". This merged with a scientific society, the Neophilosophers, to become in 1785 the Irish Academy of Science, Polite Literature and Antiquities, which received its charter from George III in 1786 as the Royal Irish Academy.'

Nettlemas night [folk festival]. 30 Apr. **1972** Diarmaid Ó Muirithe, *A Seat behind the Coachman:* 'May Eve, the last day of April, was called Nettlemas night in Cork. The Halls [Mr & Mrs S.C. Hall] tell us that on this night it was the custom for boys and girls to parade the streets with large bunches of nettles, "availing themselves of the privilege to sting their lovers".'

New Agenda [polit.]. Precursor of Democratic Left Party (1992). **1998** Fergus Finlay, *Snakes and Ladders:* '... Proinsias De Rossa and all of his colleagues in the Dáil, with the exception of Tomás MacGiolla, had started a party of their own, called New Agenda.'

New Departure Party [polit.]. Failed political party (1985). **2000** Rosita Boland, *Irish Times,* 26 Aug: 'Lord Mount Charles did have discussions with [Desmond] O'Malley, but he went on to set up his own party, the New Departure Party, which he described as "radical, left of centre, but not socialist". It never became established, a fact which caused some widely-reported amusement at the time.'

Newfoundland (Street) [Dub.] **1956** J.L.J. Hughes, *Dublin Historical Record,* 'Dublin Street Names': '... the foreign-sounding name Newfoundland Street as explained by Evans in the *Irish Builder,* 1893 .... Is probably alright. In mentioning some new streets marked out in 1773 on the **North Lotts**, a district of recently reclaimed land, he says one of these streets was, at a later date, appropriately called Newfoundland Street.' **1986** Vincent Caprani, *A View from the DART* : 'From here to **Connolly** Station the line runs through the East Wall/North Strand/Amiens Street district – all land reclaimed from the sea ... and once known, for obvious reasons, as Newfoundland.'

New Grange/Newgrange [archaeolog., Ir. *Brugh na Bóinne,* palace of the [River] Boyne, Co. na Mí/Meath]. Bronze Age tumulus. **1912** R.A.S. Macalister, *Irish Review,* Feb: 'It is much to be wished that either that name [Brugh na Bóinne] or (perhaps preferably) the more specific name of *Achad Alldai* ... should take the place of the foolish name "New Grange"; for the structure neither is *new* nor is it a *grange!* Such a label would be appropriate enough for the villa of one of the blameless if undistinguished residents in some dull London suburb or other, but it is wholly unworthy of the grave-mound of Bronze-age Kings of Ireland!'

New Light [religion]. Presbyterian sect. **1921** D.J. Owen, *History of Belfast:* 'The Presbyterians in the north of Ireland did not form one united church but were divided into several bodies ... The non-subscribers represented what was popularly known as the "New Light", and the old General Synod the "Old Light" or orthodox party.'

Newman [typog.]. Typeface designed by George Petrie and commissioned by John Henry Newman (later Cardinal) (1857). **1992** Dermot McGuinne, *Irish Type Design:* '... in order to avoid confusion in name with the earlier round Petrie designs, it seems more correct and appropriate that this type, heretofore referred to as the Keating Society type ... be called the Newman Irish type.'

Newtownmountkennedy [Baile an Chinnéidigh, Co. Chill Mhantáin/Wicklow]. **1994** K.S. Daly, *Ireland, an Encyclopaedia for the Bewildered:* 'Believed by many to be the longest place name in Ireland, except by those who have heard of Muickeenachidirdhásháile ('soft place between two seas') in Co. Galway, or Castletownconyersmaceniery in Co. Limerick.'

Niall of the Nine Sausages [<Niall of the Nine Hostages, High King (AD 380-405); nickname]. Niall Boden, entertainer and presenter of commercial RTÉ Radio programme for Donnelly's sausages (1950s). See **Don 'n' Nelly**.

Nicky Kelly Wrongly convicted (1976) of involvement in train robbery, freed 1984. Hence **Free Nicky Kelly** [slogan; graffito]. **2000** Sam Smyth, *Sunday Tribune,* 26 Nov: 'An international campaign seeking his release made the "Free Nicky Kelly" slogan almost as ubiquitous as Budweiser's current "Whassup" catchphrase.' (local graffiti artists added '... with every packet of Kellogg's Corn Flakes.')

Night of the Big Wind, the [Oíche na Gaoithe Móire]. Meteorological phenomenon. **1999** Peter Costello in W.J. McCormack (ed.), *The Blackwell Companion to Modern Irish Culture:* 'An appalling storm on the night of 6-7

January 1839. The deaths and damage done passed into folk memory, the topic of many Gaelic poems.'

Nighttown [nickname, coined by James Joyce]. Dub. brothel district. **1922** James Joyce, *Ulysses*: '(*The Mabbot Street entrance to nighttown, before which stretches an uncobbled tramsiding set with skeleton tracks …*'). **1979** Peter Somerville-Large, *Dublin*: 'She [Mrs Mack, brothel madam] was so well known that the area which Joyce called Nighttown was sometimes known as Macktown.'

NINA [acronym, UK]. Graffito. **1998** Angeline Morrison, *CIRCA*, review of Brendon Deasy, *The State We're Out*, Autumn: 'The image of Mr Deasy puzzling over a sign on some factory gates which reads "NINA" – standing for "No Irish Need Apply" – is poignant in the extreme.'

NIPPLES [acronym]. (1) **1996** Fintan O'Toole, *The Ex-Isle of Erin*: 'Joe O'Connor has captured the style of the NIPPLES (New Irish Professional People Living in England) …' (2) **1998** Seán O'Driscoll, reviewing David Rowan, *Glossary for the 90s, Sunday Tribune*, 1 Nov: '… you may be confused to learn that the boom in the economy has produced an abundance of NIPPLES, New Irish Professional People living in London Executive Suites.' (3) **1999** Neil Mackay, *Sunday Tribune*, 11 Apr: 'Ever heard of NIPPLES – Northern Ireland Professional People Living in Edinburgh? Well, my cousin's one…' See also **Nipplies**

Nipplies [acronym]. **2000** Jamie Doward, *Observer* (London), 23 Jul; 'Of the near 1,000 IT graduates from Northern Ireland's two universities, Queen's and Ulster, 40 per cent end up

leaving Northern Ireland each year … There's a word for the latter: Nipplies – "Northern Ireland professional people living in England".' See also **NIPPLES**

nixers.com [<Ir. sl. idem, <colloq. Germ. *nix* (<*nichts*, nothing + endearment suffix]. Web site. **2000** Michael Clifford, *Sunday Tribune*, 2 Apr: 'Previously the preserve of word of mouth, the staple currency of the black economy, the nixer has been hijacked by the world wide web. Welcome to "nixers.com", the site for those who want to earn a few extra bob on the side.' **2001** Derek O'Connor, *Irish Times*, 10 Mar: 'Young Marco [Herbst] then set about tracking down the Korean gentleman who – believe it or not – owned the domain name "nixers" (there's a company called Nix in Korea; he was trying to outsmart them …'

NODDI [acronym]. Fathers seeking joint custody of their children. **2000** Christine Newman, *Irish Times*, 19 Jun: 'The group, which calls itself Non-Disposable Daddies Ireland (NODDI), marched to the Dáil to highlight what it described as the marginalisation and discrimination against it by the family law court system.'

No Name Club Temperance org. **2000** *Stage Left* (Portlaoise/Naas), Oct: 'Founded in Kilkenny in 1978, the No Name Club set out to provide an alternative to the pub. "The idea was that adults and young people could get together in surroundings that had all the comfort of the pub without the alcohol", explains Tommy [Hannon].'

Northern Athens, the [<supposed cultural affinity]. Belfast. **1938** *Irish Times*, 1 Apr: 'It is not only in political thought that Belfast has departed from the spirit

of 1798, when she was Ireland's principal centre in art, literature and music, so that the town became known as "the Northern Athens.' See **Athens of Ireland**; **Athens of the North**

North Lotts [Dublin]. **1977** Dillon Cosgrave, *North Dublin, City & County:* 'It is called the North Lotts because the Corporation in 1717 drew lots for the distribution amongst themselves of the land to be acquired here by the construction of the North Wall.' See also **Newfoundland**

North Mon [abbrev., nickname]. Cork school. **1971** Seán Beecher, *The Story of Cork:* 'Close by St Vincent's is the Monastery of Our Lady's Mount, the school of the Christian Brothers, known nationally as the "North Mon".'

North Side Gang see **Bugs Moran**

North, the [colloq.]. Political entity of Northern Ireland, esp. as perceived from the Republic. **1999** Gerry O'Brien, in *Thought Lines 3*, 'Metaphor in Word and Image': 'The east bank of the Foyle is largely Loyalist and is in "the province" of Northern Ireland, i.e. "the North". Ironically, for the citizens of Derry "the South" lies west and "the North" lies to the east.'

Nose Tax, the [nickname]. Poll tax. **1895** E. Cobham Brewer, *Dictionary of*

Phrase & Fable (new ed.): 'In the ninth century the Danes imposed on Irish houses a poll tax, historically called the "Nose Tax" because those who neglected to pay the ounce of gold were punished by having their nose slit.'

NTH [acronym]. Newtownhamilton, Co. Ard Mhacha/Armagh. **1999** Toby Harnden, *'Bandit Country'*: 'Just eight miles north of Crossmaglen is Newtownhamilton … soldiers consider it the "softest" posting in South Armagh and some joke that the acronym NTH stands for "No Terrorists Here".'

Nua [tradename]. **1999** Sandra Burke, *Irish Times,* 20 Sep: 'Some names fare better than others. Nua, the name chosen by the Irish Internet services company, is a good name … It is easy to pronounce, has an Irish connotation, most people know it means new, and it ties in well with the newness of the emerging Internet economy.'

Nugent Robert, Earl Nugent (1702–1788), b. Carlanstown, Co. na hIarmhí/Westmeath]. Hence **Nugentise** Marry advantageously. **1988** Henry Boylan, *A Dictionary of Irish Biography* (2nd ed.): 'Inherited an estate of £1,500 a year. This he augmented by his skill in marrying rich widows, which caused Horace Walpole to invent the description "to Nugentise".'

O

Oakboys [politic, Ulster]. Secret society (1763-). **1988** R.F. Foster, *Modern Ireland 1600-1972:* 'the "Oakboy" movement in the north sprang up against taxes levied for road-building … it mobilised Catholics as well as lower-class Presbyterians and Anglicans.'

Oaken-footed Elzevir [<his loss of a leg; nickname]. George Faulkner (c1699-1775). **1972** Robert E. Ward, *Prince of Dublin Printers:* 'Faulkner's preference for a type called Elzevir prompted many of his competitors to call him the "oaken-footed Elzevir" and to laugh at his "wooden understanding".'

Obemdub [?<*Abhainn Bhuí* or *Abhainn Dubh*, placenames not certainly located]. Projected port of disembarkation for Spanish expedition (1601). **1601** Diego Brochero, *letter to Philip III*, 26 Jul: '… considerando mas conveniente donde disembarcar esta gente para que con facilidad se junte con lost católicos ha parecido que sea en las costas del norte en el puerto que llaman Obemdub' ['considering the most convenient place to disembark these people so that they may link up with the Catholics it has appeared that it should be on the northern coastline at the port called Obemdub']. **1964** John J. Silke, *Irish Sword,* Winter: '"Obemdub", the conclusion is, means Donegal bay, including certainly the ports of south-west Donegal but probably not excluding those of Sligo and north Mayo as well.'

O'Brien see **Lanna Macree**

O'Donnell, Leopoldo [Spanish/Irish military leader (C19). Hence **Calle O'Donnell** [street name]. **1999** John de Courcy Ireland, *Irish Times,* 25 Jan: 'An O'Donnell led an expedition from Ceuta in 1860 that captured the Moroccan city of Tetuan. There is an O'Donnell Street in Ceuta, and in Melilla.'

O'Donoghue's white horse [Lakes of Killarney]. Natural phenomenon. **1895** E. Cobham Brewer, *A Dictionary of Phrase and Fable* (new ed.): 'Those waves which come on a windy day, crested with foam. The spirit of the hero re-appears every May-day, and is seen gliding, to sweet but unearthly music, over the lakes of Killarney, on his favourite white horse.'

Odyssey Centre [Belfast]. Sports/leisure/educational facility. **2000** Eddie O'Gorman, *Irish Times,* 8 Aug: 'It comprises a 10,000-seat arena, a science centre, an IMAX theatre, and an entertainment and leisure pavilion … making Odyssey one of Ireland's largest entertainment and leisure projects.'

Óglaigh na hÉireann [<Ir. *óglach,* (young) warrior; volunteer]. (1) The Irish Volunteers (1913); (2) Regular Army (1923-). **1991** J.P. Duggan, *A History of the Irish Army*: 'The hallowed title, *Óglaigh na hÉireann*, had persisted and was reaffirmed. To the present day it remains the proprietory statutory title of the Defence Forces …'; (3) title subseq. usurped by the **Real IRA**. **2000** Gregory Allen, *Irish Times,* 28 Aug: 'In my green uniform as a member of Oglaigh na hÉireann, I was proud to meet a man who had seen the Tricolour hoisted over the erstwhile second city of the Empire.' **2001** J.P. Duggan, *Irish Times,* 21 Mar: 'I wish to protest in the

strongest possible terms at your misuse of the hallowed Defence Forces title – Óglaigh na hÉireann, in an IRA context … You are obviously oblivious to the Defence Forces' sensitivity and anger at this hijacking of their cherished title.'

O'Hanrahan's [sport]. GAA Club, Carlow. **2000** Seán Moran, *Irish Times,* 2 Dec: 'The eponymous O'Hanrahan was Michael, a 1916 activist who was executed after the failure of the rising. A Dubliner and founder member of the Leinster Council [of the GAA], he lived in Carlow for a number of years before his death. He is also commemorated by the New Ross club, Geraldine O'Hanrahan's in Wexford.'

Oirish [adj., derog.]. Applied to those claiming nationality with scant justification, esp. 'Irish' eds. of Brit. newspapers. **1997** Ciaran Carson, *The Star Factory:* '… and James Mason's notoriously unstable "Oirish" accent [in the film *Odd Man Out*] offers a further ambiguity, less that of the nationalist leader who comes from elsewhere, like Hitler, Napoleon, or Seán Mac Stiofáin (John Stephenson) …'

Old Comber [brandname]. Whiskey. **1931** Lynn Doyle, *The Glensman* (Cushendall), Dec: '… it is twenty years since I drank the Old Comber, and I know whiskey mellows better in the memory even than the wood – but I do not believe there are enough words of praise in the English dictionary to flatter that whiskey.' See **Lynn C Doyle**

Old Lady of D'Olier Street [<office location; nickname; media]. *The Irish Times* newspaper. **2000** Sam Smyth, *Sunday Tribune,* 10 Sep: '… presumably, like a stopped clock, the Old Lady of D'Olier Street must be occasionally right, even if it is by default.'

Old Lady, the [nickname]. Lady Augusta Gregory (1852-1932), playwright and theatre director. **1985** Mary Lou Kohfeldt, *Lady Gregory*: 'The Abbey rejected a play … by Denis Johnston. Reportedly it was returned to him with "The Old Lady says No" scrawled across the cover. He renamed it accordingly and got it produced elsewhere. (Lennox Robinson insisted, rather improbably, that no one at the Abbey ever referred to her as "the Old Lady"…).'

Old Lammas Fair, the see **Yellowman**

Old Light [nickname]. Orthodox Presbyterian party, Ulster (1642). **1921** Rev. Henry Dooke, quoted in D.J. Owen, *History of Belfast:* 'In Belfast they are in the habit of saying that a man when he first comes into the town walks to what they call the "Old Light" House; if he gets a gig, they say he rides to one of the **"New Light"** Houses, which are more fashionable; and when he has a carriage he is driven to church.'

Old Mister Brennan [advert.]. Character created for Brennan's Bread, Dub. **1997** Frank McNally, *Irish Times,* 20 Dec: 'I don't know about you, but I think I've had just about enough of Old Mister Brennan. You know who I mean. The old codger who turns up on the radio 26 times a day telling humorous yarns about bread … followed by bouts of wheezy guffawing in which you can almost smell the stale porter on his breath.' **1999** Brennan's Bread, *Wholemeal wrapper:* '"I've seen the light!" exclaimed Old Mr Brennan. He was, of course, referring to his latest masterpiece. A softer, lighter traditional style batch bread.' Hence **Young Mr Brennan** [media]. **Early 1990s** RTÉ Radio, *Scrap*

Saturday: used to satirise Séamus Brennan, **Fianna Fáil** politician.

Old Red Socks (nickname, Ulster). The Pope. **1998** Conor Cruise O'Brien, *Sunday Independent,* 3 May: 'I personally cannot throw any stones at Mr Paisley for his occasional anti-Papal references. I have done worse in that line than make occasional – comparatively genial – references to Old Red Sox [*sic*].'

Old Toughs [nickname]. Royal Dub. Fusiliers, former Brit. army regiment. **1939** Sean O'Casey, *I Knock at the Door:* '"The Royal Dublin Fusiliers", he said a little thickly, "the Old Toughs, by the right, quick march for foreign lands …"'

O'Ligarchy [nonce word]. **1999** Renagh Holohan, *Irish Times,* 18 Dec: 'The *Independent* of London's review section recently told us about some new English language vocabulary. Along with plastic fatigue (anger caused by carrying too many cards) … they gave us O'Ligarchy. This, they say, means "influential professional people in Ireland". News to **Quidnunc**.'

Olocher see **Dolocher**

One-Line Railway [nickname]. Listowel-Ballybunion **Lartigue** monorail (1897-1924). **1924** *Irish Times,* 8 Oct: Known locally as the one-line railway, the Lartigue was an object of curiosity to all visitors to the district. The single rail which carries the engine and carriages stands some feet above the ground and is supported by trestles shaped like the letter A.'

Operation 'Green' [politic.]. German invasion plan (1940). **1983** Robert Fisk, *In Time of War:* '… the invasion of Ireland, code-named Operation

"Green" – *Fall Grün* – was to have been a bold and extremely hazardous affair. From the French ports of Lorient, St Nazaire and Nantes, an initial force of 3,900 troops were to be landed on an eighty-five mile front …'

Operation Oíche [<Ir. *idem,* night]. Garda patrols and surveillance to combat night-time crime and violence in Dub. **2000** John Moran, *Irish Times,* 9 Sep: 'The operation is being orchestrated by the assistant Garda Commissioner for Dublin, Jim McHugh, whose Operation Oíche is attempting to reclaim the night.'

Operation Samhradh [<Ir. *idem,* summer]. Road accident prevention programme. **2000** *Irish Times,* 9 Aug: 'Operation Samhradh, the current Garda traffic operation targeting the three "killer offences" of speeding, drink-driving and non-wearing of seatbelts, was enabling the force to "hold its own" against the fatality rate.'

O'Raifeartaigh Theorem [<Lochlainn O'Raifeartaigh, physicist (1933-2000). **2000** *Irish Times,* 25 Nov: 'While at Syracuse [University, USA] he made an important discovery, known now as the O'Raifeartaigh Theorem. In it he showed the impossibility of combining relativistic symmetry with other symmetries in a non-trivial way.'

Orange Peel [nickname]. Robert Peel, Chief Sec. for Ire. (1812-18). **1966** J. C. Beckett, *The Making of Modern Ireland 1603-1923:* '… Peel was firmly opposed to any extension of the political rights of the Roman Catholics. "Orange Peel", O'Connell dubbed him, "a raw youth, squeezed out of the workings of I know not what factory in England …"

Orange Society [politic., Ulster (1795-)]. Militant Protestant organisation. **1921** D.J. Owen, *History of Belfast:* 'The society took its name from William of Orange, and, as part of its ritual, decided to celebrate every anniversary of the Battle of the Boyne.' Hence **Orangies** [colloq.] Orangemen/Unionists. **2000** Ciarán MacCionnaith, quoted by Nell McCafferty, *Sunday Tribune,* 2 Jul: 'I thought all my Christmases had come at once. But the Orangies walked out, rang Downing Street, and demanded that the negotiator be sacked.'

O'Reilly, Alexander. See **Bloody O'Reilly**

O'Reilly's money [<Count O'Reilly, Lord of Breifne; numismatics]. Unofficial coinage. **1986** Patrick Logan, *Fair Day:* 'In different parts of the country locally made coins were being widely used, as substitutes for the official coinage. Such forgeries had probably been made and used for centuries but little was done about the problem until Edward IV (1461-83) became king [of Eng. and Lord of Ire.]. One of these counterfeit issues was known as O'Reilly's money.'

Ormo [<Ormeau; brandname]. Belfast bakery and its products. See **Lower Ormeau**

Ormond Money [numismatics]. Silver coinage (1643). **1979** Patrick Finn, *Irish Coin Values:* 'This issue has been traditionally titled "Ormond" money because it was thought to have been struck on behalf of Charles I by the Viceroy, James, Marquis of Ormond. Ormond had been in charge of the King's armies in Ireland from the start of the rebellion, but since he did not take over the duties of Lord Lieutenant until much later, it may possibly be more accurate to name this coinage "The Lord Justices 2nd Issue 1643".'

Orrery [<3rd Earl of Orrery; astronomy]. Clockwork mechanism demonstrating the movement of the planets. **1895** E. Cobham Brewer, *Dictionary of Phrase and Fable* [new ed.]: '... invented by George Graham, who sent his model to Rowley, an instrument maker ... Rowley made a copy of it for Charles Boyle, third Earl of Orrery, and Sir Richard Steele named it an orrery out of compliment to the earl.'

Orthodox Celts Trad. band. **2000** Gillian Sandford, *Irish Times,* 3 May: 'The audience is the Irish Regiment, part of the peacekeeping force in Croatia. The band is the Orthodox Celts – which is made up of Serbs, none of whom have ever been to Ireland ... The group was formed in 1992, when several members began to express their love for Irish music.'

Ould Lammas Fair see **Yellow-man**

Ould Sod see **Auld Sod**

Oul'Mahoun [nickname, <OFr *Mahon*, a principal devil; Ulster]. The devil.

Oure [invented name; lit.]. River Avonbeg, Co. Chill Mhantáin/Wicklow. **1590/96** Edmund Spenser, *The Faerie Queene:* 'The spreading Lee that like an island fayre/Encloseth Corke with his divided flood;/And baleful Oure late staind with English blood ...' **1911** P. W. Joyce, *The Wonders of Ireland:* 'I have elsewhere observed that the poet often bestows fictitious names, generally borrowed from some neighbouring features ... So here "Oure" is merely the last syllable of Glenmalure, or Glenmalour as he himself calls it in his *View of the State of Ireland.*'

Ouzel Galley [maritime]. Merchant vessel which was dispatched from Dub. (1695), returning (1700) having been given up for lost. Hence (1) **The Ouzel Galley Society** Dub. commercial arbitration body and dining club (1705–1888). **1983** L.M. Cullen, *Princes & Pirates:* 'The Society was confined to a maximum of 40 members, i.e. a number corresponding to the size of the crew of the *Ouzel Galley.* Its officers were denominated as the Captain, two Lieutenants, Master, Bursar, Boatswain, Gunner, Carpenter, Master's Mate, Coxswain, Boatswain's Mate, Gunner's Mate and Carpenter's Mate.' (2) [colloq. phr.]. **Ouzel lost** Not really lost, reappearing after a long time.

P

Paddy [dimin. of Patrick, often derog.]. Generic Irishman, esp. overseas usage; gen. derog]. **2000** Ann Marie Hourihane, *Sunday Tribune*, 19 Nov: '"England was the only place I was treated like any other Irishman", says [Traveller] Johnny Collins. "Over there, you were just a Paddy, like every Irishman".' Hence (1) **Paddy/'s Land**, Ireland; (2) **Paddy's market**, market selling secondhand goods, etc; (3) **Paddy wagon** [US sl., poss. <abbrev. of 'padlock' or inference that most US police would be Irish]. Vehicle in which those arrested are transported to the local police station or gaol. See also **Expat**; (4) **Plastic Paddies** [nickname]. Children of first-generation immigrants in Britain. **1966** Nuala O'Faolain, *Irish Times*, 17 Feb: 'There are many kinds of London Irish – the ones who came with cardboard suitcases and broken hearts in the old days; the modern ones, who happen to be in London but might be in Paris or New York; and the "plastic Paddies" ... who are mostly like the urban young anywhere.'

Paddy Flaherty [<Paddy O'Flaherty; brandname]. Whiskey, subsequently **Paddy**. **1980** Malachy Magee, *1000 Years of Irish Whiskey:* 'In the 1920s Cork Distilleries had a very popular and resourceful company representative called Paddy O'Flaherty. The genial Paddy extolled the virtues of the company's fine old Cork whiskey so successfully among his trade customers that in submitting their repeat orders they simply asked for "Paddy Flaherty's whiskey." Astute company executives rewarded their diligent salesman by naming their product after him ...'

Paddy Go Easy World Wide [company name]. **2000** *Sunday Business Post*, 28 May: 'Yet again the Registrar of Companies has succeeded in entertaining readers of his recent strike-off list ... Kondopogabumprom Newsprint Paper is just one that has been threatened ... Others on the list include Shoot the Crows; Paddy Go Easy World Wide; Just a Game ... and The Beat on the Peat & a Day On the Bog.'

Paddy Kelly's Budget [media]. (1) Periodical (1832-4). **1952** B.P. Bowen, *Dublin Historical Record,* 'Dublin Humorous Periodicals of the 19th Century', Mar-May: 'The journal known as Paddy Kelly's Budget was another of this [political] class of publication ... it was succeeded by Young Paddy Kelly's Budget, which continued to December 1835, or perhaps later. This was a topical journal with a tendency to vulgarity.' (2) Periodical, Aust. **1987** Patrick O'Farrell, *The Irish in Australia:* 'Generally, their [the Irish] centrality to city low-life is suggested by the name of one of Sydney's tattle sheets of the 1840s, *Paddy Kelly's Budget* ...'

Paddy Sugarstick [nickname]. **1940** Robert Gahan, *Some Old Street Characters of Dublin:* 'One of the most adaptable of all Dublin's characters was "Paddy Sugarstick", whose real name was Charles Donnelly. "Paddy", who was a perfect whip of a man, some six-feet-two high and very lean, would introduce himself to a street as a ragman ... he would open his sweetmeat box and display its delicious contents to the youngsters, saying "Go and get me an oul' jam-jar, or a porter bottle, and I'll give you a big lump of sugarstick"...'

Paddy the Cope [<local pronun. of 'co-op'; nickname]. Patrick Gallagher (1873-1964), founder of pioneering Templecrone (Co. Donegal) Co-operative Society. **1916** *Irish Homestead,* 11 Nov: '"Paddy the Cope" was not only a good fighter but a man of business of the type which is not infrequently born on an Irish bog and ends his days as an American millionaire.'

Pale, the [<Fr. *Pal;* Lat. *palus,* stake; politic.]. Area of Eng. hegemony. **1981** Art Cosgrove, *Late Mediaeval Ireland:* '... the earliest known use of the term occurs in 1446-7 when the Gaelic Irish leader, Hugh Roe McMahon, under-took "to carry nothing out of the English Pale". The area of the pale was not yet as strictly delineated as it was to become in the late fifteenth and early sixteenth centuries.' Hence [colloq.] Greater Dub. in contradistinction to the rest of the country. **2000** Elaine Larkin, *Irish Times,* 22 Sep: 'Operating business from beyond the "Pale" is an attractive option also for companies that do not have to be located in the capital to operate.'

Pana/Pa'na/Panah [nickname]. Patrick St., Cork. **1992** Tom McElligott, *Six O'Clock all over Cork:* 'I relish the oddi-ties that show in their vocabulary and positively rejoice when I hear the suffix "ah" which the Cork idiom tends to add to certain words so that Patrick Street becomes *Panah,* Barrack Street *Barrackah*, Farranferris *Farranah.*'

Paper, De see **De Paper**; **Irish Examiner**

Papish [nickname, derog.]. Roman Catholic, esp. Ulster. **1849** Pop. ballad: 'But we loosed our guns upon them and we quickly won the day/And we knocked five hundred papishes right over Dolly's Brae.'

Parker [<Stephen Parker foundry, Dub., typog.]. Typeface (1787). **1992** Dermot McGuinne, *Irish Type Design:* 'This Parker type, together with its model, the earlier Paris face, represents an isolated and unique departure in the development of Irish type design ...'

Parliament whiskey [nickname]. Whiskey legally distilled under new Govt. regulations (1780s-) as opposed to illicit spirits or *poitín* [poteen]. **1988** John McGuffin, *In Praise of Poteen:* 'One important result of this was that the quality of legal (or "parliament whiskey" as it was called) declined as distilleries were forced to work faster and faster.'

Patent [<?] Alcoholic beverage. **1941** Sean O'Faolain, *An Irish Journey:* 'By the way, the favourite Galway drink is a Patent, i.e. half a pint of porter and a bottle of Guinness in it. In Cork this is called a Predom. I have also heard it called a System, and a Half-in-Half.'

Pearse, Padraig Revolutionary & edu-cationalist (1879-1916). Hence **Padraig Pearse** [rhyming sl.]. Fierce, gen. as intensitive modifying 'bad', 'serious', 'acute', etc. **1998** Anto Byrne, *Sunday Tribune,* '... now I'd a few on me fair enough, say I to um, de pen and ink [stink] offa you is only Padraig Pearse, know what I mee-in.'

Pee [nickname, <initial]. Padraig Flynn (1939-) politician and former EU com-missioner. **1998** Fergus Finlay, *Snakes and Ladders:* 'Eventually Pee Flynn burst in again. He sat beside me and slapped me on the knee. "Quick!", he said. "Quick! 9.2 becu – '92 prices. What is it?"' **1999**

Sunday Tribune, 14 Mar: 'It will be a different story this year, however, as Pee celebrates his last Paddy's Day as a commissioner (barring a miracle).'

Peel's Brimstone [nickname, < Robert Peel (1788-1850), Brit. statesman and prime minister]. Indian corn distributed for famine relief (1845-9) which caused severe digestive problems. **1962** Cecil Woodham-Smith, *The **Great Hunger***: '… at first the Government's Indian corn-meal had been loathed − it was called 'Peel's Brimstone' from its bright yellow colour.'

Peep o'Day Boys [<their daybreak arms searches on Catholics; nickname]. Protestant peasant movement (1784-). **1998** R.F. Foster, *Modern Ireland 1600-1972:* 'the government was evidently incapable of disciplining the Protestant "Peep o'Day Boys" who claimed they were simply enforcing the Penal Laws reneged upon by the gentry.'

Peggie's Leg [<Eng. dial. *Peggy*, wooden implement for agitating washing in a tub]. Stick of boiled sweet. **1930** *Irish Times*, 18 Oct: 'The village shop is yet to be found that does not supply that time-honoured favourite of our childhood's days, known as "Peggie's Leg." … Travel as you will throughout the country, you will rarely fail to find, even in the humblest shop window, a few sticks of tawny hue displayed for sale in the neat jackets of wax paper.'

Penguin, the [nickname]. George Mitchell, Dub. underworld figure. **2000** Barry O'Kelly, *Sunday Business Post:* 'Under his nickname, The Penguin − given to him by the Sunday World and later repeated in the Dáil by TD Tony Gregory − Mitchell became virtually a household name, along with The

Zombie and The Psycho.'

Pete Briquette [stage name]. Pat Cusack, member of the Boomtown Rats rock group (1975-). **1986** Bob Geldof, *Is That It?:* 'We changed Pat Cusack's name because we thought it sounded too Irish. We made it more Irish. We changed it to Pete Briquette, which was a pun on the fuel cakes made in Ireland from compressed peat.'

Peter the Packer [<his practice of packing juries; nickname]. Peter O'Brien, Lord Chief Justice (1842-1914). **1932** Edward Marjoribanks, *The Life of Lord Carson:* 'Peter O'Brien gained for himself the title "Peter the Packer" by his extensive exercise of the Crown right, under an Irish Juries Act, of directing jurors summoned for criminal cases, when called, to stand aside, and so excluding from the jury-box those who, it was believed, would not under any circumstances convict a prisoner.'

Petrie [<George Petrie (1790-1866), antiquary and type designer; typog.]. Series of typefaces. **1992** Dermot McGuinne, *Irish Type Design:* 'Liala Allman, who returned to work at the [Dublin] University press for her father in 1945, recalls having seen a box of punches of the Petrie type at that time.'

Pfizer Riser [nickname, <name of manufacturer]. The drug Viagra, prescribed for erectile dysfunction, produced in Co. Cork. **1998** Renagh Holohan, *Irish Times*, 13 Jun: '… do you know what they are saying about Viagra, the Pfizer Riser, in New York? You have to swallow it quick or you could get a stiff neck.' **1998** Rob Brown, *Independent on Sunday* (London), 21 Jun: 'A few weeks ago, people in the Village Inn were reported to be merrily

joking about how the "Pfizer riser" would turn Ringaskiddy into the "erection section".'

Phoenix Park [< Phoenix House, Dub; built 1611, ?< Ir. *fionn uisce*, (spring of) clear water & by assoc.,/confusion with 'phoenix' [<OE *fenix*, mythical bird]. Largest enclosed park in Europe. **1930** *Irish Times*, 4 Feb: 'It was this same Lord Chesterfield who, in 1745, erected the Corinthian column with the phoenix on top of it to explain the name of the estate; but he was wrong in his explanation.' Hence (1) **Park, the** Áras an Uachtaráin, residence of the President of Ire. and/or its appurtenances. **1996** Jack Norton, *Sunday Tribune*, 21 Jan: 'With the prospect of a vacancy in "The Park" in the not too distant future, I hope there will not be any "cosy little cartels" deciding the issue ...' (2) **Phoenix** [brandname]. Ale and stout. **1939** James Joyce, *Finnegans Wake:* '... no matter whether it was chateau bottled Guinness's or Phoenix Brewery Stout it was ...' ; (3) [politic.]. Secret Society. **1972** Diarmaid Ó Muirithe, *A Seat Behind the Coachman:* '... while England was busy putting down the Indian Mutiny in 1857-8, James Stephens ... established a secret society, the Phoenix Society, in the south of Ireland.'

Pigeonhouse Fort [Dub.]. **1930** *Irish Times*, 6 Nov: 'The familiar landmark at **Ringsend,** the Pigeonhouse, takes its name from a man called Pidgeon, who established a sort of restaurant there in the eighteenth century, long before the fortress was built for the defence of the Port of Dublin.'

Pigsback [<Ir. *ar mhuin na muice*, on the pig's back, reflecting that animal's former economic importance; website].

2000 *Irish Times,* 21 Jul: 'Pigsback.com, a new personalised offers and rewards website, providing a unique approach to consumer e-marketing, has been announced.'

Pimlico Parliamentary Reporter, The [<street in the Liberties, Dub., <street in London]. **1952** B.P. Bowen, *Dublin Historical Record,* 'Dublin Humorous Periodicals of the 19th Century', Mar-May: 'One of the first journals of this type ... was published about 1800 as a satire on the Union and to ridicule its supporters. This was The Pimlico Parliamentary Reporter, being Proceedings and Debates of the Parliament of Pimlico. It was published by Vincent Dowling from the Apollo circulating library which he kept at 5 College Green and ran for only 28 numbers. The price was "Four Camacks" [< Dub. river *Camac*].'

Pink [<colour of scarf, etc; nickname]. Dublin University sporting colours (-1936). **1936** *Irish Times,* 4 May: 'The "Pink" was instituted in 1927 ... It was an effort to get something that would correspond to the "Blue" of Oxford and Cambridge ...'

Pinkindindies [<'pink', to thrust, stab; dindy (cf. Fr. d*inde*), turkey, turkeycock]. Association of C18 bucks. **1847** John Edward Walsh, *Ireland Sixty Years Ago:* 'Others were known by the sobriquet of Sweaters and Pinkindindies. It was their habit to cut off a small portion of the scabbards of the swords which everyone then wore, and prick or "pink" the persons with whom they quarrelled with the naked points ...'

Pink Smokers [<?] Sweets. **1997** Michael Hamilton, *Down Memory Line:* 'Friday, the ten shilling pension day, was

a great day for sweets. Our favourites were "pink smokers" – round and small with a sweet smell.'

PINT [acronym]. Pressure group. **2000** Michael Cronin, Peter Sirr, *Irish Times*, 15 Feb: 'PINT (Protection of Indigenous Noiseless Taverns] is an association established to campaign for the removal of piped music from public houses. We invite your readers who are concerned about the scourge ... to send expressions of support to our email address at quietpint@ireland.com ... It is not too late to save the Quiet Pint.'

Pipewater Johnston [nickname]. **1921** D.J. Owen, *History of Belfast:* 'In 1773 a lease was granted at the nominal rent of twenty shillings a year to William Johnston, of Newforge, of "all waters, rivers, brooks, wells and water streams adjacent and contiguous to the town of Belfast" .... Johnston, who became known as "Pipewater Johnston", provided water for the town through wooden pipes ...'

Plain People of Ireland, the [latterly iron.]. *Vox populi.* **1919** Éamon de Valera [see **Dev**] to Sinéad de Valera, 19 Jul: 'the plain people of Ireland at any rate accept and recognise the Irish Republic.' **1968 Myles na Gopaleen**, *The Best of Myles:* '*Myself* ... What trade is that at which a man will succeed only by sticking it? *The Plain People of Ireland (eagerly):* What is it? *Myself:* Bill-posting. *The Plain People of Ireland:* O HA-HA-HA-HA-HA!' (Sounds of thousands of thighs being slapped and the creak of coarse country braces ...)'

Planxty ['... may come from the Latin *plangere* (supine, *planxtum*), on the model of the existing Irish word *planncaim*, which means to strike (the harp) ... The term probably originated with Carolan, as it does not appear to be found before his time, nor does it occur except in connection with his tunes.' (Donal O'Sullivan, *Carolan* (1958)]. Traditional music band. **1991** Nuala O'Connor, *Bringing it all Back Home:* 'The instigator of Planxty (the name comes from a title for a type of seventeenth-century harp tune) was Christy Moore who returned to Ireland in the early seventies ...'

Plastic Paddies see **Paddy**

Pogues [<Ir. *póg mo thóin*, kiss my arse]. Rock group. **1991** Nuala O'Connor, *Bringing it all Back Home:* 'Their name The Pogues is an abbreviation of their original name The Pogue Mahones. Pog Mahone ... is a put-down in Irish, literally "kiss my arse". The name-change came about when a Gaelic-speaking television producer rumbled it.'

Pollbinn [Ir. *poll binn,* sweet/melodious hole]. Cave, Co. An Chláir/Clare. **1965** J.C. Coleman, *The Caves of Ireland:* 'The local people in the absence of a name tend to call potholes (or sinkholes) *Poulatoon* [Ir. *poll talmhan*] (a hole in the ground). Since I started exploration work, the necessity for titles (for unnamed sites) became apparent. In some cases I was "guilty" of inventing names such as Pollbin and Pollnua [Ir. *poll nua,* new hole] (Co. Clare) but with other sites it was found more practical to use the prefix "Poll" (a hole) before the name of the townland in which the cave was situated (e.g. Pollcahercloggaun).'

Polly Woodside [<Mrs Marian ('Polly') Woodside, owner's wife; transport]. Sailing ship; subseq. renamed *Rona*; now restored and located in Melbourne, Aust., bearing orig. name. **1978** Vin Darroch, *Barque 'Polly Woodside' ('Rona'):* On the

forenoon of Saturday 7 November 1885 the iron barque *Polly Woodside,* Yard Number 38, was launched from Slip Number 2 at the North Ship Building Yard of Workman Clarke and Co. Ltd., Spencer Basin, **Queen's Island,** Belfast, for William J. Woodside and Co., shipowner, etc., of 104 Corporation Street, Belfast.'

P. O'Neill [*nom de guerre*]. Name appearing as signatory to IRA press releases, statements, etc. **1999** *Irish Times,* 3 Dec: 'A statement issued last night by the IRA said: On Wednesday 17 November, the IRA leadership announced that following the establishment of the institutions agreed on Good Friday last year, they would appoint a representative to enter into discussions with the IICD (International Independent Commission on Decommissioning) ... The statement was signed "P. O'Neill".' **2000** Diarmuid Doyle, *Sunday Tribune,* 14 May: '...in years to come, when historians look back on that history, they will notice how the name of P. O'Neill played a small but significant part in its outcome. And they will wonder about these people who adopted a pseudonym so that there could be some personal interaction between the provisional movement and the outside world. Who were they, what kind of lives did they lead, why did they choose that name and not K. Murphy or N. Fitzgerald?'

Poor Mouth Theatre Company [<Ir. *béal bocht*, persistent complaint of poverty]. **2001** Dick Hogan, *Irish Times,* 16 Jan: 'The latest arrival on the theatrical scene in Cork is Poor Mouth Theatre Company ... As its name implies, the company is not cash rich but what it lacks in resources it replaces with enthusiasm.'

Pope's Brass Band, the [politic., nickname]. Political faction. **1990** Cornelius F. Smith, in Cornelius F. Smith & Bernard Share (eds), *Whigs on the Green:* 'Elected MP for Carlow 1847, he [John Sadlier] later sat for Sligo, and became one of the leaders of the group known as "the Pope's Brass Band" ... Dickens based the character of Mr Merdle in *Little Dorrit* on Sadlier.'

Pope, the [nickname]. Eoin O'Mahony (1904-70), barrister, genealogist and great eccentric. **1988** Henry Boylan, *A Dictionary of Irish Biography:* 'of the various accounts of how he acquired the nickname, probably the most reliable ascribes it to a remark he made when a schoolboy at Clongowes [Wood College] ... taken (mistakenly) to show an ambition to be Pope.'

Poynings' Law [<Edward Poynings, Brit. soldier and statesman]. Act of Parliament (1495) declaring Eng. statutes to be in force in Ire. **1930** W.C. Sellar & R.J. Yeatman, *1066 And All That:* 'Henry VII was very good at answering the Irish Question, and made a Law called Poyning's [*sic*] Law by which the Irish could have a Parliament of their own, but the English were to pass all the Acts in it.'

Prancing Provost, the [nickname]. John Hely-Hutchinson (1724-1794), Provost of Trinity College Dublin 1774-. **1982** R.B. McDowell & D.A. Webb, *Trinity College Dublin* 1592-1952: 'The first volume of lampoons against the Provost [1775] owes its title *Prancriana* to the ridicule heaped on the proposal for a riding school in College ...' **2001** David Norris, *Irish Times*, 10 Mar: 'He was less successful at attempting to set up professorships of fencing and horse-riding, which ... earned him the nickname of the Prancing Provost.'

Predom see **Patent**

Premier County [? <from residence of prominent Butler family]. Tiobraid Árann/Tipperary, esp. in GAA context. **1996** 'Having failed in the recent past to win Munster titles with some indisputably talented teams, the Premier County now stands more or less an even chance ...' **2000** Headline, *Sunday Tribune*, 3 Sep: ''99 leader still stokes the Premier County fire.'

Pride of the Coombe see **Mrs Mulligan**

Prince John [nickname]. John O'Connell (1811-58), son of Daniel. **1876** Edward Forbes, *The Potato Commission:* 'King Dan had said, "the horrid cracks on/ The skin were the work of the hoof of the Saxon!"/Back'd by Prince John and Smith O'Brien,/His word Repealers all rely on.'

Prod/Proddie/Proddy [abbrev. + endearment suffix, gen. derog.] Protestant. **2000** 'Lorraine from Portadown', quoted in Susan McKay, *Northern Protestants, an Unsettled People:* 'There he [Breandán Mac Cionnaith] is sitting in one of those houses in Churchill Park surrounded by phones and wires and computers ... Us Prods are like big babies walking around with out nappies down to our knees beside these people.' Also **Proddy-dog**; **Proddywoddy**; **Proddywhoddy**. **1989** Hugh Leonard, *Out After Dark:* '"Only don't let them know you're a Catholic. If they [the Orangemen] ask you, say you're a Proddy-dog".' See also **Sally Rod**

Progressive Democrats [politic]. Political party (1985-). **2000** Michael D. Higgins, *RTÉ/BBC TV* 'Seven Ages', Apr: 'It's always interesting when a party give themselves a name, and when the PDs gave themselves that it asked the question as to what it was that was democratic about them.' **2000** Miriam Donohoe, *Irish Times,* 24 Oct: 'A special joint meeting of the PD national executive and parliamentary party has unanimously turned down Mr [Michael] McDowell's demand to rename the PDs the **Radical Party** ... Mr McDowell said the party label was "dated and carried a lot of negative baggage". The new title would suggest "youth, vision and vigour".'

Prosperous [Co. Chill Dara/Kildare; village]. **1837** Samuel Lewis, *Topographical Dictionary of Ireland:* '... from the flattering prospect of success which grew with every attempt, the town rather prematurely derived its name.' **1991** Con Costello, *Guide to Kildare & West Wicklow:* 'The name chosen by Robert Brooke in 1776 for the town virtually created by him as a place of cotton manufacture. The venture was never financially successful and within a decade it had failed.'

Protestant herring [**Munster**, derog.]. **1910** P.W. Joyce, *English as we speak it in Ireland:* 'Originally applied to a bad or stale herring, but in my boyhood ... applied, in our neighbourhood, to almost anything of an inferior quality: "Oh that butter is a Protestant herring".'

Provies [nickname]. Provisional IRA. **1998** Billy Wright, quoted in *Irish Times*, 3 Jan: '**King Rat** is a name identified by many as putting two fingers up to the Provies.'

Puck and Piper see **Slua Sí**

Puck Fair see **Gathering, the**; **King Puck**

Punt [Ir. *idem*, pound; numismatics]. Unit of currency (–2001). **2000** David Brown, *Independent on Sunday* (London), 10 Dec: 'City of London detectives have recently completed … a series of raids on what they say is by far the biggest counterfeiting operation in Britain. They estimate it had been producing more than £14m in foreign currency, including Spanish pesetas, US dollars, Irish punts and sterling …' Hence **2000** Róisín Ingle, *Irish Times,* 31 May: 'The days when wily Southern shoppers trekked North to make savings are long gone and a new breed of cross-Border bargain hunter has emerged. Meet the Ulster Punt-er – by their shopping bags ye shall know them.'

Puss Sunday [<Ir. *pus,* mouth, sulky expression; nickname]. First Sunday in Lent. **1986** Padraic O'Farrell, *'Tell me, Seán O'Farrell':* 'so called because the girls that didn't get married before Lent couldn't marry till Easter so they went round with a "puss" on them.' See also **Chalk Sunday**; **Cock Tuesday**

Pussy Book [nickname]. Financial ledger. **2000** Frank McDonald, *The Construction of Dublin:* 'The [Flood] tribunal was told that Bovale maintained an unorthodox record of under-the-counter cash payments to a variety of people, including employees; it was known as the Pussy Book because it had a picture of a kitten on the cover.'

Q

Quaker [<characteristics of religious soc.; sport]. Cricket term, **1992** Maurice J. Wigham, *The Irish Quakers:* 'Quaker honesty has often come in for comment, and in the days when local cricket teams were more frequent, the straight ball of no pretensions which simply removed your middle stump used to be known as a "Quaker".'

Quark [nonce word]. (1) [physics]. **2000** Dick Ahlstrom, *Irish Times,* 12 Feb: '... he [Murray Gell-Mann] chose the name quark to describe the family of particles he discovered, a word that appears in Joyce's *Finnegans Wake:* "Three quarks for Muster Mark! Sure he hasn't got much of a bark. And sure any he has it's all beside the mark."' (2) [political science]. Corrupt practices. **2000** John Waters, *Irish Times,* 5 Jun: 'The worldwide infestation of modern politics by corruption is chiefly a function of what political scientists call "the quark". It is appropriate perhaps, since the word has its origins in the work of an Irish writer, that Irish politics is now dominated by this phenomenon also.'

Queen's Island see **Dargan's Island**

Quidnunc [Lat., 'what now?']. **1895** E. Cobham Brewer, *A Dictionary of Phrase and Fable* (new ed.): 'A political Paul Pry; a pragmatic village politician ... Quidnunc is the chief character in Murphy's farce of *The Upholsterer, or What News?*' Hence [media] formerly anon. *Irish Times* column, 'An Irishman's Diary', 1927-. **1951** QUID-NUNC (Séamus Kelly), *Irish Times*, 13 Nov: 'While I object to being addressed as "Dear Pound-Now" by a Corkman who signs himself "The Dumb Ox" his letter is worth reproduction ...' **1991** Tony Gray, *Mr Smyllie, Sir:* 'Smyllie chose the pen-name "Quidnunc" ... a fairly common pseudonym for columnists in the eighteenth century, and he achieved an approach to a homogenous style by dictating the column, making minor changes in the contributions from other members of his staff, so that they conformed more closely with his own style, or lack of it.'

Quid Rides [Lat. idem, 'why do you laugh?']. **1895** E. Cobham Brewer, *A Dictionary of Phrase and Fable* [new ed.]: 'It is said that **Lundy** Foot, a Dublin tobacconist, set up his carriage and asked Emmet to furnish him with a motto. The words of the motto chosen were *Quid Rides.*'

Quiet Pint see **PINT**

R

Radical Party [politic.]. Proposed new name for **Progressive Democrats**. **2000** Justine McCarthy, *Irish Independent,* 28 Oct: 'It can hardly have escaped the gimlet-eyed that, were the name expanded to the Radical Irish Party, its acronym would neatly sum up the PDs' current morbid fears.'

Rafferty [media]. Archetypical Irishman, Aust., derog. **1987** Patrick O'Farrell, *The Irish in Australia:* 'The typical scurrilous pamphlet of the [1920-30] period, *Rafferty, King of Australia*, detailing the alleged Irishness of such Australian politics, carried such chapter headings as "Irish Politicians", "Gathering of the Kernes", "Bhoys and Blackthorns".'

Rahery horse Strong breed of horse. **1986** Patrick Logan, *Fair Day:* '… there was a small and highly serviceable type of horse kept in many parts of Ulster. These were called "Rahery horses" and, as their name implies, they may have originated in Rathlin [Reachlainn] Island off the north coast of Antrim.'

Rajah from Tipperary, the [nickname]. George Thomas, b. Roscrea, Co. Tipp., (c1756); adventurer and commander of the army of the Begum Sumuru of Sirdhana, India. **1988** Henry Boylan, *A Dictionary of Irish Biography* (2nd ed.): 'He …transferred to the service of Appa Rao, the Muhratta governor of Meerut. Shortly after the death of Appa Rao in 1797 he seized power and made himself rajah of a wide territory …'

Rakes of Mallow see **Mallow**

Rancher, the [nickname]. Jeremiah McCarthy **1971** Seán Beecher, *The Story of Cork:* '"The Rancher" in his [election] campaign expected a volume of support from the suburb of Blackpool, the home of Glen Rovers Hurling Club … The support did not materialise …. Shortly afterwards a poem attributed to the "Rancher" and entitled "The Rancher's Curse" was circulated in the city. His rancour against the Glen who had just completed an unprecedented and equalled run of nine uninterrupted victories in the Cork senior hurling championship impregnated the poem and included lines like "Nine Counties won but never again/Up the Barrs [See **Finbarr**] and F … the Glen."'

Ranter Member of Primitive Methodist body (early 1800s-). **1876** Anon ('E.A.S'): *Talk of the Road* (3rd ed.): '"Why, the next day," said Pat, "Father John comes down just the same way and goes into every house the readers were in the day before, and 'Where's the books and papers the Ranters left with you?' says he."'

Rasherhouse [nickname, from *rasher* [sl.], sexual intercourse]. Women's prison, Mountjoy (see **Joy, the**), Dub. **1997** Alan Roberts, *The Rasherhouse:* '"Ay Betty", a voice Mags had not heard before, shouted from a window. "Who's the new bit of stuff in the Rasherhouse?".'

Ra, the [nickname, abbrev.]. Irish Republican Army (Provisionals). **1995** Sam McAughtry, *Sunday Tribune,* 27 Aug: 'Neither the Ra nor the army was much interested in the effects of the bombing. The game was the thing.'

Rats [pet name]. Mongrel dog which attached himself to Brit. army patrols around Crossmaglen (c1978). **1999** Tony Harnden, *'Bandit Country'*: 'At the end of the summer of 1979, a BBC television crew discovered Rats … The Army press office saw the attention on Rats as a way of promoting "good news" stories about the military presence in South Armagh.'

Raytown [<fishing assoc., nickname]. **Ringsend**, Dub. **1988** Vincent Caprani, *Cara*, 'Raytown', Mar-Apr: '… the locals have left the scholars to their disputations and have happily settled for the time-honoured appellation of "Raytown". That nickname pays affectionate tribute to their rich ancestry.'

Real IRA [<Irish Republican Army]. Dissident republican group. **1999** Tony Harnden, *'Bandit Country'*: '… the name "Real IRA" entered common usage when dissidents staged an illegal roadblock in Jonesborough in early 1998 and told motorists: "We're from the IRA. The real IRA".' **1999** Catherine Cleary, *Sunday Tribune,* 31 Oct: '… The Real IRA, or **Óglaigh na hÉireann**, as it increasingly refers to itself, is reported to have recruited around 100 members, including those who joined the **Continuity IRA** after the Provisional ceasefire.'

Real Taoiseach [nickname]. Jack Lynch (1917-99), **Taoiseach** 1966-1973 & 1977-1979. **1999** Mark Brennock, *Irish Times,* 21 Oct: 'Referring to Mr Lynch as "the *real* Taoiseach – as he was known in his native Cork whether in government or opposition – Mr [Bertie] Ahern spoke of his great feats of outstanding sportsmanship and unique personal charisma.' Hence **Lynchspeak. 1999** Joe Carroll, *Irish Times,* 21 Oct: 'His

modest, even diffident style of leadership, coupled with an ambiguity in the use of language dubbed "Lynchspeak", often lead to his achievements being underestimated or even dismissed.'

Rebel County, the/Rebels [nickname, < 'Rebel Cork', characterisation attrib. to the fact that the mayor of the city and his son were executed (1499) with Perkin Warbeck, pretender to Eng. throne]. Cork, esp. in GAA games context. Hence **Rebel County Lager** [brandname]. **2000** Breda Shannon, *Ireland of the Welcomes,* 'A Special Brew', May-Jun: Five brews are crafted here [the Franciscan Well Brewery, Cork] by Russel Grant: a distinctive *German Wheatbear; a Rebel County Lager* … a *Blarney Blond* … a *Round Tower Red Ale* … and a *Shandon Stout.'*

Red Cow Roundabout [junction M50/N70, Dublin]. Epitome of **DART** speech ('red kye ryndabyte') as exemplified by **Roadwatch** radio traffic bulletin.

Red Hand [heraldry]. The cognizance of the province of **Ulster**, a red hand *apaumée*, or facing forward. Adopted as political symbol of Unionism. **1939** James Joyce, *Finnegans Wake:* 'Gently, gently Northern Ire! Love that red hand!' Hence **Red Hand Defenders** Loyalist paramilitary org. **2000** Susan McKay, *Sunday Tribune,* 6 Feb: 'The protesters demanded that "the **free state** reporter" note down "the writing on the wall", which was all to do with the Red Hand Defenders, the UVF, the Young Citizens Volunteers, illustrated with big red Ulster fists, dripping blood.'

Rednecks see **Bogmen**

Red Square [Waterford/Port Láirge]. **2000** Chris Dooley, *Irish Times,* 14 Jun:

'Red Square in Waterford is no more –
but try telling that to residents of the
city. From now on, officially at least, the
top of the newly pedestrianised
Barronstrand Street is to be known as
John Roberts Square, in honour of the
18th century architect who designed
many of Waterford's most prominent
buildings. Business leaders are delighted
with the name, believing the Red
Square tag to have contributed to the
city's image as a hotbed of militant trade
unionism. The name had a much more
innocent origin, however, deriving
from the red paving stones placed in the
square more than a decade ago. It has
taken root, however, too firmly to
remove from common usage … At the
other end of the city centre you'll find
Times Square, so named when a clock
was erected at the site of the apple
market … Such names, says Mr [Jim]
Nolan, are the "poetry of the street".'

Ree Raw [nickname, <Ir. *rí-rá, rirá,*
hubbub, uproar]. (1) Dub. character.
1788 *Hibernian Magazine,* 'Luke Caffrey's
Ghost': 'Oh! De time-piece had cum to
de twelves,/De fardins burn'd blue in
deir sockets,/When Ree Raw and I be
ourselves/De bottle took out of our
pockets …' (2) [media]. Magazine. **2000**
Sue Carter, *Irish Times,* 17 May: '…
Smurfit now publishes a monthly magazine aimed at the 18- to 30-year-old
market. *Rí Rá* provides news, reviews,
features, listings and interviews to the
young Irish community in London …'

Regular Ireland [US]. Republic as dis-
tinct from NI. **2000** Liam Ó Muirthile,
Irish Times, 11 May: 'Skyblue martini atá
á ól sa tábhairne ag fear an chaipín base-
ball … Fiafraíonn sé "Are you from the
North of Ireland or from regular
Ireland?" Níl **irregular** gan bhrí fós in
Éirinn.' [The man in the baseball cap

was drinking Skyblue martini in the
pub. He asked … 'Irregular' is still not
without significance in Ireland].

Rehan, Ada [pseudonym]. Ada Crehan
(1860-1916), actress. **1988** Henry
Boylan, *A Dictionary of Irish Biography*
(2nd ed.): 'Born Limerick … She was
billed in Philadelphia as "Rehan" by a
printer's error, and retained the name.'

Reilly as in **Life of Reilly** Synonym for
excellence, success. **1968** John Healy,
The Death of an Irish Town: '… we
couldn't go wrong if we grew beef and
produced milk. And both by the ton,
and the job was Reilly.'

RGDATA [acronym; ex. of *multum in
parvo*]. Trade body. **1987** Enda McKay,
in Barbara Hayley and Enda McKay
(eds.), *Three Hundred Years of Irish
Periodicals:* 'In March 1943 the journal
[*Irish Grocer*] became "the mouthpiece
of the (recently formed) R.G.D.A.T.A.
– The Retail Family Grocers'
Purveyors' and Dairy Proprietors' and
Allied Trades Association.'

Rí [Ir., king]. Individual exercising
informal arbitratory powers, West of
Ireland. **1999** Kevin Whelan, 'An
Underground Gentry?' in J.S. Donnelly
jr. & Kirby Miller (eds), *Irish Popular
Culture 1650-1850:* 'The Rí regulated
internal customary practices and also
represented the community to the outside world. Frequently, the Rí was the
scion of an ancient landed family …'

Ribbonmen [nickname, <insignia of
organisation]. C19 anti-Protestant agrarian movement. **C19** Ballad, *The Battle of
Garvagh:* 'The day before the July fair/
The Ribbonmen they did prepare/For
three miles round to sack and tear/The
loyal town of Garvagh.'

Richardson, John Grubb Industrialist and founder (1845) of Bessbrook model village, Co. Ard Mhacha/Armagh, named after his wife Bess +brook <Camlough river or 'brook'. Hence [brandname] Fertiliser. **1999** Tony Harnden, *'Bandit Country'*: 'A few miles from the barn where the South Quay bomb was mixed, a mock advertisement declares "Richardson's Fertiliser. Tried and tested at home and abroad by P.I.R.A." [Provisional IRA – as bomb-making ingredient].'

Ridgid Tool [tradename]. **1998** Fergus Finlay, *Snakes and Ladders:* 'I had gone to work for an American multinational in Cork, a good company but with the unlikely name of Ridgid Tool. I counted it already among my achievements that I had persuaded them to change the name of the company, at least for the purpose of incoming phone calls, to Ridge Tool!'

Rightboys [nickname]. Secret agrarian soc. (c1785). Maureen Wall, 'The Whiteboys', in T. Desmond Williams (ed.), *Secret Societies in Ireland:* 'The third major outbreak of violence … seems to have started on the borders of Cork and Kerry – where people began taking an oath to obey Captain Right – hence the name Rightboys …'

Ringsend car [nickname, <Ringsend, Dub.]. One-horse hackney vehicle. **1847** John Edward Walsh, *Ireland Sixty Years Ago:* 'The earliest and rudest of these [one-horse vehicles] were the "Ringsend cars" so called from their plying principally to that place and Irishtown, then the resort of the *beau monde* …' See also **Raytown, Ringsend Uppercut**

Ringsend Uppercut [< Ringsend, Dub.]. Kick in the groin. **1991** John B.

Keane, *Love Bites and Other Stories:* 'the most devastating of all blows in the common street confrontation was the Ringsend Uppercut.'

Riordans, the see **Leestown**

Rí Rá see **Ree Raw**

Rising Pints, the see **Éirí na Gréine**

Riverdance [enter't]. Irish dance stage show. **1996** Fintan O'Toole, *The Ex-Isle of Erin*: '… it was, in racing parlance, by The Eurovision Song Contest out of James Flannery's production of W.B. Yeats's *Cuchulain Cycle* at the Abbey Theatre in 1989. It began life as the interval act at the Eurovision [30 Apr 1994] …' Hence **2000** Seán O'Driscoll, *Sunday Tribune,* 14 Apr: 'At present, there are (deep breath) three troupes of *Riverdance*, three of *Lord of the Dance*, as well as productions of *Feet of Flames, Dancing on Dangerous Ground, Gael Force, Rhythm of the Dance, Spirit of the Dance, Magic of the Dance, Celtic Feet, Celtic Fusion, Rhythm of the Celts* and *Wild Irish Feet,* and that's only a start …'

Riverrun [nonce word]. First word of James Joyce's novel *Finnegans Wake* (1939). Hence [*idem,* brandname]. (a) Paperback book series publ. Allen Figgis, Dub., (1960s), (b) Architect. Consultancy. **2000** Frank McDonald, *The Construction of Dublin:* 'Seán O'Laoire recalls putting forward the case for "competitive schools for middle class kids" after the Riverrun consortium was commissioned to draft the Docklands master plan …'

Roadwatch AA (Automobile Assoc.) traffic information broadcasts, RTÉ radio. Hence **Roadwatch accent**, as perceived to be employed by its presenters, characterised by pronun. of *ou* diph-thong. **2000** Tom Doorley, *Sunday Tribune*, 30 Jan: '… it would do much to stave off the pangs of hunger which had started in the vicinity of the celebrated (by AA Roadwatch) Kinsale Road *ryndabyte*.' See also **DART**; **Red Cow Roundabout**

Roaring Meg [nickname]. Siege gun, **Derry**. **1950** Richard Hayward, *Ulster and the City of Belfast:* 'In the Double Bastion [of the city walls] is that grand old cannon, *Roaring Meg*, which played such an important part during the siege [of 1690] …'

Rob Roy [rhyming sl.] Mountjoy jail, Dublin. **1997** Tom Widger, *Sunday Tribune:* 'Last week, Paddy [O'Gorman] was confronted with visitors to Dublin's Rob Roy.' See **Joy, the**

Róisín Dubh [Ir., 'Dark Rosaleen']. Personification of Ire., esp. in poem trans. by J. C. Mangan. Hence **Róisín** [naut.] Naval patrol vessel. **2000** Lorna Siggins, *Irish Times*, 28 Oct: 'The ship's name also proved to be contentious. The Minister [for Defence] departed from the recommended shortlist supplied to him from the Naval Service and chose *Róisín Dubh*, symbolising Ireland, but also the name of a good music pub in Galway. It was subsequently shortened to *Róisín* to suit international maritime communications requirements.'

Roman collar [< Roman Cath. priest's garb; nickname]. Over-generous head on pint of draught stout. **1966** Patrick Boyle, *At Night All Cats are Grey,* 'The **Metal Man**': 'We all sat watching Jonty put the Roman collars on the pints with a few skites of fresh porter from the barrel.'

Ronnie Delany [1935-, athlete]. Winner of 1500m. at Melbourne Olympics 1956. Hence **1998** Gene Kerrigan, *Another Country:* 'Anyone who ran fast, even for a bus, was called Ronnie Delany.' Also **do a Ronnie Delany**, travel rapidly.

Roscrea/Ros Cré [Co. Thiobraid Árann/Tipperary]. Hence [brandname] Meat products. **2000** Radio advt., May: 'Roscrea rashers and sausages – satisfy your Roscreaving!'

Rosenbach manuscript [<Abraham Rosenbach]. Ms of drafts of the 18 episodes of James Joyce's novel *Ulysses*. **2000** Terence Killeen, *Irish Times,* 10 Jun: 'The Rosenbach manuscript is so named after the Philadelphia book dealer and collector, Dr Abraham Simon Wolf Rosenbach, who acquired it in 1924 from the New York lawyer and art patron, John Quinn.'

Rossmore setter [<Rossmore Park, Co. Mhuineacháin/Monaghan]. Breed of dog. **1999** Jane Falloon, *Throttle Full Open:* 'Mary [Bailey] was also passionate about dogs, and photographs from her childhood show her surrounded by them. A type of setter, known as the Rossmore setter, was bred for many generations on the estate.'

Round the House and Mind the Dresser Trad. dance. **1997** Michael Hamilton, *Down Memory Line:* 'After a time some would take the floor for a half-set. "Mind the dresser" would ring out as a side plate often ran the risk of being dislodged …'

Royal College of St Canice [<patron saint of Kilkenny]. Third-level inst. **2000** Naoise Nunn, *Irish Times,* 5 Aug: 'A university, the Royal College of St

Canice, was briefly established by James II at Kilkenny College in 1689 ...'

Royal County, the [< Tara, former seat of kings/high kings]. Co. na Mí/Meath, esp. in GAA games context. **1996** Frank McNally, *Irish Times,* 12 Sep: 'Back in the 1950s and early 1960s, a government resettlement programme introduced farmers from the west to available land in Meath. Since then, there have been little pockets of the Royal County which are forever Mayo.'

Royal Irish Academy see **Neophilosophers**

RUC/Royal Ulster Constabulary NI police force (1922-). **1999** Suzanne Breen and Patsy McGarry, *Irish Times,* 1 Dec: 'The Progressive Unionist Party, the UVF's political wing, has said that renaming the RUC is "equivalent to changing Windscale to Sellafield or **Long Kesh** to the Maze."' **2000** Deaglán de Bréadún, *Irish Times,* 20 Jan:

'Early in the week it was being put about that the name of the RUC would be retained, in parallel with a new title such as the Northern Ireland Police Service ... No less than choosing names for children, picking titles for police forces is an activity with many pitfalls. Patten Commission members considered and rejected PSNI because of a fear that it would become known in common parlance as "Pizny". Mr Patten opted instead for the Northern Ireland Police Service, or NIPS, but heaven knows what fate that name would have suffered in the rough playground of common speech.' **2000** Peter Donnelly, *Irish Times,* 17 May: 'Sir – If "RUC" must appear in the name of Northern Ireland's new police force then, for peace sake, call the body "TRUCE".' **2000** Mary Kenny, *Irish Independent,* 27 May: 'Why should the Royal Ulster Constabulary have to change its name, when the Royal Irish Academy, and the Royal Dublin Society, are permitted to keep theirs without anyone objecting at all?'

S

Saint Patrick's Cross [heraldry]. **2000** Séamas Ó Brógáin, *Irish Times,* 16 Jun: 'Arthur Allshire (June 10th) writes: "What harm would there be if the flag of St Patrick was used on public buildings in the North – especially as this flag was born aeons before there ever was a border." Except that it wasn't. It was invented by Dublin Castle in the 17th century as a counterpart of St George's Cross. It was never used as a flag (except briefly by the **Blueshirts**), and has nothing whatever to do with St Patrick.'

Sally O'Brien [advt.]. Character created by Frank Sherwin for Guinness Harp TV advertising (1980s). **1999** *Irish Times:* '"… I learned more about mindsets in Northern Ireland from that poem than I ever learned at home or at school", stated Sara. Mrs O'Brien gave Sara a stare that bore no resemblance to Sally O'Brien-and-the-way-she-might-look-at-you.' **2001** Eddie Holt, *Irish Times,* 3 Mar: '… even long before "Sally O'Brien and the way she might look at you", drink, like almost everything else, was being flogged by advertisers as a deliverer of sex.' Hence **Sally O'Briens** [pub] (1) Thorncastle St., Dublin; (2) Moscow. **2000** Séamus Martin, *Irish Times,* 2 Jun: 'Mr Mark McDonagh, from Cratloe, Co. Clare, runs Sally O'Brien's, the larger of the two Irish-run pubs in the city.'

Sally Rod [<Ir. *saileach,* willow]. Instrument of chastisement. **1997** Ciaran Carson, *The Star Factory:* 'It occurs to me that "sally-rod" is Ulster rhyming slang for "**Prod**" i.e. "Protestant".'

Sally's Bridge [Dub.]. **1938** *Irish Times,* 13 Jun: 'The demolition of Parnell Bridge (commonly called Sally's Bridge) has been followed with the deepest interest by the locals … It is interesting to recall that this bridge was originally a toll bridge, the tolls being collected (when they were paid) by an old woman named Sally. Legend has it that she had a busy time intercepting officers from Portobello Barracks and "young men from Rathmines" …'

Sam [abbrev. of 'Sam Maguire', Gaelic sportsman and republic activist (d.1927); nickname]. The Sam Maguire Cup, trophy for annual All-Ireland Senior Football Championship (1928-). **2000** Martin Breheny, *Irish Independent,* 9 Dec: 'But tonight, when the achievements of the 145 medal winners are celebrated at the Mount Brandon Hotel, Tralee, Sam will be smiling down contentedly on all of them.'

Sam and Ella [< salmonella; media]. Cartoon characters to educate children in food hygiene. **2000** *Irish Times,* 6 Apr: 'The video recounts the adventures of two cartoon bugs – Sam and Ella – who start their life in the sewer, then travel into the bathroom and finally under unwashed fingernails.'

Samson and Goliath [nickname] Cranes, Harland & Wolff shipyard, Belfast. **1999** Mike Gerrard, *Independent on Sunday* (London), 19 Dec: 'As we drive out of the compact city centre Michael [Johnston] points out two huge yellow cranes over in the docks. "They are Samson and Goliath and they helped build the *Titanic* in 1911".' **2000** Róisín Ingle, *Irish Times,* 2 Aug: 'Norman also points out the famous Harland & Wolff cranes … They are called either Samson and Goliath or William and Harry depending on whether you prefer your references biblical or royal.'

Sanglier, Sir [attrib. name; lit.]. Shane O'Neill, chieftain (1530-67). **1583** Edmund Spenser, *The Faerie Queene*, Book V: 'It was not long before he overtooke/Sir Sanglier (so cleeped was that knight),/Whom at the first he ghessed by his looke,/And by the other markes which of his shield he tooke …'

San Patricio [Sp., Saint Patrick]. Hence (1) [brandname]. Sherry produced by Bodegas Garvey, Jerez de la Frontera, Spain. (2) **San Patricios** [milit.]. Ir. force in Mexican army. **2000** Con Howard, *Irish Times,* 16 Aug: 'Sir, the Society of St Brendan … joins the Mexican Government and people in their annual moving, impressive and colourful salute to the San Patricios – "the Irish soldiers of the heroic Battalion of St Patrick" – who fought for Mexico in the war of 1846-1848 against the US.'

Saor Éire [Ir., free Ireland; politic.]. Revolutionary organisation. **1967** Kevin B. Nowlan in Francis Mac Manus (ed.), *The Years of the Great Test 1926-39:* 'The Saor Éire organisation, with the influential backing in I.R.A. and radical labour circles, was established in 1931. Its programme was boldly socialist; to create "an independent revolutionary leadership of the working class and working farmers towards the overthrow in Ireland of British imperialism and its ally, Irish capitalism".'

Saorstát [<Ir. *Saorstát Éireann*, Irish **Free State**]. Employed occasionally in bilingual context. **1992** Mary C. Daly, *Industrial Development and Irish National Identity:* '… the Federation of Saorstát Industries collapsed, and efforts by the DIDA [Dublin Industrial Development

Association] to become a national protectionist lobby by changing its name to the National Agricultural and Industrial Development Association (NAIDA) in 1929 proved ineffective.' Also **Saorstát na hÉireann** [politic.]. **1976** Michael McInerney, *Eamon de Valera:* 'Two days later [on 14 July 1921] Lloyd George and de Valera began their historic talks. At their meeting de Valera suggested that the words Irish Republic could best be translated as "Saorstát na hÉireann". Lloyd George thought the name apt.'

Sassenach [<Ir. *Sasanach*, Eng. person; Protestant]. As thus, gen. derog. **1961** Dominic Behan, *Teems of Times and Happy Returns:* 'it's one thing announcing to all and sundry that you intend killing every Sassenach … but quite a different matter is the business of getting them within shooting distance.'

Saul Road [<Capt. J.P. (Paddy) Saul (1895-1968), navigator, *Southern Cross* transatlantic flight (June 1930)]. Dub. street. **1997** Michael Traynor, *Through the Clouds over Limerick and Beyond:* 'Two streets are named in his honour in Dublin – Saul Road and Southern Cross Avenue, something which Paddy was particularly proud of.' Also **Southern Cross Road**, Bray, Co. Chill Mhantáin/Wicklow.

Saxon Shilling [term of contempt]. Payment made to recruits in Ire. to the Brit. army. **1843** Kevin Buggy, *The Nation*, 15 Apr, 'The Saxon Shilling: Go – to leave on Indian soil/Your bones to bleach, accused unburied/Go – to crush the just and brave,/Worse wrongs with wrath the world are finning!/Go – to slay each brother slave - /Or spurn the blood-stained Saxon Shilling!'

Saygulls [<imit. pronun., *recte* 'seagulls'; nickname]. Coastwatching Volunteers

during the **Emergency**. **1999** Donal MacCarron, *'Step Together!':* 'The Saygulls were allowed to live at home, and their pay and conditions reflected this. They were given minimal military training, and were the butt of many jokes by comedians, and the fighting troops.'

Scalder [<? Nickname]. Native of Enniscorthy, Co. Loch Garman/ Wexford. **1994** Vonnie Banville-Evans, *The House in the Faythe:* 'I don't know why she felt that way. Probably because … she was an "Enniscorthy Scalder" among all the **Yellow-Bellies**".'

Scruffy Murphy's [<?]. Dub. pub. Hence **2000** Paul O'Kane, *Sunday Tribune*, 20 Feb: 'Irish bars were the hot ticket in the British pub scene in the mid-1990s as Ireland suddenly became trendy. The major pub operators rushed into the market, with chains such as O'Neill's, Scruffy Murphy's, Lafferty's and Finnegan's [sic] Wake …'

Seán Citizen Archetypical man in the street. **1977** Wesley Burrowes, *The Riordans:* 'Benjie and Gillian were found in a compromising position, changing out of clothes and provoking a phone call from my old friend Seán Citizen.'

Seceders [religious movement]. **1921** D.J. Owen, *History of Belfast:* 'There was also the "Presbyterian Synod of Ireland, distinguished by the name of Seceders", it having originated in 1818 by a union of associated Synods of burghers and anti-burghers.'

Setanta [myth]. Original name of Cúchulainn (see **Cú Uladh**). **2000** Dave Hannigan, *Sunday Tribune*, 10 Sep: '… any ball tracing its lineage back to Setanta and the Red Branch Knights is bound to provoke debate. When the

seven-year-old prodigy was confronted by the rabid hound at the gates of Culainn's smithy all those centuries ago, legend has it that the ball was made of solid silver. Setanta was renamed Cuchulainn and every sliotar [hurling ball] that came after gained a complex.'

Seville Place [Dub.] Street name (1821). **1955** J.L.J. Hughes, *Dublin Historical Record*, Sep: 'The only explanation I could find is a humorous one sent to the *Irish Builder* in 1882 by a correspondent signing himself "Drumcondrian". He wrote that since oranges come from Seville therefore Seville Place was either built or baptised by an Orangeman.'

Shades Club [<Shelta *séideog*, policeman]. Youth project. **2000** Éibhir Mulqueen, *Irish Times*, 24 Jun: 'Shades Club, one of a series of youth development projects in a socially-disadvantaged area of Limerick, was named after the gardaí who became involved in the inter-agency initiative. The selection of the name, a slang word in Limerick for gardaí, met with unanimous approval from the youngsters of Moyross …'

Sham Fight [politic.]. Annual Unionist festival, Scarva, Co. Ard Mhacha/ Armagh. **2000** Róisín Ingle, *Irish Times*, 14 Jul: 'King William III emerged victorious from a sword fight with King James II amid a hail of blank gunfire … The Sham Fight, as it is called, recalls the battle between the celebrated enemies who fought at the Boyne [1690] and is the high point of the day.'

Sham Squire [nickname]. Francis Higgins (1746-1802), lawyer and informer. **1988** Henry Boylan, *A Dictionary of Irish Biography* (2nd ed.): 'Born of poor parents … He became an attorney's clerk, converted to

Protestantism and, by posing as a landed gentleman, induced a lady of means to marry him.'

Shanavest [<Ir. *sean*, old + *bheist*, waistcoat; nickname]. Agrarian secret society (C18-19). **1824** R.H. Ryland, *History, Topography and Antiquities of the County and City of Waterford:* 'The Shanavests were called Paudeen Car's Party. Q. Why were they called Shanavests? A. Because they wore old waistcoats.'

Shankill Butchers [<Belfast location + brutal method of killings; nickname]. Loyalist murder squad. **1996** BBC Northern Ireland TV, *Newsline,* 28 Oct: 'Nearly all the 19 people murdered by the Shankill Butchers were Catholics. Most were tortured before being killed.'

Shan Van Vocht [<Ir. *sean bhean bhocht,* poor old woman]. Personification of Ire. **1798** Pop. ballad: 'Will Ireland then be free?/Said the Shan Van Voght [*sic*]/Yes Ireland shall be free/From the centre to the sea,/Hurrah for liberty!/Said the Shan Van Voght.' (2) *idem* [media] Periodical (first publ. 1896). **1988** R.F. Foster, *Modern Ireland 1600-1972:* 'The small but influential Irish feminist movement used Gaelicist channels too: through the journal *Shan Van Vocht* founded in Belfast by Alice Milligan and Anna Johnston ...'

Shanwick [<Shannon+Prestwick; aviation]. Joint North Atlantic control authority, with radio base in Ballgireen, Shannon. **2000** *Irish Air Letter,* Dec: 'A recent UK Air Accidents Investigation Branch (AAIB) Bulletin described an incident which occurred to British Airways Concorde G-BOAC on 25 May 1998 which well highlighted the cumbersome nature of HF communications with Shanwick Oceanic Control.'

Shea's Acres [<?]. Land measure. **2000** Flann Ó Riain, *Irish Times,* 16 Oct: 'Earlier measures of land included Burgage Acres, Great Acres, Irish Acres, Clanwilliam Acres and **Cunningham Acres**, but a 1782 lease in *The Inchiquin Manuscripts* concerning the land of Cahersherkin in the Co. Clare parish of Clooney, has a saving clause "for all Mines, Minerals and Shea's Acres".'

Sheila [also **Shela, Sheelah,** etc., Aust., (formerly Brit.) sl. <Ir. proper name *Síle*]. (1) Girl or young woman. **1828** *Monitor* (Sydney), 22 Mar: 'Many a piteous Shela stood wiping the gory locks of her **Paddy**, until released from that duty by the officious interference of the knight of the baton.' **1943** *Bulletin* (Sydney), 27 Oct: '"I wouldn't have cared if he'd been a good lookin' feller", lamented Bill, "but an ugly-looking cow like that beatin' a man to a sheilah".' (2) **Sheela** [nickname]. **1910** P. W. Joyce, *English as we speak it in Ireland:* 'Man or boy who takes an interest in affairs properly belonging to women.' (3) **Sheela na Gig** [Ir. *Síle na gcíoch,* <*síle,* effeminate person; *cíocha,* breasts]. C14-15 stone fetish representing a woman with displayed genitalia, poss. fertility symbol. **2000** Dick Hogan, *Irish Times,* 6 Dec: 'A Sheela na Gig being held in a crate at a Dúchas depot in Mallow should be returned to the community which is its rightful owner, a local development association has claimed.'

Shelbourne [Dub.]. Hotel. **1999** Rosita Boland, *Irish Times,* 20 Nov: 'The hotel was set up in 1824 by Martin Burke. He didn't think his own name was grand enough for the sort of hotel he wanted to establish, so he gave to it a name which had a historical connection with the hotel's site, adding a vowel in the process, from *Shelburne* [<William

Petty, 2nd Earl, b. Dub. 1737] to Shelbourne.' **2001** George Huxley, *Irish Times,* 17 Jan: 'The Shelbourne Hotel is a historical monument. Its name evokes much Irish history. The present owners, lacking a historical sense, propose to change the name to Meridien. The proposal is deplorable.' Hence [maritime] Sailing ship. **1992** John de Courcy Ireland, *Ireland's Maritime Heritage:* 'The celebrated Limerick firm of J.N. Russell and Sons both owned ships and built them locally. The largest sailing ship built at Limerick was the 372 tons wooden barque Shelbourne, which traded with the West Indies.'

Shelbourne University [see **Shelbourne**]. Bogus institution. **2001** Yvonne Healy, *Irish Times*, 23 Jan: 'She had been browsing the Internet, she said, and had discovered that she could gain a bachelor's degree in hotel management from the Shelbourne University in Dublin ... On the letterhead of the "university", its address was given as the Shelbourne Dublin Building, 27 St Stephen's Green – in fact, the Shelbourne Hotel.'

Shenanigan, Mr Justice [<US sl. *idem*, poss. <Ir. *sionnachuadh*, 'act of playing the fox, japing' (Dinneen) or Native Amer. or prop. Name 'Seán Hannigan', identity unknown]. (1) [advt.] **2000** *Radio commercial:* 'At this point Mr Justice Shenanigan said that anyone who booked a holiday without going to Limerick Travel needed not only their bank account examined but their head as well. This is Mary McMuckian at the Shenanigan Tribunal.' (2) [pub]. **Shenannigans**, Skerries, Co. Dublin.

Shinner [<*Sinn Féin*, nationalist movement/party, (1905-); nickname, gen. derog.] Applied to members of the party and it sympathisers; nationalists in general. **2000** Suzanne Breen, *Irish Times*, 10 Feb: 'There was hardly a Shinner in sight yesterday. Those party members who recently walked Stormont's grand marbled corridors as if they had been doing it all their lives were nowhere to be seen.'

Shook [nickname]. James Stephens (1825-1901), chief founder of the **Fenian** revolutionary movement. **1968** E.R.R. Green, in T.W. Moody (ed.), *The Fenian Movement:* 'Despite rumours flying about the country of the mysterious *Shook* or *Shooks* (variants of *seabhac siubhlach* [wandering hawk], the name given Stephens by O'Mahony of Bandon) the authorities did not realise for some time that they were dealing with a national organisation operating from Dublin.'

Short Kesh [nickname, play on **Long Kesh**]. Refugee accommodation. **2000** Seán MacConnell, *Irish Times*, 25 May: 'The 400 asylum-seekers expected in Athlone will probably not arrive until early next month ... A site which is being prepared for them just off the Athlone bypass has already earned the local nickname "Short Kesh".'

Shraft/Saraft/Shrass/Scraff [<Shrove]. Shrovetide; Shrove Tuesday. **1867** Patrick Kennedy, *The Banks of the Boro:* 'I was in Iniscorfy [Enniscorthy], you see, on Sraft [*sic*] Tuesday.'

Sick and Indigent Roomkeepers' Society [Dub.]. Charitable body. **1984** Mary E. Daly, *Dublin, the Deposed Capital:* 'The Sick and Indigent Roomkeepers Society was an eighteenth century institution of exclusively Dublin origin. Unlike the Society of St Vincent de Paul it was non-sectarian and had no moral or religious purposes.' (Often corrupted in demotic Dublinese to 'Sick and Indignant Roomkeepers …')

Sign of the Three Candles/ Candlesticks [<'*Trí caindle forosnat cách ndorcha: Fír, Aicnéd, Ecna*' ('Three candles that light up every darkness: Truth, Nature and Knowledge'); tradenames]. Printers/publishers. (1) **1958** Thomas Wall, *The Sign of* **Dr Hay's Head**: '[Patrick] Lord in this emergency [1755] apealed … to one "old Browne" who was no doubt Thomas Browne, the patriarch of Catholic printers who "at the Sign of the Three Candlesticks" in High Street had been for many years past quietly publishing religious books …' (2) **1928** Colm Ó Lochlainn, *Irish Book Lover,* May-Jun: 'In 1926 when I decided to set up my printing press in Fleet Street [Dub.], it gave me great joy to find that a large sign board hung outside the premises. This I took down and painted with the sign of the Three Candles …'

Silent Sister, The [<its poor C18 academic publishing/research record; nickname]. Trinity College Dublin. **1954** Oliver St John Gogarty, *It Isn't This Time of Year At All!:* 'Mahaffy was the best known of all the scholars whose industry had sent the fame of "The Silent Sister", as Dublin University was called in Oxford and Cambridge, over all the world.' **1928** R.B. McDowell & D.A. Webb, *Trinity College Dublin 1592-1952:* 'It was in this second quarter of the eighteenth century … that Trinity College earned for itself the nickname of the "Silent Sister", and although the reproach lived on long after it had ceased to be true, it was at this period deserved.'

Silk of the Kine [<Ir. Síoda na mBó, poem]. The fatted calf. **1936** Oliver St John Gogarty, *As I was Going down Sackville Street:* '"With the Silk of the Kine slaughtered, the slums increasing, and the cream of our youth transported by thousands, de Valera is about as good a nation-builder as an advocate of birth-control".'

Simon Pure [<? Nickname]. Good quality poteen [illicit whiskey]. **1908** Lynn Doyle, *Ballygullion:* 'Here's somethin'll console ye. This is the rale Simon Pure this time.'

Sin é [Ir. That is it]. New York pub. **2001** Shane Hegary, *Irish Times,* 17 Mar: 'Only in Sin é, the bar that famously acted as a magnet for the Morrisson and Donnelly Visa generation, does he [Gary Jermyn] find the Irish American he hopes for …'

Single-Speech Hamilton [nickname]. **1895** E. Cobham Brewer, *A Dictionary of Phrase and Fable* [new ed.]: 'The Right Hon. W.G. Hamilton, Chancellor of the Exchequer in Ireland, spoke one speech, but that was a masterly torrent of eloquence which astounded everyone (November 13th 1755).'

Six Counties/Six County [polit.]. Antrim, Armagh, Down, Fermanagh, Londonderry and Tyrone as constituting Northern Ireland. Gen. employed by those indisposed to recognise that entity. **1949** All-Party Anti-Partition Conference, *Ireland's Right to Unity:* 'The Six County area cut off in 1920 had never existed before as an entity in history or politics or economics. It was not **Ulster**, which is a province of nine counties. It had no natural boundaries. It had no unity within itself.'

Skelligs List [<Sceilig/Skellig Is., Co. Chiarraí/Kerry]. Anonymous defamatory

verses which were circulated annually. **1976** Des Lavelle, *Skellig:* 'Skellig Lists ... some of them containing up to forty verses – humorous, satirical, vicious – were common throughout **Munster** from Dingle to Cork for at least the past 140 years ...'

Skibbereen [An Sciobairín. Co. Chorcaí/Cork]. Village. Hence (1) [media]. **Skibbereen Eagle** Local newspaper. **1895** E. Cobham Brewer, *A Dictionary of Phrase and Fable* (new ed.): 'It was the *Skibbereen,* or *West Cork Eagle* newspaper, that solemnly told Lord Palmerston that it had "got its eye both upon him and on the Emperor of Russia".' **2000** Breda O'Brien, *Irish Times,* 10 Jun: '... I heard the researcher ask about RTÉ news. In his innocence, the researcher had wandered into a household where the *Skibbereen Eagle*'s eye on Russia would be as nothing compared to this home's eye on RTÉ.' (2) [transport] **Skibbereen Perseverance** Stage coach. **1843** W.M. Thackeray, *The Irish Sketch-Book:* 'That light four-inside four-horse coach, "the Skibbereen Perseverance", brought me fifty-two miles today, for the sum of three-and-sixpence ...'

Skin-the-Goat [<? nickname]. James Fitzharris, car driver involved in the assassination of Brit. officials Burke and Cavendish by the **Invincibles** (1882). **1996** Éamonn Mac Thomáis, RTÉ Radio (rebroadcast), 6 Feb: 'James Fitzharris was known as Skin-the-Goat, but you wouldn't call him that to his face. Though you could call him Skin. For some reason he didn't mind that.'

Slán Abhaile [Ir., safe home; tradename]. Chauffeur service. **2000** *Irish Independent,* 9 Dec: 'Others have positively benefited from the [taxi] dispute.

Slán Abhaile, the group that drives you and your car home if you've had a few drinks, has been overwhelmed by enquiries.'

Slieve Donard Coat see **Ulster**

Slow, Lazy and Never Comfortable [nickname]. Railway. **1941** Sean O'Faolain, *An Irish Journey:* 'In body I went on the SL and NC Railway, which is supposed to mean Sligo, Leitrim and North *(recte* Northern*)* Counties, but which is locally, more accurately, interpreted as the Slow, Lazy and Never Comfortable.'

Slua Sí [Ir., fairy host]. Russian trad. group. **2000** Seamus Martin, *Irish Times,* 3 May: 'Slua Sí, or *Voinstvo Sidov,* as they style themselves in Russian, is now the foremost group among the traditionalists, and its equivalent on the progressive side is Sídhe Mhór.'

Small Nation, the [media]. Organ of Irish Self-Determination League of Australasia (1921-). **1987** Patrick O'Farrell, *The Irish in Australia:* 'The league sought, fairly successfully, to absorb the various small Irish groupings in a large movement, had strong American links, and published a journal, *The Small Nation.'*

Smithfield (1) Belfast. **1993** Marcus Patton, *Central Belfast: An Historical Gazeteer:* '... this was a rectangular square between Castle Lane, Millfield, North Street and Royal Avenue. It was laid out in July 1788 in an area at the end of Berry Street known as "The Rails", to replace the markets held till then in the High Street. It may have been named after the London meat market, but there is a record of John Gregg leasing "grazing for two cows" at

"Smith's Field" in the early 18c.' (2) Dub. **1999** Noel Keating, *Irish Times,* 31 Dec: 'I read with great pleasure your article on the rejuvenation of Smithfield plaza … You quote the words used by the architect … followed by a reference to the original Irish name for this part of Dublin – Margadh na Feirme (the Farm Market). Would not this have been an opportunity to restore the original name to this central part of Dublin rather than retaining an imperial import?'

Snail Box, The [<?] Pub. **2000** *Irish Times*, 23 Mar: 'The remains [two skulls] … had been found by workmen digging a trench for a septic tank beside The Snail Box Pub, near Kilmoon Cross, north of Ashbourne (Co. Meath).'

Soda Cakes [<second siege of Limerick (1691); nickname]. Inhabitants of the Thomondgate area. **1998** Criostóir O'Flynn, *There is an Isle:* '… the garrison of a small outpost on the Clare side of Thomond Bridge were supplied at their posts with soda bread baked by the natives of that area.'

Soldiers of Destiny [politic.]. Pop. mistranslation of **Fianna Fáil**; gen. mildly derog. **2000** Miriam Lord, *Irish Independent,* 1 Jul: 'Midnight at the oasis, and the exhausted Soldiers of Destiny put their camels to bed. A merciful relief … It has been a long, parched crawl through the final miles of a cruel political desert for the Government.'

Soldiers of the Rearguard [nickname]. 26th (Old IRA) Battalion recruited for service in the **Emergency**. **1961** Dominic Behan, *Teems of Times and Happy Returns:* 'I should really say a word or two about the "Soldiers of the Rearguard" … This force was composed of men who had fought in the Easter Rising and the War of Independence, and the average age must have been about fifty …'

Sonas [tradename]. Unsuccessful development co. **2000** Justine McCarthy & Jerome O'Reilly, *Irish Independent,* 10 Jun: 'In 1996, the project suffered a major set-back when the rainbow coalition formally decided not to introduce legislation permitting casino gambling … It must surely be the final irony for Roy Dixon and his fellow directors that they put such careful thought into the chosen name for their project from the outset. The Irish word *sonas* is supposed to mean "luck, happiness".'

Soodlum [nickname]. Street character. **1940** Robert Gahan, *Dublin Historical Record,* Mar: 'It was in Francis Street that he was born, his real name being Healy; doubtless he would have preferred being so called, but the children of Dublin decreed otherwise, and when they bestowed the name of Soodlum upon him, Soodlum he had to be, and the name went with him to the grave.'

Sourface [nickname]. Protestant, or those exhibiting perceived Prot. characteristics. **1995** Patrick Maume, *D.P. Moran:* 'Moran gazed at the long faces in the [Rathmines, Dub.] tram, ostentatiously sorrowing for the dead queen [Victoria] and coined his most famous nickname: "Sourface". Ostensibly, "Sourface" stood for a particular affectation of superiority, and Moran repeatedly denied it meant "Protestant". It was sometimes applied to Catholic Unionists, but such people were called "Catholic Sourfaces" …'

Southern Cross [astronom.]. The constellation of *Crux Australis*, employed as symbol on Aust. Flag. Hence (1) [transport]. See **Saul Road**. (2) [media]. **Southern Cross, the** Ir-Argentine newspaper, Buenos Aires (1875-). **1975** Liam Cosgrave (**Taoiseach**), *Southern Cross,* Número del Centenario [centenary issue]: 'For one hundred years The Southern Cross has been the sole newspaper in Argentina – indeed throughout Latin America – which has catered specifically for the descendants of the many Irish immigrants who have made their homes in Argentina.' (3) *Idem.* [transport]. E-W motorway S. of Dub. **2000** Frank McDonald, *The Construction of Dublin:* 'The Southern Cross section of the M50, linking Firhouse with Sandyford, was approved in August 1992 ... and should have been open to traffic by the end of 1997.' *(It was not.)*

South Pole, the Pub, Annascaul, Co. Chiarraí/Kerry, named by Tom Crean, who accompanied E.H. Shackleton (1874-1922) on his 1914 Antarctic expedition. **1999** Maureen Keane, *RTÉ radio* 'Sunday Miscellany', 19 Dec: 'When Tom Crean got back to Annascaul he opened a pub, called it the South Pole and never left it again till he died in 1938.'

Soyer [<Alexis Benôit Soyer (1809-58), French chef]. Soup devised as famine relief for the Irish poor at a cost of £1 per 100 gallons. **1847** Anon. (?) James Clarence Mangan *A Vision of Connaught in the Nineteenth Century:* 'But neither of bones/Nor of juicy meat/Could I ever the faintest perfume smell./A greasy slime/The water appears/As Soyer, the great enchanter, knows ...'

Sparrow [< *Sp[anish]* +*Arrow*, service mark of **Iarnród Éireann** Dub. outer suburban rail service]. Spanish-built Arrow units. **1999** *Railway Preservation Society of Ireland Newsletter,* Nov: 'Based

in **Connolly** during the summer, the locomotive is likely to return to Inchicore for the winter months, especially now that space is at a premium with the arrival of the new Sparrow diesel DMUs [diesel mechanical units].'

Spike, the [nickname]. Proposed 'Monument of Light' for O'Connell St., Dub. **2000** John Kelly, *Ireland on Sunday,* 16 Jul: 'The man who spiked the "Spike" in the middle of O'Connell Street with a successful High Court action has now launched an attack on the newly released Environmental Impact Statement (EIS) ... The court ordered that after public consultation, Environment Minister Noel Dempsey should make the decision on the hypodermic-like "spike".'

Spud [< 'murphy', sl. name for potato; nickname]. Applied to male individual with surname 'Murphy'. **1949** Tom Barry, *Guerilla Days in Ireland:* 'Immediately the action started I sent Jim Murphy (Spud) and eleven riflemen to reinforce Kelleher.' See also **Murphia**

Squad, the [nickname]. Assassination unit in War of Independence (1919). **1990** Tim Pat Coogan, *Michael Collins:* 'The Squad was a group of assassins, a specially-selected hit-squad directly under Collins' orders.' See also **Big Fella**; **Twelve Apostles**

Stab City [<reputation for violence]. Limerick. **2000** Eibhir Mulqueen, *Irish Times,* 29 Jan: 'But any negativity stemming from *Angela's Ashes* is benign compared to the "Stab City" nickname, which appears to stem from Christmas 1982, when there were three unconnected murders in Limerick, one of them a Libyan student ... *Scrap Saturday,* the former satirical radio programme, is blamed for popularising it.'

Starry Plough [heraldry]. Flag of the Citizen Army, Labour party strike force (1913-). **1940** *Irish Times,* 1 Apr: 'Sean O'Casey, who was associated with the Citizen Army in its early years, took the title of his play "The Plough and the Stars" from its banner the Starry Plough. He returns to that inspiration in his recent play, "The Star Turns Red".'

State, the [<Irish **Free State**; abbrev.]. NI usage. **1999** Theresa Judge, *Irish Times,* 12 Mar: 'Now, ironically, children from "the State" – as the Republic is termed – are coming to Cashel [Co. Fermanagh] community hall for Irish dancing classes every weekend.'

Statue, the [Cork city]. Memorial to Fr Mathew, temperance advocate (1790-1856) by J. H. Foley. **2000** Dick Hogan, *Irish Times,* 4 Jul: '"The Statcha" is on the move ... Father Mathew is to be uprooted and moved further down the street, nearer to Winthrop Street, as part of the modernisation and rejuvenation of tired old St Patrick's Street ... "The Statcha", in Cork parlance, is much more than a memorial, it has deeper connotations than that. Visitors were told to take their bearing from the statue when catching buses or waiting to be collected.' *(The move was subsequently rescinded.)*

Steelboys/Hearts of Steel Agrarian secret society, Ulster (1770s). **1921** D. J. Owen, *History of Belfast:* '... it was the body of "Steelboys", or "Hearts of Steel" that became notorious in Ulster, where a grievance existed in connection with the estate of the Marquis of Donegall (an absentee landlord) ...' **1895** Quoted J.A. Froude, *The English in Ireland:* '"Petition of those persons by the name of Hearts of Steel. That we are all Protestants and Protestant

Dissenters ... That we who are all groaning under oppression, and have no other possible way of redress, are forced to join ourselves together to resist.'

Stephen's Green Club Dub. (1837-). **1990** Cornelius F. Smith, in Cornelius F. Smith & Bernard Share (eds), *Whigs on the Green:* 'The omission of "Saint" from the Club's name had little to do with ecumenism. The Dublin street directories all were "un-sainted" at that time.'

Stick/Stickie [nickname <adhesive on identity badge]. Member of the Official Sinn Féin, following the split leading to the formation of the Provisionals [see **Provies**] (1970). **1995** Tim Pat Coogan, *The* **Troubles***:* 'The Provisionals, also known as the "Provos", "Provvies" and, sometimes, "Pinheads", used to fix their labels to their lapels with pins. The Officials used gum ...'

Stolen Railway, the [nickname]. Parsonstown & Portumna Bridge Rly (1868-1878). **1976** K.A. Murray & D. B. McNeill, *The Great Southern & Western Railway:* 'When the lease expired in 1878 ... the other creditors now set out to pay themselves. Looting began; everything portable was taken – the timber station building at Portumna Bridge disappeared in a single night ... Today, the "Stolen Railway" may be traced by the course of its overgrown earthworks, monuments to the optimistic hopes of those who built it.'

Street, The [<Ir. *sráid,* level ground around a house, hence 'the dogs on the street', canines slow in comprehension]. Airside retail development, Dub. airport. **2000** *Irish Times,* 26 Apr: 'A shopping mall to rival any other will open at Dublin airport in the late summer ...

The new mall will be called "The Street" and 400 sq. m. of retail space on The Street are now up for grabs.'

Stroke City [nickname <forward slash between Derry/Londonderry]. **2000** Róisín Ingle, *Irish Times,* 18 Nov: '[Gerry] Anderson wrung the whole debacle out of his system in a book, *Surviving in Stroke City* (1999), his widely recognised nickname for Derry.' See also **Derry/Londonderry**

Substitution of Service, the [legal]. **1895** E. Cobham Brewer, *A Dictionary of Phrase and Fable* (new ed.): 'Instead of serving a process personally, the name of the defaulter was posted on the walls of a Catholic chapel in the parish or barony, or in some other public place.'

Sugar Island [Newry, Co. an Dúin/Down]. **2000** Tony Canavan, *Inland Waterways News,* Autumn: 'By 1769, the channel to Carlingford Lough had been deepened to accommodate bigger ships, making Newry an international port handling French wine, Baltic timber and West Indies sugar, giving the town's Sugar Island its name.'

Suite [Fr., continuation; lit.]. Short story by Samuel Beckett. **2000** John Banville, *Irish Times,* 29 Apr: 'The first story he wrote in French was called, typically for Beckett, "La Fin" (The End). Its original title was "Suite"... Beckett began writing it in English, but after 29 handwritten pages he drew a line a third of the way down the page – surely one of the most significant dividing lines in 20th-century literature – and continued on in French.'

Swaddler [poss. < 'the babe in swaddling clothes' referred to by a Methodist and overheard by a Dub. priest; nickname

(1745-)]. Methodist; Protestant; Catholic who converts for material benefit. **1922** James Joyce, *Dubliners,* 'An Encounter': 'and so we walked on, the ragged troop screaming after us *"Swaddlers! Swaddlers!"*, thinking that we were Protestants.'

Swastika [tradename]. Dub. laundry. **1983** Niall Quinn, *Voyovic, Brigitte* and *other stories*: '... one day in my formative years I stood sheltered under the mothering arms of Mrs Woolfson as the silent, electric van of the Swastika Laundry crept ... past the concrete air raid shelters in the middle of the road.' **2000** Eileen Battersby, *Irish Times,* 20 Jul: 'Kavanagh senior drove a van. "He worked for the Swastika Laundry" he says and mentions the chimney stacks which bore the company trademark which, he points out "was a sun symbol before the Nazis ever adopted it. It's a wonder the chimneys didn't confuse the German pilots in thinking they were back at home".'

Sweep, the [abbrev; nickname]. Irish Hospital Sweepstakes (1930-) **1996** David Hanly, *Sunday Tribune,* 3 Nov: 'You will remember the Lottery's predecessor ... once a part of our culture. The "Sweep" made some families fabulously wealthy (and the winners didn't do too badly either).' See **Irish Swoop**

Sweetie [nickname]. Charles J. Haughey (1925-), politician & **Taoiseach** (1979-81, 1982 & 1987-1992); popularised by his lover Terry Keane in her *Sunday Independent* gossip column. **1999** Brenda Power, *Sunday Tribune,* 16 May: '... no other publication, nor commentator, nor rival columnist dared to expand upon what Keane announced each week. A profile of her in *In Dublin* in the late 80s appeared without so much as a glancing reference to Sweetie.'

Swift [tradename; transport]. Fast passenger vessels, Grand Canal. **1968** Harold W. Hart, *Dublin Historical Record,* Jan: 'The "Swift" boats were established in June 1835 for daytime travel, during a period when marked reductions were being made in passenger fares, road competition then being strong.'

Swing [nickname]. Street character. **1940** Robert Gahan, *Dublin Historical Record,* Mar: 'One has to follow Swing for a little while to discover just why he is so named. As he approaches a street corner ... there is a shout of "Swing, you devil, Swing!" and the advice is taken by our friend, who swings his stick in a circle in the hope of striking one of his tormentors ...'

Synge-song [on analogy of 'sing-song', <J.M. Synge, playwright (1871–1909), gen. derog.]. Perceived characteristic of his writing style. **2000** Leo Daly, *Ireland of the Welcomes*, May-Jun: 'Despite the perpetual Synge-song of summer schools and recent Celtic Aran Renaissance activity, the new Leachta [sic] Cuimhne [cenotaph] at Cill Éinne received little notice from the media ...'

System see **Patent**

T

Taca/TACA [<Ir. *idem.*, prop, support; freq. capitalised as if an acronym]. Fund-raising scheme for **Fianna Fáil** (1960s-70s). **2000** Sam Smyth, *Irish Independent,* 1 Jul: '… businessmen discreetly lined up to contribute money to the party via the Taca organisation … Opening Taca to the great unwashed was the beginning of the end and the discreet little club of movers and shakers faded into oblivion.' Hence **Tacateer** [nonce-word]. **2000** Dick Walsh, *Irish Times,* 1 Apr: 'And you could always find a commentator or two to take the side of the po-faced crowd maundering on about the national interest when what was really at stake was the profits of Tacateers.'

Tallaght Strategy [<Tallaght, Co. Átha Cliath/Dublin; polit.]. Policy pronouncement at this location (1987). **1998** Fergus Finlay, *Snakes and Ladders:* 'Alan Dukes and **Fine Gael** had, in our view, opted out of opposition altogether. Dukes had declared, in a speech which came to be known as the "Tallaght strategy", that he would not oppose just for the sake of it.' **2000** Medb Ruane, *Irish Times,* 5 May: 'The Tallaght Strategy initiated by Alan Dukes reframed the economic crisis by creating a cross-party political consensus … A Tallaght Strategy for the immigration, asylum-seeker and refugee issue cannot be modelled on that template.'

Tánaiste [Ir. *idem., '*second, next, substitute' (Dinneen); tanist]. Deputy Prime Minister. **1937** *Bunreacht na hÉireann/ Constitution of Ireland,* 6.1.2: 'The

Tánaiste shall act for all purposes in the place of the **Taoiseach** if the Taoiseach should die, or become permanently incapacitated …' **1937** *Irish Times,* 3 May: 'I also seem to remember that the ancient Tanist had to be "tall, noble and free from blemish". And if these qualifications are to be obligatory for our Deputy Prime Minister, I can foresee a possibility of trouble. When they said "free of blemish" in those days, they meant it.'

Tans see **Black and Tans**

Taoiseach [Ir. *idem.,* 'chief, head, leader or prince' (Dinneen)]. Prime Minister. **1937** *Bunreacht na hÉireann/Constitution of Ireland,* 13.1.1: 'The President shall, on the nomination of Dáil Éireann appoint the Taoiseach, that is the head of Government or Prime Minister.' **1937** *Irish Times,* 3 May: 'The pity is, of course, that pretty well everybody will prefer the humdrum expressions "President" and "Prime Minister" to the euphoniousness of "Uachtarán" and "Taoiseach".' Hence **Teflon Taoiseach** [<brand of resistant plastic material; nickname]. Bertie Ahern, Taoiseach (1997-). **2000** 'Drapier', *Irish Times,* 29 Jan: 'The Denis Foley development shows yet again that if there is any threat to this Teflon Taoiseach it is likely to come from one or other, or both, of the tribunals.'

Tariff Commission [polit.]. Govt. body instituted to implement economic protection policy (1926). **1992** Mary C. Daly, *Industrial Development and Irish National Identity, 1922-1939:* 'While the Tariff Commission remained in existence until 1938, its sole task was the comic-opera function of deciding whether to protect prayer books, a task completed in 1934.'

Tá Sé's [Ir., it is]. (1) [nickname]. First (Ir.-speaking) Battalion, Ir. army. **1973** Noël Conway, *The Bloods*: 'Among those who had come to say "good-bye" to the "Bloods" at this time [1940] was Lt. Seán Collins, who had come to the Battalion a decade earlier from the "Tá Sé's".' (2) **Taw Shay** [nickname, derog.]. Enthusiastic but incompetent learner/speaker of Irish. See **Law Braw**

Tá Tú [Ir., you are]. Pub. **2000** Chris Heaney, *Irish Times*, 2 Dec: '"Belfast's got the buzz" – this supremely memorable and naff slogan of yore has, in fact, never been truer, as a quick tour of new designer bars and restaurants will testify, with places like Tá Tú and Apartment now offering alternatives to a pint 'n' pie in the Crown.'

Tay Pay [<Hib.E. pronun. of initials]. T[homas] P[ower] O'Connor (1848–1929), journalist and politician. **1922** James Joyce, *Ulysses*: '... Paddy Hooper worked with Tay Pay who took him on to the *Star*.' Hence **T.P.'s Weekly** [media]. Literary paper (1902-4). **Nd** P. & B. Rowan, Belfast, *Books and Periodicals of Irish Interest*, Cat. 50B: 'In 1887 he founded "The Star" with the innovative object of creating a radical paper with the "human touch", and followed it with "The Sun" in 1893. This non-political weekly is however the most important of his publishing enterprises.'

Teflon Taoiseach see **Taoiseach**

Teig/Taig/Teague [<Ir. *Tadhg*, proper name; nickname & adj., gen. derog.]. Irishman; [Ulster] Roman Catholic. **1718** John Durant Breval, *The Play is the Plot*: 'CARBINE Thou has the brogue a little sure. JEREMY As well as any Teague of em all Sir, if that can do your honour

any kindness.' Hence **Teagueland** [nickname; derog.] Ireland. **1984** Liz Curtis et al., *The Same Old Story*: 'The Joe Miller book of "Teagueland Jests and Bog Witticisms", published in 1789, was prefaced with the words: "The bulls and witticisms that too frequently drop from Irish mouths has made them the discourse and entertainment in all sorts of companies. Nothing more recommends Teague and his countrymen than their national stupidity".'

Tel-el-Kebir [<battle between Brits. & Egyptians (1882); brandname; Dub.]. Dairy. **2000** Patrick Comerford, *Irish Times*, 9 May: 'His [Sir Garnet **Wolseley**'s] victory at Tel el-Kabir [*sic*] earned him a peerage from Gladstone and gave an exotic name to a Dublin dairy, the TEK.'

TempleBrau [<Temple (Bar), Dub. + Germ. *brau*, brew, brewery; brandname]. Beer. **2000** Breda Shannon, *Ireland of the Welcomes*, 'A Special Brew', May-Jun: 'Peter Mosley, the head brewer at The Porterhouse, produces eight brews: *TempleBrau* is a well-defined sharp pilsner ... Then there's *Chiller*, a refreshing American-style beer ... *An Brainblasta* – [Ir. *An Braon Blasta*, the tasty drop] suitably named for its heavyweight 7% strength – is perhaps best avoided by those of us who don't suffer hangovers gladly.'

Terry Alts [<?]. Agrarian secret society, related to **Whiteboys**, Co. Thiobraid Árann/Tipperary (1830s). **1999** Robert Graham, *The Irish Journals of Robert Graham of Redgorton, 1835-1838*: 'The peasantry have rough and unpleasant manners and at several places they turned out and jeered at the driver of His Majesty's mail car which he tried to turn off as a joke, calling them Terry Alts.'

The Edge [stage name]. Dave Evans (1961–) lead guitarist with **U2**. **1993** Dave Bowler & Bryan Dray, *U2:* 'Dave Evans was given an honorary name, The Edge, chosen by **Bono** after a hardware store that he would pass on his way into the city [of Dub.]. The name was apparently chosen because it matched the shape of his head ...' **2000** Eddie Holt, *Irish Times,* 4 Mar: 'It's ironic that some of these big names are, literally, such small names. Bono and Edge appeared. Though cool and cutting edge 20 or more years ago ... these single, four-letter names have dated now.'

The Hot Irishman [brandname]. Drink mix. **2000** Ella Shanahan, *Irish Times,* 29 May: 'The Hot Irishman is the brainchild of former computer executive Mr Bernard Walsh and his wife Rosemary. The reaction to this Irish coffee mix has been "super", he reported.'

These Islands [polit./geog]. Ire. & Britain. **1992** John de Courcy Ireland, *Ireland's Maritime Heritage:* 'It [Harland & Wolff] is still the largest, most innovative and most successful shipyard in what we like to refer to as "these islands".' **2000** Dick Hogan, *Irish Times,* 21 Aug: 'The fact that the Merriman Summer School was able to discuss "these islands" as a viable region was an indication of how greatly the political and cultural environment had changed in the last 20 years.'

Thesiger, Captain [lit.]. Character in E. OE. Somerville and Martin Ross, *The Real Charlotte* (1894) who subsequently reappears as **Captain Cursiter**. **1999** 'Sadbh', *Irish Times,* 20 Nov: '"When we were going through the text of *The Real Charlotte*, we discovered that one of the minor characters – who appears sailing up and down the lake in

chapter three – reappeared on the lake in chapter nine with a different name", says [publisher] Tony Farmar, with a hint of glee in his voice.'

The Thinking Man [advt.]. Character created by Kapp & Peterson, Dub., and embodied (early C20) in slogan 'The Thinking Man smokes a Peterson's pipe'.

Thing, the see **Tomb of the Unknown Gurrier**

Thin Lizzy [<character in comic *The Beano* (UK)<nickname, 'Tin Lizzie', of early Ford car.] Pop group. **1991** Nuala O'Connor, *Bringing It All Back Home:* 'In March 1973 ... an Irish single went into the English charts and reached number six. The singer was Phil Lynott, an Irishman born in England of an Irish mother and a Brazilian father. The band was Thin Lizzy.'

Thirteen [numismatics]. **1895** E. Cobham Brewer, *A Dictionary of Phrase and Fable* (new ed.): 'A thirteen is an Irish shilling, which, prior to 1825, was worth 13 pence, and many years after that date, although reduced to the English standard, went by the name of "thirteen".'

Thoroughbred County [<equine associations; nickname/tradename]. Co. Chill Dara/Kildare. **1999** Colman Cassidy, *Irish Times,* 16 Nov: 'Kildare has adopted the horse as its official logo by assuming a new identity as the "thoroughbred county". The brand image was officially introduced yesterday by the Minister for Finance, Mr McCreevy, at his Straffan home.'

Three Fs [polit.]. Policy of Land League (1880s). **1966** J.C. Beckett, *The Making of Modern Ireland 1603-1923:* '... the bill that he [Gladstone] introduced in April [1881] virtually conceded the basic demands of the Land League agitation, popularly known as the "three Fs": fair rent, to be assessed by arbitration; fixity of tenure, while the rent was paid; freedom for the tenant to sell his right of occupancy at the best market price.'

Tibb's Eve [<'St Tibb's Eve', evening of the last day, Day of Judgement]. Day that will never come. **1944** Francis MacManus, *Pedlar's Pack:* "'Do you know you could keep running from this until Tibb's Eve without striking Christian country!'"

Tiger Roche [nickname]. Dub. 'buck' (b. 1729]. **1988** Henry Boylan, *A Dictionary of Irish Biography:* 'Killed a watchman in a drunken riot, fled to North America and fought with the French against the Indians. Accused of stealing a fowling-piece from a brother-officer, convicted at a court-martial and dismissed the service in disgrace. Attacked his guard with such ferocity he was called "Tiger".'

Tim [Scots. <Ir. *Tadhg*, proper name, see **Teig**; nickname]. **2000** Pat McGoldrick, *Irish Times,* 10 Jan: '... I was becoming increasingly agitated, especially as some of the Rangers players had heard there was a "Tim" (Celtic fan/Catholic/Irishman) in their midst and were giving me some good-natured stick.'

Times Square see **Red Square**

Tintawn [<Ir. *tinteán,* hearth, as in *níl aon tinteán mar do thinteán féin*, there's no hearth like your own hearth; brand-name). Sisal carpeting. **2000** Terry Prone, *Irish Times,* 21 Oct: 'In my teens I had the whole thing worked out ... We might not be much economically,

but look at Tintawn. Tintawn was a gruesome distant cousin of carpeting. It had the sensual appeal of a distressed sack, but it resonated with self-sufficiency and frugal patriotism.'

Tintown [<corrugated iron construction; nickname]. Prison camp, The Curragh, Co. Chill Dara/Kildare, used by the Brits during the War of Independence and subsequently by the **Free State** in the Civil War; internment camp for over 500 suspected IRA activists during WWII. **1973** Noël Conway, *The Bloods*: 'some 80 Bloods had been attached to the Engineers to assist in building the internment camp, later to be known as Tintown.'

Tipperary [Tiobraid Árann, Co. & town]. Hence (1) [Song] 'It's a Long Way to Tipperary', popular Brit. army song (World War I). **1940** *Irish Times,* 12 Sep: '"Tipperary" was not a war song, though it became famous through the war, but it was popular at least a year before August, 1914.' (2) [*idem.,* brand-name]. Cheese manufactured by Dairygold Food Products, Mitchelstown (also Tipperary Spring Water and other products). (3) **Tipperary boys** Irish-Aust. insurrectionists. **1987** Patrick O'Farrell, *The Irish in Australia:* 'A branch of O'Connell's Repeal Association was formed in Sydney 1842 and the elections of the following year – the first elections in the colony – saw "Tipperary boys" (a curiously constant phenomenon in Australian public history) on the rampage.' (4) **Tipperary lawyer** [sl.] Cudgel. (5) **Tipperary fortune** [sl.]. Breasts, pudenda and anus. **1811** Captain (Francis) Grose, *A Dictionary of Buckish Slang, University Wit and Pickpocket Eloquence:* 'Two townlands, stream's town, and ballinocrack, said of Irish women without fortune.' (6)

Tipperary Gully [Aust.] **1987** Patrick O'Farrell, *The Irish in Australia:* 'Take the Bungaree-Dunnstown area just out of Ballarat, with its economy of potato growing, and its reputation, into the 1940s, of being "Tipperary Gully", "wild Irishman country"…'

Tirconnell/Tyrconnell [Ir. *Tír Conaill*, land of Conall (Gulban), ancestor of O'Donnell family of Donegal]. Former name of Donegal. Hence (1) **The Tyrconnell** [brandname] malt whiskey. **1999** Advt: 'In 1876 the Watt Family entered a horse appropriately named "The Tyrconnell" in the Irish class, "The Queen Victoria Plate" horse race. Incredibly it won at 100-1 odds. The event went into racing folklore and the company celebrated the event with a special commemorative label. The same name lives on today in this fine whiskey.' (2) **Tyrconnell Downs** [Aust.] Queensland property. **1987** Patrick O'Farrell, *The Irish in Australia:* '… William Martin, writing to his father in Ballycastle, Co. Antrim, in December 1873, from Tyrconnell Downs near Roma, was totally opposed to his sisters or female relations coming to join him.'

Tír na nÓg [Ir., land of youth; myth.]. Otherworld preserve of perpetual youth; hence any such agency, etc. producing such a state. **2000** Peter Cunningham, *Irish Independent,* 12 Aug: 'Locked in the bathroom, I spewed out massive gobs of stuff [hair dye] like pink ice cream and rubbed them into my locks. This Tír na nÓg business can be tricky. After five minutes, my face in the mirror looked like that of a fire-fighter in *Towering Inferno* …'

Titanic [transport]. White Star Liner *Titanic*, built (1911) by Harland & Wolff, Belfast; sunk 1912. Hence (1)

Titanic Bar Pub, Cóbh, Co. Cork. **2000** Clodagh Finn, *Irish Examiner,* (Cork) 22 Aug: 'Maybe the dead will be remembered with dignity in the Titanic Bar too, but I just can't quite reconcile the sound of clinking glass with the cries of those drowning men Mary McGovern [survivor] saw being beaten by oars.' (2) **Titanic Quarter** [Belfast]. City development on redundant shipyard site. **2000** Monika Unsworth, *Irish Times*, 4 Apr: 'The [science] park will occupy a 23-acre site in the newly created Titanic Quarter at Queen's Island, adjacent to the Harland & Wolff shipyard in the east of the city.'

Todd [nickname]. C.S. Andrews (1909-85). Revolutionary and public servant. **1979** C.S. Andrews, *Dublin Made Me*: 'A curious feature of my Terenure life was the fact that nearly all the boys and many of the men had nicknames – Tipp Dwyer, Nauch McGrath, Giller Guilfoyle, Monkey Donovan – and in due course I acquired my own nickname, Todd. It was derived from a character in the *Magnet* [boys' magazine] who was called Alonzo Todd whom I resembled in appearance. "Todd" stuck to me so firmly that it became my Christian name, even amongst my own family …'

Tomb of the Unknown Gurrier aka **The Thing** [<play on 'Tomb of the Unknown Warrior', Paris *et al*; nickname, Dub.]. Concrete trough featuring plastic 'flame' erected on O'Connell Bridge to mark first **An Tóstal**. **1991** Tony Gray, *Mr Smyllie, Sir:* 'the whole contrivance was so vulgar and nasty that a crowd of engineering students tore the plastic flame from its fixings … and threw it into the Liffey. **Myles [na gCopaleen]** had already christened it the Tomb of the Unknown Gurrier.'

Tom the Devil [<his torturing of victims during the 1798 Rising; nickname]. Thomas Homann, sergeant, North Cork Militia. **1996** Patrick Comerford, *Irish Times,* 2 Sep: 'the greatest abuse [by Wexford hurling teams] was reserved ... for Cork. And this was so because the memory of "Tom the Devil" was alive in Wexford for a century after the rising.'

Tonehenge [<Theobald Wolfe Tone (1763-98), revolutionary leader + *(Stone)henge*, Brit. prehistoric monument; nickname, Dub.]. Memorial to Tone, St Stephen's Green. **1993** Vincent Caprani, in *The Berlitz Travellers [sic] Guide to Ireland:* 'Tone's statue ... was no sooner unveiled when some Dublin wag christened it "Tone-henge" (the nicknaming of the city's statues being something of a traditional pastime).'

Torrens, Robert (1814-86) Ir. political economist; major figure in colonisation of South Australia and its first premier. Hence (1) **Lake Torrens**; **River Torrens**, South Australia. (2) **Torrens System/Title** [politic.]. Land Act. **1990** Magnus Magnusson (ed.), *Chambers Biographical Dictionary:* 'He sponsored the Real Property Act of 1857 which introduced the Torrens system, whereby title to land was secured by legislation.'

Tory [<Ir. *tóraidhe*, a robber, a highwayman, a persecuted person (Dinneen)]. Brit. political nickname (1679) and party name (1689). **2000** Paul Muldoon, *To Ireland, I:* 'He [James Butler, earl of Ormond] seems to have been the first person to use the word "tory" of the "idle boys" and "plunderers" operating as highwaymen on Irish roads, many of them being Royalists who refused to give up their arms after 1601.'

Tóstal, An [Ir., pageant, array or muster,

parade, display, pride (Dinneen)]. 'Ireland at Home' festival designed to appeal to returning Irish-Americans (1953-). **1953 Myles na Gopaleen,** *Irish Times*, Apr: '... I would like to record what happened the Tóstal in the town of Carlow. They had a great week of it altogether, with no less than Charles Lynch playing the piano. *Not one single stranger was in town!*'

Tottenham in his Boots [nickname]. Charles Tottenham (1685-1758), politician. **1952** Maurice Craig, *Dublin 1660-1860:* 'A dispute had arisen between the Government and the patriotic party [1731] ... When it came to a division the numbers were exactly equal. But at the crucial moment in came Colonel Tottenham ... covered in mud and still wearing a huge pair of jackboots. He had ridden all through the night, nearly sixty Irish miles, to cast his vote for the patriots. For many a long year after that "Tottenham in his Boots" was a standing toast in patriotic circles.'

Traitors' Gate [<*idem*, Tower of London; nickname]. Dub. monument. **1999** Mary Russell, *Irish Times,* 9 Dec: 'James [Walsh] never came home – which is why his name is to be found on the granite arch at the entrance to Dublin's St Stephen's Green. The arch, sometimes known as Traitors' Gate, was erected in memory of the officers and men of the Royal Dublin Fusiliers who died in the Anglo-Boer War.'

TransAer see **Translift**

Translift [aviation]. Charter airline (1991-2000). **2000** *Irish Air Letter,* Dec: 'The name selected for the new airline was Translift Airways Ltd ... inspired by a combination of Trans Meridian and Heavylift ... N8083U was registered

EI-TLA on 26 February 1992 and was delivered Venice to Shannon the following day, carrying the name *Tomas Shligigh* ... The new era for Translift dawned on 07 October 1993 when Airbus A320 EI-TLE was delivered Southend-Dublin in a new colour scheme, carrying the name *Caitlin Shligigh* ... The original choice of name had been influenced by the initial concentration on cargo operations, but it was realised that the Translift name was not entirely appropriate to its current type of all-passenger operation ... In February 1997 the company announced a change of name to TransAer ...'

Trenche's Remedy [< J. Townsend Trench, Kenmare, Co. Kerry, land agent (late C19); brandname]. Quack medicine. **1993** Philomena McCarthy, *Kenmare and its Storied Glen:* 'Trench claimed to have discovered a cure for epilepsy and the [Lansdowne] Lodge had bottles of "Trenche's Remedy" stacked all over the place. It was widely advertised in newspapers and magazines ... Later it was analysed and proved to contain nothing beyond natural water and harmless colouring.'

Troubles, the [euphem.]. Applied to Ir/Brit., Pro-/Anti-Treaty, Republican/ Loyalist wars, civil wars and violence (1920s and 1969-). **1988** John Healy, *No One Shouted Stop!:* 'Ireland became a two-sided country once again as "The Troubles", that happy Irish euphemism for civil war, grew more murderous by the year ...'

Trowis [lit.]. River Drowes, Donegal/ Leitrim border. **1590/96** Edmund Spenser, *The Faerie Queene:* 'Sad Trowis that once his people over-ran.' **1911** P.W. Joyce, *The Wonders of Ireland:* '... it is clear that the poet [Spenser] thought it

was an anglicised form of an Irish word ... *truaghas*, sadness, wretchedness, from *truagh*, sad. The poet's fancy is not correct, for the ancient name of the river is not *Truaghas* but *Drobhaois* ... a very different word.'

Tuam Unical [typog.]. Typeface, designed by Jarlath Hayes, 'commended' in 'Design and Irish Typeface' competition (1978). Name suggested by Liam Miller. (The present writer was unsuccessful in his attempt to have him name it *Cló Ceo*.)

Tuatha Dé Danann [Ir., the people of the goddess Dana]. Pre-Christian deities common to the Celtic peoples. Hence [*idem*]. Trad. music group. **2000** Ian Kilroy, *Irish Times*, 3 May: 'In Italy, Tuatha Dé Danann are keeping the flame alight for Irish traditional music composed between 1400 and 1800 – I'd call that specialised ...'

Tullamore [Co. Uíbh Fháilí/Offaly]. Hence [brandname] **Tullamore Dew** [< Daniel Edmond Williams]. Whiskey. **1980** Malachy Magee, *1000 Years of Irish Whiskey:* 'One of the most inspired slogans ever applied to a brand of whiskey, "Give every man his Dew", certainly made Tullamore Dew universally known. The "Dew" artfully incorporates the initials of the company, D.E. Williams Ltd.' **1997** Seán MacConnell, *Irish Times*, 27 Nov: 'The people of Tullamore, Co. Offaly, have just discovered that naming their heritage centre after a famous drink associated with the town may cost them more than £400,000 in lost grants. They want to call it the Tullamore Dew Heritage Centre, after the well-known tipple. But a sub-committee in Bord Fáilte dealing with EU grants want them to drop the Dew.'

Tullymander [<James Tully, politician, Minister for Local Govt. 1973-7 + *(gerry)mander*; polit.]. Perceived attempt to gerrymander constituencies in his 1974 Electoral (Amendment) Bill. **1998** Stephen Collins, *Sunday Tribune*, 22 Mar: 'The so-called "Tullymander" boomeranged badly on its authors and helped **Fianna Fáil** to a record victory in 1977.'

Turfburner, the [nickname <peat fuel]. Last steam locomotive built in Ir. **1992** Tom Ferris, *Irish Railways in Colour:* 'The locomotive, officially numbered CC1, but widely known as the Turfburner, was completed at Inchicore in the summer of 1957 …'

Twelfth/Twalth [<12 July 1690, Battle of the Boyne; imit. of Ulster pronun.]. **1939** *The Irish Times*, 16 Feb: 'Here's a story from the "City of Light". Orange Wullie John met **Papish** Pat a few days before the "Twalth". They were good friends.'

Twelve Apostles, the [nickname]. Hit squad recruited by Michael Collins (see **Big Fella, the**) during War of Independence (1920). **1990** Tim Pat Coogan, *Michael Collins:* 'in January 1920 Collins added Tom Keogh, Mick O'Reilly and Vincent Byrne. The expanded **Squad** became known as the "Twelve Apostles".'

Tyrconnell see **Tirconnell**

U

Uisce [Ir., water]. Street sign. **1940** *Irish Times*, 29 Jul: 'Recently I commented upon the fact of some of our hotels introducing Irish on to their menu cards. Strolling along Rathmines Road a day or two ago, I made note of more progress. In place of the old DCWW [Dublin Corporation Water Works] on some of the iron traps of the water mains the single word Uisce was stamped … this department seems to make more use than any other of the public services of Irish. All its new lorries and bus-like cars are named in Irish, even some of its pneumatic drills.'

Ulster [<Ir. *Ulaidh* + Scand. *Staðr*, place] (1) Trad. 9-county Province. (2) The six counties of Northern Ireland (1922-). Hence (1) *idem.*, **1895** E. Cobham Brewer, *A Dictionary of Phrase and Fable:* 'A long loose overcoat, worn by males and females, and originally made of frieze cloth in Ulster.' **1948** *Belfast Street Directory:* 'M'Gee and Co. Ltd., Military, Naval and Ladies' Tailors, Inventors of the Ulster Coat and Slieve Donard Coat.' (2) *idem.,* abbrev. of Ulster King of Arms, heraldic officer (est. 1552). c**1967** Patrick Kennedy, *Sketches Collected Chiefly from the Records in Ulster's office and Other Authentic Documents by Patrick Kennedy, Herald Painter.* (3) **Ulster County Gazette** [media]. **197?** Daniel Nolan, *The Provincial Press in the Changing Economy:* 'One of the most prized possessions of [the US] Congress is an original copy of the *Ulster County Gazette,* published in Kingston, New York, during the rule of the first President of the United States

…' (4) **Ulster Custom** [agrarian] **1972** Diarmaid Ó Muirithe, *A Seat Behind the Coachman:* 'The *Ulster Custom* left the tenants in Ulster in a much better position than those in other provinces. It was a practice or usage by which a tenant paying rent to his landlord should not be evicted without being paid by the incoming tenant, or by the landlord, the full market price of his interest in the farm …' (5) **Ulster Defence Regt**. 2000 Jim Cusack, *Irish Times,* 1 Jul: '[Bernard] O'Mahoney had a deep dislike for the sectarian local militia of the Ulster Defence Regiment he served alongside. He and his fellow English "professionals" had a low regard for the local UDR men − "not one of the British Empire's better ideas" − known as the "Utterly Defenceless Regiment".' (6) **Ulster Fry** [gastronomy] Trad. calorific breakfast. **2000** Róisín Ingle, *Irish Times,* 27 Dec: 'The outsider will notice that the Ulster Fry, aka Heart Attack on a Plate, is nevertheless more varied than a southern breakfast …' (7) **Ulster Volunteer Force** Anti-Home Rule militia (1913). **1921** D.J. Owen, *History of Belfast:* 'It had of course been realised that something more would be needed than a mere drafting of Articles [of the Provisional] Government [for Ulster] and therefore an "Ulster Volunteer Force" had been formed.'

Ulysses [Homeric hero]. Title of novel by James Joyce (1922). Hence (?) [transport]. Ship's name. **2000** Martin Wall, *Sunday Tribune,* 13 Feb: 'It's all Greek to Geraldine. Early bird listeners to *Morning Ireland* were taken aback by the business news bulletin on Thursday. In reporting on the naming of Irish Continental Lines' new craft, Geraldine Harney said that "in keeping with the company's Irish image", it would be naming the ship *Ulysses*.' [2] [brandname] Furnishings designed by Eileen Gray (b. Enniscorthy 1877). **2000** Patricia O'Reilly, RTÉ *Sunday Miscellany,* 5 Nov: 'She opened a gallery [in Paris], designed a range of rugs which she called "Ulysses", after the novel by James Joyce.'

Unapproved Road [politic.]. Crossing between NI and the Republic unauthorised by Customs authorities. **1999** Tony Harnden, *'Bandit Country'*: 'Price differentials between the two jurisdictions and the existence of dozens of "unapproved" roads without customs posts meant that smuggling could be a profitable sideline or, for some, a principal occupation.'

Uncle see **Hamlet**

Uncle Arthur [cf. Sp. *tío*, uncle, as in *Tío Pepe,* in same affectionate/respectful sense; nickname]. Arthur **Guinness** (1725-1803), founder (1759) of the eponymous Dub. brewery; his heirs and successors. **2000** *Ireland on Sunday*, 16 Jul: 'Uncle Arthur losing his touch. The Irish are turning their backs on the black stuff.' **2000** Jerome Reilly, *Irish Independent*, 29 Jul: 'For the workers in Dundalk who jumped for joy when they got the letter of appointment to a plum permanent job with Uncle Arthur, that worldwide success is no comfort.'

Uncle Paythur [<Peter Flynn, character in Sean O'Casey, *The Plough and the Stars* (1926)]. Persistent begrudger/complainer. **1989** John Healy, *Magill*, Oct: 'not since Dr Conor Cruise O'Brien [see **Cruiser**] condemned the Labour Party as "poltroons" and "Uncle Paythers" [*sic*] and then joined the party will we have seen so great a switcheroo.'

Uncle Tim's Cabin [<Tim Healy, first Governor-General of the Irish **Free**

State (1922]; nickname]. Viceregal Lodge, **Phoenix** Park, Dub., subseq. Áras an Uachtaráin. **1979** Peter Somerville-Large, *Dublin:* 'At the Viceregal Lodge Tim Healy … took over from the Lord Lieutenant as Governor-General … [Oliver St John] Gogarty … called the rechristened Arus [*sic*] an Uachtaráin "Uncle Tim's Cabin".'

Uncrowned King of Ireland, the [nickname]. Charles Stewart Parnell, statesman/politician (1846-91). **1977** S.F. Pettit, *This City of Cork, 1700-1900:* 'As the procession wound down Shandon Street and North Main Street the people would come out in crowds … to savour the excitement of seeing the "Uncrowned King of Ireland" go by.'

Undertakers [nickname]. C18 Ascendancy power-brokers who controlled borough politics with govt. connivance. **1999** W.J. McCormack (ed.), *The Blackwell Companion to Modern Irish Culture:* 'Parliamentary managers who acquired their distinctive name from the fact that they "undertook" to pilot legislation through the Irish House of Commons on behalf of non-residential lord lieutenants in return for power and preferment.'

Under the Clock [Dub.] **1955** J.L.J. Hughes, *Dublin Historical Record,* 'Dublin Street Names', Sep: 'If you said you would meet someone Under the Clock this used to mean the Ballast Office clock in Westmoreland Street but now-a-days it stands for Clery's in O'Connell Street, especially for visitors from the country.'

United Arthritis Club [nickname, <perceived age/infirmity of members]. United Arts Club, Dub. **1975** John Ryan, *Remembering How We Stood:*

'Among its considerable accomplishments was to have "blackballed" Patrick Kavanagh. It was generally known around town as the United Arthritis Club.'

Unknown Gurrier see **Tomb of the Unknown Gurrier**

Urination Once Again [nickname, <poem by Thomas Davis, 'A Nation Once Again' (1846)]. Statue of Davis, College Green, Dub., by Edward Delaney (1966) and its spasmodically eructating fountain.

Urney [An Urnaí, Co. Thír Eoghain/ Tyrone; village]. Hence (1) [brandname]. Chocolates & confectionery. **1999** Eamonn Mac Intyre, *Irish Times,* 'Urney chocolates were first produced in the townland and parish of Urney, between Strabane and Clady; it was initially a cottage industry ... Mr Gay Byrne's first broadcast words were for Urney chocolates on its sponsored programme. As he says in his autobiography, "In those days people used to shout across the street,

'Any time is Urney time.'".' (2) **Urney pudding** [gastronomy]. **1983** Theodora Fitzgibbon, *Irish Traditional Food:* 'Urney pudding – Maróg Urnaidhe. This is a steamed pudding from the north of Ireland.'

U2 Rock band. **1993** Dave Bowler & Bryan Day, *U2:* '... [Steve] Averill's suggestion of U2 came from the name of a US military aeroplane which was shot down in 1960 and caused a heightening of East-West tension ... In the context of a band, the name U2 seemed rootless, ambiguous, inclusive in the sense of "you too" and yet almost anonymous ...' Hence **2000** Róisín Ingle, *Irish Times,* 20 Mar: 'Apparently the latest Freemen of Dublin had scanned the small print and discovered that one of their privileges was the right to graze sheep on common ground ... A seemingly unperturbed **Bono** said looking after the lambs was like tending his own musical flock, henceforth known as Ewe2. "They crap on me too," he joked.' See also **The Edge**

V

Vanessa [pet name]. Hester Vanhomrigh/ Esther Van Homrigh, friend/lover(?) of Jonathan Swift. See **Cadenus**; **Varina**

Varina [pet name]. Jane Waring, daughter of the Archdeacon of Dromore, to whom Jonathan Swift proposed marriage (1696). **1985** David Nokes, *Jonathan Swift:* 'As with Esther Johnson (Stella) and later with Hester Vanhomrigh (**Vanessa**), he Latinised Jane Waring's name to Varina. The device was a common enough feature of the amatory lyrics of the time, but in Swift's case his habit of renaming these fatherless girls is a distancing process that both elevates them to mock divinities and reduces them to pets.' (The Waring family gave its name to Waringstown, Co. Down).

Vermin Jelly [tradename]. **1930** *Irish Times,* 23 Aug: 'In the good old days of Queen Anne, one John Nelson, who lived at "The Blue Rowling Pin in Bride Street, Dublin", offered for sale to the general public "Extraordinary Vermin Jelly at one shilling and threepence a pound … In his advertisement, which appeared in *Dublin Intelligence* (1711), he stated that he was selling thus cheap "for the service of the public, as well as the encouragement of the said John Nelson"… As the name of this delicacy is not attractive, we presume that the advertiser meant "Vermicelli Jelly" which, perhaps, may have been called colloquially "Vermin Jelly" by Dubliners of the period.'

Village Quarter [Dub.]. Commercially-orientated development project. **2000** John Moran, *Irish Times,* 8 May: 'Last Christmas Dublin Bus's late-night services took to naming the Camden Street-Wexford Street-Harcourt Street end of the stretch as "The Village Quarter", clearly with the Greenwich Village area of New York in mind.' **2000** *Sunday Business Post,* 26 Jun: 'An initiative by local business people to upgrade and enhance the area between St Stephen's Green and Portobello in Dublin will be launched tomorrow by the Minister for Tourism, Sport and Recreation … The official launch of the Village Quarter, as the area has been named, will take place at 5.30pm in the **Iveagh** Gardens.'

Vinegar Hill [Co. Loch Garman/ Wexford, <Ir. *Fiodh na gCaor,* the wood of the berries, by imitative assonance]. Site of major battle of 1798 rising. Hence [Aust.] Password in Dec. 1854 revolt at Eureka, Victoria goldfields. **1954** C.H. Currey, *The Irish at Eureka:* 'The Irishmen who formed the core of the stand made at Eureka were of a later vintage than "the men of '98", yet the password for admission to their stockade was "Vinegar Hill".'

Virtual Irish Pub [website]. **2000** William Hederman, *Irish Times,* 30 May: 'If you find yourself [abroad] in a town with an Internet café but no Irish pub, you could visit a chat room at an Irish website. The well-known Virtual Irish Pub *(www.vip.ie)* is an obvious choice here.'

Viva [Dub.]. Pub. **2000** Edel Morgan, *Irish Times,* 27 Sep: 'Viva, Cocoon, **Dakota**, AKA – these are the names of only a few of the ultra cool bars revolutionising life on the Dublin social scene … Pubs which fail to fit in with the expectations and lifestyle of sophisticated but fickle 21st century Celtic cubs are being left off the circuit. The Daniel O'Connell on Aston Quay … is a case in point.'

W

Walking Day/Sunday [nickname]. (1) [Dub.]. Viewing day, Donnybrook Fair (C19). **1996** Con Costello, *Leinster Leader* (Naas) 6 Jun: 'Crowds of people flocked there [Donnybrook] on Walking Sunday (a custom also adopted at Punchestown where the first meeting was held in 1850) to see the booths ...' **2000** Joan Walsh, *Leinster Leader* (Naas), 4 May: 'Record crowds basked in sunshine as Walking Sunday at Punchestown attracted one of the largest crowds in memory.' (2) [Co. Dub.]. Sunday before Rathfarnham Fair (10 Jun.). **1943** George A. Little, *Malachi Horan Remembers:* 'The Sunday previous to the fair was called "Walking Sunday", as it was on that day that people who lived at a distance commenced walking their stock.'

Walking Gallows [nickname]. Edward **Hepenstall**, officer of the Wicklow Militia Regiment during 1798 Rising. **1998** Dick Grogan, *Irish Times*, 4 Mar: 'An amateur historian, Vincent O'Reilly, will expound on the lurid career of Edward Hepenstall, who came to be known as "The Walking Gallows" ... He perfected the technique of "half-hanging", suspending his victim by the neck over his shoulder. Being well over 6ft tall and of immense stature, he was ideally built for this method.'

Warhouse, the [nickname]. Widow McCormack's house, The Commons, Co. Thiobraid Árann/Tipperary. **1998** Dick Grogan, *Irish Times,* 29 Jul: '"The Warhouse", as the building is known locally, was the site of a minor battle when a couple of hundred largely unarmed local followers of the **Young Ireland** leader, William Smith O'Brien, besieged a party of armed police in the house of the young Widow McCormack and her children.'

Washer of the Ford, the Personification of Ireland, said to have appeared, among other instances at the battles of Magh Rath (637) and Corofin (1318). **1865** Samuel Ferguson, *Congal; a Poem in Five Books:* '... "Who art thou, hideous one; and from what curst abode/Comest thou thus in open day the hearts of men to freeze;/And whose lopp'd heads and severed limbs and bloody vests are these?"/"I am the Washer of the Ford," she answered; "and my race/Is of the Tuath de Danann line of Magi ..."' Also **Grey Washer by the Ford**. **1895** E. Cobham Brewer, *A Dictionary of Phrase and Fable:* 'An Irish wraith which seems to be washing clothes in a river, but when the "doomed man" approaches she holds up what she seemed to be washing and it is the phantom of himself with his death wounds from which he is about to suffer.'

Water Club, the [maritime]. **1945** Anthony T. Lawlor, *Irish Maritime Survey*: 'The oldest Yacht Club in the world did not commence life under the title of later days [Royal Cork]; it originated about the year 1720, when a number of gentlemen interested in sailing formed "the Water Club of Corke Harbour".'

Waterford/Port Láirge [city and Co.]. Hence [brandname] crystal glass. **1996** Fintan O'Toole, *The Ex-Isle of Erin*: '... the answer that the research provided was that, indeed, very few American consumers associated Waterford with Ireland. It was the news that Tony O'Reilly wanted to hear: that the process of branding Ireland that he had begun over 30 years before had now reached the point where a part of the country had become, finally, no more than a brand, a name without a face, a placeless image, freed at last from history.'

Water Rat [nickname] (Ulster). Customs officer. **1996** Seamus Deane, *Reading in the Dark:* 'We ducked into the darkness of the hedgerow. "Water rats", said Brendan Moran, peering up after them. It was the nickname given to customs officers "looking for smugglers …".'

Waterwag [maritime]. One-design sailing craft. **1945** Anthony T. Lawlor, *Irish Maritime Survey:* 'Dun Laoghaire has the honour of fostering small open boat-racing. In 1887, the Waterwag's Association was started.'

Wavers Club Commuters' club, Belfast and County Down Rly. (mid C20). **2001** Brian McDonald, *Five Foot Three,* Belfast: 'Also travelling [on the last train, 22 April 1950] was a large group called the Wavers Club … it was the custom of some of the commuters to wave to their wives from the train on leaving Millisle Road Halt at Donghadee. The custom spread to other commuters, who also began waving to the ladies, and so the Wavers Club was formed.'

Waxie's Dargle [<use of wax-end for stitching leather + Dargle river, synonymous (late C19) with holiday resort]. Annual gathering of cobblers at Irishtown Green, near **Ringsend**. **1981** Brendan Behan, *After the Wake:* 'Why can't you write about something natural? Like the time we all fell into the water at the Waxie's Dargle.'

Welsh choir [nickname]. Construction workers from Wales working in Dub.

2000 Frank McDonald, *The Construction of Dublin:* 'Since the mid 1990s … the construction industry is so stretched that electricians, plumbers and carpenters are commuting from Holyhead every Monday on the Stena HSS service … They have become known collectively as "the Welsh Choir".'

West Briton/West Brit. [nickname, gen. derog.]. Ir. man/woman professing, or assumed to profess, loyalty to UK, or aping Eng. manners. **1995** Patrick Maume, *D.P. Moran:* 'The romantic nationalism of his boyhood, the political activities of his youth were clumsy imitations. All his life he had been a West Briton without knowing it.' **1995** Ronnie Drew, *Irish Times,* 4 May: 'It [Dún Laoghaire] was a very strange place, sort of colonial … There was a West Brit feel about the place.'

Westlife [enter't]. Boy band. **2000** *Irish Independent,* 13 Dec: 'In the beginning they sang and played around Sligo. There were six guys in the band and they called themselves I.O.U … Louis [Walsh] cut I.O.U. in half. He dropped three of the I.O.U. guys and he kept Shane, Kian and Mark. He soon changed the name of the band to Westlife (because they had started in the West of Ireland).'

Wexford/Loch Garman [Co. & city] Hence **Wexford Senate** [1798-]. Revolutionary parliament. **2000** Chris Dooley, *Irish Times,* 19 Apr: 'The original Wexford Senate, based on the French revolutionary model, had a membership of 500 and lasted just three weeks during the 1798 rebellion … It reconvened at Johnstown castle 200 years later in a project originally conceived as a fundraiser towards the construction of the National 1798 Visitor Centre in Enniscorthy.'

Whiteboys [nickname]. Secret agrarian society (1761-). **1999** Kevin Whelan jr. & Kerby A. Miller (eds), *Irish Popular Culture 1650-1850:* '... the adoption of the Stuart colour (white) by the agrarian redresser movements of the 1760s instantly conferred a political coloration on **Munster** Protestants' attempts to understand the phenomenon ...'

White Caps [nickname]. Kerry vigilante group. **1895** E. Cobham Brewer, *A Dictionary of Phrase and Fable* (new ed.): 'An influential family ... who acted a similar part as Judge Lynch in America. When neighbours became unruly, the white caps visited them during the night and beat them soundly. Their example was followed about a hundred years ago in other parts of Ireland.'

Whitefeet [nickname]. Secret agrarian society (C19). **1973** Joseph Lee in T. Desmond Williams (ed.), *Secret Societies in Ireland:* 'The Whitefeet asked in Leix [Laois] and Offaly in 1831, only two years after Catholic emancipation, "What good did emancipation do us? Were we better clothed or fed ...?"'

White Vicar [nickname]. Ghostly visitation. **1930** *Irish Times*, 11 Feb: 'There exists an old tradition in the parish of Stradbally, Co. Waterford, that the ghost of the "White Vicar" still appears. Local historians state that he was a member of the Augustinian Order, but, as their habit is black, it is difficult to reconcile his appearance in a white monastic robe with membership of that Order. According to local tradition he was killed about 1700 ...'

White Widow [nickname]. Ghostly visitation. Duchess of Tyrconnell, wife of Richard Talbot, Lord Deputy of Ireland under James II. **1895** E. Cobham Brewer, *A Dictionary of Phrase and Fable* [new ed.): 'After the death of Talbot, a female, supposed to be his duchess, supported herself for a few days by her needle. She wore a white mask, and dressed in white.'

Wild Flowers of Tullahogue [<eponymous perfume; nickname, derog.]. Jurymen newly qualified for service under the Juries Act (1871). **1932** Edward Marjoribanks, *The Life of Lord Carson:* 'When [Lord] O'Hagan carried his Act, which lowered the qualification for jurymen, and admitted to the jury-box a class of peasants largely illiterate and quite unfitted for the discharge of judicial duties, his new juries were immediately called "The Wild Flowers of Tullahogue".'

Wild Geese [<migratory flight; nickname]. Soldiers and scions of leading families who, after the broken Treaty of Limerick (1603) left for mainland Europe, many to serve in Continental military forces. Hence (1) [*idem*]. Pub. **2000** Alison O'Connor, *Irish Times,* 21 Jun: 'Dubliner Sean Ó Conaill has just opened an Irish pub in Paris ... according to estimates, Sean's pub, The Wild Geese, is around the 50th Irish pub now operating in the French capital.' (2) **Wine Geese**, those who entered the wine & spirits business; and by extension to the Irish in the same field elsewhere. **1998** Mary Dowey, *Irish Times,* 18 Apr: 'He [Ted Murphy] is a living encyclopaedia on the so-called Wine Geese – those families who migrated from Ireland, mainly between the 17th and 19th centuries, and ended up in the wine trade.' **1999** [advt.]. 'The Australian Wine Geese are back ... After 150 years McGuigan's have returned to their homeland.'

Wimpey [tradename]. UK building firm employing many emigrant Irish, esp.1950s–60s. **1999** *RTÉ TV,* 'The Irish Empire': glossed as acronym 'We Import More Paddies Every Year.'

Witches' knickers [nickname]. Vagrant plastic bags. **2000** Katharine Blake, *Irish Times,* 23 Dec: 'Irish retailers alone use almost 300,000 tons of plastic a year, one-third of which is categorised under "not for resale" – which includes all the plastic wrapping on goods. Two-thirds of this is plastic carrier bags, which end up in land-fill or blowing about in trees and hedges (now known colloquially as "witches' knickers").'

Wolseley [<family name; brandname]. Motor car. **2000** Patrick Comerford, *Irish Times,* 9 May: 'The Wolseley family gave its name to Mount Wolseley in Co. Carlow, while Garnet's younger brother, Frederick York Wolseley, gave his name to Wolseley motor cars. Both brothers were born in Dublin in Goldenbridge House, now part of the famous convent and school in Inchicore.'

Women's Little Christmas [cf. Ir. *Nollaig na mBan,* Women's Christmas]. 6 January, feast of The Epiphany in Christ. **19??** Kevin Danaher, *The Year in Ireland: A Calendar:* '[the name is explained by] the assertion that Christmas Day was marked by beef and whiskey, men's fare, while on Little Christmas Day the dainties preferred by women – cake, tea, wine – were more in evidence.

Woodenworks [nickname]. Boardwalk. **2000** Maria Pepper, *Irish Times,* 27 Sep: 'The Viking town of Wexford has got its heart back with the opening of a newly extended quay front to replace the century-old "Woodenworks" which

was at the centre of a preservation campaign in the 1980s.'

Wood's Halfpence [numismatics]. Debased coinage minted for use in Ireland by William Wood (1722-24), a patent for the right of coining copper money having been granted to the Duchess of Richmond, George I's mistress, who sold it to Wood. **1724** Jonathan Swift, *A Letter to Mr Harding the Printer, upon Occasion of a Paragraph in his News-Paper of August 1st 1724, relating to Mr Wood's Half-pence:* 'In your News-letter of the First Instant, there is a Paragraph … relating to Wood's Halfpence, whereby it is plain, which I foretold in my *Letter to the Shop-Keepers, &c.,* that this vile Fellow would never be at Rest; and that the Danger of our Ruin approaches nearer …' See also **Drapier**

Workers' Republic [media]. Political publication(s). **1967** Donal Nevin in Francis Mac Manus (ed.), *The Years of the Great Test 1926-39:* 'The term "Workers' Republic" had a history long associated with Labour in Ireland and was probably peculiar to Ireland. It was the title given to the weekly organ of the Irish Socialist Republican Party established by James Connolly in 1898 and was again used by him for the paper he edited in 1915 and 1916.'

Wran Boys [local pronun. of 'wren']. Those who follow (26 Dec.) pre-Christian trad. of 'following' or 'hunting' the wren, victimised in Christian era as betrayer of St Stephen. **2000** Gillian Ní Cheallaigh, *Irish Times,* 19 Dec: 'The Wran Boys made an early visit to the Mansion House in Dublin yesterday at the launch of the 17th Wran Revival meeting … One of the co-founders, Tom Ahern, has been "following the wran" for 50 years.'

X

X-Case [legal]. *Cause célèbre* involving pregnant teenager, 'Miss X', prevented from travelling to Britain for an abortion (1992). **1998** Fergus Finlay, *Snakes and Ladders:* 'I was of many thousands who found the actions of the state in the X case totally repulsive.'

XMG [acronym; milit.]. Crossmaglen/ Crois Mhic Lionnáin, Co. Ard Mhaca/ Armagh. **1999** Toby Harnden, *'Bandit Country':* 'For the British soldier, Crossmaglen – known as XMG to the military, and Cross to locals – is a place of hostility, isolation and the constant threat of death.'

Y

Yahoo [lit.]. Creature of low intelligence in Jonathan Swift, *Gulliver's Travels* (1726). **2000** Paul Muldoon, *To Ireland, I*: '... *Eochaid* means "horse-rider", the *eoch* element being cognate with *equus*. It occurs in myriad forms in Irish literature, as Eochai, Echuid, Echaid ... Eochy. And Eochu. It also occurs. I want to suggest, in that book I mentioned earlier ... as "Yahoo". Having offered us horse-humans in the guise of the Houyhnhnms, Swift presents us with a crypto-current version of their opposite image in the vile Yahoos.' Hence (1) individual of low moral standard; (2) **Yahoo!** [tradename]. Internet supplier. **2001** Delphine Denuit, *Le Figaro* (Paris), 4 Jan: 'Quel revirement! La société américaine Yahoo! Inc. a provoqué la surprise hier en décidant d'interdire la vente d'objets nazi sur ses services d'enchères en ligne.' ['What a sudden change! The American company Yahoo! Inc. caused a surprise yesterday in deciding to ban the sale of nazi items on its on-line auction services.']

Yank [abbrev. of *Yankee*, <Du. *Jan Kees*, John Cheese, nickname for Du. and Eng. settlers in America]. **1998** Medb Ruane, *Irish Times*, 7 Jul: 'But Bill Clinton is actually an American, not a Yank. The term Yank was specially reserved for Irish-Americans, all other Americans being more or less a separate breed ... Yanks were Irish-Americans who might spend money visiting Ireland, but were no more than tourists in what we knew to be "our" culture ...'

Yellow-bellies [nickname<colour of GAA strip]. Wexfordmen, esp. in sporting context. **1866** Patrick Kennedy, *Legendary Fictions of the Irish Celts*: 'Queen Elizabeth [I of Eng.] once witnessed a hurling match, the conquering party being Wexfordians, distinguished by yellow silk kerchiefs tied round their bodies. "Oh", cried her majesty, rapping out an oath, "what brave boys these *yellow bellies* are!"'

Yellow Card [<soccer disciplinary warning; milit.]. **2000** *Irish Times*, 31 Mar: 'The so-called Yellow Card, which contains the standing instructions for soldiers in Northern Ireland as to when they can open fire, was revised four times between September 1969 and November 1971, and twice more in July and November 1972 ...'

Yellow Dragoons [milit.]. Regiment engaged in Battle of the Boyne (1690). **1990** Robert Shepherd, *Ireland's Fate*: '"There is no place of excuse for the dragoons" [John] Stevens wrote, "especially the Earl of Clare's, commonly known by the name of Yellow Dragoons, being the colour of their clothes, who were the first that fled having scarce seen the enemy".'

Yellow-man [nickname]. Toffee made from golden syrup, brown sugar, butter, vinegar and sodium bicarbonate, assoc. with Ballycastle. Co Antrim. **Nd** Pop. ballad: 'At the Ould Lammas Fair, boys,/were you ever there,/Were you ever at the fair in Ballycastle O?/Did you treat your Mary Ann to dulse and Yellow-man ...'

Yellow Polly see **Donegal Red**

Yeo [abbrev., nickname]. Yeomanry corps under officers commissioned by Brit. Crown (1796). **1978** John Hewitt,

The Rain Dance,'The True Smith of Tieveragh': 'There is a ballad rooted in the Glens/about a rebel smith the Yeos pursued.' See also **Killyman Wrackers**

Yorick [<defunct humorist in Shakespeare's *Hamlet*/character in Sterne's *Tristram Shandy* (1759); media]. Humorous journal. **1952** B.P. Bowen, *Dublin Historical Record,* 'Dublin Humorous Periodicals of the 19th Century', Mar–May: '… he [Richard Dowling] returned to Dublin about 1876 and started a new paper called Yorick which was half literary and half comic … The venture only lasted about six months.'

Young Ireland [politic.] Group within O'Connell's Repeal Assoc. (1840s). **1987** Richard Davis, *The Young Ireland Movement:* 'Young Ireland was not a clearly articulated movement but a group of Repealers, working with Daniel O'Connell in the 1840s.' Hence (1) **Young Ireland Branch** (of the United Irish League) (1900s). **1995** Patrick Maume, *D.P. Moran:* 'These [party members] were joined by young

intellectuals associated with the Young Ireland Branch … These Y.I.B.s (as they were known) used *The Leader* to advocate greater freedom of debate…' (2) **Young Ireland Association, the** Politic. movement (1933). **1967** T. Desmond Williams, 'De Valera in Power', in Francis Mac Manus (ed.): *The Years of the Great Test 1926-39:* 'The banned national guard was then renovated on allegedly constitutional lines. Its new title became The Young Ireland Association – as a legitimate branch of United Ireland.'

Young Mr Brennan see **Old Mr Brennan**

Young Tigers [nickname] Political faction. **1984** Fergal Tobin, *The Best of Decades; Ireland in the 1960s:* 'Esso developed an enormously successful advertising campaign ("Put a Tiger in your Tank") aimed at the ever-growing motor market; the slogan was later picked up by James Dillon, TD, who dubbed the Fine Gael liberals the "Young Tigers", a name that stuck.'

Z

Zanzibar see **GUBU**

Zig and Zag [media]. TV puppet characters created by Ciaran Morrison and Mick O'Hara (1987). **2000** Derek O'Connor, *Irish Times,* 23 Dec: 'Originally guest stars on a show called *Dempsey's Den*, one day's work a week became two, the three ... next thing you knew, Zig and Zag were a genuine cult phenomenon.' See also **Dustin**

Zozimus [<his recitation of history of St Mary of Egypt; nickname]. Michael Moran (1794–1846), blind Dub. balladeer. Hence (1) [media] humorous journal. **1952** B.P. Bowen, *Dublin Historical Record,* Mar–May: 'In 1870 the best of the early comic papers Zozimus was started by A M Sullivan from the **Nation** office ... In his selection of a name for the paper Sullivan showed his journalistic acumen. He called it after the well-known Ballad–Singer, Michael Moran, who was nicknamed Zozimus from one of his ballads. The name was one which drew attention by reason of its unusual character ...' Hence (2) [media] **Zoz.** Humorous journal. **1952** B.P. Bowen, *op. cit:* 'In 1876 another humorous paper arose from the ashes of **Ireland's Eye**. This was called Zoz, or the Irish Charivari.'

Select Bibliography

Standard dictionaries have been omitted, as have the majority of references and citations in the text, except where these involve a work of more general onomastic application.

Akin, Salih (ed.), *Noms et Re-noms: La denomination des personnes, des populations, des langues et des territoires* (Rouen 1999)

An Irish C.C., *Dysert-Diarmada; or Irish Place-Names. Their Beauty and their Degredation* (Dublin 1919)

Anon., *Ainmneacha Gaelige na mBailte Poist* (Dublin 1969)

Clerkin, Paul, *Dublin Street Names* (Dublin 2001)

Comerford, T., *History of Ireland* (4th ed., Cork 1807)

Corran, H.S., 'Genghis is ghoon for you', in *The Harp* (Dublin 1990)

Craig, Maurice, *The Elephant and the Polish Question* (Dublin 1990)

Daly, Mary E., *Industrial Development and Irish National Identity, 1922-1939* (New York 1992)

Ellis, Peter Berresford, *A Dictionary of Irish Mythology* (London 1987)

Flanagan, Deirdre, *Béal Feirste agus Áitainmneacha Laistigh* (Galway 1982)

Flanagan, Deirdre & Laurence Flanagan, *Irish Place Names* (Dublin 1994)

Grose, Francis, *A Dictionary of Buckish Slang, University Wit and Pickpocket Eloquence, compiled originally by Captain Grose* (London 1811)

Joyce, Gerry, *Limerick City Street Names* (Limerick 1995)

Joyce P.W., *The Origin and History of Irish Names of Places* (3rd ed., Dublin 1871)

Le Rouzic, Pierre, *Un Prénom pour la Vie* (Paris 1978)

Leerssen, Joep, *Mere Irish and Fíor-Ghael* (Cork 1996)

Leerssen, Joep, *Remembrance and Imagination* (Cork 1996)

McKay, Patrick, *A Dictionary of Ulster Place-Names* (Belfast 1999)

MacLysaght, Edward, *The Surnames of Ireland* (6th ed., Dublin 1985)

M'Cready, Charles T., *Dublin Street Names, Dated and Explained* (Dublin 1892)

Mac Giolla-Domhnaigh, Padraig, *Some Anglicised Surnames in Ireland* (Dublin 1923)

Miles, Joyce C., *House Names Around the World* (Newton Abbot 1972)

Morgan, Jane *et al.*, *Nicknames, their Origins & Social Consequences* (London 1979)

O'Connor, Charles, *Dissertations on the Ancient History of Ireland* (Dublin 1753)

Ó Corráin, Donnchadh & Fidelma Maguire, *Gaelic Personal Names* (Dublin 1981)

Ó Dochartaigh, Cathair, 'Irish in Ireland' in Glanville Price (ed.), *Languages in Britain & Ireland* (Oxford 2000)

Ó Maolfabhail, Art (ed.), *The Placenames of Ireland in the Third Millennium* (Dublin 1992)

Ordnance Survey/An tSuirbhéireacht Ordanáis, *Gazetteer of Ireland/ Gasaitéar na hÉireann* (Dublin 1989)

O'Reilly, Camille C., *The Irish Language in Northern Ireland* (Basingstoke/New York 1999)

Porlan, Alberto, *Los Nombres de Europa* (Madrid 1998)

Rémi-Giraud, Sylvianne & Pierre Rétat, *Les Mots de la Nation* (Lyon 1996)

Room, Adrian, *Dictionary of Irish Place-Names* (Belfast 1986)

Share, Bernard, *Slanguage, A Dictionary of Slang and Colloquial English in Ireland* (Dublin 1997)

Theisse, Anne-Marie, *La Création des Identités Nationales* (Paris 1999)

Woulfe, Patrick, *Irish Names for Children* (Dublin 1974)

Woulfe, Patrick, *Sloinnte Gaedheal is Gall/Irish Names and Surnames* (Dublin 1923)